The Films of Oliver Reed

ALSO BY SUSAN D. COWIE
AND TOM JOHNSON

The Mummy in Fact, Fiction and Film
(2002; paperback 2007)

The Films of Oliver Reed

SUSAN D. COWIE *and*
TOM JOHNSON

Forewords by
Sir Christopher Lee *and* Ron Moody
Afterword by Michael Winner

McFarland & Company, Inc., Publishers
Jefferson, North Carolina, and London

LIBRARY OF CONGRESS CATALOGUING-IN-PUBLICATION DATA

Cowie, Susan D.
The films of Oliver Reed / Susan D. Cowie and Tom Johnson; forewords by
Sir Christopher Lee and Ron Moody; afterword by Michael Winner.
p.   cm.
Includes bibliographical references and index.

ISBN 978-0-7864-3906-5
softcover : 50# alkaline paper ∞

1. Reed, Oliver, 1938–1999 — Criticism and interpretation.
I. Johnson, Tom, 1947–   II. Title.
PN2598.R426C79   2011   791.4302′8092 — dc23   2011033379

British Library cataloguing data are available

Cover image: Oliver Reed as Bill Sikes in *Oliver!,* 1968
(Columbia Pictures/Photofest)

Manufactured in the United States of America

*McFarland & Company, Inc., Publishers
Box 611, Jefferson, North Carolina 28640
www.mcfarlandpub.com*

To Sir Christopher Lee, CBE, who was there at the beginning of both Oliver Reed's career and this book, and to Jimmy Sangster, who died while this book was being edited.— TPJ

To my darling hubby Colin, the reason I wake up in the mornings and the bravest man I know.— SDC

Acknowledgments

This book would have been impossible to write without the sterling help of Randy Vest, who tracked down most of the videos we needed to see.

Thanks also to the British Film Institute, the Lincoln Center Library for the Performing Arts, Dick Klemensen, Mark A. Miller, Karen Schleicher, Terry Tait, Elaine Hahn, Jerry Ohlinger's Movie Material Store, Denis Meikle, Wayne Kinsey, Mark Walter, Ernest J Harris, Gary Richards and the wonderfully useful Internet Movie Database.

Among the co-workers of Oliver Reed who answered our call were Catherine Feller, Janette Scott, Suzan Farmer, William Hobbs, Joyce Broughton, Jimmy Sangster, Anthony Hinds, John Cater, Michael Ripper, Mark Lester, and Jennie Linden.

Author Denis Meikle graciously allowed us to reprint an interview he conducted with Reed, and Colin Cowie provided the sketch on page 54.

We have made every effort to credit the correct copyright holders with the illustrations in the book; copyright is vested in the company that made the film depicted unless otherwise stated. Please accept our apologies for any errors detected which will be corrected in any further editions published.

We are truly grateful to Sir Christopher Lee, CBE, and Ron Moody who provided the forewords and to Michael Winner, OBE, who wrote the afterword. We hope that what appears in the middle is as informative and entertaining.

Susan D. Cowie and Tom Johnson

Contents

Foreword by
Sir Christopher Lee, CBE

My association with Oliver Reed began in 1959 — at the beginning of his career, over fifty years ago in a little film called *Beat Girl*. I played a sleazy strip club manager and Oliver played a sort of beatnik. We didn't meet, either on or off screen, but did so often over the next forty years.

I actually met and acted with Oliver in a Hammer film called *The Two Faces of Dr. Jekyll* (1960). He played a tough (to put it mildly) nightclub bouncer — which he'd actually been — who came on a bit too strong with Paul Massie (as Hyde) and myself as Hyde's deplorable friend. We beat Oliver mercilessly; I had to stop Hyde killing him!

Oliver became a star soon afterwards in Hammer's *The Curse of the Werewolf* (1960), filmed as were most of the company's films at that time at Bray Studios. I had some business there and stopped at the dining room for lunch. Bray had wonderful lunches! There was Oliver, drenched in blood and fur, eating — or trying to — alone. No one would sit with him, let alone eat with him. Having been in similar circumstances at Bray, I sympathized with him and sat down. He seemed very grateful.

Oliver and I next appeared on screen, for Hammer again, as two of *The Pirates of Blood River* (1961). I was the pirate chief, Oliver was one of my chief henchmen. I had just bought a second-hand Mercedes and would pick up Oliver and fellow actor Denis

Shaw on the way to Bray. Denis was like Oliver, something of an extrovert, and occasionally got Oliver into trouble. Specifically, Denis would start fights in pubs and Oliver would finish them. This, sadly, was the case a few years later when Oliver was seriously injured by a broken bottle when he was attacked in a London club. His face was badly scarred and his budding career nearly ended.

Oliver sat in the back of my Merc and alternated between sleeping — we had to be at the studio very early — and wondering, out loud, whether acting was the right career for him. He was very young, and like most young actors, very unsure of himself. This, despite being the nephew of Sir Carol Reed, one of the great film directors. I tried to assure him that most young actors — myself definitely included — had the same doubts. He was, I think, grateful for the advice.

Oliver repaid my kindness for the rides and advice years later when I was the subject of a *This Is Your Life* episode by telling the television audience that I'd charged him for the petrol! This was not true. I countered by saying that, if we'd done it now, I could have made a fortune!

Oliver next pointed out that I would spend the trip singing. Loudly. This was true. I had to do something to keep us awake. He specified that I would sing "Doe, a deer, a female deer..." This was not true. The song, which appears of course in *The Sound of Music*, had yet to be written!

Oliver looked as much like a pirate as anyone could have, and behaved like one as well. He could be quite dangerous with a sword in his hand. Everyone got out of his way — he would swing, wildly, in all directions. Everywhere. Oliver was a very strong, athletic young man, always into the physical element of his role.

Having had quite a bit of swordfighting experience myself, I attempted, vainly, on this film and others to come, to teach him some discipline in his fighting. In one key scene he and Peter Arne are blindfolded — on my order — to fight to the death over Marla Landi. It was nearly that. It was very frightening to watch; I'm not sure how well, if at all, they could actually see. It's amazing no one was injured.

In another scene, I was leading my band of cut-throats across the lake at Black Park, which stood in for Blood River. The lake was, to say the least, filthy. As we were crossing, Oliver thought that the scene could use a bit of livening up, so he started — unscripted, mind you — a fight with another pirate. Both of them went underwater. Oliver paid for his impulse with a case of bright red, badly infected eyes and a trip to hospital.

He was right, though. The scene was improved. This was typical of Oliver; he would impulsively create a bit of business not in the script — often during a fight — if he felt the scene needed it. This did not always endear him to directors and other actors but he was often proven to be right by the result on the screen.

My assessment of Oliver Reed at this time was that he was an extremely intelligent, extremely physical young man whose mind was always working on the set. Sometimes his instincts were wrong, but just as often they were right. He was extremely undisciplined but had great presence and charm.

He was pleasant, courteous and respectful to all concerned, especially towards Peter

Cushing and myself. We gave him a great deal of advice on acting and other matters, and he took it to heart, despite calling us his "maiden aunts"!

To be honest, he became a much bigger star than, at that time, I thought possible. But I wasn't surprised when he did. He had all the necessary qualities.

As Bill Sikes in *Oliver!* (1968), directed by his uncle Carol, he became a huge star. Naturally, Oliver emphasized the physical aspect of his role; I preferred Robert Newton's more mental approach in David Lean's *Oliver Twist* (1948). But that's simply my opinion. For Oliver, it was a part very well played. It brought him a great deal of attention and made his career. He deserved it.

Oliver and I next met on screen in *The Three Musketeers* (1973). The film was shot in Spain and was quite long. The producers, incredibly, decided to release it as two films, despite paying the cast and crew for one! No one was pleased. Oliver and I were on opposite sides; he, as Athos, led the Musketeers and I, as Rochefort, was the Crown's chief henchman. We had a terrific fight in a blazing barn — real swords, real daggers. My character wore, among other cumbersome things, an eye patch; I certainly kept my other eye wide open, remembering Oliver's tendencies with a sword in his hand! Oliver even used his cape as a weapon, flapping it in his opponent's eyes. I'm not sure if that was scripted or not! He came at me, both hands on the hilt, swinging wildly. I stopped. When he inquired why, I informed him that this was not how the fight had been rehearsed. He apologized. And did it again!

This time I parried his coming blows and whacked him across the thighs with the flat of my sword. He stopped. I asked him who had originally taught him to use a sword. He hung his head, apologized again, and said, "You did. And not like this. I'm sorry." It didn't happen again.

I rode with Oliver and his mate Reg Prince, returning from filming at an ancient monastery. We stopped at a country inn for a drink. I requested a white wine. By the time I got back in the car, I was feeling poorly — I had a pounding headache and could hardly see. Oliver sheepishly admitted that he'd spiked my wine with vodka! I was not amused, and Oliver apologized — again. He thought behavior like that was funny; Oliver meant no harm but his impulsivity caused harm on occasions.

I was one of the few on the film who could match him with a sword. Even the Spanish stuntmen, among the toughest in the business, were reluctant to fight him. I took Oliver aside and cautioned him they might retaliate. "I've been very naughty," Oliver said. "No," I said, "bloody stupid." The behavior stopped.

Oliver Reed's off-set behavior had gradually become the property of the tabloid press, but this did not happen in my presence. He was always prepared and cooperative if, as I've said, a bit creative and impulsive. As he became a better and more important actor — and he became very good and very important — I'd hoped that he'd look after himself more and become an even bigger asset to his profession. But...

Our last professional association was on *Treasure Island* (1989). As we were playing a scene, I was about to deliver my dialogue and Oliver decided his character should have a heart attack ... unscripted, of course. His grunts and gasps drowned out my lines, but I kept at it, thinking, "Well, it's just Oliver." Naturally, when I saw the scene on screen, it worked.

I was sitting at home on May 2, 1999, when I received a phone call from Malta. Rosemary Burrows, who was married to Eddie Powell, Hammer's stuntman, was working on *Gladiator*. She informed me of Oliver's death in a pub he'd adopted. The tabloid press was, naturally, quite descriptive of the drinking that had taken place. I was saddened but hardly surprised.

When seeing *Gladiator*, I thought, "At least Oliver went out at the top of his game." He gave the film's best performance.

I can't say that I knew Oliver Reed well, but I knew him for forty years; I knew him well enough to like him and admire his talent. I met his widow Josephine and his children Mark and Sarah, and liked them too.

Oliver Reed was a very good actor and, in my opinion, could have been a great one had he not chosen the path he trod. That said, he left behind a remarkable body of work. It's sad that many people are interested only in his occasional seamy adventures and forget about the positive aspects of his life, including his ability as an actor.

Sir Christopher Lee, CBE
December 2007, London

Sir Christopher Lee, CBE, was a veteran of 45 films and a star at Hammer when he met the fledgling Oliver Reed on The Two Faces of Dr. Jekyll *(1960). He taught Reed how to handle a sword and himself during this period of his growing fame. They were reunited on* The Three Musketeers *(1973) after both had broken through as stars in mainstream productions.*

Foreword by Ron Moody

The first time I met Oliver Reed was on the film *Oliver!* when we attended pre-production meetings and dinners. John Box, the production designer, was usually present as well as John Green, the music supervisor. As for my first actual sighting of Ollie, I can't really remember, which is odd because he usually made quite a first impression!

His uncle, Sir Carol Reed, was the greatest director I ever worked with, as well as the greatest teacher of film technique. He was responsible for me learning an awful lot about how to prepare on film. He was also a gentleman — the word is now out of date — and he was a kind, kind man. Very good-hearted, and he got on well with the children for that reason. They realized that they were in good hands. His films *The Third Man* and *Odd Man Out* are among the finest ever made. I've always admired him so much. One of the peak moments on *Oliver!* was when I was skittering along the cobblestoned alleyway, he said, "You remind me of F. J. McCormick from *Odd Man Out*." What a compliment!

Ollie and I used to eat lunch together nearly every day in the commissary. One day we were doing the jewelry scene where Ollie, as Bill Sikes, takes all the jewelry out of his coat and I, as Fagin, drop them one by one into a bag. "Beeaauutifuul ... beauutifuul." On that day, round about lunch time, we were doing that scene and we had covered Ollie's close-ups.

After lunch, we were going to do my close-ups. At lunchtime, we always had a bottle of wine — or two. It never actually affected our work. This day, dear Ollie, with a little glint in his eye, ordered the second bottle. I thought, "What's this for?" But I drank my share, the same as he did. And by the time lunch was over, I was a bit high. So we went back to the set and I staggered on and I carried on with the scene, and there was this peculiar gleam in my eye that I could never have acted. Sort of a glow. And a wildness, like a torch shining in the eyes but it was mischief and greed. All the qualities that I would like to have got into it that I can't normally do. The second bottle of wine helped give me the look! It was one of my best scenes in the film thanks to my mischievous friend.

I don't know to this day if he intended for that second bottle to get me kicked over the edge. But he was certainly capable of it.

I told him I collected clown portraits, and he decided to collect them as well. I think the reason was that he was as much of a clown as I was. He was basically a very mischievous little boy. He loved to frighten people. He loved to chase people. He loved to tease people.

He loved to shock people. He did it in his work, and in his life, too.

One day on the lot, I didn't have anything in particular to do, so I was stuck inside learning my lines or rehearsing a number. I came out for some air, and Ollie and I were talking and Jacquie Darrell, one of the dancers whom I quite fancied, walked past. And I said, "Hello — do you know Oliver?" and that was it. They were married soon after, I think.

Another incident was when we had a party; the whole *Oliver!* crowd, most of the actors and dancers and a few of the crew. It was great. We were enjoying the sense of presence of having the *Oliver!* crowd. There were a lot of the general public in the restaurant and they were obviously looking at our table because we had a few film stars there. And suddenly Ollie stood up. I think he was on his fourth bottle — who knows? Then he stood on his chair. I can't remember if he made a speech or if he sang. But as he did it he ripped open his trousers and he exposed his Y-fronts (underwear). I don't know why! He just felt like it, I suppose. It was certainly unexpected.

He loved being an eternal child. He loved to play games. And he had to win. He was absolutely obsessed. He used to play with his stand-in (Reg Prince), a big hulking great character. After shooting they would usually meet up in the pub and have a few drinks before they went home. They nearly always ended up playing games.

I arm-wrestled with him once and I held him. I had a sudden feeling that maybe, because I was very strong in the arms then, if I held him and I could start to go back, I could win. But I couldn't, because he had to win. There was a kind of aura coming from him — a need to be the best. He had to win. So everyone, whether they could have won or not, didn't. It's one of those things you never know, isn't it?

He was a competitor. He was a clown. We got on very well. We had a mutual respect which was evident from both of our attitudes.

He was also a very generous actor. He was very generous with ideas. He once taught me the great Spencer Tracy gag. Tracy would walk up to somebody with his eyes on the floor and then, when he got close to them, he'd suddenly look up. You got the shock look up from the floor up to the person's face. Apparently, the idea was that Spencer Tracy used to look at his mark on the floor, walk up to it, his eyes on it all the time. Then suddenly he'd look up into the face of his co-actor. I used it quite a few times myself. It's very effective.

No matter how late Ollie was out the night before — we didn't know what sort of carousing went on — he would roll in looking absolutely knocked out, as if he had really been up all night. But he never fluffed a line and he was never late. He was 100 percent professional. In the end, people didn't mind him being a hellraiser because he was such a pro. He had this very professional streak that kept him going, although he must have weakened himself by drinking too much at different times.

It once again gives me the thought that maybe this frightening man who loved to terrify people with his glare (he would sit down with somebody he didn't know and just stare at them, those great eyes piercing into the person who was probably terrified) was actually very shy. That's all he wanted, he just wanted to frighten people.

It was all part of this marvelous mischief that was in him. The secret was that he was really very shy. He had a great deal of authority and self-control in his work. You wouldn't normally think of him being shy. But when you really think about it, he never really bossed anybody, never really tried to come out on top of anybody. Only if you knew him well would you know that.

When we met again in *A Ghost in Monte Carlo* it was different. We didn't have lunch every day. I only met him a few times on the set and he seemed less matey. I guess that was just me; it wasn't a very happy shoot. I didn't get along well with the director.

I was invited to appear in Ollie's *This Is Your Life*. I came on after doing my intro and walked up to him beaming away, and he was beaming away; and without changing his expression he grabbed me by the testicles. I let out a shriek and there was a huge laugh, but they castrated the scene.

He came on my *This Is Your Life*, immaculately dressed. He was so well-behaved, he really was unbelievably civilized. He wasn't the mad Ollie at all. Josephine must have mellowed him, but if she did, what was in him before that made him such a wild one? They were in love and she was looking after him; someone to look after the wild boy.

This covers our relationship. There weren't that many times that we worked together but they were all enjoyable.

Ron Moody
April 2009, London

Ron Moody shone as Fagin in Oliver!, *the Best Picture of 1968 and Oliver Reed's breakthrough in mainstream film. The film changed the course of both their careers with Reed becoming an international superstar. Ron Moody continues to work on stage and television to great acclaim.*

Preface

When the news broke of the death of Oliver Reed in Malta on Sunday, May 2, 1999, there was a general sadness because a light had gone out in the world. Oliver was always good for a headline, an eye-popping appearance on TV or a tale lovingly told. What most forgot at the time was that he was also a world-class actor who had the distinction of appearing in good examples of almost every film genre and that his work ethic put many to shame.

We were reminded of an incident, wryly retold by Liza Minnelli when asked about her late mother, the great Judy Garland, whose mega-stardom always seemed to obliterate her personal happiness. "Was she always so sad?" Liza was asked. She replied that her mother, within the family, was happy and loving, but when outsiders came to her dressing room and began conversations with cooing sympathy, expecting her to be depressed, she would sigh and look sad with drooping shoulders, lapping it up and sharing the joke with any member of her family who happened to be present.

In recent years it has become apparent that Reed also appreciated that his public had a picture of him that required him to appear the worse for wear — and he was so good an actor that he was frequently believed to be in his cups when he was just giving his public what it wanted. Unfortunately, this is the image which remains for millions of moviegoers.

We waited a long time for someone to write about Oliver Reed's films in detail. And while his tongue-in-cheek autobiography and books about his extraordinary life are available, any book about his films appears to be selective and subjective. So we have written our own and hope it meets with your approval, dear reader.

And may we say we love and respect him even more than we did when we started.

A Note to the Reader

The purpose of our book is to present the film career of Oliver Reed, a career we

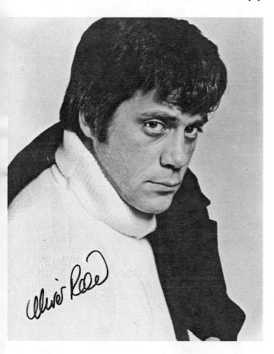

Publicity shot of Oliver Reed with autograph (Susan D. Cowie collection).

feel is among the best, most interesting and varied of any actor from any era.

We are well aware that Reed's personal life often intruded into the perception of him as an actor by the public, reducing him to a "personality."

We have no knowledge, personally, of Oliver Reed; we know only what we have seen on the screen. We have no interest in or any intention of delving into that aspect of his life that has fascinated the tabloids, other than when it intrudes into the work.

For those interested in that personal information, we recommend Cliff Goodwin's excellent biography *Evil Spirits* (Virgin, 2000).

Among the Missing

The following films have appeared on various Oliver Reed filmographies and have presented various problems for the authors.

The Age of Pisces (1972). We could find no evidence that the film exists at either the British Film Institute or the Lincoln Center Library for Performing Arts. Neither were there copies to be had from a myriad of dealers and collectors.

99 Women (1983). Again, no evidence of it having been made at either reference source and no copies from dealers or collectors.

Frank and I (1983). This was a well-produced, reasonably tasteful softcore porno film produced by Harry Alan Towers. Reed has been listed as a "guest star" but was not visible in the print viewed by the authors. Since Reed had worked for Towers previously, it's possible that he did appear in the film but the film may have several versions since it was an international production.

Blue in the Face (1992). This was a Harvey Keitel production based on a play. Reed is not mentioned in any of the literature we found on the film and we were unable to locate a print.

The People vs. Larry Flint (1996). This excellent biography of the infamous *Hustler* publisher features an Oscar-worthy performance by Woody Harrelson — but no Oliver Reed. At least not *our* Oliver Reed; an actor by that name plays a small role as a political figure.

A Brief Biography of Oliver Reed

Robert Oliver Reed was born to be an actor. His grandfather, Sir Herbert Beerbohm Tree, was a Victorian stage star and his uncle, Sir Carol Reed, directed, among other excellent films, *The Third Man* (1949).

Reed was a child of the Blitz (born February 13, 1938, in Wimbledon, London), and his schooling was erratic at best, complicated by his undiagnosed dyslexia and a problematic home life. Marcia, his mother, left the family in 1940 and his father, Peter, was a conscientious objector which limited his employment options during wartime and earned him Oliver's scorn (which must have been a received opinion from his mother as he was far too young to comprehend the term). But, showing the determination that would make him a film star, Oliver kept at it, doing well enough in general to get by and excelling in athletics.

After a particularly serious argument with his father, the seventeen-year-old Reed left both school and home. He was in danger of becoming dangerous; the angry, physically powerful young man prowled the seedy Soho district of London, often finding trouble. He eventually found a job as a club bouncer.

Oliver had no clue as to what to do with himself; he was more likely to end up in prison as on a film set. But, while working at a hospital, he learned that a film was to be shot nearby. For a laugh he inquired about working as an extra and was hired (but never paid) to appear in a crowd scene in *Value for Money* (1955). He was seventeen; in six years he would be starring on screens worldwide in *The Curse of the Werewolf*.

Reed's eighteenth birthday was acknowledged by a letter drafting him into National Service. After completing his basic training he became an officer candidate, but his dyslexia prevented him from scoring adequately on the written exam. He was posted to Hong Kong where he experienced, not for the last time, alcohol and sex. Unsure of his future, although he was sure it would not be in the military, he decided to become a film star. He never once considered becoming "just an actor."

At age 20, Reed (back in London) joined the Film Artists' Association, looking again for work as an extra — a stop he realized he had to make on his way to the top. He scored with a call to play a photographer in *Hello London* (1958) but other parts — and money — were in short supply.

Oliver felt it was time to visit Uncle Carol again. When he dropped in late in 1958, Oliver was stunned to find that the famed film director was no more willing to help him onto a film set than he'd been in 1956 when he turned down a request from his nephew to cast him in *Trapeze*.

Uncle Carol did not believe in nepotism, but he did believe in giving good advice; see as many films as possible and learn to recognize good acting from bad. Oliver took to the plan instantly although he rejected out of hand his uncle's suggestion that he join a rep company.

Oliver made himself known around London's casting offices and, somehow, landed the part of Richard of Gloucester in the BBC drama *The Golden Spur* (1959). He soon met aspiring model Kate Byrne whom he married in January 1960. They would have a son, Mark, born in January 1961.

After appearing in ten films, mostly extra work, Oliver joined forces with Hammer Film Productions which, along with Michael Winner and Ken Russell, would be the main influence in his film career. "Michael gave me my money," Reed often said, "and Ken gave me my art. But Hammer gave me my technique."

Hammer Films was founded in 1934 by Will Hinds (a comedian who billed himself as Will Hammer) and Enrique Carreras. After a fitful start, interrupted by World War II, the company found international success in 1957 with *The Curse of Frankenstein* starring Peter Cushing and Christopher Lee. Hammer remade many of the classic Hollywood horrors and, in 1959, got around to *The Two Faces of Dr. Jekyll*. Oliver was given the small but showy part of a nightclub bouncer — a job with which he was well acquainted. The following year Hammer began casting for a werewolf...

At age 22, Oliver had, in retrospect, rather quickly become a film star. True, it was "only" a Hammer Horror, but a very well-made one, and he gave an electrifying performance under the practiced hand of director Terence Fisher. During the next three years Oliver would appear in five Hammer productions in a row, eventually totaling nine in all. Despite his identification with Hammer Horror, *The Curse of the Werewolf* was his only appearance in that type of film; half of his roles were in costume adventures.

In 1962 Oliver joined with the second of his major career influences, director Michael Winner, who cast him in *The System*.

Oliver played — expertly — a slightly over-aged, too-smart-for-his-own-good beach photographer who developed a "system" for meeting girls on holiday for casual sex.

Just as everything seemed to be going his way, Oliver walked into the Crazy Elephant club near Piccadilly and left with only half of his face. A drunken patron took exception to an innocuous remark made by Oliver and smashed a glass or bottle against his left jawbone. He was left with permanent facial scars and probably a few internal ones as well. He began drinking far too much, a behavior that would plague his personal and professional life until the end.

Director Ken Russell soon became influence number three. He noticed Oliver as a panelist on, of all things, the TV series *Juke Box Jury* and contacted him for an interview. Russell had been planning to film a biography of the composer Debussy — and Oliver was a dead ringer, without the scars. Fortunately for the careers of both men, Russell was big enough to overlook them. With the encouragement of Winner, Oliver took the part in the spring of 1965.

For the next ten years or so, Oliver was one of the world's biggest stars and best actors (not always the same thing). Winner's *The Jokers* (1966) and *I'll Never Forget What's 'Isname* (1967) established Oliver as an icon of "swinging London." *Oliver!* (1968), directed by Sir Carol, was voted Best Picture; during this period, Oliver met dancer Jacquie Daryl and they became lovers. Kate divorced him; he and Jacquie subsequently had a daughter, Sarah. *Women in Love* (1969), directed by Ken Russell, was perhaps his best all-around film and performance. *The Three Musketeers* (1973), *The Four Musketeers* (1974) and *The Return of the Musketeers* (1989), all directed by Richard Lester, had Oliver headlining all-star casts. Throw in *The Devils* (1971, Ken Russell), *Tommy* (1975, Russell) and *Royal Flash* (1975, Lester) and the 1970s pretty much belonged to Oliver Reed.

Then, gradually, it was over. For every

quality production like *The Prince and the Pauper* (1977) there was nonsense like *The Great Scout and Cathouse Thursday* (1976), *Maniac* (1976) and *Touch of the Sun* (1979). His final forty films included ten "guest appearances" and one firing. Oliver's outrageous behavior (often faked, just for laughs) got more press than his film roles.

He married his third wife, Josephine Burge, in September 1986; her influence helped to calm Oliver down some, but not enough. He somehow made around 25 films from 1986 to 1990 with few of them, including *Castaway* (1986), of any real interest. Then he was reunited with Michael Winner.

Oliver played a small but pivotal role in *Parting Shots* (1999), a black comedy about a man who, believing he's dying, hires a hitman (guess who?) to even the score with some "old friends." Oliver's winning performance indicated that his career was indeed salvageable and that he needed one more break to get back on top.

Sir Ridley Scott's *Gladiator* (2000) was certainly the biggest film of Oliver's career and contains one of his best performances. As Proximo, trainer of Maximus (Russell Crowe in an Academy Award–winning performance), Reed simply devoured the camera and dominated every scene in which he appeared. *Gladiator* was Reed's second film to win Best Picture and he might have received a Best Supporting Actor nomination (and statue) had he not died, unexpectedly, on May 2, 1999, before the completion of the film. He was only 61, certainly young enough to complete his comeback.

As the record stands, Oliver Reed appeared in more than 100 films over a career that spanned five decades. Not all were wonderful. But 25 or so were among the best of their kind. Few actors can claim to have appeared in top-quality dramas, musicals, literary adaptations, horror, science fiction, westerns, swashbucklers, comedies and war pictures.

Oliver Reed probably would not have made that claim either. He just made the films.

Friends and Colleagues
Remember Him

Janette Scott

Janette Scott is show business royalty, with parents in the business and having had a career in the movies from the time she was a child. Oliver Reed starred as her psychotic brother in *Paranoiac*, though he had been an extra on a much earlier film that she starred in and knew her by sight and reputation.

I thought if I am to turn my memory all the way back to *Paranoiac* whatever year it was, it might be better to just let my mind flow "stream of consciousness" rather than work on a set piece for you.

Freddie Francis was the director. I had worked for him before and we were great friends. His wife Pam was "continuity girl" or as they now call it "script girl." I had not worked with Olly [Note: most people spell Reed's nickname "Ollie"] before and I really don't think I knew anything about him at all when we started to film on location in beautiful summer weather. We became instant friends. I'm sure, looking back in hindsight, I must have been very naive, but I didn't realize until long afterwards that he must have been married at the time. He never mentioned his family at all and seemed, beneath the brooding dark looks, rather shy and nervous. I would take a picnic basket to the location every day and very soon I was sharing it with Olly who always seemed to be at my shoulder when I turned around. He almost seemed embarrassed to be taking our work seriously and would joke perhaps a little too much until he realized that I, who had been bought up in "the business," wanted to be as professional as possible. I remember Freddie Francis being quite glad that I would check upcoming scenes with Olly. We all got on extremely well and it was a happy film set.

Olly could not "hold a tune." He was hopeless at singing any song. Danny Kaye had made the film *Hans Christian Andersen* (1952) in which he sang a song called "Inchworm." The melody is sung with the words "Inchworm, inchworm/measuring the marigolds/you and your arithmetic/you'll probably go far," etc. Meanwhile there is a counter-melody behind which goes "Two and two are four/four and four are eight/ eight and eight are sixteen/sixteen and sixteen are thirty-two." Now the reason I bother to tell you this is, for some daft reason I tried to teach Olly the counter-melody while I sang the verse. Not only could he not hold the melody, he also had no sense of rhythm whatsoever. It was hopeless — but he wanted to succeed at this silly song so much that we worked on it daily for the whole film!

I'm pretty certain he must have been living alone — separated from his wife perhaps? Remember, I didn't know he was or had been married — but I remember several night-time calls — very late, midnight and beyond where he would talk for hours and not want to put the phone down. I realized this was someone who was very needy and did not want to face the silence of being alone. Once or twice I thought he had been drinking a bit — but since we never drank while we were working, it didn't enter my mind that this was (or would become) a problem for him. My mother [actress Dame Thora Hird] and my father had a country cottage not far from my home near Ottershaw in Surrey. Because he seemed so alone I asked him to come down to the country during the filming for a couple of weekends. These were great fun. Olly and my mother and father got on wonderfully well. It seemed he enjoyed being "one of the family" and I have a vivid memory of Olly having climbed up a walnut tree in their cottage garden to gather walnuts for my mother to pickle, getting stuck and all of us with ropes and buckets and finally a ladder trying to get him down, but laughing so much there was little energy left to help him.

Work progressed and everyone seemed pleased with the film. By the time it ended, my mother was doing a summer season in the theatre in Blackpool in the North of England and at the "wrap" of the film I said goodbye to my friends at Bray Studios and went up to visit my parents and see the show. While up there I got a call from Freddie Francis to say that he had been asked to do some work on a film of John Wyndham's *The Day of the Triffids* and would I come south and be in it with Kieron Moore as my co-star. Trusting Freddie completely, and without seeing the script, I came back to London and MGM Studios where filming was to take place for five or six weeks.

After a couple of days filming, Olly suddenly appeared on the set. I thought at first he must be filming on another set at MGM, but this was not the case. He had found out that Freddie and I were working together again and had come to visit. This was very nice and we were social for a while, but, of course, we had to get on with the work. He left. The next day Olly was back again. It was afternoon and he had obviously had a "good lunch" and was a little bit too loud. He had to be asked to be quiet or leave. The next day he arrived very drunk and had to be removed from the set. When I drove out of the studio that night he followed me in his car and forced my car off the road at one point, so I pulled into the drive of a pub and spent some time calming him down. But he had scared me and the next day the gate men at the studio turned him away. I know he came several

times more and I think Freddie Francis dealt with him — so I'm sure it was done in a kind way, because Freddie was a lovely, gentle man. However, I'm truly sad to say I never spoke to Olly again. Some time later I saw him in a London restaurant — he was at the far end of the room and I was horrified to see a great scar on his face.

I realize, to quote your letter, that you have "no interest in his private life," so for that reason I have not gone into too many details, but it's a hard tightrope to walk. Where does the acting life end and the private life begin, I wonder. Certainly we did not talk of acting techniques or "getting into the characters we were portraying." We were jobbing actors. We were expected to turn up at the studios on time — which we did. Know our lines — which we did. And give a reasonable performance without too much fuss or taking up too much time on what was a low-budget film. We did just that.

Remembering Olly as a unique person with extraordinary looks ideal for the big screen is easy. Remembering him as a gentle, shy, nervous and witty person, who took me to see his primary school in Guildford, who insisted we go to the cinema together on an afternoon off, who adored my mother and father and who changed in a dramatic way a short time after we worked together, is both a pleasure and a sadness. I hope these memories are of use to you both for your book.

Catherine Feller

Catherine Feller was Oliver Reed's first leading lady, a fresh new face at Hammer to match his new role as movie star. Feller had worked in films and television before *The Curse of the Werewolf*. She continues to work and live in Italy.

The Curse of the Werewolf was my first really big part in a film. I was very young — which is my excuse for many of the opinions I'm going to give. In that film I was in fairy-tale-land ... and it was wonderful! It was all so glamorous. The director, Terence Fisher, was very kind — I remember feeling no fear. It was, you know, all done in little bits. Much easier than the theatre! I had no problems in the scenes with my leading man, Oliver Reed, not in the scenes....

I thought, and everyone thought, he was very handsome. I was aware that he was very special ... already a kind of star ... or seemed to be. He was very easy — not "leading man-nish"— none of that. But off the set there were some problems. We argued a lot. About the future!

I don't know how I dared really. He'd been asked to go to Stratford-upon-Avon to do Shakespeare. I said, "You're a great actor — you shouldn't take those film offers, you should go there." He said, "No. I know what I'm doing. I'm going to make film after film after film and I'll get money, money, money and power, power, power, then I can choose what I want to do at Stratford. I can always go to Stratford once I have the money and the power." Now I realize that he was right and I was wrong. It's a wonder that he didn't put an impediment in my way! He was very good to me on set. If I met me now, as I was then, I would not, perhaps, like myself. That girl, then, did this: When we were on night loca-tion, when Oliver had to climb that church and was killed as the werewolf, we were there all night. We had this big meal in an enor-mous tent. We were the leading lady and the leading man — we were placed at one table. And I just looked at him and said, "Oh, Oliver! I can't eat looking at all that blood and pus ... with your face like that." I just flounced off! I wouldn't eat with him! Later, people said, "What! Oliver Reed!" People were dreaming of him! But I — I refused to break bread with him! I suppose he couldn't easily get over that. But he never made a fuss. I think he just dismissed me. And also, he wasn't at all attracted to me — he was, I think, married at the time so that's as it should have been! And I wasn't to him — and I've worked out why!

Over the years so many girls and women in Italy, in England, have said, "Oh, it had to be wonderful, kissing Oliver Reed." But he meant nothing to me and I've figured out why. It was me, not him! I think I have been attracted to men all my life that had a sort of feminine streak in them. And he didn't. He was an absolute *man*! He was indomitable! You couldn't move him. I couldn't wheedle

around him. He was a man! And that didn't attract me — he was too much of a man for me!

When my 60th birthday approached, one of my friends in Milan who had moved to London with his wife said, "When you be-come 60, if you come to London, I'll give a big party for you." And he did. I chose to have twenty of my best friends. There was a lot of whispering going on. Suddenly I heard, "But she didn't really care for him." What it was — on that day, Oliver had died. They knew I had made the film with him, and they were all whispering, keeping it under cover. And this friend said, "Why? She really didn't get on with him all that well." But it did give me a very strange feeling. Of course, I didn't really know him that well, but it was a shock. I realized how much everybody admired him. Suddenly, Jennie Linden said, "Oh, Olly!" She was very struck because she'd made *Women in Love* with him. He was so full of life...

I'd like to make a sort of tribute to Oliver's father. He was a conscientious objector, and he suffered for it and seemingly made people in his family suffer for it. He fought by not fighting, and Oliver Reed became a fighter. It's like a full circle. I think his father and he were very alike. In the later years they came together again. I had conflicted admiration for Oliver Reed. My arguments about his fu-ture showed that I thought he was very good. But the rest of the time it was blissful indif-ference. And no harm done. It says some-thing good about him.

Your historical records may show that he was not yet a star ... was just becoming a star. But it didn't feel like that. It feels as if he was. He had star quality. I don't remember him asking questions like an actor on the way up. I feel that he was already up! It was quite ob-vious that Christina, the girl I was playing, would fall for him. He was very special. He was very, very handsome; particularly in his white shirt, his face above a high collar. Very strong face and maybe, a face unlike any other. His stardom was in part due to his face. You don't say, "Oliver Reed looks like..." Nobody ever said he looked like someone. Oliver Reed looked like Oliver Reed.

Jennie Linden

Jennie Linden met Oliver Reed during the filming of Women in Love *and remained fond of him thereafter. She is an accomplished actress and stalwart of many television series in the 1960s and '70s.*

Oliver as one of those actors you couldn't fail to like, or indeed admire. His personality was huge, funny and over the top! In *Women in Love* I discovered Oliver was extremely kind; also I discovered he liked a drink, or six, loved to party and indulge in clever pranks. He was *always* dramatic "on" and "off." He could have been a very interesting actor. He was being very subtle in *Women in Love*. Very exciting to watch. But he sabotaged himself again and again. However, he was a great liver of life, one of the few "Hollywood stars" of the English film industry. He died as he lived, absolutely "full on." I was so pleased to have worked with him.

Mark Lester

As a small boy, Mark Lester worked with Reed, taking the title role in *Oliver!* Much later, he starred with Reed in *The Prince and the Pauper*, where they had as much fun off screen as on. Lester now works as a therapist in England.

SUSAN D. COWIE: All the stuff I've read about *Oliver!* said that you, Jack Wild and the other children didn't get to see Oliver Reed as himself, he was always Bill Sikes. Is that so?

MARK LESTER: That was pretty much the case. We were all terrified of him.

SC: He did look rather scary, that is true.

ML: You should have met him [*laughs*]!

SC: There's a wonderful juxtaposition between himself and little Oliver who's the quintessential innocent, which is absolutely beautiful. Apart from being scared of him, do you have any memories you would like to share about making *Oliver!*?

ML: I think because he was a sort of Method actor he used to come on the set in the guise of Bill Sikes so we just thought that that was how he was. It was only really at the very end of the film when we were having our after-filming party in the Shepperton Studios restaurant that Oliver Reed sort of let his hair down and I think he got Jack and me drunk on vodka. He said he would add something spicy into our lemonade; I do remember having three or four of these and going home and I think I remember my mum said I got into the bath with all my clothes on at the age of nine!

SC: Oh dear, not a good sign

ML: Well, she wasn't very impressed

SC: No, I bet she wasn't. And then later, were you not a bit bothered about working with him?

ML: Oh no, no, no! I really wanted to work with him. He was very fine and it was a really good experience working with him on *The Prince and the Pauper*.

SC: Very different, I imagine.

ML: Yes it was different. Again, he was a very powerful character but obviously I was older then and felt kind of wiser to it; I went on a couple of drinking expeditions out with Mr. Reed—I couldn't keep up [*laughs*].

SC: I don't think many people could, not even Michael Ripper. Ripper used to make the most lethal lager at home and he really could pop it away, God bless him, but even he said he couldn't keep up with Oliver.

ML: I remember we went out to a restaurant to celebrate his daughter's birthday—I think Oliver would have celebrated the opening of an envelope—and we had this meal and he decided that we were going to eat pudding first and then continue backwards. I don't think we actually got any further than the pudding because we were thrown out of the restaurant for throwing gooey chocolate pancakes as we had a food fight. In Budapest—the old town of Buda—it was still in Communist times and they weren't too impressed with us having a food fight. Everyone got covered in chocolate sauce and we were asked to leave the restaurant. I remember the next day going off filming and I think Oliver didn't — he never really used to drink if he was having to work the next day, only when he wasn't working. Anyway, I had to, and I remember coming home back to the hotel in the evening and the two chambermaids outside my room going, "Oh you're horrible. You're disgusting" and I asked, "What are you talking about?" and they said, "Look at the bed." And they hadn't changed the bed and it was covered in chocolate and they obviously thought it was something else! So I tried to explain to them that it wasn't what they thought it was and I sort of put my finger on it as if to taste it and they all screamed [*laughs*].

SC: Definitely a difficulty of communication!

ML: Yes it was — and that was a night to forget, I think! I was very, very drunk but then you know Oliver would go on and carry on drinking afterwards — he would have started before us and carried on after. I don't know how he could do it.

SC: He must have had the most amazing capacity.

ML: Absolutely!

SC: So after *The Prince and the Pauper*, did you have to do the rounds with the promos for it?

ML: No! They didn't promote it. I think they didn't have any money to promote it. [The producers] had tied up all their money in *Superman* and they didn't really do any promoting — there wasn't even a premiere.

SC: I'm not even sure that I actually saw it at the movies, though I've seen it on satellite TV and video.

ML: It didn't do very well at the cinema but it's done better latterly on DVD.

SC: It's enormous fun.

ML: It's a good romp!

SC: It's one of the good versions of *The Prince and the Pauper*.

ML: It had a great cast, there were a lot

of good people in it: George C. Scott, Ernest Borgnine, Raquel Welsh, Charlton Heston, megastars.

SC: So you had fun.

ML: Yes, I was very fortunate to work on it.

SC: Would you have worked with Oliver again at a later date?

ML: Oh God, yeah! Yeah, yeah! Definitely.

SC: That's nice to know. We have a sort of dividing line between the people who absolutely refused to talk to us that he *really* must have annoyed, and others who were kinder.

ML: Well, I know David Hemmings and he had a big falling out — I think that was over Raquel Welch — and then they did a fight scene and Oliver Reed didn't pull any of his punches.

SC: He never did, though. William Hobbs, the fight arranger for the Musketeers movies, said when Olly went into it, he went into it heart and soul so you always had to be careful if you were on the other end.

ML: Yes — a lot of the stunt team who were Hungarian were very wary of him!

SC: Sounds like the Spaniards on *Musketeers*!

William Hobbs

A formidably talented fight arranger, William Hobbs met Reed when coaching him for the first Musketeers movie. He subsequently worked on the others. Hobbs also created fights for *Royal Flash*. He continues coaching actors and opera singers with a variety of dangerous weapons so they appear experts on stage and screen.

SUSAN D. COWIE: When did you first meet Oliver?

WILLIAM HOBBS: I first met Oliver prior to shooting *The Three Musketeers*. I asked for the leading actors to undertake some training before shooting started and this work began with Michael York and Richard Chamberlain in London. Oliver, however, wanted me to go to him and work at his mansion house in Dorking. I went down to this very impressive stately English home [Broome Hall], and was ushered into an enormous wood-paneled room with a huge picture window overlooking the garden. There was nobody in the room and I thought it rather strange but became aware of a very high-backed chair facing the window and eventually Oliver's face appeared around the side of the chair. A good entrance, I thought, and perhaps well planned for new visitors. After introductions and a brief chat (I remember Oliver to be a man of few words), he took me out to the garden where I was to work with him, stomping around in the very long grass. I began some exercises, showed him positions and got him briefly lunging and parrying when suddenly, after only a few moves, he complained about his leg, saying he had pulled a muscle. The session for me was therefore disappointingly cut short, but maybe not for Oliver. As we all know, he was a very fine actor. Of course, he was a big man and he may quite genuinely have felt a few aches. That was our first meeting and the only training session I ever had with Oliver. The next time we met was on location in Spain when I was devising the opening sequence of fights between the Musketeers and the Cardinal's Guard.

TOM JOHNSON: Were you familiar with his movies? Had you heard of him before?

WH: I knew of him but no more than that, really. I think I had seen his name in some Hammer horror pictures. I knew he was respected in the business but found out a lot more as we started to work together.

SC: Obviously it takes a lot of discipline because it's jolly dangerous, what you do.

WH: Shall we say, some actors have more discipline than others. Oliver, in my experience, was extremely professional and I recall that he was always first on the set in the mornings. However he wasn't a theatre actor or to my knowledge had had a theatre training. He was a natural, and the notion of rehearsing over and over again to improve a

scene or a piece of action wasn't Oliver's way. In the fights, he would learn the moves by coming to one session, then on to the following day's shoot but knowing every move. This was impressive, but maybe not so impressive for his courageous cinema opponents who would have welcomed longer rehearsals. Even the tough Spanish stuntmen used to raise their eyes to Heaven when selected to fight with Oliver. Oliver actually had the very first fight to be shot on *The Three Musketeers* and I gave him the head Spanish stuntman to meet in combat during the early scene in the garden of the Cloisters. The man was tough and experienced but on his very first attack Oliver felled him with a bad hit on the head and he lay puking on the ground.

I believe it was after this that straws were drawn by the stunt crew as to who should fight with Oliver! This was not the best way to commence shooting an action adventure film. After a suitable recovery period, the same fight was shot again and it was performed with tremendous brio and passion but it was pretty hairy, which was down to the fact that it was insufficiently rehearsed. The danger that came across in his acting was of course compelling but putting "opponents" into real danger was not beneficial, except that his acting during the fights came across superbly on the screen, showing that Athos meant business.

TJ: The fights were so well rehearsed that they look unrehearsed.

WH: Well, some sequences were well rehearsed and others were not as well as I would have liked. I need to rehearse the actors as much as possible both for safety and the look of the end result. I'm a maddening perfectionist.

TJ: When you compare them to an Errol Flynn movie, the fights in *The Three Musketeers* looked real.

WH: Hopefully they did, as I tried to make them look as genuine as possible. I remember talking to Richard Lester before we started shooting about what level of panache, brio, violence or comedy he wanted and we talked about the old Gene Kelly version (*The Three Musketeers*, MGM, 1948). Richard wanted the fights to be as real as they could be. The comedy would come out of the characters and situation, so we never played for comedy. The feeling of reality which ultimately came across on the screen, at times, had something to do with the simplicity of the routines, which with more rehearsal might have become too complex. We had plenty of rehearsal for duels such as the climactic sequence between D'Artagnan and Rochefort.

Praise must be given to those wonderful actors who gave their all in performance. Regarding weaponry, I particularly did not want the Musketeers all to have the same swords, looking like the Tiller girls, not that those particular actors ever would, so with Richard's approval I gave each different weapons to provide more of a personal identity to the characters in action. D'Artagnan fought with a sword only, Athos with a sword and cloak, Aramis with sword and dagger and Porthos with sword and anything he could lay his hands on.

SC: The weaponry in the *Musketeers* movies doesn't look anachronistic. In some versions it looks almost as though they've borrowed stuff from the Olympics but the weapons in all four *Musketeers* movies look accurate to the period. If you're a pedant about history, things like that matter.

WH: They matter very much and great care was taken in selecting the correct weaponry and choosing a different style of sword guard for each of the principal characters. I began by selecting the long rapier blades of the period which Richard Lester wanted but had to go back to him and say that they were too long and heavy for the actors to handle convincingly, particularly when having to perform a sequence of combat over and over again. We made a compromise, chopping down the length of the blade just a little, so that it was still heavy and cumbersome in order that the actors would not be able to wield them like a fairy

wand or a modern Olympic foil, thus maintaining a period feel to the action.

TJ: As it must be — like boxers going twelve rounds and barely able to stand up.

WH: Well of course, and I loved Richard Lester's humor. It was gratifying too that he allowed me to incorporate my own pieces of comic invention into the fights and shot everything I came up with. I recall one particular moment I was pleased with at the end of the fight in the washing room: when the heroes had vanquished the guards and, thinking there were no more to deal with, fell exhausted into each other. Then one lone guard moved forward to attack and they glanced at each other, unable to do anything as the guard fell before them.

TJ: And the humor counterpointed the ferocity of the fight?

WH: Exactly — it was nothing like Olympic fencing. At least I hope not!

SC: D'Artagnan's so much younger than the rest of them that if they're in that sort of big fight, the older guys are going to be more tired than he is.

WH: They were also wearing wonderful but very heavy costumes. Oscar-winning designs by Yvonne Blake. When I first looked at the designs, my heart fell as I thought the actors would be unable to move in them and fight at the same time. What happened of course was quite the reverse. It was because the costumes were voluminous and heavy that together with the weighty swords they gave the action a gritty, historically accurate feel.

SC: We've been reviewing all the movies you did with Richard Lester and the last one I looked at was *Royal Flash* where you were hanging on a hook in the kitchen scene and that's different fighting.

WH: Yes, it was — a later period. I worked on five films for Richard and I learned a tremendous amount about filming from him. Oliver was of course in that film as well as in the three *Musketeers* movies. He again gave a wonderful performance, but working on fights with Oliver was not easy.

In *Royal Flash*, in order to preserve his opponent Malcolm McDowell, keep Oliver under control and my own sanity, I got my own back by choreographing sword moves which gave Oliver no attacks but only parries. Oliver was a natural attacker but he didn't realize what I had done until, on the set at the moment of shooting, and I recall with a certain amount of pleasure of which I'm not particularly proud, the expression on his face change from glowering menace to one of surprise as he held in his need to attack to being trapped in a routine of constant defense. Working with Oliver however was never easy, as we had different ideas as to how much rehearsal was required. I'd like to rehearse as much as possible, whilst Oliver only wanted to do the minimum, as I believe he knew that he could give a good showing merely on the day of shooting. Not so good for his film opponents. He would prefer to get rehearsal over with and nearly always turn up on the day of the shoot knowing all his moves, which in some cases was pretty alarming for his opponents who hadn't had sufficient rehearsal. That was the way Oliver worked and the end result never failed.

During the filming of *The Return of the Musketeers*, in a fight routine I had Oliver making a kick at an opponent, which he didn't want to do and I was forced to change the move. I wasn't happy about doing this as it seemed exactly the right move. However, that night after shooting, when I was back in my hotel the phone rang and it was Oliver on the phone. "It's Oliver here," he said. "I'm in the bath and now I realize why you wanted that." After all I had experienced with him, I was truly delighted, as well as being very surprised, for we were anything but bosom buddies.

TJ: He's been presented as a drunk in books, which was part of him I guess. We don't know him, so I don't know what to believe. He's always been presented as personal life first and movies as an afterthought. There's a new book out called *Hellraisers* about Oliver, Burton, Harris and O'Toole.

WH: I worked with three of them!

TJ: It's just a rehash of all their drinking exploits and that's not right for Oliver Reed — he never had the other side. So what we're interested in, and that story you just told us is perfect, is that as an actor there had to be more to him than just being drunk and carrying on and that's what we're trying to get across. We don't care about the other stuff. It's been done to death.

WH: Well, as I said to you, I remember Oliver as being the first on the set ready for work and in all the times we worked together I was never aware of him having a hangover when filming. If he did, then he concealed it admirably. I remember him as good as gold when waiting under canvas in the morning on *The Return of the Musketeers*, always with a book in hand, glasses on and constantly reading. Apart from the way he went about the fights, I thought he was tremendously professional. When we were making *Royal Flash* in Germany, Malcolm McDowell said to me, "You know, Ollie's arrived. We'll all have to pull our socks up now." As an actor, I think his fellow cast members also had respect for him. It's a great pity, I think, that he didn't have the chance to further enhance his work, and play some classical roles. He could have been a great Cyrano or Falstaff.

SC: When he made *The Curse of the Werewolf*, his co-star Catherine Feller nagged him because he'd been approached to do Shakespeare and he said to her, "Not yet. Later. I'm going to establish myself as a movie star and then I'm going to go and do Shakespeare."

WH: He could have done so many classical roles, with that amazing, soft but caressing voice, but I do wonder how it would have projected in the theatre. I've known a number of film actors who are wonderful on screen but lack the technique to project in theatre. [But] I don't think Oliver would have been lacking in that requirement. More likely, the long, detailed rehearsals would not have suited him.

SC: He had such a range of things he

could do. People tend to think of him in horror films or falling over drunk but the range of characters he played was quite phenomenal.

WH: That's right. For example the Ken Russell films such as *Women in Love*. I think he was very underestimated.

TJ: Christopher Lee told us about Oliver's spontaneity which was more often right than wrong in improvising a scene but could be difficult for those around him. And as you said, there was danger as you never knew what he was going to do

WH: I agree completely with that. When performing the fights, he was at times quite terrifying to others. Some Spanish stuntmen even drew cards to determine who would fight him. I recall one occasion before we were due to rehearse on set and he tried to parry on the left when it was meant to be on the right, which caused his opposing stuntman to stab him in the arm. The result was a night in hospital for Athos. When he returned to shooting, he was angry when he walked through the routine at forgetting the moves. He started shouting and throwing swords around. The crew ducked and moved out of the way whilst I was left standing my ground and the flack. There is no doubt that if he could have improvised the swordplay, he would have been a good deal happier. However, there is equally no doubt that he always came out looking great in all his combats. One of the reasons may be that he shouted and acted fury against his opponents when fighting. There was no tinkle, tap, tap, tap of blades when he was in action. He would also drive his opponents back, forever moving after them. In *The Three Musketeers*, having lunch with Christopher Lee in a local simple Spanish restaurant outside Madrid where Christopher and I had been rehearsing the final confrontation between D'Artagnan and the villain Rochefort, I told Christopher of a letter in my pocket that I had written to Richard Lester resigning from the film because of the difficulties I had experienced working with Oliver. I had felt hamstrung in

that I wasn't able to do my work in the way I wished and was deeply unhappy about it. Filming wouldn't be filming if there weren't any problems, and my only serious problem was working with Oliver. In retrospect these could well have been down as much to my inexperience at the time, as to Oliver's preference for improvisation and attitude to rehearsals. Christopher said that if I handed in the letter to Richard, I would never work in the industry again. His advice brought a return to sanity for me. I pocketed the letter which had never been opened to this day and I shall forever be grateful to Christopher's wise and helpful words of wisdom. I had to tell myself that Oliver's and my ideas of how to achieve the best results were different and leave it at that. I truly liked and respected Oliver. Such larger-than-life film stars don't seem to be around much any more, or maybe they aren't wanted these money-driven days. Were he still around, there is no doubt that his charisma would still light up the screen whilst his japes and at times outrageous behavior would even moreso today hit the front pages of papers.

As for my career, although I had already worked on *HMS Defiant* and Polanski's *Macbeth*, it was Richard Lester's wonderful *The Three Musketeers* that gave it lift-off, and after this Ridley Scott's first feature *The Duellists*. I was fortunate that it was the time that intelligent as well as entertaining adventure stories were being made into pictures. Nowadays it seems that action is being made by fast pop video style cutting in the editor's room. No one cares any more, it appears about character and situation; action in which you are led by motivation and the people involved. The Gene Kelly version was splendid but for me Richard Lester's was superior with its mixture of realism, high drama and comedy. There were great film actors then, macho and with real charisma. You only have to think of Oliver, Christopher Lee and Charlton Heston amongst the other fine actors in our version. The film is still to this day frequently shown on television. The hardships we went through in the filming were all worth it and brought the cast and crew together. The heat may have been brutal, the costumes and weaponry incredibly heavy; and personally I was concerned about the dangers of accidents occurring during the fight scenes. Thank goodness the few we had were not serious, but still the fighting and the action were alarming whilst providing a pretty fair sense of reality. One day I must bring myself to open that letter of resignation I wrote. Well, perhaps not!

Readers of this book should know that Oliver Reed, whether his routines were always to my liking or not, whether they always went right or not, livened up every fight scene in which he appeared. Fights with Oliver were pretty damn near real. I have a great deal of admiration for him as he could be extremely courteous and charming. He may have described himself as a "public school thug" but I suspect that was the image he liked to present.

Samantha Eggar

Samantha Eggar first met Oliver Reed during the war when they were both small children. Later they encountered each other again when they were cast as leads in Cronenberg's *The Brood*. Eggar received an Oscar nomination for *Molly McGuires* and has an extensive career in films and television.

In his memoir he once reminded me, I was his first girlfriend, aged three! I made him a Plasticine cake. (If you are American, this is what English kids made models of. It is like putty and came in colors.) We were all living in a village called Bledlow in Buckinghamshire, probably in safety from the bombing of London. His mother and mine were friends.

Next meeting I think was when we were both young actors. Probably out of sequence but not memory, we were shooting a film in Paris called *Lady in the Car* and I had my two young children with me. We were living in a flat on the Avenue Foche and Ollie came to tea. His relationship with the kids was instant and all fun. He played "the carpet game": wrapped them up in a huge Persian carpet and then picked up one end and rolled them out. "Again" was heard all afternoon, amidst screams of laughter. My kids (now with children the same age) remember him very fondly.

Adults taking time to acknowledge one's children is a very good sign.

As an actor and maybe a person, he had a duality. His softness in voice and feelings and body language juxtapositioned the brawn of the bar room and its sometimes humorless eventualities, i.e., some poor chap knocked out cold. But the bluster and the fevered rant was always quieted in the end and I personally, though going through once on the receiving line of "language," evermore ended up loving him. If you are a good bastard, you win.

THE FILMS

Value for Money (1955)

Group Film Productions Ltd.; released by J. Arthur Rank Film Distributors in the U.K. in 1955 and by Rank Film Distributors of America in the U.S. in 1957

Crew—Director: Ken Annakin; from a novel by Derrick Boothroyd; Writers: R.F. Delderfield, William Fairchild; Producer: Sergei Nolbandov; Executive Producer: Earl St. John; Original Music: Malcolm Arnold; Cinematographer: Geoffrey Unsworth; Film Editor: Geoffrey Foot; Casting (uncredited): Weston Drury Jr.; Art Director: Alex Vetchinsky; Costume Design: Julie Harris; Makeup Artist: W.T. Partleton; Hair Stylist: Iris Tilley; Production Manager: H.R.R. Attwool; Assistant Director: Pat Marsden; Third Assistant Directors (uncredited): Colin M. Brewer, Geoffrey Helman; Draughtsman (uncredited): Lionel Crouch; Sound Recordist: John Dennis; Sound Editor: Archie Ludski; Sound Mixer: Gordon K. McCallum; Dubbing Crew (uncredited): Bill Daniels, C. Le Mesurier; Boom Operator (uncredited): Robert T. MacPhee; Sound Camera Operator (uncredited): Ken Rawkins; Camera Operator: David Harcourt; Still Photographer (uncredited): Norman Gryspeerdt; Color Consultant: Joan Bridge; Music Recordist: Ted Drake; Conductor: Muir Mathieson; Production Controller: Arthur Alcott; Choreographers: Irving Davies, Paddy Stone; Continuity: Kathleen Hosgood; Furrier: Molho; Production Secretary (uncredited): Teresa Bolland.

Cast—John Gregson (Charley Broadbent), Diana Dors (Ruthine West), Susan Stephen (Ethel), Derek Farr (Duke Popplewell), Frank Pettingell (Mayor Higgins), Charles Victor (Lumm), Ernest Thesiger (Lord Dewsbury), Hal Osmond (Mr. Hall), Jill Adams (Joy), Joan Hickson (Mrs. Perkins), James Gregson (Oldroyd), Donald Pleasence (Limpy), John Glyn-Jones (Arkwright), Leslie Phillips (Robjohns), Ferdy Mayne (Waiter), Charles Lloyd Pack (Mr. Gidbrook); uncredited: Oliver Reed (Bit), Julia Arnell (Ruritanian Doll), Peter Burton (Hotel Receptionist), Cyril Chamberlain (Hotel Manager), Ronald Chesney (Harmonica Player), Peggy Ann Clifford (Fat Mother), Irving Davies (Dancer), Pamela Davis (Topsy Doll), Carol Day (Doll), Jane Dore (Zulu Doll), Eleanor Fazan (Leopard Doll), Christine Finn (Reporter), Mavis Greenaway (Doll), Florence Gregson (Mrs. Walker), Hermione Harvey (Rabbit Doll), Guido Lorraine (Head Waiter), Gillian Lutyens (Jeweler's Assistant), Jill Melford (Muriel), Aleta Morrison (Baby Mink), Diana Munks (Topsy Doll), Sheila O'Neil (Indian Doll), Francis Pidgeon (Ferry Doll), Sheila Raynor (Mrs. Hall), Diana Satow (Poodle Doll), Ruth Sheil (Twin Doll), Cyril Smith (Writ Server), Paddy Stone (Dancer), Ann Sullivan (Doll), Terence Theobald (Audition Producer), Mavis Traill (Cat Doll), Mollie Weir (Mrs. Matthews), Ian Wilson (Extra), Vic Wise (Stagedoor Keeper), Patricia Webb.

Synopsis

Charley Broadbent (John Gregson), a young Yorkshireman, inherits a sizable fortune from his father. He decides to try the nightlife in London and meets a beautiful young girl (Diana Dors) performing in a night club. She plots to take him for every penny he possesses and he is quite happy to be taken, causing him to momentarily forget Ethel, the girl he really cares for.

Comment

The authors were unable to find a copy of this movie to review. A superb cast gives the hint that this was an above-average offering for its time. ("Will give considerable amusement to unsophisticated local audiences."—*Variety*, August 17, 1955.) Oliver Reed was fortunate to find a number of these productions while learning his craft.

Hello London (1958)

Kinran Production; released by 20th Century–Fox in the U.K.; no U.S. release

Crew—Writers: Guy Elmes, Ken Englund, George Fowler, Herbert Sargent; Producers: George Fowler, Sonja Henie; Executive Producer: Alan Neuman; Original Music: Philip Green; Cinematography: Otto Heller; Film Editor: Oswald Hafenrichter; Casting: Maude Spector; Art Director: Scott MacGregor; Makeup Artist: George Partleton; Hair Stylist: Barbara Ritchie; Production Manager: Clifford Parkes; Assistant Director: Kip Gowans; Sound Editor: Robert Winter; Wardrobe: Maude Churchill; Musical Director: Philip Martell; Choreographers: George Baron, Ted Shuffle; Continuity: Betty Harley.

Cast—Sonja Henie, Michael Wilding, Dora Bryan, Roy Castle, Robert Coote, Lisa Gastoni, Eunice Gayson, Ronny Graham, Charles Heslop, Stanley Holloway, Oliver Johnston, Trefor Jones, Dennis Price, Joan Regan (Themselves), Oliver Reed (Press Photographer), Ruth Lee (Woman).

Synopsis

Sonja Henie, world-famous ice-skater and movie star, arrives in London on a world tour with her ice show. She is asked to stay one more night than she intended in order to attend a charity performance. She begs her tour manager to arrange it and, with all her famous friends and acquaintances, puts on a good show.

Comment

In 1958, Sonja Henie, a Hollywood legend, was a little past her sell-by date but still good box office. She had an idea for a series of movies of her ice show traveling the world and showcasing major cities, hoping it would revive her flagging career, and she personally paid for this film to be produced. The authors were not able to see a print, but it was said that the skating sequences were magical and the plotline unmemorable. And it gave Oliver Reed something of a star-spangled introduction to the movies, and a lifestyle to aim for.

The Square Peg (1959)

The Rank Organisation; released by J. Arthur Rank Film Distributors in the U.K. in 1958; no U.S. release

Crew—Director: John Paddy Carstairs; Original Screenplay: Jack Davies, Henry Blyth, Norman Wisdom, Eddie Leslie; Producer: Hugh Stewart; Executive Producer: Earl St. John; Original Music: Philip Green; Cinematographer: Jack Cox; Film Editor: Roger Cherrill; Art Director: Maurice Carter; Costume Design: Yvonne Caffin; Makeup Artist: Geoffrey Rodway; Production Manager: Charles Orme; Assistant Director: Bert Batt; Set Dresser: Vernon Dixon; Sound Recordists: Gordon K. McCallum, Leo Wilkins; Camera Operator: James Bawden; Song "The Square Peg" composed by Michael Carr, Philip Green; Production Controller for Pinewood Studios: Arthur Alcott; Continuity: Susan Dyson.

Cast—Norman Wisdom (Norman Pitkin), Honor Blackman (Lesley Cartland), Edward Chapman (Mr. Grimsdale), Campbell Singer (Sgt. Loder), Hattie Jaques (Gretchen), Brian Worth (Henri Le Blanc), Terrence Alexander (Capt. Wharton), John Warwick (Colonel Layton), Arnold Bell (Gen. Hunt), Andre Maranne (Jean-Claude), Victor Beaumont (Jogenkraut), Frank Williams (Capt. Ford), Eddie Leslie (Medical Officer), Richard Marner (Bit Part), John G. Heller (German Officer at Gate); uncredited: Martin Boddey, Oliver Reed, Harold Goodwin, Richard Warner, Ian Wilson, Fred Griffiths (Lorry Driver), Victor Maddern (Motor Pool Corporal), Sheila McGibbon (Annie McQuillan), Hazel Sutton (Blonde).

Synopsis

During World War II, Norman Pitkin (Norman Wisdom), a council road-digger, and his boss Mr. Grimsdale (Edward Chapman) are proud of their war effort in keeping the town's roads fit for the many military vehicles that have to use them. Mr. Grimsdale is very aware of his own importance, and Norman is more than happy to revel in reflected glory. Working outside the army camp, they come into conflict with the military, and Norman is taken to the camp jail. Being Norman, and still in possession of his spade, he digs his way out, appropriates a female uniform and narrowly misses being seduced by Sgt. Loder (Campbell Singer). The army, angry at the subterfuge, arranges to have the whole council road gang called up for military service — shocking, as these men's jobs were exempt from service during the war. Aghast, Grimsdale and company report for duty and their induction course. Needless to say, Norman is a perfectly hopeless soldier and has many mishaps during basic training. Downhearted because of his situation, he is nonetheless overjoyed to meet the soldier whose uniform he had stolen, the lovely Lesley Cartland (Honor Blackman), who is preparing to be parachuted into occupied France as a Resistance operative. She is amused by Norman's adulation, and he, knowing his place in wartime British society, is content to worship from afar and dream. Shortly after the end of basic training, Norman's group is told that they are going to France. Due to a mix-up at the pub where they are having a farewell drink, Norman and Mr. Grimsdale find themselves aboard an aircraft over France, not having done any parachute training. After a hair-raising descent, they find themselves in the wrong place and having to find a unit to report to. In a nearby town, Norman gets strange reactions from the German soldiers lolling by the bars because he is the spitting image of the German general in charge of the district. As a French freedom fighter prepares to kill him in the bar, Lesley recognizes him and sees a chance to use his resemblance to the general to free her captured comrades from the German headquarters. Norman is happy to try — anything to stay close to Lesley. The men dig a tunnel under the wall of the headquarters; Norman makes his way to the general's room only to find that gentleman having an amorous adventure with the Junoesque Gretchen (Hattie Jacques), star of the Berlin Opera. Norman hides while the two serenade each other; seizing an opportunity to steal the general's clothes, he bluffs his way into the dungeon and rescues the resistance fighters. On their way out, Norman is caught and sentenced to be shot. The firing squad members stand him against the wall; the general delights in Norman's impending doom. The officer in charge of the squad tells Norman to move away from the newly painted wall and the blindfolded prisoner disappears down his own hole! Norman returns the hero and gets the girl.

Comment

Sir Norman Wisdom was the British film industry's answer to Charlie Chaplin. Although he never achieved Chaplin's worldwide recognition, he had a much longer active film career and is adored across Eastern Europe to this day. When he recently died (after suffering from dementia for years), the whole of the Isle of Man turned out for his funeral. Wisdom created a hapless, innocent, moral, endearing character, usually named Norman Pitkin, who could make the audience laugh, weep in sympathy and empathize as he battled all kinds of Establishment tyrants through his movies. Comedy is said to be the hardest discipline, but Wisdom made it look effortless. When, in later years, he evolved into a fine dramatic actor on TV, many critics were surprised; they shouldn't have been. Don't blink or you'll miss Oliver Reed square bashing with the other squaddies. "Mildly amusing comedy with a number of hilarious situations among dullish patches." — *Variety*, December 31, 1958.

The Captain's Table (1959)

The Rank Organisation; released by J. Arthur Rank Film Distributors in the U.K. in 1959 and by 20th Century–Fox in the U.S. in 1960

Crew—Director: Jack Lee; Screenplay: Bryan Forbes, Nicholas Phipps, John Whiting; from a novel by Richard Gordon; Producer: Joseph Janni; Original Music: Frank Cordell; Cinematographer: Christopher Challis; Film Editor: Frederick Wilson; Art Director: Michael Stringer; Costume Design: Joan Ellacott; Makeup Artist: George Blackler; Hair Stylist: Stella Rivers; Production Manager: Arthur Alcott; Production Manager: Peter Manley; Assistant Director: Stanley Hosgood; Sound Recordists: Bill Daniels, Geoffrey Daniels; Sound Editor: Arthur Ridout; Camera Operator: Dudley Lovell; Continuity: Penny Daniels; Publicity Director: Harry Gillard.

Cast—John Gregson (Captain Ebbs), Peggy Cummins (Mrs. Judd), Donald Sinden (Shawe-Wilson), Nadia Gray (Mrs. Porteous), Maurice Denham (Major Broster), Richard Wattis (Prittlewell), Reginald Beckwith (Burtweed), Lionel Murton (Bernie Floate), Bill Kerr (Bill Coke), Nicholas Phipps (Reddish), Joan Simms (Maude Pritvhett), Miles Malleson (Canon Swingler), John Le Mesurier (Sir Angus), James Hayter (Earnshaw), June Jago (Gwenny Coke), Nora Nicholson (Mrs. Lomax), John Warner (Henry Lomax), Harry Locke (Hole), Joseph Tomelty (Dalrymple), Ed Devereaux (Brickwood), Rosalie Ashley (Annette), Donald Churchill (Jay); uncredited: Oliver Reed, Yvonne Buckingham, Lynne Cole, Beth Rogan, David Aylmer, Steven Berkoff, Harry Brunning, Peggy Ann Clifford, Roland Curram, Heather Downham, Harold Goodwin, Lilian Grassom, Fred Griffiths, Sam Kydd, Herbert Osman, Wendy Peters, Robert Readon, Totti Truman Taylor, Tony Wager, Gillian Watt.

Synopsis

After decades as the captain of cargo vessels, Captain Albert Ebbs (John Gregson) is embarking on his first voyage aboard the South Star liner *Queen Adelaide* as its master, out from Tilbury, bound for Sydney, Australia. If this first voyage goes well, his appointment will be made permanent. Ebbs is well looked after by his personal steward "Tiny" Burtweed (Reginald Beckwith) who is embarrassingly considerate. First officer Shawe-Wilson (Donald Sinden), who has been used to having his head when running the ship, resents the new captain's authority. The first officer's main interest is pretty girls, none of whom are safe from his attentions. Prittlewell (Richard Wattis), the chief purser, is conducting a profitable smuggling business using the ship's supplies; he takes delight in pointing out to the captain that, as well as commanding the ship, he must run all kinds of social functions, talent competitions, beauty contests, old-time dances and so on.

Among the passengers invited to dine at the captain's table are several pretty, unattached women who see him as one of the perks of a long sea voyage, a novelist, an Australian traveler, a deaf old lady and her son and Major Broster (Maurice Denham), a personal friend of the shipping line chairman who expects to be treated like royalty. Ebbs realizes that Broster must be kept happy if his promotion is to be permanent. But things conspire against Ebbs: amorous ladies, a riotous children's tea party and a fancy dress ball where the "champagne" being served proves to be cider (another of Prittlewell's swindles). Ebbs feels that he will shortly be back at the helm of a grimy tramp steamer. But when he discovers Broster in a compromising position with Mrs. Porteous (Nadia Gray), Ebbs regains his confidence while Broster loses his. When the ship docks in Sydney, Ebbs is confident that Broster will send a glowing report to the company chairman in London. He and the supportive Burtweed look forward to many more happy voyages.

Comment

The authors were unable to find a copy of the movie to review. Reed was in a scene with a bucket on his head — the first of many "costumes" in his long career! *Daily Herald* (January 2, 1959): "[A] fairly amusing film, though there are too many weak jokes and damp situations.... I was interested in the announcement which appears after the credit titles: 'This film was made with the co-operation of the Orient Line — who gravely disapproved of the whole thing.'... I imagine 'disapproved' is an understatement." *Variety*, January 14, 1959: "Somewhat scrappy but amusingly light-hearted comedy."

Upstairs and Downstairs (1959)

The Rank Organisation; released by J. Arthur Rank Film Distributors in the U.K. in August 1959 and by 20th Century–Fox in the U.S. in 1960; 101 minutes; Color

Crew—Director: Ralph Thomas; Producers: Betty Box, Ralph Tomas; Screenplay: Frank Haney; Camera: Ernest Steward; Editor: Alfred Roome; Music; Philip Green.

Cast—Michael Craig (Richard), Anne Heywood (Kate), Mylene Demongeot (Ingrid), James Robertson Justice (Mansfield), Claudia Cardinale (Maria), Sidney James (PC Edwards), Joan Hickson (Rosemary), Joan Sims (Blodwen), Joseph Tomelty (Farrington), Nora Nicholson (Mrs. Farrington); uncredited: Oliver Reed.

Synopsis

Two newlyweds find more problems than they bargained for when they try to hire a servant; one applicant for the job is a near-prostitute, another has a large sheepdog, a third gets drunk and ruins a party and a fourth uses the position to cover an attempted bank robbery.

Comment

The authors were unable to find a print of this movie to review. "Most of the fun comes from the performances, most of them exaggerated but hilarious."—*Variety*, August 19, 1959.

Beat Girl (1959)

Willoughby Film Productions; made in 1959, released by Renown in the U.K. in 1960 and by Victoria in the U.S. in 1962; filmed at MGM British Studios, Borehamwood, and on locations in London; 96 minutes (U.K.), 85 minutes (U.S.); U.S. title: *Wild for Kicks*

Crew—Director: Edmond T. Greville; Producer: George Willoughby; Story & Screenplay: Dail Ambler; Cinematographer: Walter Lassally; Camera Operator: Neil Gemmell; Editor: Gordon Pilkington; Music: John Barry; Lyrics: Trevor Peacock, Hyam MacCoby; Wardrobe Supervisor: Harry Haynes; Art Director: Elven Webb; Production Manager: Al Marcus; Casting Director: Harvey Woods; Makeup: Sidney Turner; Hairdresser: Anne Box; Assistant Director: Kip Gowan; Recording Supervisor: A. W. Watkins; Dubbing Editor: Don Challis; Sound Recordists: J. B. Smith, Gerry Turner.

Cast—David Farrar (Paul Linden), Noelle Adam (Nichole), Christopher Lee (Kenny), Gillian Hills (Jennifer), Shirley-Ann Field (Dodo), Adam Faith (Dave), Peter McEnery (Tony), Claire Gordon (Honey), Nigel Green (Simon), Delphi Lawrence (Greta), Oliver Reed (Plaid Shirt), Michael Kayne (Duffel Coat), Anthony Singleton (Green Pants), Robert Raglan (FO Official), Nade Bell (FO Official's Wife), Margot Bryant (Martha), Norman Mitchell (Club Doorman), Pascaline (Stripper).

Synopsis

Jennifer (Gillian Hills), a precociously sexy teenager, rebels against her father Paul (David Farrar) and his new wife Nichole (Noelle Adam) by sneaking out to a coffee bar called the Off-beat during the evenings to dance with her friends. Trying to befriend Jennifer, Nichole meets her at the Off-beat for lunch, but Jennifer insults and embarrasses her. As Nichole leaves, Greta (Delphi Lawrence) greets her warmly. Jennifer notices this and talks to Greta, a stripper who works across the street in a club called Les Girls, managed by Greta's boyfriend Kenny (Christopher Lee). When Jennifer visits the club to talk further with Greta, she meets Kenny. He is immediately attracted to her. Greta tells Kenny and Jennifer that Nichole had once been a stripper and a close friend of hers in Paris.

When Nichole tells Kenny that she will call the police if he allows the under-age Jennifer in the club again, he tells her he knows of

Oliver Reed (wearing a plaid shirt) as Plaid Shirt flanked by Jennifer (Gillian Hills, far left), Dave (Adam Faith, far right) and unknown actors in *Beat Girl* (Renown/Victoria, 1959).

a secret past. As a result, Nichole confesses to her husband that poverty had led her to become a stripper and a prostitute in Paris long before they met and that he had saved her from her degrading life. He maintains he still loves her and together they go looking for the missing Jennifer. At the club, Kenny offers to take Jennifer to Paris where he assures her she would be a star as an "exotic dancer." He makes sexual advances but Greta intervenes, stabbing him to death. Jennifer is briefly suspected of the murder by the police. Chastened, sadder and wiser, she is released into the care of Paul and Nichole.

Comment

Beat Girl was released in the U.K. on October 28, 1960, but the U.S. audience had to wait until 1963 to see this tight little thriller. As Johnson and Miller note in *The Christopher Lee Filmography*, "*Beat Girl* distinguishes itself from most other JD films of this type by its interesting glimpse of London's teens during a brief but distinct period of beatniks and jazz-pop music, a scene that would soon change with the coming of the Beatles and the Rolling Stones."

Beautifully, moodily shot in black and white, it has the feel of a documentary. The leading lady, 13-year-old Gillian Hills, discovered by Roger Vadim and convincing as a petulant 16-year-old, was a joy. The rest of the splendid cast did the production proud. Adam Faith, flavor of the month in the pop world at the time, here made his acting debut; in his later years he became an accomplished actor and entrepreneur. The film's soundtrack was crafted by John Barry, who would shortly become synonymous with the James Bond theme; it was the first film soundtrack to be available on disc and began a multi-million dollar industry!

Oliver Reed can be seen in the Off-beat coffee bar, dancing wildly (a habit he never grew out of on the screen!), but registers with the audience by his sheer charisma. It was obvious that the camera loved him and that he was literally throwing himself into learning his craft.

All the bit parts at this time were giving him experience in front of the camera and the opportunity to observe at close hand those actors he had watched assiduously from the stalls in the movie theatres of his teenage years; he learned the lessons well. During filming of an episode of the TV series *The Saint*, for instance, "Reed ... is gunned down ... and killed. As the blank cartridge was fired Reed dramatically hurled himself backwards and knocked himself out cold. 'It was the best example of method acting I have ever seen,' said the show's production manager Johnny Goodman" (Sellers, 85).

Beat Girl's reviews were rather harsh: "Horrifying!" (*Daily Express*); "It's no worse than others of its kind" (*London Times*); "It's left at least one beat critic" (*Daily Mail*).

Life Is a Circus (1960)

Vale Film Productions; released by British Lion Film Corporation in the U.K. in 1958 and by Allied Artists and Schoenfeld Films in 1962 in the U.S.; U.K. Certificate: U

Crew—Director: Val Guest; Writers: Val Guest, Len Heath, John Warren; Producers: John Pellatt, E.M. Smedley-Aston; Original Music: Philip Green; Cinematographer: Arthur Graham; Film Editors: James B. Clark, Bill Lenny; Art Director: Anthony Masters; Costume Design: Beatrice Dawson; Sound Recordist: Buster Ambler; Sound Editor: John Glen; Choreographer: Denys Palmer.

Cast— Bud Flanagan (Bud), Teddy Knox (Sebastian), Jimmy Nervo (Cecil), Jimmy Gold (Goldie), Charlie Naughton (Charlie), Eddie Gray (Eddie), Chesney Allen (Ches), Shirley Eaton (Shirley Winter), Michael Holliday (Carl Rickenbeck), Lionel Jeffries (Genie), Joseph Tomelty (Joe Winter), Eric Pohlmann (Rickenbeck), Harold Kasket (Hassan), Maureen Moore (Rose of Baghdad), Edwin Richfield (Driver), Peter Glaze (Hand 1), Sam Kydd (Removal Man), Geoffrey Denton (Policeman), Marian Collins (Girl in Bookshop), Fred Johnson (Mr. Deaken); uncredited: Oliver Reed (Spectator at Sideshow), Josephine Bailey (Child).

Synopsis

Rickenbeck, owner of a big circus, determines to break his rival, Joe Winter. Carl, Rickenbeck's son, falls in love with Shirley, Winter's attractive daughter, and does all he can to help Winter, but the situation rapidly worsens. Crazy Gang member Bud, working as a general handyman for Winter, buys an old lamp from Ches, a junk man, gives it a rub, and Aladdin's genie appears. Bud orders the genie to make the circus a success but the genie is preoccupied with a scantily clad harem girl doing the dance of the seven veils. But the circus becomes successful and Shirley and Carl plight their troth as the Crazy Gang become the genie's slaves.

Comment

The film starts slowly, but picks up once the genie appears. Bud Flanagan, Jimmy Nervo, Teddie Knox, Jimmy Gold, Charlie Naughton, Eddie Gray and Bud's old partner Chesney Allen (coming out of retirement just to sing the duo's monster hit "Underneath the Arches") work themselves tirelessly, as they always did in their live shows. The Crazy Gang were favorites of King George VI and Queen Elizabeth (who was not yet the Queen Mother) and were guaranteed of royal attendance whenever they opened in the theatre, and assured of being bill-toppers at any Royal Command performance. You either loved or hated them; their mixture of downright silliness, slapstick, double entendres and saccharine songs was the benchmark for variety shows.

Once again, the rapidly learning Oliver Reed found himself in one of the year's prestigious productions. Shirley Eaton, an attractive ingénue (later to become famous as a golden corpse in *Goldfinger*) was an effective love interest and personable Michael Holiday, an English Guy Mitchell, was well cast as the well-meaning rich boy. Lionel Jeffries makes the screen sparkle with his performance as the distracted genie. Apart from fun at the expense of the genie (who is understandably annoyed at being parted from the dancing girl), trapeze tomfoolery and a Wild West sketch generate the loudest laughs. The staging was professional and a couple of catchy tunes added to the fun.

"Big Top comedy extravaganza, presented against realistic backgrounds.... The Crazy Gang's humour is unsubtle but Lionel Jeffries' amusing performance as the genie ... keep its modest end up"—*Kinematograph Weekly*.

The Angry Silence (1960)

Beaver Films; released by British Lion Film Corporation in the U.K. in 1960 and by Valiant Films in the U.S. in 1960

Crew—Director: Guy Green; Screenplay: Brian Forbes; from an original treatment for the screen by Michael Craig and Richard Gregson; Producers: Richard Attenborough, Brian Forbes; Associate Producer: Jack Rix; Original Music: Malcolm Arnold; Cinematographer: Arthur Ibbetson; Film Editor: Anthony Harvey; Casting: Maureen Goldner; Art Director: Ray Sim; Makeup Artist: Harry Frampton; Hair Stylist: Barbara Ritchie; Assistant Directors: Julian Mackintosh, Basil Rabin; Set Dresser: Ken Bridgeman; Sound Recordist: Buster Ambler; Sound Mixer: Red Law; Dubbing Editor: Alastair McIntyre: Camera Operator: Gerry Massy-Collier; Wardrobe: Laura Nightingale; Continuity: Beryl Booth; Production Secretary: Inez Easton.

Cast—Richard Attenborough (Tom Curtis), Pier Angeli (Anna Curtis), Michael Craig (Joe Wallace), Bernard Lee (Bert Connolly), Alfred Burke (Travers), Geoffrey Keen (Davis), Laurence Naismith (Martindale), Russell Napier (Thompson), Penelope Horner (Pat), Brian Bedford (Eddie), Brian Murray ("Gladys"), Norman Bird (Roberts), Beckett Bould (Arkwright), Oliver Reed (Mick), Edna Petrie (Harpy), Lloyd Pearson (Howarth), Norman Shelley (Seagrave), Daniel Farson, Alan Whicker (Themselves), Irene Barrie, Karal Gardner (Teenage Girls), Roland Bartrop (TV Producer), John Charlesworth (Intern), Tony Doonan (Matthews), Eve Eden (Betty), Joe Gibbons, Alfred Maron (Lorry Drivers), Marilyn Green (Cathy), Ronald Hines (Ball), Noel Hood (Miss Bennett), Bernard Horsfall (Pryce-Evans), David Jarrett (Chuck), Piers Keelan (Keyes), Michael Lees (Harris), Stephen Lindo (Brian), Dolores Mantez (Nurse), Roger Maxwell (Collins), George Murcell (Jones), Lisa Page (Julia), Frederick Peisley (Lewis), Redmond Phillips (Ambulance Man), Michael Raghan (Porter), Graham Rowe, Brian Forbes, Clive Strutt (Reporters).

Synopsis

Tom Curtis (Richard Attenborough) is a dedicated employee of Martindale Engineering Company. His job barely enables him to support his Italian wife Anna (Pier Angeli) and two children — and she's expecting a third. To make ends meet, they have taken in Joe (Michael Craig), Tom's friend and co-worker, as a lodger. Travers (Alfred Burke), a labor relations agitator, arrives and joins forces with Connolly (Bernard Lee), who has ambitions to become a big-time union leader. He and Davis (Geoffrey Keen), the works manager, have an uneasy relationship that tips over into antagonism when Davis refuses to grant the workers' demands, chiefly their desire to have a "closed shop" (effectively banning non-union labor). Connolly organizes an unauthorized strike, which greatly concerns Martindale (Laurence Naismith) who fears they may lose a national contract. The next day Tom and 11 others decide to "scab." At first they are the subject of insults, followed soon by vandalism to their homes. The walkout ends, but not the strikers' animosity towards Tom. He is given the silent treatment, even by Joe. After an emotional confrontation with Anna, Joe moves out. The situation escalates when Tom is tricked into a newspaper interview by a reporter (Graham Rowe) that incites the whole factory. The TV and national papers take up the story, making matters worse for all concerned. After Tom's small son Brian (Stephen Lindo) is tarred and feathered by the bigger boys at school and calls Tom a dirty scab, Joe erupts in the factory dining hall. Travers creates a rumor that there will be mass firings due to the troubles and the workers stage a wildcat strike. Tom comes to work alone and is jostled by Mick (Oliver Reed), "Gladys" (Brian Murray) and Eddie (Brian Bedford). That night he's knocked down in a hit-and-run and Eddie blinds him in one eye with a kick of a boot. Joe, enraged, tracks Eddie down on his motorbike. After giving Eddie a savage beating, Joe drags the punk to a huge meeting in the factory courtyard. Joe takes the microphone from the official speakers and exposes the crime—and his own guilt for initially helping create the situation. Faced with this, the strikers are appalled at their behavior. Travers, seeing that his plots have failed, scuttles back to London.

Comment

Although Oliver Reed had relatively little to do with the success of *The Angry Silence,* the film was one of the best with which he was associated and would look good on anybody's filmography. The story of labor problems in a small factory and the workers' violent repression is as topical, hard-hitting and engrossing now as it was at the time of release; *The Angry Silence* is a production that, due to its concern for human weakness, will never go out of date.

After seven previous films, *The Angry Silence* finally provided Oliver with main title billing. Listed fourteenth in a cast of fifty, Reed's Mick is on screen for two minutes and speaks but a few lines, but he manages to make a visual impact. Wearing a black jacket and trousers and a black and white striped shirt, and his hair a bit too long, Mick is insolent, cocky and a nasty piece of work. If one is judged by one's associates, Mick is instantly spotted as heading for trouble. His mates at the factory, "Gladys" (Brian Murray) and Eddie (Brian Bedford in an excellent, film-stealing performance) are worse than he is. It doesn't take too much effort to envision this trio chucking the factory and starting a street gang *à la The Damned.* They typify the great divide between the young and the not-so-young, not only at Martindale's but throughout Britain (and America) in 1960. These lads have little respect for their elders— screw World War II—and they're going to have what they want. And they'll have it right now, thank you. When an elderly worker (who probably fought in both world wars) attempts to speak out at a union meeting against striking, Mick will have none of it.

OLD MAN: You all know me.

MICK (smirking): Who are you?

Mick doesn't have much to do in the film—he seems to always be lurking at the edges—but Oliver Reed makes his presence felt in the few opportunities given to him. Anyone watching this film (as someone at Hammer must have been) could see a star in the making.

The Angry Silence was filmed on location in Ipswich, Suffolk, and at Shepperton Studios with an estimated budget of £98,000 in the summer of 1959. It was trade shown on February 2, 1960, premiered at the Plaza on March 10, and went into general release on March 28 to rave reviews.

Being an anti-trades union film, this was initially banned in Wales where the cinema chains were controlled by the miners' unions. It was only when Richard Attenborough personally intervened and screened it for the union leaders that the ban was revoked.

"Provocative, up to the minute tale, handpicked cast, strong woman's angle, impressive highlights. The controversial, explosive tale has the benefit of expert acting; Richard Attenborough gives a splendidly disciplined performance and Pier Angeli wrings the heart as the sympathetic wife—and masterly direction."—*Kine-*

matograph Weekly, February 4, 1960; "It packs a lesson to be felt and thought about" — *The New York Times*, December 13, 1960.

The Angry Silence was nominated for a slew of awards including an Oscar for Best Writing, Story and Screenplay — Written Directly for the Screen. It won a BAFTA for Brian Forbes for Best British Screenplay; also BAFTA-nominated were Richard Attenborough (Best British Actor), Guy Green (Best British Film and Best Film from Any Source) and Pier Angeli (Best Foreign Actress); it won Guy Green the FIRRESCI prize, the OCIC Award and other honors.

Oliver Reed later recalled, "I finally got some regular work as an extra on films. My first speaking role was in *The Angry Silence* because another actor didn't turn up on the day. It all built up slowly from there" (*Daily Express*, March 6, 1976). His career was kicking in; one year (and nine films) later, he would star in *The Curse of the Werewolf*.

The League of Gentlemen (1960)

Allied Filmmakers; released by Rank Film Distributors in the U.K. in 1960 and by Kingsley-International Pictures in the U.S. in 1961; 116 minutes

Crew — Director: Basil Dearden; Producers: Michael Relph, Basil Dearden; Screenplay: Bryan Forbes; Cinematographer: Arthur Ibbotson; Editor: John Guthridge; Music: Philip Green.

Cast — Jack Hawkins (Hyde), Nigel Patrick (Race), Roger Livesey (Mycroft), Richard Attenborough (Lexy), Bryan Forbes (Porthill), Kieron Moore (Stevens), Robert Cook (Bunny), Terence Alexander (Rupert), Melissa Stribling (Peggy), Norman Bird (Weaver), Patrick Wymark (Wylie), Nanette Newman (Elizabeth), David Lodge (CSM), Doris Hare (Molly), Gerald Harper (Capt. Saunders), Bryan Murray (Grogan); uncredited: Oliver Reed (Man Looking for Audition Room).

Synopsis

Hyde (Jack Hawkins), angry at being kicked out of the army, decides to recruit seven down-and-out ex-officers to rob a bank. They use their military skills, which have been overlooked by the military, and nearly pull it off.

Commentary

The film is one of the most important of its year. The cast was exemplary and the technical staff at the height of their powers — a splendid tutor group for an up-and-coming actor. Oliver Reed appears as a rather precious young man, looking for an audition room; he interrupts the gang's planning meeting at a supposed orchestral rehearsal. It's a glorious couple of minutes; once again, the camera loves him and you remember him after the film is done.

"It would have been possible for *League of Gentlemen* to have been written and played entirely for thrills and suspense ... but by electing to infuse a lot of comedy into the film the producers have broadened its appeal" — *Variety*, April 20, 1966.

The Two Faces of Dr. Jekyll (1960)

Hammer Film Productions; released by Columbia Picture Corporation on October 24, 1960, in the U.K. and by American International Pictures on May 3, 1961, in the U.S.; 88 minutes; Technicolor; Megascope; filmed at Bray and Elstree Studios; U.S. title: *House of Fright*; U.K. Certificate: X

Crew — Director: Terence Fisher; Producer: Michael Carreras; Associate Producer: Anthony Nelson-Keys; Screenplay: Wolf Mankowitz, based on Robert Louis Stevenson's novelette "The Strange Case of Dr. Jekyll and Mr. Hyde"; Cinematographer: Jack Asher; Music and Songs: Monty Norman and David Hencker; Music Supervision: John Hollingsworth; Supervising Editor: James Needs; Editor: Eric Boyd-Perkins; Production Design: Bernard Robinson; Production Manager; Clifford Parkes; Camera Operator: Len Harris; Continuity: Tilly Day; Sound: Jock May; Makeup: Roy Ashton; Hairdresser: Ivy Emmerton; Costume Designer: Mayo; Wardrobe: Molly Arbuthnot; Dancer: Julie Mendez; Assistant Art Director: Don Mingaye; Casting: Dorothy Holloway; Stills: Tom Edwards; Assistant Director: John Peverall; Second Assistant: Hugh Marlow; Sound Editor: Archie Ludski; Masks: Margaret Robinson.

Cast — Paul Massie (Jekyll/Hyde), Dawn Addams (Kitty), Christopher Lee (Paul Allen), David Kossoff (Litauer), Francis De Wolf (Inspector), Norma Marla (Maria), Joy Webster, Magda Miller (Sphinx Girls), Oliver Reed (Young Tough), William Kendall (Clubman), Pauline Shepherd (Girl in Gin Shop), Helen Goss (Nannie), Dennis Shaw (Hanger-on),

Felix Felton (Gambler), Janine Faye (Jane), Percy Cartwright (Coroner), Joe Robinson (Corinthian), Joan Tyrill (Major Domo), Douglas Robinson (Boxer), Donald Tandy (Plainclothes Man), Frank Atkinson (Groom), Arthur Lovegrove (Cabby).

Synopsis

London, 1874; Dr. Henry Jekyll (Paul Massie) is living a reclusive life, having been shunned by his peers because of his theories on the duality of man's nature. His wife Kitty (Dawn Addams) is stifled, without servants and trapped on a solitary round of socializing with their acquaintances; her one escape is the affair she is having with Paul Allen (Christopher Lee), Henry's "friend," who sees Henry as a personal banker who will take care of his (Paul's) negligently acquired debts. Henry's remaining loyal colleague Litauer (David Kossoff) tries in vain to prevent Henry from pursuing his experiments.

Henry injects his deadly serum after Kitty refuses to stay at home with him and the transformation begins. The young Mr. Hyde (also Massie), handsome and totally amoral, goes in search of pleasure, released from Henry's moral code. At the Sphinx, a club catering to rich men's foibles, Hyde initially takes up with a prostitute but, spying Kitty and Paul, he abandons the woman in the middle of the dance floor. When she protests he hurts her and introduces himself to the lovers as a friend of Henry's. Dancing with Kitty, he agrees not to mention seeing her with Paul. On returning to their table he is accosted by a handsome bouncer (Oliver Reed) who gets tough on behalf of the slighted tart. Hyde beats him nearly to death, stopped at the last minute by a horrified Paul. Hyde acquires all Paul's debts and is introduced to the seamiest side of the city in exchange. Using the debts as bait, Hyde attempts to seduce Kitty into buying Paul's life back with her favors. She refuses, making it clear that she is not anybody's woman but that she loves Paul with all her heart. Hyde then pretends that Henry will agree to Kitty's departure, and arranges a final dinner at the Sphinx; he kills Paul with the exotic dancer Maria's (Norma Marla) boa constrictor, rapes Kitty and leaves her to find Paul's body. Overcome with shock and grief, Kitty falls to her death through the club's skylight. Hyde meantime has given Henry's house and all Kitty's finery to Maria.

But Hyde cannot be happy and after making love to Maria, strangles her, waking as a distraught Henry. Stronger than Henry, Hyde kills and burns a laborer in the laboratory, making up the lie that Henry had died in the fire after trying to murder him. The coroner and police are convinced. Slyly congratulating himself, Hyde is praised for his courage by the court only to have Henry, using his last vestiges of willpower, regain his body. Litauer and Jekyll are happy that Hyde is defeated, but the price is the death of Jekyll.

Comment

The Two Faces of Dr. Jekyll was an enormous gamble for Hammer. As Johnson and Del Vecchio remark, "Although the film contains little visual horror, its plot elements are morally repellent. And, earlier in 1960, Hammer's *comedy* version of the same subject, *The Ugly Duckling*, was released. With all this against the film, it remains a fascinating failure that deserves credit for at least daring to be different.... Although it is difficult to defend many of its lapses, the picture deserves credit for finding a new way to film an old story" (Johnson and Del Vecchio, 177).

Making his Hammer debut, one Oliver Reed. He recalled in his autobiography (98), "When I came out of the army, I went to my Uncle [director Sir Carol Reed], and he said to go into repertory if I wanted to be an actor. It was good advice, so I ignored it completely. I took my photos around, and got a bit in *Jekyll* (98)."

The Two Faces of Dr. Jekyll was the first association between American International and Hammer, friendly rivals since 1957. James Carreras signaled his intention to remake the Stevenson classic in *Kinematograph Weekly* (March 12, 1959): "[O]ur script boys have come up with an astonishing new approach. This new concept is so brilliantly original, and yet so simple, that a lot of filmmakers will be kicking themselves silly that they never thought of the idea themselves." Filming commenced on November 23 and ended on January 22, 1960. The film premiered at the Pavilion in London on October 7, following a trade show at the Columbia on August 20; general release on the ABC circuit began on October 24 to mixed reviews.

The London Times (October 10): "An ingenious, though repellent variation"; *The Sunday Times* (October 9): "Massie does what he can to save something from a wreck alternately risible and nauseating"; *The Observer* (October 9): "A vulgar, intentionally foolish work"; *The Spectator* (October 14): "It has peculiarly horrid moral inversions"; *Kinematograph Weekly* (October 6): "Characterization bold, climax stern and spectacular"; *Variety* (October 19): "Terence Fisher's direction is done effectively with few holds barred. The Victorian atmosphere is well put over"; *The New York Herald Tribune* (August 24, 1961): "A colorful, ingenious remake." Released in the U.S. as *House of Fright* with few references to its literary origins in the advertising, it quickly sank.

Reed told Denis Meikle in 1992,

I came out of the army and I wanted to be an actor so I went around lying to everybody that I had been in rep in South Africa and Australia, because I never thought that anybody had been to South Africa or Australia. And one of the people I spoke to was a man called Stuart Lyons who used to be a casting director for a film company. One of the people I'd lied to was making a series on Richard III and the War of the Roses and I was cast as Richard — and I'd never really acted before in my life — and it was for the BBC — and I don't know who was more surprised than me. I was an extra, in crowds.... One of the people who saw me was Stuart Lyons who was casting for Hammer. And I was about to get a job, really, as a gigolo — not a proper gigolo really, because the girls I was looking after fired me because they got emotionally involved with me so I wasn't very successful. So I was about to sell washing machines in the interim. The fellow who interviewed me said, "Of course you know you visit the ladies at lunchtime, but they won't commit until the husband comes home at night so you'll probably have to do a bit of the business while the husband's away." I wanted the job so badly I said, "No, I don't mind that at all." I returned to my flat and there was a call from Stuart Lyons, and they cast me in *The Two Faces of*

Dr. Jekyll, then *The Sword of Sherwood Forest.* That saved my bacon!

When I came back from *Sword of Sherwood Forest* [Hammer associate producer] Anthony Nelson-Keys phoned me up and said, "We're making a film called *The Curse of the Werewolf*, would you come and test for it," and that was the only test I've ever done in my life.

So I say, "Yes" and I went down and did the test. In *Jekyll* I'd played "the strongman"; I'd been a bouncer in a strip-joint near Wardour Street — I just wore louder clothes in the film! I'd say, "And now comes the lovely Yvonne!"

For Reed it was a chance to make a mark. His good looks and athleticism, and having actually *been* a bouncer, made him a natural for the tiny role. It brought him to the attention of people with the power to make his career progress. On a slightly skeptical note: Does anyone believe that slender Massie could have beaten buff Mr. Reed? "Suspension of disbelief," our dear friend Terence Fisher once remarked, in a slightly different context!

The Bulldog Breed (1960)

The Rank Organisation; released by J. Arthur Rank Film Distributors in the U.K. in 1960; no U.S. release

Crew—Director: Robert Asher; Original Screenplay: Henry Blyth, Jack Davies, Norman Wisdom; Producers: Hugh Stewart; Executive Producer: Earl St. John; Original Music: Philip Green; Cinematographer: Jack Asher; Film Editor: Gerry Hambling; Art Director: Harry Pottle; Costume Design: Anthony Mendleson; Makeup Artist: Geoffrey Rodway; Production Manager: David Orton; Assistant Director: Bert Batt; Set Dresser: Peter Lamont; Sound Editor: Jack T. Knight; Sound Recordist: John W. Mitchell; Camera Operator: H.A.R. Thompson; Continuity: Joan Davis.

Cast—Norman Wisdom (Norman Puckle), Ian Hunter (Admiral Sir Bryanston Blyth), David Lodge (CPO Knowles), Robert Urquhart (Comdr. Clayton), Edward Chapman (Mr. Philpots), Eddie Byrne (PO Filkins), Peter Jones (Diving Instructor), John Le Mesurier (Prosecuting Counsel), Terence Alexander (Defending Counsel), Sydney Tafler (Speedboat Owner), Brian Oulton (Bert Ainsworth, Cinema Manager), Harold Goodwin (Streaky Hopkinson), Johnny Briggs (Johnny Nolan), Frank Williams (Mr. Carruthers), Joe Robinson (Tall Sailor), Liz Fraser

(NAAFI Girl), Penny Morrell (Marlene Barlow), Claire Gordon (Peggy, Girl in Bar), Julie Shearing (WRN Smith), Leonard Sachs (Yachtsman), Glyn Houston (Gym Instructor); uncredited: John Arnatt (Briggs), Oliver Reed, Philip Locke (Teddy Boys in Cinema Fight), Michael Caine (Sailor in Cinema Fight), Cyril Chamberlain (Jimmy the Landlord), Larry Dann (New Dalton's Boy), Robert Desmond (Sailor on Bridge), Sheila Hancock (Doris), Rosamund Lesley (Peggy), Bryan Pringle (PTI), William Roache (Space Center Operator), Anthony Sagar (Instructor's Assistant), Anne Scott (Polynesian Girl).

Synopsis

When grocery delivery man Norman Puckle's (Norman Wisdom) girlfriend jilts him, he makes several unsuccessful attempts at suicide. Proving hopeless at self-destruction, he is inveigled into joining the Royal Navy, believing all the promotional spin he is offered. Life in the navy is not all about gorgeous girls, as he had been led to believe, but really hard work as Norman gets to take care of the admiral's bulldog as part of his duties. Norman gets into all sorts of trouble making mistakes in training including getting his crewmates leave which is subsequently cancelled, throwing the whole crew overboard, trouble with his diving costume, boxing mishaps, a fight with Teddy Boys at the cinema, a court martial and being chosen to be the first man into space because said bulldog pulls him into the training building. The rigorous space training is a minefield for the hapless Norman and so he is replaced, only to end up in piloting the spacecraft having chased a dog and a rabbit on board.

Having, surprisingly, managed the space flight adequately by desperately pushing all the buttons and hoping for the best, he crash-lands near an island and gets his just rewards by meeting a beautiful native girl with whom he spends a romantic interlude before the navy rescues him.

Comment

This movie's topicality — the current space race — and the fun it poked at great institutions like the Royal Navy, made it a winner in British cinemas. The action included the slapstick comedy that everyone expected from a Wisdom movie and a good laugh was had by all.

The Bulldog Breed was filmed in August 1960 at Beaconsfield Studio and on location in Portsmouth and Weymouth. The movie was Wisdom's eighth for Rank. Reed can be glimpsed as a Teddy Boy in the cinema, but don't blink or you'll miss him! He would report to Bray Studios the following month to film *The Curse of the Werewolf* and would return to Weymouth as a star the following spring for *The Damned*.

Variety (December 15, 1960): "The film stands or falls by Wisdom and though the actor, as always, seems to be trying rather too hard, his genial good humor and energy carry him through the various situations entertainingly. *The Bulldog Breed* serves its undemanding purpose." *Kinematograph Weekly* (December 15, 1960): "Clean fun, box office star, popular supporting players, slick direction, polished technical presentation, neat verbal cracks. Capital British light booking."

The Sword of Sherwood Forest (1960)

Yeoman Films in association with Hammer Films Productions; released by Columbia Pictures in the U.K. on December 26, 1960, and by Columbia Pictures in the U.S. in January 1961; 80 minutes; Copyright length: 96 minutes; Technicolor; Megascope; filmed at Bray Studios, England, and County Wicklow, Republic of Ireland; U.K. Certificate: U

Crew— Director: Terence Fisher; Producers: Sidney Cole, Richard Greene; Executive Producer: Michael Carreras; Screenplay: Alan Hackney; Music: Alun Huddinott; Music Director: John Hollingsworth; Cinematographer: Ken Hodges; Supervising Editor: James Needs; Production Managers: Don Weeks (England), Ronald Liles (Ireland); Art Director: John Stoll; Camera; Richard Bayley; Makeup: Gerald Fletcher; Hairdresser: Hilda Fox; Wardrobe Supervisor: John McCorry; Continuity: Pauline Wise, Dot Foreman; Horsemaster: Ivor Collin; Construction Supervisor: John McCorry; Production Secretary: Judith Walsh; Assistant Director: Bob Porter; Editor: Lee Doig; Original Songs: Stanley Black; Songs Sung by Dennis Lotis; Sound: Alban Streeter, John Mitchell, Harry Tate; Wardrobe Mistress: Rachel Austin; Casting Director: Stuart Lyons; Master of Arms: Patrick Crean; Master of Archery: Jack Cooper; Main Titles: Chambers & Partners.

Cast— Richard Greene (Robin Hood), Peter Cushing (Sheriff of Nottingham), Richard Pasco

Melton (Oliver Reed), Newark (Richard Pasco), Ollerton (Patrick Crean) and the prioress (Vanda Godsell) in conference to commit treason in *The Sword of Sherwood Forest* (Hammer/Columbia, 1960).

(Newark), Sarah Branch (Marian), Niall MacGinnis (Friar Tuck), Nigel Green (Little John), Dennis Lotis (Alan A'Dale), Jack Gwillim (Hubert Walter, Archbishop of Canterbury), Oliver Reed (Melton), Edwin Richfield (Sheriff's Lieutenant), Vanda Godsell (Prioress), Brian Rawlinson (Falconer), Patrick Crean (Ollerton), Derren Nesbitt (Martin), Reginald Hearne (Man at Arms), Jack Cooper (Archer), Desmond Llewellyn (Traveler), Charles Lamb (Old Bowyer), Aiden Grennell (Outlaw), James Neylin (Roger), Barry de Boulay (Officer), John Hoey (Old Jack), Andrew McMaster (Judge), John Franklin (Walter's Secretary), Maureen Halligan (Portess).

Synopsis

Robin Hood (Richard Greene) and Little John (Nigel Green) come to the aid of a wounded man in Sherwood Forest. Shortly after, they come upon the lovely Marian (Sarah Branch) bathing in a woodland pool. She and Robin, mutually attracted, agree to meet at the Owl Inn despite Little John's warning that it is a trap. At the inn, the Sheriff of Nottingham (Peter Cushing) waits to offer Robin a pardon in exchange for the wounded man. When Robin refuses, the sheriff attempts to capture him, much to the annoyance of Marian. At the outlaws' camp the man dies after warning of danger at Bawtry Priory. Robin passes the warning to Friar Tuck (Niall MacGinnis). He then goes to meet the Earl of Newark (Richard Pasco) who is so impressed with the outlaw's bow skills that he hires him as an assassin whose target is unnamed. At Bawtry the sheriff attempts to claim an estate for Newark, knowing that the earl plans to build a castle in defiance of the king. The claim is blocked by the archbishop of Canterbury (Jack Gwillim), who is Robin's unnamed target. The archbishop is joined on the road to London by Marian. Ambushed by Newark's men, they take refuge in the Priory. The sheriff, apprised of Newark's plan to kill the prelate, objects. He is stabbed by Melton (Oliver Reed), a young lord keen to fix his place in the pack of traitors to the king.

Newark attacks the Priory and is killed by Robin, who thereby wins Marian's hand and can end his life of outlawry.

Comment

Hammer's long-delayed sequel to *Men of Sherwood Forest* began shooting on May 23, 1960, with a cast far above its material and a star closely identified with his role: Richard Greene spent from 1955 to 1958 filming *The Adventures of Robin Hood* for CBS-TV. Filming ended on July 8 followed by a trade show in November. The reviews were positive. *Kinematograph Weekly* (November 24, 1960): "Jolly, disarmingly naive adventure comedy melodrama"; *The New York Times* (January 26, 1961): "Better than usual. This Robin isn't nearly so bedraggled as the last twenty or so"; *The New York Herald Tribune* (January 25, 1961): "There is some effort to make the dialogue sound reasonably lively."

Although past his prime physically, Greene transferred his TV persona to the big screen with professional ease. Cushing's complex sheriff, who has limits to his treason, was a superb foil to the simply honest outlaw. "Nottingham's murder was the film's shocking highlight, as audiences expected a traditional duel between him and Robin. Unfortunately, the film dies with him. The supporting cast, especially Richard Pasco, is fine, but Oliver Reed delivers an embarrassingly awful performance" (Del Vecchio & Johnson: 191). "It was a dream come true for Reed, running around a forest with a sword emulating his childhood hero Errol Flynn. The great swashbuckler of Hollywood's golden age had only recently died. Reed was in a pub when he heard the news and ordered a Guinness; standing to attention he downed the pint in a single gulp" (Sellers, 75).

Reed acquired a new skill in what was essentially a bit part: sword play, a talent which was to become extremely useful in years to come. Master of arms Patrick Crean is not on record as having had problems with Oliver rehearsing. "Reed ... delivers a performance difficult to define. His simpering voice and attitude are ridiculous and it's hard to believe that he is the same actor who was so convincing in *The Curse of the Werewolf* [1960]" (Del Vecchio and Johnson, 142). He also gained more experience in front of the camera and must have learned a great deal about not over-egging a part when he saw the finished result. That Terence Fisher did not attempt to alter the performance was a surprise, since he always attempted to get the best from all his actors. The slightly longer part in his second Hammer outing was good practice for Reed, starting him on his journey to become one of the screen's most effective villains and adding the costume adventure genre to his repertoire.

His and Hers (1961)

Sabre Film Productions; released by Eros Films in the U.K. in 1961 and by Favorite Films in the U.S. in 1962; U.K. Certificate: U

Crew—Director: Brian Desmond Hurst; Screenplay: Stanley Mann, Jan and Mark Lowell; Cinematographer: Ted Scaife; Musical Director: John Addison; Editor: Max Benedict.

Cast—Terry-Thomas (Reggie Blake), Janette Scott (Fran Blake), Wilfrid Hyde-White (Charles), Nicole Maurey (Simone), Billy Lambert (Baby), Joan Sims (Hortense), Kenneth Connor (Harold), Kenneth Williams (Policeman), Majer Tzelniker (Colin McGregor), Joan Hickson (Phoebe), Oliver Reed (Poet), Barbara Hicks (Woman), Francesca Annis (Wanda), Dorinda Stevens (Dora).

Synopsis

A publicity stunt becomes the real thing when Reggie Blake (Terry-Thomas), a well-known travel writer, is lost in the desert. When he later returns home, having sampled the Bedouin way of life, he expects his long-suffering wife Fran (Janette Scott) to adopt the practices and mores of the Bedouin. When she refuses, they divide the house and each lives according to their preference. Reggie has a sultry French filmmaker to stay in his half, and Fran is stung into writing a catty book lampooning her husband's travels. She also plans a divorce, but changes her mind. Once reconciled, they each write a bestseller and their publisher chooses one of the four Bedouin wives gifted to Reggie to have for his own.

Comment

The authors were not able to obtain a print of the movie; since there is the ubiquitous "beatnik party" scene, we're sure Oliver Reed might be spotted strutting his stuff as well as reading his poetry. He really had a guardian angel looking over his career, as this is another high-status British film of its day with a superb cast and the cream of comedy actors. This is the first time he came within Janette Scott's orbit; the next time they would meet as co-stars.

"Intermittent rib-tickling, artful distaff slant, box office stars, provocative label..."— *Kinematograph Weekly*, January 24, 1961.

No Love for Johnnie (1961)

Five Star Films Ltd.; released by J. Arthur Rank Film Distributors in the U.K. in 1961 and by Embassy Pictures in the U.S. in 1962

Crew—Director: Ralph Thomas; Screenplay: Nicholas Phipps, Mordecai Richler, from Wilfred Fienburgh's novel; Producer: Betty E Box; Executive Producer: Earl St. John; Original Music: Malcolm Arnold; Cinematographer: Ernest Steward; Film Editor: Alfred Roome; Art Director: Maurice Carter; Set Decorator: Arthur Taksen; Costume Design: Yvonne Caffen; Makeup Artist: W.T. Partleton; Production Manager: Charles Orme; Assistant Director: Stanley Hosgood; Sound Mixer: Gordon K. McCallum; Sound Recordist: Dudley Messenger; Sound Editor: Don Sharpe; Camera Operator: James Bowden; Continuity: Gladys Goldsmith.

Cast—Peter Finch (Johnnie Byrne), Stanley Holloway (Fred Andrews), Mary Peach (Pauline West), Peter Barkworth (Henderson), Hugh Burden (Tim Maxwell), Marian Collins (Pretty Girl), Rosalie Crutchley (Alice Byrne), Fenella Fielding (Sheila), Michael Goodliffe (Dr. West), Gladys Henson (Constituent), Mervyn Johns (Charlie Young), Geoffrey Keen (The Prime Minister), Donald Pleasence (Roger Renfrew), Dennis Price (Flagg), Paul Rogers (Sydney Johnson), Peter Rogers (Sydney Johnson), Peter Sallis (MP); uncredited: Oliver Reed.

Synopsis

In the North of England in Earnley, Johnnie Byrne is elected to Parliament and travels to London to take up his seat. He is already sneeringly dismissive of those who elected him and sure that he is destined for higher things. When he goes home to his Communist Party–supporting wife he finds her cold and uninterested and so he starts to stray. Meanwhile, he is planning with other MPs to oust his own prime minister. At a party he meets Pauline West (Mary Peach) and his plans to scupper the government get lost in a lovers' tryst.

Having been outed for his sins he gets a severe warning, but his luck holds as he is tipped to replace a terminally ill minister — providing he "loses" his politically incorrect wife. His hopes of a reconciliation vanish as he dumps her without a moment's hesitation. Putting his feet up on the government front bench, his "love" will now be his rising political career.

Comment

One of the major movies of its decade, *No Love for Johnnie* resonates into the 21st century as — to the cynical — nothing much changes in politics. The book was written and published in 1958 by Wilfred Fienburgh, who was an MP from 1951 to 1958. The book is very cynical and horribly apposite as seen against the scandals of the House of Commons in 2009–11. The film was shot at Pinewood in August 1960 and released in 1961 with a first class cast of the best the British film industry had to offer and was yet another magnificent classroom for the young Oliver Reed who lapped up the experience and stored it away for future reference.

Reed appears at an offbeat Bohemian party, doing the "Reed dancing" we came to know and love. It's another "don't blink or you'll miss him" episode, but it put him in the midst of a superb cast and splendid technicians. Who could want for a better classroom?

Released in the U.K. on Valentine's Day (!) 1961, the film was well-received. *Eve* (December 9, 1961): "One of the year's finest British films. It is honest, realistic and adult"; *Time* (December 8, 1961): "[L]ike its zero of a hero, it's a political animal that tries to be all things to all men."

The Rebel (1961)

Associated British Picture Corporation; released by Warner-Pathé Distributors in the U.K. in 1961 and by Continental Distributing in the U.S. in 1961; color; 105 minutes

Crew—Director: Robert Day; Writers: Ray
Galton, Alan Simpson, Tony Hancock; Producer:
W.A. Whittaker; Original Music: Frank Cordell;
Cinematographer: Gilbert Taylor; Film Editor:
Richard Best; Casting: Robert Lennard; Art Direc-
tor: Robert Jones; Set Decorator: Scott Slimon; Hair
Stylists: Ivy Emmerton, Polly Young; Makeup: Tony
Sforzini; Production Manager: R.E. Dearing; Assis-
tant Director: Kip Gowens; Second Assistant Direc-
tor: Gordon Gilbert; Paintings: Alistair Grant;
Sound Recordists: Leonard Abbott, Ronald Abbott,
Len Shilton; Recording Director: A.W. Lumkin;
Dubbing Editor: Arthur Southgate; Camera Oper-
ator: Val Stewart; Wardrobe: Dora Lloyd; Costume
Designers: Alan Sievewright, Margit Saad; Musical
Director: Stanley Black; Titles: James Baker; Con-
tinuity: Doreen Dearnaley; Scenario Editor: Fred-
erick Gotfurt.

Cast—Tony Hancock (Anthony Hancock),
George Sanders (Sir Charles Broward), Paul Massie
(Paul), Margit Saad (Margot), Gregoire Aslan (Car-
reras), Dennis Price (Jim Smith), Irene Handl (Mrs.
Crevatte), John Le Mesurier (Office Manager), Liz
Fraser (Waitress), Mervyn Johns (Manager of Lon-
don Gallery), Peter Bull (Manager of Paris Gallery),
Nanette Newman (Josey), Marie Burke (Mme. Lau-
rent), Bernard Rebel (Art Dealer), Sandor Eles
(Artist), Oliver Reed (Artist in Cafe), Neville Becker
(Artist), Marie Devereux (Yvette), John Wood (Poet),
Victor Platt (Dock Official), Mario Fabrizi (Coffee
Bar Attendant), Barry Shawin (Bistro Owner);
uncredited: Bandana Das Gupta (Foreign Beauty),
Sally Douglas (Jim Smith Acolyte), Marie France
(French Girl), Hugh Lloyd (Man on Train), Jean
Marsh (Strange Woman at Party), Patrick Newall
(Art Gallery Patron), Edna Petrie (Ghastly Woman),
Dani Seper (French Girl), Brian Weske (Laughing
Sailor).

Synopsis

Anthony Hancock (Tony Hancock) is a
downtrodden office worker who paints and
sculpts in his free time to alleviate the boredom
of his daily life. When his landlady Mrs. Crevatte (Irene Handl) discovers his paintings and
a huge sculpture in his rooms, she gives him
notice to quit. He slams the door on her, and
the vibrations make the statue plummet through
the floor. Hancock takes his paintings and
sculpture to Paris, where he intends to join the
art community. The sculpture has its head
knocked off at the docks and falls in the water;
Hancock leaps in after it and loses his ticket.
He hitches to Paris in the rain and finds a friend
in artist Paul (Paul Massie) who is truly talented. Paul shares his studio with Hancock and

is captivated by the drivel Hancock spouts as
his "theory of modern art." Soon Hancock is
all the rage at bohemian parties. Paul quits and
goes to London, leaving his paintings to Hancock as a gift.

Wealthy art dealer Sir Charles Brewer
(George Sanders) offers Hancock money for
Paul's paintings, and Hancock becomes a
wealthy man. Carreras (Gregoire Aslan), a
wealthy shipping magnate, commissions Hancock to sculpt his man-eater wife; she tries to
seduce Hancock who rejects her and narrowly
misses being shot by her. At the unveiling, Carreras is insulted by the naive quality of the
statue, but Hancock escapes as the statue falls
through the yacht's deck. Sir Charles has taken
Hancock's own paintings to exhibit in London. Hancock catches up to Paul who gives
him his latest paintings. Sir Charles realizes that
Paul is the true artist and Hancock throws off
his rich artist's clothes shouting, "You're all raving mad!" Returning to his flat, he begins work
on his statue again, using his landlady as a
model.

Comment

Tony Hancock's successful TV writing
team Galton and Simpson scripted this film.
They knew their character intimately — a little
man, slightly at war with himself and his fel-
lows, but quick to grasp an opportunity to get
on. There are many amusing scenes: Hancock
revolting against the office manager, the arty
Left Bank parties with more than a nod to "The
Emperor's New Clothes" with respect to knowledge about art, and Hancock painting a picture
by daubing paint on a canvas and riding a bicycle over it.

When the British Film Institute showed
it, David Sharp described it thus: "In this film,
comic rebellion places artists as the antithesis
of workers and there is a kind of lazy shorthand
at work that conflates artists with Paris, exis-
tentialism, angry young men, beatniks and beat
poets. Cod philosophical discussions of what
art is about permeate the film, but this reflects
the times accurately and allows Hancock to get
in his 'you're all raving mad' catchphrase as he
quits the exhibition and its phony artists, art-
works and moneyed hangers-on. The coda has

him remaining true to himself, re-creating the Aphrodite statue once more, now with Irene Handl as his model. In an absurdist echo down the years, Aphrodite and the other works seen in the film were re-created by the London Institute of Pataphysics in 2002. Hancock would have loved the irony." And there we were, thinking it was just a jolly comedy film!

"[Oliver Reed] was mesmerizing and it was obvious that the camera loved him," remembers Hancock's genius scriptwriter Alan Simpson.

But he kept fluffing his lines. Now on a film you have a tight schedule and for one little speech there's a limit to how many takes they're going to do. And he was so good, but he kept fluffing it and the director yelled, "Cut. Go again." I think they got up to seven takes and Reed fluffed every one. The producer was standing next to the director and witnessing all this, shaking his head in dismay, according to Galton. "He was saying to the director, 'He's got to go, if he doesn't get it right now he's got to go, we can't waste any more film, it's costing money.'" I don't know whether anybody said anything to Oliver because on the next take he was absolutely perfect and it made the final cut [Sellers, 74].

Reed told Denis Meikle in 1992, "The director was a very well known homosexual — and I think he fancied me. He had some original Picassos, I believe. So I went up to see him; I kept talking about my Uncle Carol to let him know that, if he so much as put his hand on my knee, I'd tell my Uncle Carol." Learning his trade amidst the cream of British comedy talent at the time, collating all the information on the technicalities of filming and watching the experts at work seemed to Reed to be a better way of honing one's skills than drama school or repertory theatre. In his case, he was right.

The Curse of the Werewolf (1961)

Hammer Film Productions–Hotspur Production; released by Universal Pictures in the U.K. on May 1 and in the U.S. on June 7, 1961; 88 minutes; filmed at Bray Studios; U.K. Certificate: X

Crew— Director: Terence Fisher; Producer: Anthony Hinds; Associate Producer: Anthony Nelson-Keys; Executive Producer: Michael Carreras; Screenplay: John Elder [Anthony Hinds], based on Guy Endore's *The Werewolf of Paris*; Cinematographer: Arthur Grant; Music: Benjamin Frankel; Production Design: Bernard Robinson; Art Director: Thomas Goswell; Assistant Art Director: Don Mingaye; Supervising Editor: James Needs; Editor: Alfred Cox; Camera: Len Harris; Sound: Jock May; Continuity: Tilly Day; Makeup: Roy Ashton; Hairstyles: Frieda Steiger; Wardrobe: Molly Arbuthnot; Special Effects: Les Bowie; Production Manager: Clifford Parkes; Casting: Stuart Lyons; Stills: Tom Edwards; Assistant Director: John Peverall; Second Assistant: Dominic Fulford.

Cast— Clifford Evans (Professor Carrido), Oliver Reed (Leon), Yvonne Romain (Servant Girl), Catherine Feller (Christina), Anthony Dawson (Marquis Siniestro), Hira Talfrey (Teresa), Richard Wordsworth (Beggar), Francis De Wolff (Landlord), Warren Mitchell (Pepe), George Woodbridge (Dominique), John Gabriel (Priest), Ewan Solon (Don Fernando), Peter Sallis (Don Enrique), Michael Ripper (Old Soaker), Sheila Brennan (Vera), Martin Matthews (Jose), David Conville (Gomez), Anne Blake (Rosa), Denis Shaw (Jailer), Josephine Llewellyn (Marquesa), Justin Walters (Young Leon), Renny Lister (Yvonne), Joy Webster (Isabel), John Bennett (Policeman), Charles Lamb (Chief), Desmond Llewelyn (Footman), Gordon Whiting (Second Footman), Hamlyn Benson (Landlord), Serafina DiLeo (Zumara), Kitty Attwood (Midwife), Howard Lang (Irate Farmer), Stephen W. Scott (Another Farmer), Max Butterfield (Cheeky Farmer), Ray Browne (Official), Frank Siernan (Gardner), Michael Peake (Farmer in Cantina), Rodney Burke, Alan Page, Richard Golding (Customers), Loraine Caruana (Servant Girl as a Child).

Synopsis

Eighteenth-century Spain. As a punishment for offending the sadistic Marquis Siniestro (Anthony Dawson) at his wedding celebration, a beggar (Richard Wordsworth) is cast into a dungeon where over the years he becomes more animal than human. When a serving girl (Yvonne Romain) refuses the marquis' sexual advance, she is thrown into the beggar's cell where she is raped. After killing the marquis she runs into the forest where she is found by the kindly Professor Carrido (Clifford Evans). Nursed by his housekeeper (Hira Talfrey), the girl gives birth to a son on Christmas Day, and then she dies.

Leon (Oliver Reed) meets his mother (Yvonne Romain)—who died in childbirth!—in a publicity shot from Terence Fisher's horror classic *The Curse of the Werewolf* (Hammer/Universal-International, 1961).

A few years later, young Leon (Justin Walters) is identified as a werewolf by the local priest (John Gabriel) after a series of attacks on livestock, but due to the love and care of his adoptive parents, he grows up to be a normal adult (Oliver Reed). While working at a winery, Leon falls in love with Christina (Catherine Feller), but her father (Ewan Solon) blocks the romance. Taken reluctantly to a brothel by Jose (Martin Matthews), Leon responds to the full moon and his sordid surroundings by morphing into a wolf, murdering Jose and a prostitute (Renny Lister).

The priest explains his condition to him and Leon realizes that only Christina's love can save him. They are separated when the police arrest and jail him. Leon again becomes a wolf and kills his cellmate (Michael Ripper). Leon escapes from the cell and is shot by Carrido with a silver bullet after terrorizing the town.

Comment

The conception of *The Curse of the Werewolf* was almost as twisted as that of poor Leon.

Hammer Films was planning a picture to be set during the Spanish Inquisition. *The Rape of Sabena* was to have started filming on September 5, 1960, but due to (1) the disapproval of the screenplay by the British censor, (2) potential outcries from the Catholic Church and (3) cold feet by company director Sir James Carreras, himself a Catholic, the plug was pulled.

To fill the gap, producer Anthony Hinds' werewolf movie, which was to have been shot next, was moved up. Since Spanish sets had already been constructed, Hinds was stuck with them which was problematic, the script being based on Guy Endore's 1939 novel *The Werewolf of Paris*. Problem #2: Hinds' (writing as John Elder) script had been red-penciled by the censor on August 22 which would result in an ongoing battle. The censor won and the film has only comparatively recently been restored, prompting Jonathan Rigby (2000, 87) to write, "Viewing the restored version of the film, it's sobering to reflect on how much less of a success [the finale] was in the old BBFC-approved print, which was more thoroughly mangled than any of Leon's victims."

With production scheduled to start on September 12, two new problems presented themselves. Who should play the werewolf, and what should he look like? Hammer's previous monsters had been played — superbly — by Christopher Lee, but at 38 he was well above the age required. Also, Lee was balking about reprising the Dracula character and it is doubtful that he was interested in donning fangs and fur. What was required was a young unknown who could be gotten cheaply!

Reed had had a small part in Hammer's *The Two Faces of Dr. Jekyll* and a somewhat larger role in *The Sword of Sherwood Forest,* both pictures directed by Terence Fisher who had also made *The Curse of Frankenstein, Horror of Dracula* and *The Mummy. The Curse of the Werewolf* was his first truly starring role and he remembered it thus: "I was 22 but told them I was older because I knew they were looking for someone more mature. I was paid ninety pounds a week. It was a fortune. But I had nobody to celebrate with because Kate [his wife] was working at the time, which was very brave of her since she was terribly pregnant. So I danced all round the house with Pudding the cat" (Reed, 103). The young couple must have been delighted to have Reed's talents recognized and to be able to pay the bills for a change — a double victory!

Reed told Denis Meikle in 1992,

I don't know if anyone else was in the running or not. We did all of the werewolf makeup scenes at the same time because it was easier that way ... it took a long time to put the stuff on and off. Hammer Films was a most amazing place — I remember the bread-and-butter pudding — wonderful! It was just like a big family at Bray — right on the river. It was superb. I was asked to dine with the directors ... Anthony Hinds [producer] ... James Carreras [owner] ... then I knew I'd made it, because that's where Peter Cushing and Christopher Lee used to have lunch. When I was doing the bit in *Jekyll* I ate with everyone else, then in *Werewolf* I was invited into the private dining room which wasn't nearly as much fun because all I could do was drink milk through a straw — you know, you can't eat with fangs, long nails. I really frightened little Michael Ripper and big Dennis

Shaw in the prison scene when I threw the cell door at him. It wasn't balsa wood either. I was fitter in those days.

Terence Fisher was a wonderful, gentle man who loved his "bevy." He and Stuart Lyons tried to put me on a private contract so you'd have a director and a casting director who would have acted as my managers. Stuart went on to cast *Cleopatra* and he tried to get me on that.

Terry had probably seen me as Richard III. In *Werewolf* I think I did fine. They taught me my craft. I knew what a mark was and I knew what a key light was, and I knew what lenses were because I'd listened. I found Terry very easy — he didn't get involved too much. I spent about a month on the film. I got £120 a week. A pint of beer was nine pence — I could have a drink and pay the rent. I wasn't offered any more monster roles, because what happened was, Joe Losey came along and we made *The Damned*. I did *Pirates of Blood River* and then that ridiculous film *The Brigand of Kandahar* and then I called it a day because I could see that I'd learned enough from Hammer and I saw what was happening

Roy Ashton's incredible makeup for Leon (Oliver Reed) in *The Curse of the Werewolf* (Hammer/Universal-International, 1961).

to Peter Cushing and Christopher Lee in terms of them being cast in those sorts of roles all the time.

Roy Ashton began his career in makeup in 1933 when he entered an apprenticeship program at Gaumont British Studios. His first credited job was on *Tudor Rose* (1936). Twenty years later Ashton found himself assisting Phil Leakey on *The Curse of Frankenstein*. When Leakey left Hammer in 1958, Ashton was a willing replacement and remained with the company for 13 years. Ashton first encountered Reed on *The Two Faces of Dr. Jekyll*. When Ashton was engaged for *The Curse of the Werewolf* he immediately went to the Natural History Museum and began taking photographs of a large stuffed wolf, combining lupine and human features in his subsequent design. Hammer was then undecided on its werewolf actor and Anthony Hinds asked Ashton's opinion.

"I suggested Oliver Reed since he seemed exactly right — his bones and everything," Ashton recalled. "His powerful bone structure was just right for the appearance and his gifts as an actor were perfect for the part. In addition, he resembled a wolf anyway when he's very angry"

The transformation of Leon is a classic example of Hammer's craftsmen overcoming the limitations of the budget. "I suggested the wolf-man's transformation by only showing his hands," Ashton recalled (Goodwin, 77). "To do this we had to lock the cameras off in the same position for each shot.... I prepared a cast out of plaster with their imprints, so that, every time they stopped the camera, we could take Oliver away to apply more hair and to make the nails a little longer. When he came back he put his hands in the cast again, as it had been before.... [T]he whole treatment took about two hours."

At the close of the day Reed would have to spend an hour and a half peeling the makeup off hair by hair. Reed reportedly said, "I'd just be ready [after being made-up] and they would shout 'Lunch, everybody!' and I'd be left strutting around the studio covered in fur and teeth. I would slowly make my way up to the restaurant and drink three pints of milk through a straw.... Sometimes I wouldn't bother taking [the makeup] off completely. It was great fun sitting in the car at the traffic lights" (Sellers, 75–76).

The Curse of the Werewolf falls halfway between the ancient techniques of *The Wolf Man* and the modern techniques of *An American Werewolf in London* but Ashton's makeup procedure was definitely in the former camp. "First of all you have got to reproduce the actor's head," said Ashton. "That means casting and molding in plaster. I made an appliance which fitted underneath his eyes and went right over the top of his head and over the ears. I pushed out his nostrils with a pair of candles. I made the eyebrows up a little more massively as well. I made a series of beards which I fastened around the neck so that they just slipped around when the artist moved. A succession of hair falls, rather like overhanging sheaths, were fitted to the back of the neck and towards the shoulders. The main trunk was fitted with a leotard and yak hair was put all over this to simulate the coat of a wolf. Contact lenses were inserted for extreme close shots. Teeth were extended — canines made and fitted. It was quite a complicated job. It took about an hour and a half to two hours."

In a break with tradition established in *The Wolf Man, The Curse of the Werewolf* eschewed the often effective — but just as often ineffective — time lapse dissolves to show the transformation. Other than seeing hair sprout on Reed's hands, his transformation is achieved though gradual makeup application, cutting and lighting effects. When Reed makes his first and only on-camera metamorphosis, his face is away from the camera. As his cellmate Michael Ripper looks on, Reed suddenly launches towards him — and the camera — with his face partially distorted. The camera turns to the now retreating Ripper, then reverts to a fully transformed Reed. Terence Fisher staged the scene so well that few viewers ever noticed, or cared about, the lack of a standard transformation. Hammer regular Michael Ripper told the authors in 1975, "Oliver was superb as the werewolf. We had a scene in the jail cell where he changed from Leon to the wolf. The power of his performance — he scared the shit out of me!" Ripper had great respect for Reed as an actor and an all-round "good bloke" and always reminisced fondly on the times they worked to-

gether. There were, and still are, complaints about the werewolf's limited screen time: the transformation takes place with about ten minutes of screen time remaining.

Another break with tradition is that, after being killed, Leon does not change back to human form. Our final viewing of the werewolf's bloody corpse is more effective than the expected — and clichéd — transformation to reveal him at peace. There's no peace for this werewolf, or for Christina who stands sobbing.

While *The Curse of the Werewolf* clings to the full moon–silver bullet notions of its predecessors, the film breaks with tradition in a third major way. The cause of Leon's lycanthropy is not due to a gypsy curse or science run amok but, as explained by the kindly priest, "a werewolf is a body where the soul and the spirit are constantly at war. The spirit is that of a wolf ... and whatever weakens the human soul — vice, greed, hatred, solitude — especially during the cycle of the full moon when the forces of evil are at their strongest — these bring the spirit of the wolf to the fore. And, in turn, whatever weakens the spirit of the beast — warmth, fellowship, love — raise the human soul." Some have said this is a valid description of Reed when in his cups.

The ideology adapted by Hinds from Endore's novel is what gives *The Curse of the Werewolf* its distinction among genre films. The entire production, notably Reed's star-making performance, follows this lead, making *The Curse of the Werewolf* a bit more than a hairy face and bloody fangs. That, naturally, didn't stop the British critics turning werewolves themselves and savaging the film. The *British Film Institute Bulletin* reviewer remarked, "Even by Hammer standards, this is a singularly repellent job of slaughter-house horror.... Surely the time has come when a film like this should be turned over to the alienists for comment: as entertainment its stolid acting, presentation and direction could hardly be more preclusive."

One critic broke ranks to describe Reed's performance as "mesmerizing." *The Hollywood Reporter*, however, remarked, "As often in Hammer's productions, this one attempts to humanize, to give logic and motivation to what — to modern minds — is ludicrous, cruel or incomprehensible.... It is presented with intelligence and sympathy, not horror for its own sake."

Anthony Hinds said, "[A]lthough I have not seen it for many years, I am rather fond of *Curse of the Werewolf*. Oliver Reed, who played the wolf, was the most patient and self-disciplined of actors. I heard he's a bit wilder now, but at the time he was sitting patiently in the chair for hours, while Roy Ashton built up that marvelous makeup, hair by hair!" (Jan van Genechten, 53). According to Terence Fisher, "He gave a tremendous performance! He had to play for two things at the same time. He really made you feel when the inevitable change, the curse of the werewolf, took possession of him, and, at the same time, he made you feel his great love for the girl...." Asked what it was like to direct Reed in his first major film, Fisher said, "I loved working with him. He was young and ambitious in those days. I found he was a delight to work with.... I have never seen him do anything better since. I think this was his best performance ever; he was superb in that

A young actor about to become a star: Oliver Reed in a publicity shot from *The Curse of the Werewolf* (Hammer/Universal-International, 1961).

film. He was right emotionally and interpretively, very, very good" (Jan van Genechten, 65). Roy Ashton said of Reed, "He was a really professional chap and very ambitious at the time, because this film offered him his big chance. He would do anything, nothing was too much trouble. As far as a professional artist goes, I thought he was marvelous. He put everything he had into that role — it was a great performance" (Jan van Genechten, 79).

From the publicity manual: "Oliver Reed is no conventional actor. There is a depth of character in his face, a mystical sombreness which is ideally suited for this type of role. On him falls the mantle of the great Lon Chaney." According to S.L. Wise, "Oliver Reed's sensitive performance as the tormented Leon, combined with his good looks and sex appeal, leave no doubt that he could have been *the* Hammer horror star. Instead, he chose to try his luck outside the genre. In the years since, he has made some good films — and quite a few bad ones — but he has never given a better performance than he did in *The Curse of the Werewolf*" (Jan van Genechten, 152). Richard Klemensen recalls, "I had the honor of sitting next to the director of the film, Terence Fisher, at a showing of *The Curse of the Werewolf* in 1977, at the Horror Elite convention in London. It's not everyone who can watch a favorite film while the creator whispers little tidbits to you, like for instance, 'You know, Ollie Reed did all his own stunts in the final rooftop chase scene. Tremendously athletic lad!'" (Jan van Genechten, 162). Reed, talking to Ian Brown of *Photoplay Film Monthly* (July 1968), said that Hammer Films "gave me a chance to gain filmmaking experience quickly, and thoroughly, and I was ready for the roles in non-horror films that came along. I used to say to myself, 'I'll take this part because this film will do me a lot of good.' It never did. Or I'd say, 'This won't do me much good, but I'll take it.' And it would turn out very well for me. I came to the conclusion that you just can't tell, so I just do the best I can with a part and see what happens."

The final thought on Reed's werewolf: "Oliver Reed plays Leon with blistering energy and sincerity, never more frighteningly so than when confined in a prison cell or bordello bedroom. His lupine moments are made all the more powerful by yet another of Roy Ashton's brilliant makeup designs, particularly when the film rallies in the final reel for a rousing, and affecting, finale" (Rigby, 87).

The Pirates of Blood River (1962)

Hammer Film Productions; released by British Lion–Columbia Distributors in the U.K. on August 13, 1962, and by Columbia in the U.S. in July 1962; 84 minutes (U.K.), 87 minutes (U.S.); Technicolor (U.K.), Eastman Color (U.S.); U.K. Certificate: U

Crew— Director: John Gilling; Producer: Anthony Nelson-Keys; Executive Producer: Michael Carreras; Screenplay: John Gilling, John Hunter; Story: Jimmy Sangster; Cinematographer: Arthur Grant; Music: Gary Hughes; Musical Director: John Hollingsworth; Production Designer: Bernard Robinson; Production Manager: Clifford Parkes; Art Director: Don Mingaye; Editor: Eric Boyd-Perkins; Supervising Editor: James Needs; Special Effects: Les Bowie; Horse Master–Master at Arms: Bob Simmons; Camera Operator: Len Harris; Assistant Director: John Peverall; Sound Recordist: Jock May; Sound Editor: Alfred Cox; Makeup: Roy Ashton; Hair Stylist: Frieda Steiger; Costumes: Molly Arbuthnot; Continuity: Tilly Day; Wardrobe Mistress: Rosemary Burrows; Casting: Stuart Lyons.

Cast— Kerwin Mathews (Jonathan), Glenn Corbett (Henry), Christopher Lee (Capt. La Roche), Marla Landi (Bess), Oliver Reed (Brocaire), Andrew Keir (Jason), Peter Arne (Hench), Michael Ripper (Mac), Jack Stewart (Mason), David Lodge (Smith), Marie Devereux (Maggie), Diane Aubrey (Margaret), Jerold Wells (Commandant), Dennis Waterman (Timothy), Lorraine Clewes (Martha), John Roden (Settler), Desmond Llewelyn (Blackthorne), Keith Pyott (Silas), Richard Bennett (Seymour), Michael Mulcaster (Martin), Denis Shaw (Silver), Michael Peake (Kemp), John Colin (Lance), Don Levy (Carlos), John Bennett (Guard), Ronald Blackman (Pugh).

Synopsis

Jason Standing (Andrew Keir) is the leader of a strict sect of Huguenots, descended from those fleeing religious persecution in France generations before. They now inhabit a wild and beautiful Caribbean island. Standing's son Jonathan (Kerwin Mathews) has no favors as the leader's son — when he falls in love with a married woman, he is sent to the penal colony the sect runs on the other side of the island; his lover has already perished for her sins, sur-

rounded and devoured by the piranhas that inhabit the shallows around the island's river. Jonathan manages to escape and comes across a pirate band led by the crippled Capt. La Roche (Christopher Lee). Though physically disadvantaged, he is no less a tough leader than the elder Standing, and he is convinced that the sect has a great treasure somewhere on the island. Crafty La Roche convinces Jonathan that he will help reform the island in exchange for a safe haven. The pirates reveal their true intentions when they attack and pillage the settlement. Brocaire (Oliver Reed) and Hench (Peter Arne), both desiring the same woman, fight a duel to the death over her, although "duel" is too polite a term for the actual event. Brocaire loses, horribly. Escalating the violence in his determination to find the treasure, La Roche discovers that a huge statue of Standing's ancestor which presides over the council chamber is in fact made of solid gold. Believing gold to be too tempting, the Founding Fathers had hidden it "in plain sight" instead of concealing it. The pirates attempt to transport the statue to their ship, hidden in a bay across the island. The people of the settlement do everything in their power to prevent it and the pirates eventually turn on La Roche. The statue, lashed to an improvised raft, is floated into the river. Jason dives in after it as the raft breaks up, and he and the pirates are engulfed by the hungry piranha.

Comment

As Jimmy Sangster told Tom Johnson in July 1997, "Hammer approached me to write a pirate picture, which was fine by me. I'd grown tired of Gothics. There was one stipulation though, due to the budget, low as always. The movie had to take place on land. A landlocked pirate movie — good old Hammer!" He did a good job, nonetheless, with an interesting take on an old theme. For students of ethics, it's hard to work out who is the most evil — the elder Standing or La Roche; they seem two sides of the same coin.

Les Bowie made a little glass matte for a brief glimpse of the pirate ship at anchor so that the audience would know how the pirate force arrived and that's the last we see of it.

The Pirates of Blood River was filmed

between July 3 and August 31, 1961, using Bray Studios and Black Park. A trade show on May 5, 1962, was followed by a July 13 premiere at the Pavilion in London. It went into general release on August 2 just in time for the school summer holidays, and was partnered with *Mysterious Island*. The queues were phenomenal, but the critics were mostly lukewarm: "Stodgy, two-dimensional costume piece" (*Monthly Film Bulletin*); "Satisfactory adventure" (*Variety*); "Thrilling story, robust characterization" (*Kinematograph Weekly*).

Reed certainly threw himself into the pirate role which is essentially a tiny part, but while he is on screen the viewer's eye is drawn to him as he is always active — though never trying to steal scenes, merely enhance them. This could lead to some dangerous situations as when crossing the lake, Reed and Lee were among the few whose heads and shoulders were above the water. Reed thought there should be more action in the slog through the water and initiated an improvised skirmish. It looked great on screen, but Black Park Lake was not a relatively hygienic studio tank: "The ooze and the sludge and the stench were appalling. Poor Oliver Reed's eyes were so badly affected that he had to be treated in hospital. The lake, without outlets, was condemned" (Lee, 203). Reed, speaking to Denis Meikle in 1992 said, "We had to cross all those bogs and poor Michael Ripper was so small ... he was panicking because he was drowning ... and Christopher Lee, he's 6'5" so he could breathe, and anyone about 6' could just about breathe. Poor little Michael was so small — he was a midget pirate. He was a great social mate of Anthony Hinds — that's why he was in so many Hammer films." Oliver endeared himself to director John Gilling by hurling himself into Gilling's suggested scenarios when even the stunt guys didn't want to know. "He sacked 'em!" Reed told a reporter.

Reed's innate acting ability was being tamed slightly as he learned his craft, but even in this small outing he proved a force to be reckoned with.

Captain Clegg (1962)

Hammer Film Productions–Major Production; released by J. Arthur Rank Film Distributors in U.K. on June 25, 1962 and by Universal in the U.S. on June 13, 1962; 82 minutes; Technicolor (U.K.), Eastman Color (U.S.); filmed at Bray Studios; U.S. title: *Night Creatures*; U.K. Certificate: A

Crew— Director: Peter Graham Scott; Producer: John Temple-Smith; Screenplay: John Elder [Anthony Hinds]; Additional Dialogue: Barbara S. Harper; Cinematographer: Arthur Grant; Music: Don Banks; Musical Director: Philip Martell; Production Designer: Bernard Robinson; Art Director: Don Mingaye; Editor: Eric Boyd-Perkins; Supervising Editor: James Needs; Special Effects: Les Bowie; Makeup: Roy Ashton; Hair Stylist: Frieda Steiger; Assistant Director: John Peverall; Wardrobe: Molly Arbuthnot; Second Assistant Director: Peter Medak; Sound: Jock May.

Cast— Peter Cushing (Dr. Blyss/Captain Clegg), Yvonne Romain (Imogene), Patrick Allen (Capt. Collier), Oliver Reed (Harry Crabtree), Michael Ripper (Mipps), Martin Benson (Rash), David Lodge (Bosun), Derek Francis (Squire Crabtree), Daphne Anderson (Mrs. Rash), Milton Reid (Mulatto), Jack MacGowran (Frightened Man), Peter Halliday (Sailor Jack Pott), Terry Scully (Sailor Dick Tate), Sydney Bromley (Tom Ketch), Rupert Osbourne (Gerry), Gordon Rollings (Wurzel), Bob Head (Peg-Leg), Colin Douglas (Pirate Bosun).

Synopsis

In 1776, on the high seas, a mutilated mulatto pirate (Milton Reid) is sentenced to death by abandonment on a desert island for attacking the pregnant wife of Captain Clegg, his leader.

Many years pass but the pirate threat does not diminish, and many pirates have turned to smuggling to survive. Captain Collier (Patrick Allen), a revenue officer, is detailed to investigate the smuggling of French brandy in the town of Dymchurch. The town boasts the grave of the executed Captain Clegg; it is also haunted by the fabled "Marsh Phantoms," terrifying apparitions on horseback that gallop across the marshes, keeping all sensible folk safely abed.

Those not so sensible who chance upon the Phantoms are apt to die of the shock. The vicar of Dymchurch, Dr. Blyss (Peter Cushing), refuses to help Collier search for smugglers, although he is unfailingly polite and "helpful" in trying to billet the revenue men during their stay. Collier is invited to dine with the local magistrate, Squire Crabtree (Derek Francis), and his son Harry (Oliver Reed) at the inn. Joining them for dinner, Blyss is attacked by

Collier's "ferret"—the aforementioned mulatto—to the surprise of all. Unbeknownst to Collier, many of the townsfolk (including innkeeper Rash [Martin Benson] and Mr. Mipps [Michael Ripper] the undertaker) are members of the smuggling team, led by Dr. Blyss, who created the Phantoms to keep the curious at bay! Harry loves Rash's ward Imogene (Yvonne Romain) but their relative social positions make marriage impossible; neither can Harry tell Imogene that he is a smuggler for fear of putting her in danger.

Disguised as a scarecrow to act as lookout for the smugglers, Harry is shot by one of the revenue men passing the time with a spot of target practice. Once Collier deduces the ruse, he is on the look-out for a wounded man and thinks he has found him in the person of Blyss, only to be embarrassed that he is wrong. Harry narrowly misses capture, hiding in Blyss' home to get medical treatment. Later, when Rash makes a clumsy attempt to seduce Imogene, she escapes to Blyss' home, worried that Rash was being truthful when he told her that she was Clegg's daughter. Blyss tells her that it is true and astonishes her when he reveals that Harry knows her true parentage and doesn't give a fig about it. The vicar informs Harry of the attack, he rushes off to punish Rash and a fight ensues. Collier breaks up the fight and is triumphant when Harry is revealed as the wounded smuggler, arresting him on the spot.

Since Harry's father is the local magistrate, Collier decides to take Harry out of town to be tried. Harry escapes and Blyss performs a wedding ceremony even as Collier's men return. Harry and Imogene escape to a new life in France. Collier reveals Blyss as Clegg to the astonished congregation who rally to the vicar who has saved them from starvation. Blyss explains that, surviving his own hanging had led to him being a "new man." During the ensuing confusion, Blyss and Mipps escape through the smugglers' tunnels to Mipps' establishment but the mulatto throws a harpoon at Mipps; Clegg throws himself in front of the weapon and saves his friend's life while sacrificing his own. Mipps, weeping, carries the lifeless body of Blyss to the empty grave in the churchyard and lays his captain to rest, watched by the silent townspeople. Collier bows in respect.

Comment

Basing their movie on Russell Thorndyke's 1915 novel *Dr. Syn*, Hammer announced (in *Kinematograph Weekly*) their intention to begin filming on September 18, 1961. Disney also intended to make a version of the same novel for American TV and a theatrical release elsewhere. Disney claimed the rights to the name, so Hammer had to retitle their offering; the structure of the story stayed much the same, save for splitting Syn's character into two—a scarecrow lookout and the smuggler-in-chief. Michael Ripper, glorying in the role of Mipps, told Tom Johnson in April 1993, "One of my favorites was *Captain Clegg*—a great part, a great story, and a great cast. I always enjoyed Peter Cushing, of course, and Oliver Reed was a lot of fun, too."

Captain Clegg was released on a double-bill with *The Phantom of the Opera* on June 25, 1962, to generally favorable reviews. *The London Times* (June 28): "An almost jolly story of smugglers and king's men"; *The New York Post* (August 23): "Don't sell this thriller short"; *New*

Oliver Reed as Harry, the squire's son and smuggler, his only (relatively) benign role for Hammer in *Captain Clegg* (Universal-International, 1962).

York Daily News (August 23); "Executed as if a big spectacle was in the making"; *Variety* (May 5): "The Hammer imprimatur has come to certify solid values, and there's no mystery why these films rate audience allegiance"; *Films and Filming* (July): "A rattling good piece of comic book adventure"; *The Observer* (June 10): "Sickening makeup effects"; and *The Monthly Bulletin* (July): "The script is feeble, the acting uninspired."

Oliver Reed told Denis Meikle in 1992, "Peter Cushing is a very specific actor who believes in writing everything down. You know, 'I touch my hand, I put my hand on the table, then I point and I scratch.' He's really so meticulous ... but actors work in different ways, but for me, a very nervous actor, I needed to be just given my head." Joyce Broughton, Peter Cushing's secretary and friend of 37 years, told us of Cushing's affection and admiration for Reed. He thought Reed had a splendid career in front of him, especially admiring Reed's beautiful speaking voice, but in later life he gently chided Reed for his drinking. When they met many years later at an event in London's Leicester Square one morning, Cushing sadly pointed out to Joyce that Reed sent someone for cans of beer while they waited because he couldn't manage without.

As a family film, *Captain Clegg* gave Reed access to another audience — children. His portrayal of Harry is a perfect mix of derring-do, romantic hero and courageous fighter; he looks and acts the part to perfection. Patrick Allen, who played Collier, told the authors in 2005 what fun they all had making the film.

The Scarlet Blade (1963)

Associated British Picture Corporation–Hammer Production; released by Warner-Pathé in the U.K. on August 11, 1963, and by Columbia Pictures in the U.S. in 1964; 82 minutes; Technicolor (U.K.), Eastman Color (U.S.); Hammerscope; filmed at Bray Studios; U.S. title: *The Crimson Blade*; U.K. Certificate: U

Crew— Director: John Gilling; Producer: Anthony Nelson-Keys; Screenplay: John Gilling; Cinematographer: Jack Asher; Music: Gary Hughes; Music Supervisor: John Hollingsworth; Production Design: Bernard Robinson; Art Director: Don Min-gaye; Editor: John Dunsford; Supervising Editor: James Needs; Special Effects: Les Bowie; Camera Operator: C. Cooney; Makeup: Roy Ashton; Hair Stylist: Frieda Steiger; Sound Recordist: Ken Rawkins; Sound Editor: James Groom; Wardrobe Mistress: Rosemary Burrows; Production Manager: Clifford Parkes; Assistant Director: Dough Hermes; Second Assistant: Hugh Harlow; Third Assistant: Stephen Victor; Production Secretary: Pauline Wise; Camera Maintenance: John Kerley; Focus: Mike Sarafian; Clapper Loader: David Kelly; Boom: Peter Pardoe; Sound Camera Operator: Al Thorne; Still Cameraman: Tom Edwards; Publicity: Brian Doyle; Assistant Makeup: Richard Mills; Costumes: Molly Arbuthnot; Studio Manager: A.F. Kelly; Construction Manager: Arthur Banks; Master Carpenter: Charles Davis; Master Painter: Lawrence Wren; Master Plasterer: Stan Banks; Property Master: Tommy Money; Property Buyer: Eric Hiller; Floor Props: John Goddard; Grip: Albert Cowlard; Transportation: Coco Epps.

Cast— Lionel Jeffries (Colonel Judd), Oliver Reed (Sylvester), Jack Hedley (Edward), June Thorburn (Claire), Duncan Lamont (Major Bell), Suzan Farmer (Constance), Michael Ripper (Pablo), Charles Houston (Drury), Harold Goldblatt (Jacob), Clifford Elkin (Philip), Michael Byrne (Lt. Hawke), John Harvey (Sgt. Grey), John Stuart (Beverly), Harry Towb (Cobb), Robert Rietty (King Charles I), John H. Watson (Fitzroy), Douglas Blackwell (Blake), Leslie Glazer (Gonzales), John Wodnott (Lt. Wyatt), Eric Corrie (Duncannon), Denis Holmes (Chaplain).

Synopsis

In 1648, England is in the throes of civil war; Oliver Cromwell and his Parliamentarians versus King Charles I (Robert Rietty). The fugitive king is hiding, protected by Beverly (John Stuart) and sons Edward (Jack Hedley) and Philip (Clifford Elkin). Colonel Judd (Lionel Jeffries) is in command of the Roundheads, supported by cocky young Captain Sylvester (Oliver Reed).

When Beverly and the king are captured by Judd's forces, the king is taken into custody and Beverly summarily executed. Judd's daughter Claire (June Thorburn) is not a supporter of Cromwell and curtsies in homage to her king when he is taken, to the annoyance of her father. Sylvester desires the beautiful Claire; a marriage to a high-ranking officer's daughter being a good way to advancement, Sylvester presses his suit with arrogance, invading her bedroom and being totally obnoxious. Claire, seeing a way to help the Royalists, encourages

Sylvester (Oliver Reed) and Claire (June Thorburn) stare each other down in *The Scarlet Blade* (Hammer/Columbia, 1963).

him to think she returns his regard and she persuades him to help the Beverly brothers in an attempt to rescue the king. Edward Beverly assumes the *nom de guerre* "The Scarlet Blade" to avenge his father and work to save the king, organizing the locals and a gypsy band led by Pablo (Michael Ripper) into a guerrilla force. Claire offers her help and she and Edward become lovers. Sylvester, realizing his hopes are dashed, turns his coat again. With Judd overseeing the king's transfer, Major Bell (Duncan Lamont) takes command of the local Roundhead forces and arrests Edward's sister Constance (Suzan Farmer) as "bait" to capture the Scarlet Blade, whose attacks on the Roundheads are causing considerable trouble. On returning to his command, Judd learns of Sylvester's treachery. Sylvester plans to use his knowledge of Claire's involvement in the plot to rescue the king as a way of escaping punishment for his own disloyalty but he reckons without Judd's feelings for his daughter. Judd

shoots Sylvester to silence him. Following a dreadful battle where Philip is killed, Edward and Claire escape and seek sanctuary in the gypsy camp. Judd, searching for the rebels, has the camp searched by his troops. During the search he recognizes his daughter and Edward in the band but does not denounce them and rides away, leaving them safe.

Comment

Hammer had a flair for making period adventures at this time; their costume and set design teams could recreate a period convincingly and this adventure excelled in strong characters. As Johnson and Del Vecchio point out, "The focus of *The Scarlet Blade* is not Edward's swashbuckling, but the moral dilemmas of Sylvester and Judd" (Del Vecchio & Johnson, 235).

Filming commenced on March 1, 1963, and finished on April 17, using Bray and locations in Black Park. It was released in London

Sylvester (Oliver Reed) and his mentor Captain Judd (Lionel Jeffries) plot against the Crown in
The Scarlet Blade **(Hammer/Columbia, 1963).**

on a double bill with *The Son of Captain Blood*; the pair achieved the second highest total of takings at an ABC cinema for the year. The film generally had favorable reviews. *Kinematograph Weekly* (June 27, 1963): "Time is taken to establish the character"; *The Monthly Bulletin* (August): "This production is attractive with a reasonably convincing period flavour and careful detail, costumes, and settings"; *Variety* (April 1, 1964): "Endowed with the cost of production polish that is a specialty of Hammer Films." According to Johnson and Del Vecchio, "Top-billed Lionel Jeffries gave a strong performance, but this is clearly Oliver Reed's film, and it becomes far less interesting after Sylvester's death" (Del Vecchio & Johnson, 235).

Reed was in his element as Sylvester, and must have annoyed Lionel Jeffries immensely

by stealing the film; so much so that Jeffries flatly refused to speak to us about Reed. Suzan Farmer recalled, "I loved working with Ollie. He was an enchanting man and very funny and kind." Michael Ripper was truly fond of Reed and chuckled over their various exploits while making the film. "Oliver was never boring — you never quite knew what he'd do next, but it always looked good on screen," he told the authors in the seventies. "All the guys had to ride, and I don't like to ... not fond of horses ... so whenever I'm on a horse in the film, under the eyeline of the camera there is a bloke holding the reins. Worked too — some film critic said I looked like I was born in the saddle!" Fighting with swords, romancing the boss' daughter and taking revenge when it all goes against him — Reed's Sylvester is a complex and interesting character with more dimensions than the two-

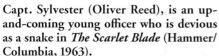

Capt. Sylvester (Oliver Reed), is an up-and-coming young officer who is devious as a snake in *The Scarlet Blade* (Hammer/Columbia, 1963).

dimensional "good guys." The moral dilemmas of Sylvester and Judd are centered on Claire and the effect her treachery to the Roundhead cause, if discovered, might have on each man's military career. That the father's love triumphs and that Sylvester gets his comeuppance is very satisfying.

Oddly, the film was re-titled *The Crimson Blade* in the U.S.—making all the characters referring to the Scarlet Blade in the film sound rather foolish.

Paranoiac (1963)

Hammer Film Production; released by J. Arthur Rank Film Distributors in the U.K. and Universal Pictures in the U.S.; 80 minutes; filmed at Bray Studios; U.K. Certificate: X

Crew—Director: Freddie Francis; Producer: Anthony Hinds; Associate Producer: Basil Keys; Screenplay: Jimmy Sangster; Cinematographer: Arthur Grant; Production Designer: Bernard Robinson; Art Director: Don Mingaye; Music: Elizabeth Lutyens; Musical Supervisor: John Hollingsworth; Supervising Editor: James Needs; Production Manager: John Draper; First Assistant Director: Ross MacKenzie; Continuity: Pauline Wise; Sound: Ken Rawkins; Makeup: Roy Ashton; Hairdresser: Frieda Steiger; Wardrobe Supervisor: Molly Arbuthnot; Special Effects: Les Bowie, Kit West; Wardrobe Mistress: Rosemary Burrows; Camera Operator: Moray Grant; Focus Pullers: David Osborne, Robin Higginson; Assistant Art Director: Ken Ryan; Sound Editor: James Groom; Boom Operator: Ken Nightingall; Sound Transfer Operator: H.C. Allan; Sound Camera Operator: Al Thorne; Second Assistant Director: Hugh Harlow; Third Assistant Director: Ray Corbett; Production Secretary: Maureen White; Still Photographer: Curtis Reeks; Studio Manager: A.F. Kelly; Construction Manager: Arthur Banks; Chief Electrician: Jack Curtis; Master Carpenter: Charles Davis; Prop Master: Tommy Money; Prop Buyer: Eric Hillier; Camera Grip: Albert Cowland; Camera Maintenance: John Kerley; Clapper/Loader: Bob Jordan; Sound Maintenance: Charles Bouvet; Boom Assistant: R.A. Mingaye; Publicist: Brian Boyle;

Assistant Makeup: Richard Mills; Master Painter: Lawrence Wrenn; Master Plasterer: Stan Banks; Floor Props Chargehand: W. Smith; Electrical Chargehands: George Robinson, Vic Hemmings; Transport Drivers: Coco Epps, Laurie Martin.

Cast— Janette Scott (Eleanor Ashby), Oliver Reed (Simon Ashby), Liliane Brousse (Francoise), Alexander Davion (Tony Ashby/Imposter), Sheila Burrell (Aunt Harriet), Maurice Denham (John Kossett), John Bonney (Keith Kossett), John Stuart (Williams), Colin Tapley (Vicar), Harold Lang (RAF Type), Laurie Lee, Marianne Stone (Women), Sydney Bromley (Tramp), Jack Taylor (Sailor).

Synopsis

Eleven years have passed since a plane crash killed the wealthy John and Mary Ashby. Their adult children Eleanor (Janette Scott) and Simon (Oliver Reed) and Mary's sister Harriet (Sheila Burrell) have gathered at the parish church — where Simon plays the organ — for the yearly memorial. The vicar (Colin Tapley) includes in the service a mention of the suicide of the eldest son, Tony, with whom Eleanor was very close. He had drowned himself eight years before, leaving only a vague note. Eleanor, who is quite frail, faints when she sees a figure in the doorway (Alexander Davion) she believes is Tony. Simon is overjoyed. A nasty, self-centered alcoholic, he stands to inherit the entire High Tor estate, if she is

Oliver Reed was the psychotic Simon Ashby in *Paranoiac* (1963) (sketch by Colin Cowie).

judged to be insane. Eleanor is being cared for by Francoise (Lilliane Bricuse), a "nurse" hired by Simon — actually his mistress. After seeing "Tony" again at High Tor, Eleanor feels that she's mad and throws herself into the sea. "Tony" fishes her out and returns her to High Tor, shocking Simon and Aunt Harriet. Simon, afraid that he'll lose the bulk of the estate, has an argument with the family solicitor Mr. Kossett (Maurice Denham) and tells his slippery son Keith Kossett (John Bonney) that he knows he's been embezzling the estate. Keith has actually done worse: He's hired a look-alike to impersonate Tony for the purpose of obtaining the estate for himself. Mr. Kossett and Aunt Harriet grill "Tony," but he's been well prepared. He tells them he faked the suicide to escape the crumbling family situation. "Tony" has now moved in to High Tor. One night, after hearing music from the chapel, he and Eleanor investigate and see Simon playing the organ and what appears to be a boy singing. Simon decides they must die and cuts the brake cables on Eleanor's car but the plot fails. "Tony" and Eleanor again hear music; this time "Tony" is attacked by a masked figure who is revealed to be Aunt Harriet. She confesses that it is Simon who is mad. She dresses up as an effigy of Tony, for whose suicide Simon feels responsible. Back in the house, "Tony" and Eleanor kiss passionately. Disgusted by what she feels is incestuous behavior, she attempts suicide, forcing "Tony" to reveal the truth. Francoise has had enough and attempts to leave but Simon drowns her in a pool. "Tony" confronts Simon in the chapel and finds the real Tony's mummified corpse. Simon admits that he faked the entire suicide and murdered his brother. He knocks out "Tony" and ties him up. When he leaves, Aunt Harriet sets the chapel ablaze. Now completely insane, Simon rushes to the chapel to save his brother. "Tony" has been freed by Eleanor, but Simon dies in the conflagration.

Comment

Paranoiac was Reed's first true starring role for Hammer. After appearing in seven previous films for the company, he was given his opportunity. Reed's character appeared in almost every scene, and he dominated each one.

Reed told Denis Meikle in 1992, "Freddie Francis was a technician — he was a lighting cameraman really. He's a technocrat — very technical, very nice fellow. Terry Fisher didn't know half that stuff. But he was more artistic — he had a great eye for the four wall setup that Hammer uses. Freddie was very charming. Directors don't register too much with me — I just get on and do my job. I don't get involved."

Paranoiac was planned by Hammer to be filmed as early as 1954 when the company bought Josephine Tey's novel *Brat Farrar*. After two abortive attempts to film Paul Dehn's screenplay in 1955 and 1959, the script was shelved, only to be resurrected in a completely different form. The project was handed to Hammer's star writer Jimmy Sangster, who then jettisoned most of Tey's novel.

Sangster told the authors,

I was a fan of Josephine Tey's work, and tried to keep as much of it as possible. That said, I didn't keep much! We didn't even put her name on the credits, for which she was probably very grateful. Due to our limited budget the horse racing segments of her novel — it really centered on the sport — had

to go. Due to this being a Hammer film, horror had to come in. One of my favorite films is *Diabolique* [1955] — a classic of plot twists and turns. I like it so much I've rewritten it quite a few times myself! After Hitchcock's *Psycho* [1960], Hammer wanted to move away from *Dracula* and *Frankenstein* so I wrote an unrelated series of similar films. *Taste of Fear* [1961] was the first — and best.

Paranoiac was the third — and second best. Screenwriters spend a lot less time on the set than most people think — practically none, actually. I don't recall meeting Oliver Reed during filming, although we did become friendly for a time afterwards. I didn't write the part for him, although it seems like I did. He was very, very, very good. I wasn't surprised when he became a big star after leaving Hammer. I'll admit he became a bigger star than I thought possible, but, looking back, I shouldn't have been. Oliver Reed had what it took.

The little that survived from *Brat Farrar* was the element of impersonation; the rest was pure Jimmy Sangster, which is as good as this type of Hammer film gets.

Paranoiac began production at Bray Studios on July 23, 1962, and wrapped on August 31. Following a September 7 trade show it was partnered with Hammer's *The Kiss of the Vampire* for a January 26, 1964, release. *Paranoiac* opened in America in May 1963, as a single feature.

Paranoiac was the first of the Hammer films to be directed by Academy Award–winning cinematographer Freddie Francis and is certainly the best. His introduction of Simon sets the stage perfectly: As the vicar eulogizes Simon's late parents, their son sits at the church organ dragging on a cigarette and smirking. Francis' handling of the entire cast is extraordinary for a fledgling director, especially that of Reed in his first starring role.

Anthony Hinds told the authors, "As the producer and writer of *The Curse of the Werewolf*, I knew we had something special in Oliver Reed. He was a born film star, really, and Hammer was fortunate that he stayed with us as long as he did. He had a wonderful attitude — he was very cooperative and didn't take himself too seriously. After *Paranoiac* I knew Oliver's

Simon Ashby is just as dangerous as he looks in *Paranoiac* (Hammer/Universal, 1963).

time with us was coming to an end. He had too much talent to stay in the type of films we could offer him. His success on an international level did not surprise me in the least."

Reviews were relatively generous for a Hammer film (which were generally undervalued). "This is good, old-fashioned chiller nonsense that does not have to be believed to be enjoyed. Clear direction and a taut script make the storyline quickly and continuously understandable. Oliver Reed revels in the growing madness of Simon" (*Kinematograph Weekly*, September 12, 1963); "Lack of experience proves no handicap for Francis ... as he has sculpted a suspenseful and smartly paced opus out of Jimmy Sangster's effective screenplay. Reed plays a scheming brother with demonic skill, blending bits of spoiled brat and sneaky madman for a menacing portrayal" (*Variety*, April 10, 1963); "Top marks for Oliver Reed and Sheila Burrell for bringing just the right degree of restraint to their hammy roles. It can go without saying that any film directed by Freddie Francis is bound to be eyetaking" (*Films and Filming*, March 1964); "Simon is one of the

Don't be fooled by his good looks and charm; Simon (Oliver Reed) is a dangerous *Paranoiac* (Hammer/Universal-International, 1963).

worst heels ever put up on the screen and I'm afraid he's a sight more sadistic than Bill Sikes. A wastrel, a pervert, drunk and otherwise demented figure well played by Oliver Reed" (*New York Mirror*, May 23, 1963).

On the verge of the big time, Reed was handed a choice role by Sangster, Hinds and Francis, and he made the most of it, delivering his best performance up to that point. Simon Ashby has been — literally — getting away with murder, due to his considerable surface charm and his family's position in the community. At first he seems merely unpleasant but is gradually revealed to be a dangerous alcoholic. He has to be watched closely; his demeanor, usually calm and overly polite, can change in the blink of an eye. He can become, quickly and inexplicably, violent as when he berates the family's long-suffering butler (John Stuart), or drunkenly turn on a harmless pub patron while brandishing a fistful of darts.

More quietly but equally disturbing, as he and Aunt Harriet watch a confused Eleanor walking in the garden, Simon wears an amused smirk which vanishes instantly to be replaced with a believable look of concern as Harriet turns to face him. Despite Simon's physical prowess, words are his main weapon; he rarely raises his voice and often speaks in a whisper. But what he says can be devastating. After the memorial service, Simon comes home late. When Aunt Harriet asks where he has been...

SIMON: I've been drinking. Now I'm going to drink some more.

HARRIET: I would have thought that on the day of the service...

SIMON: That I'd have on my sackcloth and ashes. They've been dead for 11 years. It's your idea to resurrect them once a year and parade them in front of the villagers ... not mine.

HARRIET: If you behaved like a normal human being, I wouldn't have to.

SIMON: Before you start apportioning blame, how do you think it looked letting little Eleanor behave that way in public? It must have given the villagers a marvelous tidbit.

HARRIET: Your sister is sick!

SIMON: Sick?

Keith Kossett (John Bonney) and Simon Ashby (Oliver Reed) scheming in *Paranoiac* (Hammer/Universal-International, 1963).

HARRIET: Well, she's very upset ... disturbed.

SIMON: Auntie dear, my sister is insane.

No one is safe from Simon's nastiness. As he lies in Francoise's bed, she gets on top of him. He asks her, tenderly, if she's free for the evening. She looks at him adoringly; he kisses her forehead, gets up and walks out, leaving the door open so Aunt Harriet can see her kneeling on the bed, in her lingerie.

Later, as Simon awaits the result of his tampering with Eleanor's brakes, Francoise suggests that they simply forget about the inheritance and run off together.

SIMON: You're more stupid than I gave you credit for.

FRANCOISE: What is it that makes you want to hurt people?

SIMON: I don't hurt people.

FRANCOISE: Oh yes you do, all the time. Your aunt, Eleanor ... me.

SIMON: Do I hurt you?

FRANCOISE: Sometimes ... you're cruel.

SIMON: But then you like me to hurt you, don't you?

At the film's climax, "Tony" confronts Simon after finding the real Tony's mummified corpse in the chapel.

SIMON: Now you've found out, what are you going to do about it? I'll tell you, shall I? Nothing. Because Tony isn't dead. I'm talking to him now.

TONY: How did you fake that suicide note, Simon?

SIMON: I didn't. I got him to write it in a game some weeks before. I kept it.

TONY: How long before?

SIMON: A year. Maybe two.

TONY: You made up your mind to murder him when you were only thirteen?

SIMON: About then.

TONY: And you did your best to murder me?

SIMON: Not my best.

All of the dialogue is delivered calmly, rationally and softly, making it all the more chilling. This was a style that Reed would use effectively for the rest of his career.

Reed's most startling physical acting comes at the climax as he lurches down the staircase to rescue Tony's body; his face and body twist violently as he races to the burning chapel. No one ever looked more insane on film; it is almost too believable.

Hammer Productions has now come tantalizingly close to a bullseye. This economical little chiller has some solid assets.... [It] opens with devilish adroitness and whips up considerable suspense and conviction with some sparse, succinct dialogue. What a family! There's a modern Heathcliff type (Oliver Reed) often into violent rages.—*New York Times*, May 23, 1963.

Anthony Hinds was right. Hammer could no longer contain Oliver Reed's exploding talent.

To his credit, Reed never disparaged the company or downplayed his role in it after he became a star. In fact, he praised Hammer for giving him the opportunity to learn everything he needed to know about acting. His next teacher would be Michael Winner.

The Damned (1963)

Columbia Pictures presents a Hammer Film Production–Swallow Production; released by Columbia Pictures in the U.K. in 1963 and by Columbia Pictures in the U.S. in 1965; 87 minutes (U.K.), 77 minutes (U.S.); filmed at Bray Studios; U.S. title: *These Are the Damned*; U.K. Certificate: X

Crew—Director: Joseph Losey; Producer: Anthony Hinds; Executive Producer: Michael Carreras; Associate Producer: Anthony Nelson-Keys; Screenplay: Evan Jones, based on H.L. Lawrence's novel *The Children of Light*; Cinematographer: Arthur Grant; Production Designer: Bernard Robinson; Art Director: Don Mingaye; Supervising Editor: James Needs; Editor: Reginald Mills; Music: James Bernard; Music Director: John Hollingsworth; Song "Black Leather Rock" by Evan Jones and James Bernard; Sound: Jock May; Production Assistant: Richard MacDonald; Assistant Director: John Peverall; Camera Operator: Len Harris; Costumes: Molly Arbuthnot; Continuity: Pamela Davis; Makeup: Roy Ashton; Hair Stylist: Frieda Steiger; Production Manager: Don Weeks; Casting: Stuart Lyons; Sculptures: Elizabeth Frink.

Cast—Macdonald Carey (Simon Wells), Shirley Ann Field (Joan), Viveca Lindfors (Freya), Oliver Reed (King), Alexander Knox (Bernard), Walter Gotell (Major Holland), James Villiers (Captain Gregory), Kenneth Cope (Sid), Thomas Kempinski (Ted), Brian Oulton (Mr. Dingle), Barbara Everest (Miss Lamont), Alan McClelland (Mr. Stuart), James Maxwell (Mr. Talbot), Rachel Clay (Victoria), Caroline Sheldon (Elizabeth), Rebecca Dignam (Anne), Siobhan Taylor (Mary), Nicholas Clay (Richard), Kit Williams (Henry), Christopher Witty (Wilham), David Palmer (George), John Thompson (Charles), David Gregory, Anthony Valentine, Larry Martyn, Leon Garcia, Jeremy Phillips (Teddy Boys).

Synopsis

Wealthy vacationing American Simon Wells (Macdonald Carey) is picked up by Joan (Shirley Ann Field), whose psychotic brother King (Oliver Reed) leads a "teddy boy" gang for whom she acts as a tasty decoy. Simon, beaten and robbed, is rescued by a secret military installation's security guards. Recuperating in a local hotel, Simon meets Bernard (Alexander Knox), head of the project, and Bernard's lover, sculptress Freya (Viveca Lindfors).

Joan approaches Simon on his boat, attempting to explain her behavior when the incestuously jealous King arrives. Leaving with Simon, she avoids his clumsy pass and asks to be put ashore. They break into Freya's cottage, make love in her bed and leave before King arrives. Inside the military complex, Bernard uses a television link to speak to the children in his care. The children believe they are being groomed to go into space but in reality they are part of an experimental attempt to breed a generation who could survive nuclear war. Personally immune to fallout, their touch is deadly.

The gang chases Simon and Joan into the sea, followed by King. The three are rescued by Victoria (Rachel Clay) and Henry (Kit Williams), two of the children. Too late, Bernard tries to separate the children from the adults but they are already poisoned. Misinterpreting Bernard's actions, the adults attempt to escape with the children. King and Henry make a break in Freya's car, chased by a helicopter.

Dying from the effects of radiation, King drives off a bridge. Simon and Joan are allowed back to his boat but die on board. Bernard shoots Freya, who knows too much and could be a security risk.

Comment

Oliver Reed told Denis Meikle in 1992, "I continued to be cast by Hammer because I was cheap and I gave them what they wanted. I knew my lines, I didn't knock over the furniture, I was on time. I almost worked back to back for Hammer. Anthony Nelson-Keys was my main contact. The colonel [Sir James Carreras] would smile at me as he walked around the studio because I represented something that worked. This was one of the first films Joe Losey put his name to after the McCarthy witch hunt — he was one of the people who had been chased out of Hollywood because he associated with people who wanted to ban the bomb. He believed in Socialism ... he wasn't a Communist ... he just didn't believe in war and, hence, he made *The Damned* which was really anti-bomb. He used to wear home-woven clothes ... pale green and brown. He was very generous — he used to take the cast out for dinner and preach anti-bomb stuff to us. I found him very, very left of center, very enthusiastic, very keen. The last time I saw him was in the St. Regis Hotel in New York and I think I found him, then, extraordinarily arrogant because he'd made a film that was successful.

You rarely saw producers on the set [but] they used to listen to everything because of the boom — they had it wired into Tony Keys' office. It wasn't until later, until I'd gotten a little more senior at Hammer, that I used to go in and have a drink with Tony and you could hear all the chat in the studio. It was like a spy network. I didn't know how other studios worked — I didn't know any other studios. I knew Lime Grove Studios for the BBC, and Hammer, and Black Forest or Black Park, the place we used near Pinewood Studios. I wasn't getting any offers from other companies until it was about that stage when I met Ken Russell and Michael Winner. Michael gave me my money, Russell gave me my art, but Hammer gave me my technique."

Based on H.L. Lawrence's novel *The Chil-dren of Light*, *The Damned* began filming at Bray on May 8, 1961. A *Kinematograph Weekly* reporter visited the set and spoke to Reed about making a record for Decca called "Lonely for a Girl." Director Losey was fascinated by the radiation theme but had reservations about two of his actors; he liked Reed personally but was put off by the fact that he had "no training at all, and he already had a certain arrogance, so he wasn't easy" (Del Vecchio & Johnson, 211). Shirley Ann Field was hired because she had just worked with Laurence Olivier and the producers thought she would add some cachet to the project (Caute, 143). "Losey juxtaposed the flamboyant aggression of the 'Teds' with the indirect, secret, hidden, hypocritical violence of the military-scientific establishment practicing its Orwellian experimentation deep under the cliff.... Casting Viveca Lindfors ... was a stroke of genius on Losey's part.... [D]espite a riveting performance by Oliver Reed as the gang leader, the impact of the film was blunted by performances either routine (Alexander Knox, Macdonald Carey) or mediocre (Shirley Ann Field)."

Shooting ended on June 22, 1961. Despite its topicality and internationally recognized director and stars, the film gathered dust for nearly two years; it finally premiered at the Pavilion on May 30, 1963, supported by *Maniac*. It probably would have stayed on the shelf longer had Losey not become the critics' darling via *The Servant* (1963), elevating his work to "serious study" levels. In truth, British Lion and Columbia didn't seem to have a clue about marketing a Hammer film that wasn't conventional "Hammer Horror."

The Evening News (May 23, 1963): "It carries the imprint of a master film maker"; *The London Times* (May 30, 1963): "Losey is one of the most intelligent, ambitious and consistently exciting filmmakers now working in the country. It would be a thousand pities were his latest film, after 18 months on the shelf, to go out unremarked at the lower half of a 'double X' all horror programme." "Carreras did not like what Losey had done with *The Damned* and the film was shelved for two years before being cut to 87 minutes.... Clearly nobody felt *The Damned* had been a great success, but much to the astonishment of the producers, it won top prize in Trieste at the first science fiction film festival." *The New York Times* (July 8) described it as "Orwellian," *Variety* (July 14) as "a strange but fascinating film." As Johnson and Del Vecchio noted, "If 23 minutes were removed from *Citizen Kane*, the result would be incomprehensible, too, so it is unfair to carp about vagueness and plot holes. What is left of major interest is Arthur Grant's crisp black and white photography and an outstanding job by the underappreciated Oliver Reed.... There is enough left of *The Damned*, even missing a quarter of its running time, to make it one of the decade's most interesting science fiction films" (Del Vecchio & Johnson, 212).

The System (1964)

Kenneth Shipman Productions; released in the U.K. by Bryanston Films in 1964 and by AIP in the U.S. in 1966

Crew— Director: Michael Winner; Writer: Peter Draper; Producer: Kenneth Shipman; Associate Producer: George Fowler; Original Music: Stanley Black; Cinematographer: Nicolas Roeg; Film Editor: Fred Burnley; Art Director: Geoffrey Tozer; Costume Design: Bridget Sellers; Makeup Artist: Gerry Fletcher; Hair Stylist: Betty Glasow; Production Manager: Clifton Brandon; Assistant Director: Peter Price; Sound Recordist: Stephen Dalby; Camera Operator: Alex Thomson.

Cast— Oliver Reed (Tinker), Jane Merrow (Nicola), Barbara Ferris (Suzy), Julia Foster (Lorna), Harry Andrews (Mr. Larsey), Ann Lynn (Ella), Guy Doleman (Philip), Andrew Ray (Willy), John Porter-Davison (Grib), Clive Colin Bowler (Sneakers), Ian Gregory (Sammy), David Hemmings (David), John Alderton (Nidge), Jeremy Burnham (Ivor), Mark Burns (Michael), Derek Nimmo (James), Pauline Munro (Sylvie), Derek Newark (Alfred), Stephanie Beaumont (Marianne), Talitha Pol (Helga), Dora Reisser (Ingrid), Susan Burnet (Jasmine), Victor Winding (Stan), Jennifer Tafler (Sonia), Poss Parker (Fred), Gwendoline Watts (Girl).

Nicola (Jane Merrow) and Tinker (Oliver Reed) relax on the beach in *The System* (Shipman/Bryanston/AIP, 1964). Reed's face was soon after scarred during a brawl in a Soho club.

Synopsis

Tinker (Oliver Reed) is wasting his life and whatever talent he has as a beach photographer in Roxton. He's developed a "system" for meeting girls on holiday by taking their picture — and getting their address for the duration of their stay — and sharing them with his younger mates who work on the promenade. Tinker's only rule is to avoid emotional involvement, which he breaks when he meets Nicola (Jane Merrow), a London model down for the week with her wealthy father Philip (Guy Doleman). The gang must earn enough money — and get enough sex — over the summer to last them through the rest of the year when Roxton is a ghost town. Tinker has provided for that by photographing the odd party or wedding and "romancing" Ella (Ann Lynn), the bored wife of a local comedian (Victor Winding). The gang invites itself to a party at Philip's house where Tinker makes a move on Nicola, but she is uninterested. Instead he leaves with Sylvia (Pauline Munro) after getting a vague promise from Nicola to meet the next day. He becomes upset when a mate's (Andrew Ray) girl (Jennifer Tafler) becomes pregnant. Tinker offers to connect them with an abortionist. He later meets Nicola on the beach, where she tells him she knows all about the system. She returns to his room and humiliates Tinker when he clumsily tries to initiate sex.

Mr. Larsey (Harry Andrews), Tinker's boss, notices that Tinker's productivity is down and he'd better not plan on returning next season. Tinker confronts an unlicensed photographer and a vicious fight ensues. He returns to his room with Lorna (Julia Foster); he despises himself for doing it. The next day he and Nicola go to a deserted beach and have both a swim and sex.

After being attacked in retaliation for the earlier fight, Tinker is invited by Philip to his house to discuss his relationship with Nicola. Tinker realizes how far apart their worlds are after being pummeled in a tennis game he foolishly enters. The best man at his friend's hastily scheduled wedding, Tinker gives a cynical speech, and meets Nicola at a beach bonfire afterwards. After having sex in his room, he tells Nicola that he loves her and he's returning with her to London. But — she's off to Rome on a modeling assignment for several months. She says he should come up to London when she returns but Tinker has heard that one before.

Comment

As the London express pulls into the beach resort of Roxton, the camera, mounted in the train, pans the platform. It passes several loungers, finally zeroing in on a smiling (or smirking) young man. He is handsome and dangerous looking, but somehow not. His eyes bore into the camera and a star is born.

The System may well be the single most important film in Oliver Reed's career. It marked his departure from Hammer and positioned him for the international stardom that would come with *Oliver!* and *Women in Love*. It also brought him together with Michael Winner, who would direct some of Reed's best films.

Michael Winner said in Channel 4's *The Real Oliver Reed*, "You hit this wonderful face in a big way, looking slightly dangerous, and the audience was always knocked out by this first image. *The System* examined youth that was out to have a good time, but in fact was insecure and sensitive underneath. And really, this was Oliver."

Reed told Robin Bean in a June 1967 *Films and Filming* interview, "I think Michael has a reputation for being difficult. I like him because he's very honest and there's nothing phony about him. As long as you're honest and straightforward.... We've always got on very well. Behind Winner's megaphone, voice, cigar and chair, there beats a heart of gold. Sort of."

Reed and Winner met in October 1962 when the actor brought the young director a screenplay he had written. But Winner was more interested in Reed the actor than in Reed the writer; he felt that Reed had what it took to become a major star, if only the right vehicle could be found. In his splendid autobiography, Winner writes, "I'd met Oliver in 1962 when I was casting *West 11*. I'd always thought he was a wonderful actor. He was very sensitive and quietly spoken. Unlike the image he was later to acquire as a roustabout drinker. Oliver showed me poetry he'd written. I liked him very much.

He ... was dismissed by [producer] Danny Angel as 'another B picture actor.' Oliver had only done Hammer horror films, but I thought he had more to offer" (Winner, 86).

When *The System* came his way, Winner knew whom to call. Winner owned his own production company, Scimitar Films, and, through that, made the acquaintance of writer Peter Draper. Draper had begun a novel, *The Takers*, that he had turned into a film script. They were based on his observations at the Devon coast town of Brixham: Draper was intrigued by the conflict between the locals and vacationers who, despite their dependence on each other, never seemed able to co-exist. The locals developed a sub-language, calling vacationers "grockels" so they could discuss them without causing offense. A "grockelbox" was a camera, "grocklefodder" was food and a "grockeltrap" was an amusement arcade. This concept was brilliantly transferred to the screen, mock-documentary style, with a sarcastic voice-over by Reed. But Draper's main interest was the youth of both groups who took from each other without realizing the extent of their callousness.

Tinker is a handsome, charming, talented but troubled not-so-young man, unsure of his present or his future, bedeviled by women and alcohol, but with an innate sense of decency that makes the above even more disturbing. (Perfect casting for Reed.) Tinker has stayed at the beach too long; he is becoming almost a father figure to the teenage boys who idolize him and the teenage girls he seduces. Unlike his young charges, Tinker is only too aware of his misconduct and isn't very happy with himself. In character as Tinker, Reed remarks, "I never make the same mistake twice ... I make it hundreds and hundreds of times." Prophetic?

Tinker may or may not have what it takes to make it big in London and is afraid to find out; he prefers to remain a big fish at a small beach. He's even in over his head, finally, in Roxton when he falls in love with Nicola. She is, of course, playing him like he's played hundreds of others. Worse — he knows it but can't help himself. The huge difference between them is hammered home when the smartass Tinker flippantly challenges one of her London friends to a game of tennis. This probably being the first time he's held a racquet, Tinker is casually dispatched; he's completely out of his depth, for once, and he knows it. The scene is both funny and bitter.

Tinker (Oliver Reed) and Nicola (Jane Merrow) in a publicity shot from Michael Winner's *The System* (Shipman/Bryanston/AIP, 1964).

Oliver Reed as Tinker instructs the lads (including David Hemmings, second from left) in the film that changed his career, *The System* (Shipman/Bryanston/AIP, 1964).

Winner, Draper and Reed make the viewer feel sorry for Tinker even though he hardly deserves it.

The System has a bit of everything — comedy, sex, violence, pathos and social commentary. And it all works. The comedy is mainly supplied by Reed. His dancing (always good for a laugh) and spontaneous lapses into odd dialects and mugging are perfectly realized.

Winner cuts away from the film's several sex scenes, but Reed and Jane Merrow easily get the point across. But Winner, according to *People* (September 9, 1964), nearly ran foul of the censor: "You could hardly call *The System* daring but the mere threat of possible censorship nearly killed off the whole idea. [Winner] was tipped off by the British Board of Film Censors that it didn't have much chance of getting by. Winner took a gamble. And he didn't think it would be approved. The film you will see was

eventually passed with only a single cut." Reed was tangentially mentioned as an "actor with a future."

The violence comes as a surprise and is fairly shocking. The fight at the party lasts only a minute, but Reed is terrifying in his intensity. The scene adds a great deal to our perception of Tinker, and also added censorial problems. The *Daily Mail* (no date): "After four months' deliberation, Britain's film censors are to allow a picture which includes nude bathing and a realistic fight to be shown uncut. The director, Michael Winner said, 'The censors ... must have seen it a dozen times before they made up their minds. The picture doesn't condone the boys' system. Indeed we show that, eventually, they get little pleasure from it.'"

Reed also delivers in the pathos department in several scenes in which he faces his unacceptable behavior. After conning the sadly

6646-24

Tinker (Oliver Reed) thinks Nicola (Jane Merrow) is just another conquest in *The System* (Shipman/Bryanston/American International, 1964).

naive Lorna to his room for sex, Tinker says, "I had the feeling you'd been here before ... thousands of times."

He shows up drunk at Ella's home, looking for whatever she's prepared to give him. This time, it's nothing. "We use people up, don't we?" he says. After he's come to realize that Nicola has used him, he's told by Suzie, a former lover, "There are only two kinds of people — the takers and the taken." His face tells us he completely understands.

The whole film is one continuous social commentary on the pointlessness of living for shallow pleasure. But Winner and Draper throw in an even more disturbing concept by suggesting that the "straight life" isn't much better. Tinker is horrified when his friend insists on marrying his pregnant girlfriend, and says, "You're going to end up in some ugly little bungalow full of three-ply furniture and four

square feet of lawn to mow every Saturday morning."

In *Evening News* (October 20, 1964), Peter Draper defended his bleak view of *The System*'s characters: "I found that local boys, carrying suitcases stuffed with newspapers, were travelling to Exeter to wait for the holiday expresses from London and the North. All these trains go to Torquay. The boys posed as holidaymakers, chat up the most attractive girls and have everything lined up for themselves and their pals by the time the train gets in. The girls never knew the boys are locals. Beach photographers and similar people often act as tip-off men with addresses and other details."

Reed was signed in mid–July 1963 and production on *The Takers*, as it was then titled, began in Torquay during the last week of August, continuing into October. *Kinematograph Weekly* (September 12, 1963) reported Winner as saying: "The actors are all playing their own ages. When you're on location, everything is so much more real, and it's no good making up people of 30 to look 18. It just doesn't work."

A trade show was held July 30, 1964 — quite a lag due to the censorship situation. *The System* went into general release on September 20, paired with, of all things, William Castle's *Strait-Jacket!*

Most reviewers were enthralled: "Oliver Reed, the brash but likable cut-rate Romeo, could be a find. Behind his dark and rather glowering good looks there's a wide mixture of smart alecky, genuine humor and animation. The snag for overseas is that it has no marquee appeal. However, Reed seems likely to rectify that situation if he gets the breaks."— *Variety*, August 12, 1964; "The problem it poses, that of youthful immorality, is a serious one. Oliver Reed does a strong job as the self-tortured Tinker. There are some noticeably clever directorial touches."— *Kinematograph Weekly*, August 6, 1964; "Handled with skill and tact."— *Daily Telegraph*, September 6, 1964; "It will be interesting to see how holidaymakers react, for the film is an attack both on them for their conformity and bad taste, and those involved in the resort industry who exploit them. Oliver Reed is bitter, self-pitying, eloquent, irresistible."— *The Observer*, September 6, 1964.

Reed told Denis Meikle in 1992, "I came to Michael Winner after he'd seen me in a Hammer film and tried to get me in *West Eleven* with Julie Christie [but producer] Danny Angel said that Julie Christie was a B picture actress and I was a nothing. I'm very glad to say that Julie Christie went on to do extraordinary things and was anything but a B picture actress and I hope that I was more than a nothing. And so Winner found the man who had Twickenham Studios at the time.... Ken Shipman didn't know anything about films but just was a rich man and bought the studio.... He put some money up for the first Winner film I did — *The System*. I did the Winner film when I decided to give up Hammer ... and then I got my face cut."

Winner is reported as saying, "He was a menace at night, no question. He was very professional on the set — in the evening a disaster." David Hemmings remarked, "He could drink 20 pints of lager with a gin or *crème de menthe* chaser and still run a mile for a wager."

Barry Norman added, "It was about eleven o'clock in the morning but he was well into the beer already. And we talked for a bit and then he suggested that we go off and box each other. At that point I made an excuse and left because he was in much better shape than I was and I wasn't about to be knocked out by him" (Sellers, 95).

More from Hemmings: "I was introduced to Oliver Reed, with whom I was to work (and carouse enthusiastically) on several subsequent occasions, lastly in 1999 on *Gladiator*. Ollie was never a man you could miss — broad, intelligent, funny, frightening, and deeply unpredictable. His aim always was to be larger than his already oversized self. Oliver had a grin that split his face like an early muppet, but with less of the charm" (Hemmings, 115).

The System had Oliver Reed on the starting blocks for international stardom. Some years later he admitted, "I have not told Michael Winner that he is the director with the most talent; he is undoubtedly one of the most talented" (*Playmen*, May 1972).

Monitor: The Debussy Film (1965)

British Broadcasting Corporation; televised in February 1965

Crew— Producer-Director: Ken Russell; Scenario: Melvyn Bragg, Ken Russell; Dialogue: Melvyn Bragg; Cinematography: John McGlashan, Ken Westbury; Film Editor: Allan Tyrer; Makeup Supervisor: Maureen Winsdale; Dubbing: Stanley Morcom; Wardrobe: Vera Buckle; Titles: Derek Nice; Assistants to Director: Anne James, Christopher Martin, Jack Wells.

Cast— Oliver Reed (Claude Debussy/The Actor), Vladek Sheybal (Pierre Louis/The Director), Annette Robertson (Gaby Dupont), Iza Teller (Mme. Bardas), Penny Service (Lily), Vernon Dobtcheff (An Actor), Jane Lumb (Saint Sebastian), Victora Russell (Chochou), Verity Edmett (Zohra the Slave Girl), Stephanie Randall (Secretary).

Synopsis

The Director (Vladek Sheybal) is assembling the cast and crew of his documentary on the life of French composer Claude Debussy, and we are privy to his discussions with the Actor (Oliver Reed) who plays Debussy as he tries to get him into character. This is not a difficult task since the Actor and Composer have much in common, especially their dismissive attitude to the women in their lives. The documentary opens with Debussy's funeral in 1918.

In between are random vignettes involving the Director, the Actor and the Composer (it is sometimes difficult to discern whether we are seeing the Actor or the Composer) including Debussy discussing his poverty-stricken background saying, "The only memory of my mother is she used to slap my face"; the Director lecturing the Actor on the art scene in Paris in the 1890s where the mixture of the arts caused Debussy to attempt to reproduce painting in sound; the Actor and Composer both sponging off their respective women; the insinuating presence of Louis, a pornographer and pedophile; the Actor and Director discussing Debussy's life in London; the Actor and his girlfriend dancing to the Kinks' "You Really Got Me" at a party; the Actor being put down at the party because of his interest in Debussy; and Debussy and his girlfriend fighting violently over money. The director opines that Debussy was lazy — he only wrote what he wanted when he wanted"; he further explains to the Actor that the Composer was a wastrel who could not make his lover happy. As they break for lunch, the Actor's girlfriend slaps an actress for coming on to him; she then pretends to shoot herself as Debussy's lover had done. Debussy then moves on to Lily (Penny Service) who falls ill when he is unable — and unwilling — to support her. He finds a new wealthy mistress who offers her patronage. The Director, the Actor and crew watch a small-scale stage performance of a play about Debussy, who had sued the playwright. The Composer begins work on *The Fall of the House of Usher* and identifies with Edgar Allan Poe's Roderick Usher. Before his death he declares, "I am Roderick Usher."

Comment

While a synopsis never really does justice to its subject, it is never more true in this case. *The Debussy Film* may sound like an incompre-hensible mess but is, in fact, a riveting, brilliant effort. True, it does require the viewer's rapt attention but there's nothing wrong with that. One of the film's more interesting aspects is that often viewers aren't certain whether they're watching Debussy or the Actor.

Reed, an actor important to Russell's subsequent career, is both Debussy and the actor who plays him. Vladek Sheybal plays the director and Debussy's mentor Pierre Louys. As Sheybal struggles to fix the elusive musician on film, the affairs and encounters of other members of the cast parallel and illuminate the simplified story of Debussy's life usually retailed by musical dictionaries. Story and reality interpenetrate. *The Martyrdom of St. Sebastian* — Debussy wrote incidental music for D'Annunzio's play — is recreated by the film unit on a modern beach with a crucified girl in a white sweatshirt pincushioned by arrows. Sheybal and Reed visit the man who is to play Debussy's antagonist Maeterlinck, but the actors so irritate one another that a grotesque duel is fought there and then, with walking sticks instead of swords and the playwright peppered with rubber-suckered arrows from a toy gun. If anything matters in this encounter, Russell reasons, it is the emotion and personal animosity, which are timeless. When the director struggles for strict accuracy he is merely absurd. "They *did* play with balloons — I checked it," he says triumphantly to his cast as they watch film of Debussy and his girl bumping a balloon from one to another while they drift through the park to *L'Apres-Midi d'un Faune*, ignoring the fact that slow motion, backlighting and the blend of music and image create a romantic tone poem with little to do with reality. If one wants objective truth about Debussy, it can be found only in the first line. As the composer's pathetic funeral procession struggles through the rain, a child (Xavier Russell in his first role) runs after the coffin and returns with the bleak news, "It seems he is a musician."

A furor followed the telecasting of this film (diplomatically referred to as "Impressions of the French composer" on its airing). Russell was unaware that American producer Harry Saltzman, acting on a suggestion from Michael Caine, wanted him to direct Saltzman's next feature. Russell, therefore, continued to make dramatized documentaries in a style that was palely imitated by others. Reed had reached both a personal and professional low when he went to Russell for an audition. His face (as noted in the biography section) had been badly scarred and roles were not being offered; he was forced to drive a mini-cab to pay the bills.

Ken Russell (Goodwin, 95): "When I first saw him he looked terrific. He struck me as vivacious, cheeky, and not run-of-the-mill. I remember him as being very moody and glowering. I liked his spirit — everyone else I auditioned seemed to fade into insignificance."

Russell, rightly, overlooked the facial scars. Directors for the remaining thirty-five years of his career chose to overlook them as well!

Russell (Russell, 64–65): "My association with Oliver goes back to the mid-sixties and the time I was preparing *The Debussy Film* for the BBC. I first saw him on *Juke Box Jury*, a TV pop show in which the jurors passed sentence on the Top Twenty. Two things in particular struck me about the young Mr. Reed. Firstly, he was the life and soul of the party, and secondly, he bore an extraordinary resemblance to Claude Debussy. I rang his agent and Oliver came to see me in my office at Lime Grove. He did his best to lounge on an upright chair and said, 'I hear you are considering me for Debussy.' I nodded. He fixed me with his hooded eyes, looking moody, mean and magnificent. 'What about this?' he asked, sticking out his chin. I looked. It was freshly scarred. 'Someone with a broken bottle thought I looked too pretty,' he volunteered. 'Well, thanks for coming in,' I said. He nodded and got up looking tight-lipped. 'That's what they all say when they see the scar,' he said bitterly. 'What scar?' I said. Oliver was good as Debussy, capturing the brooding sensuality and threatening calm that is so characteristic of the man and his music. For all his macho image, Oliver is a sensitive artist who approaches his craft intuitively."

The Debussy Film began as a feature planned by Russell and Melvyn Bragg. When no one was interested they took it to the BBC. It began production in the spring of 1965 as part of its *Monitor* arts series. Russell is reported as saying, "Huw Wheldon [*Monitor*'s editor] didn't dig *The Debussy Film*. He thought that I had made up some of the fantastic details until I showed him some original photographs to prove my point. Of course, the most fantastic always were true" (Baxter, 116). Reed was a dead ringer for Debussy, both physically and, in many ways, artistically. He has surprisingly little dialogue; he's most often presented in brooding poses which, of course, he did excellently. It's a remarkable performance, far different from anything he had ever done.

Ken Russell: "Both in his music and his life, Debussy was a great sensualist. There's a line of his in the film, 'Music should express things that can't be said.' A lot of artists have his quality. Lots of actors may not intellectually be able to grasp an argument or may be exactly opposed to it, but sensually can absorb the essence of the subject. Oliver was able to do that to a certain extent in *The Devils* and *The Debussy Film*" (Baxter, 116).

The Debussy Film was first broadcast on May 18, 1965. It inspired quite a controversy; one can only imagine what the "typical audience figure" made of it. Seen today, with its complexities more commonplace, the film is mesmerizing. The cast is universally excellent, particularly Vladek Sheybal as the enigmatic (and slightly slimy) Director. The black-and-white photography by John McGlashen and Ken Westbury is stunning; the sets and costumes are equally so. In all, *The Debussy Film* was quite a package and was a turning point in its star's career. As he said, "It was the point at which I began to shoot upwards. I had the misfortune to look like a prizefighter and speak like a public schoolboy. When I started, the only jobs I got were as teddy boys in leather jackets who whipped old ladies around the head with a bicycle chain and stole their handbags" (Goodwin, 98). For years Reed had been battling against his villainous looks to escape typecasting. Russell changed all that and proved Reed's artistic savior when he cast the actor in this television film.

Shortly after, Reed added his beautiful speaking voice as narrator to another Monitor production, *Always on Sunday*, about the customs officer Henri Rousseau, who could only paint on a Sunday due to his official duties. The beauty of Rousseau's work was somewhat dampened by the black-and-white photography; the painter struggled his whole life and died penniless. John Baxter wrote in his book *An Appalling Talent—Ken Russell*, "[Star John Lloyd's] presence, his Yorkshire accent ... and Oliver Reed's reading of the Melvyn Bragg-Russell commentary combine to make one of Russell's most delightful films, ending in a perfect dying fall. As Rousseau, unmourned and abandoned, lies dead in a pauper's hospital, the victim of indifference and his own desperate self-doctoring, Reed notes without rancor, 'His picture *The Dream* is in the Museum of Modern Art in New York, valued at more than one million dollars.'"

The Party's Over (1965)

Tricastle; released by Monarch Film Corporation in the U.K. in 1965 and by Allied Artists in the U.S. in 1966

Crew— Director: Guy Hamilton (uncredited); Writer: Marc Behm; Producers: Jack Hawkins, Anthony Perry (uncredited); Original Music: John Barry; Cinematographer: Larry Pizer; Film Editor: John Bloom; Art Director: Peggy Gick; Assistant Director: David Bracknell; Sound Recordist: Robert Allen.

Cast— Oliver Reed (Moise), Clifford David (Carson), Ann Lynn (Libby), Katherine Woodville (Nina), Louise Sorel (Melina), Mike Pratt (Geronimo), Maurice Browning (Tutzi), Jonathan Burn (Phillip), Roddy Maude-Roxby (Hector), Annette Robertson (Fran), Alison Seebohm (Ada), Barbara Lott (Almoner), Eddie Albert (Ben).

Synopsis

The rich and beautiful American Melina (Louise Sorel), on holiday in London, falls in love with "the Pack," a group of beatniks out for kicks and not much else. She is afraid of just about everything and is in hiding from Carson (Clifford David), her fiancé, who has been sent to bring her home by her industrialist father Ben (Eddie Albert). The Pack's leader, Moise (Oliver Reed), is a well-educated but unmotivated womanizer who is attracted to Melina, but she constantly rejects him. When Carson arrives at "the Pad," a ramshackle building where most of The Pack live, he's given the runaround about Melina's whereabouts. He is also vaguely threatened by Moise and his disturbing sidekick Tutzi (Maurice Browning).

Carson is given conflicting messages from Libby (Ann Lynn), who wants Moise, and Nina (Katherine Woodville), to whom he is attracted. Phil (Jonathan Burn), the only man to be accepted by Melina, becomes hysterical when questioned by Carson and commits suicide by jumping from a roof. Moise tells police that Phil was upset about failing an important exam. After being told more lies about Melina's whereabouts and Phil's suicide, Carson is finally given that truth by Moise: After refusing Moise's sexual advances at a party, a drunken Melina fell to her death from a stairway—but only Moise and Tutzi realized that she was dead. The other girls, thinking she was just unconscious, stripped her and placed her on a couch. Phil began to have sex with her; when he kissed her, he realized something was terribly wrong and ran out. Still thinking that Melina was just unconscious, The Pack held a mock funeral procession and her corpse was left in the street. Moise and Tutzi made it look as though she was the victim of a hit-and-run.

When Ben arrives to assist Carson, he's told by the police that his daughter is dead. Carson is willing to let Ben think that she was killed by a drunken driver and that Phil's death was an unrelated incident. As Ben has her coffin loaded onto the train, Moise arrives on the platform and tells Carson and Nina that he's going to tell Ben the truth.

They watch apprehensively as Moise approaches the grieving father but Moise softens; after saying he's sorry, he walks away in tears.

Comment

The Party's Over is Reed's most controversial film—certainly the only one to be banned for several years—and contains one of his best early performances. Production began in London in November 1962 under Guy Hamilton's direction. He had previously worked, in various capacities, on top-level British films, notably *The Third Man* (1949) as assistant director. In the summer of 1964 Hamilton would direct Ian Fleming's *Goldfinger,* arguably the best of the James Bond series. And *The Party's Over* would be perched on his shoulder like an albatross.

Being a product of the British studio system, Hamilton was enthusiastic about being able to film *The Party's Over* on location, mainly

Tutzi (Maurice Browning) and Moise (Oliver Reed) rebel against society in the controversial *The Party's Over* (Allied Artists, 1965).

on King's Road, Chelsea and Elm Park Gardens. In addition to directing, Hamilton also had money in it under the banner of Tricastle Films. His partners were Jules Buck, Jack Hawkins and Peter O'Toole. The budget — £100,000 — was partly financed by Rank.

In addition to cutting costs on filming on location, Tricastle saved a bundle with its no-name cast (excluding Eddie Albert). However, given the film's subject matter and the ages of its characters, it would have been difficult to populate *The Party's Over* with stars. Reed had just finished *Paranoiac* and was fast becoming a recognizable actor, but was hardly a household name. He was certainly the best known cast member after Eddie Albert.

According to Peter Cowie (*Films and Filming*, December 1962), Reed was living the part offscreen as well (which might explain a few things to come) by dressing down, looking scruffy in restaurants, acting tough — and reveling in the disgust of fellow patrons.

Moise's point of view was a complex one. He is clearly well-educated and is much deeper — and a better person — than he presents. But, for some reason, he is choosing to throw his life away. He hints that he had the proverbial troubled childhood, explaining, "My bath was never the right temperature." He constantly chases women — mostly Melina — but rejects Libby "because she's the only one who keeps saying 'yes.'" When he finally tells Carson the truth, he explodes:

MOISE: She was your fiancée and I dumped her dead body in the gutter. Maybe you don't care enough — if it were Nina, that would be a different story. Maybe you'd feel a little of what I feel now!

CARSON: You're not trying to kid yourself into thinking you loved Melina, are you?

MOISE: Love? I don't know what you're talking about.

Perhaps the greatest insight into Moise's character comes from Tutzi when Moise tells him that he's not afraid of anything: "You have to be alive to be afraid."

While Reed was preparing for his breakthrough role in Michael Winner's *The System* in August 1963, *The Party's Over*, six months after its completion, had run into serious trouble. The British Board of Film Censors had refused to grant the film a certificate — not even an X. Fearing that *The Party's Over*'s nihilism would have an adverse effect on British youth, the BBFC placed the film in the same category as Marlon Brando's motorcycle drama *The Wild One* (1954), still unreleased in the U.K. at that time.

Producer Anthony Perry said in *Films and Filming* (August 1963), "The censors disliked the film because it attacks the weakness of middle class morality. The Chelsea Set it portrays are none the less moral because its values may be different." *Films and Filming* opined, "After the trash given certificates by the BBFC, *The Party's Over* would have to be a very black film indeed to justify what might be regarded by many people as a display of high handed prejudice by the Board."

The Observer (October 27, 1963) reported, "A heavily cut version of *The Party's Over*, possibly the most controversial and outspoken film ever made in Britain, faces on Tuesday its last chance to escape being banned by the censor. This is the climax of ten months of wrangling between the Board's Secretary Mr. John Trevelyan and the film's producers. The dispute shows how difficult it still is for a British producer to obtain a British showing for an adult film on a serious sexual theme. The film is very strong stuff indeed (or rather, it was in its uncut version). In January, Trevelyan was shown it unofficially and said he thought it was a "horrid film" and said he "could not care for the people in it"—which the producers felt was irrelevant to his function as a censor."

The New York Times (November 29, 1963) followed with, "If and when a British film called *The Party's Over* crosses the Atlantic, all will notice right at the start two curious omissions. These will be no directors' or producers' names on the credit titles. [This was the case with the print viewed by the authors.] For the

record, the picture — but not the version to be released — was directed by Guy Hamilton and produced by Anthony Perry."

Their request that their names be removed was quite a position to take. They were disgusted by the BBFC decision to deny the film a certificate and their backers' desire to release a mutilated version to recoup their expenditure. *The Party's Over* had been partly bankrolled by the National Film Finance Corporation and the Rank Organisation, who had planned to release it. The film was ultimately released in Britain by Monarch and in America by Allied Artists.

Trevelyan felt that Mark Behm's script did not explicitly condemn the lifestyle of The Pack. The story had originally been placed in Paris with mostly American characters but, probably due to financial considerations, the location was moved to London. Trevelyan found this troublesome; he felt that "local depravity is a more dangerous example than foreign depravity." Tricastle's response: "The characters are so unhappy that no one would identify with or copy them."

When Trevelyan denied a certificate, Rank cancelled its contract to release the film. In a last bid to gain a certificate, Hamilton and Perry under protest made several small cuts — to no avail. They then walked away, their names removed. From *The New York Times* (November 29, 1963):

ANTHONY PERRY: The required cuts in certain scenes would leave audiences vague as to what happened.

JOHN TREVELYAN: Often it is better to leave things obscure.

PERRY: If you leave it vague, the audience will imagine the worst. Our version gave a sharp sense of shock that was wholly moral.

Over the next year and a half, additional cuts were made to the satisfaction of the BBFC (if to no one else), and *The Party's Over* was trade shown on May 6, 1965. *The Guardian* (May 7, 1965): "It is unpleasant and it is meant to be. The people it deals with are shockers. The censor does not like it. And the censor is wrong. I can understand the censor's concern. The film does not need to take a moral stand;

those youngsters condemn themselves with every line they say. *The Party's Over* should be shown"; *The Daily Mail* (May 2, 1965): "To me, it is not so much a shocking picture as a sickening one and a shameful specimen of British youth to show the outside world"; *The Observer* (May 7, 1965): "Perry and Hamilton regard it as a serious and moral film, since depravity is shown to bring misery. Two hundred feet have been now been cut and the orgy and funeral scenes severely modified, but it will not get a full release; it will be shown initially at a few selected cinemas in London. The uncut version has been sold to Germany and Japan."

The Party's Over premiered at the Picadilly Jacey on May 8. *The Sunday Times* (May 9, 1965): "Lest we should forget that the film was made with the very best will in the world, *The Party's Over* sets off with a firm declaration of moral intent.* But mostly the young people hang vacantly about like so many television extras in search of direction. The exception is a bearded Oliver Reed with a sense of mission. There's nothing wrong with his performance"; *Kinematograph Weekly* (May 13, 1965): "This is such a sordid subject that it is difficult to see how it can qualify as proper entertainment. Oliver Reed is well cast"; *Variety* (May 13, 1965): "There are a few performances that show promise, notably Oliver Reed."

The Party's Over, despite the cuts and controversy, is extremely well done if, of course, depressing and unsettling. What actually happened to Melina and Phil is gradually revealed through a series of flashbacks—partly truth, partly lies, partly omissions—until Moise finally comes clean. This adds a level of suspense that would have been missing had the film unfolded conventionally.

Members of The Pack look and behave like characters from *Night of the Living Dead* (1968); at one point, Tutzi describes Moise as being a zombie. They are directionless and aren't even rebelling against anything in particular. Moise has his own litany of petty grievances, but uses them as an excuse.

Reed is excellent. If the film had been

given a decent, timely release, it may have done for his career what *The System* did a bit later. He is alternatively cool, raving, callous and introspective. Reed even injects a bit of comedy by lapsing into various insolent accents and dialects.

One feels that what Moise needed to get himself on track was a good hiding, which Carson gives him, verbally, after the truth comes out: "She's dead! Phil's dead! The bucket of slop has been kicked over! Now—get out of this place and grow up!" And that's exactly what Moise, unexpectedly, does. As he walks off, crying, it seems possible that he'll reinvent himself in a more positive way.

Let's hope that *The Party's Over* is eventually given a DVD release in its original form. It was shown at the London Barbican in October 2007 as part of a series on censorship. It is well past time to give this superb film another chance.

The Brigand of Kandahar (1965)

Hammer Film Productions; released by Warner-Pathé in the U.K. on August 8, 1965 and by Columbia in the U.S. in 1965; 81 minutes; Hammerscope; Technicolor; filmed at Elstree Studios; U.K. Certificate: U

Crew— Screenplay-Director: John Gilling; Cinematographer: Reg Wyler; Producer: Anthony Nelson-Keys; Music: Don Banks; Music Supervisor: Philip Martell; Production Designer: Bernard Robinson; Production Manager: Don Weeks; Editor: James Needs; Special Effects: Syd Pearson; Camera Operator: Harry Gillman; Assistant Director: Frank Nesbitts; Sound Recordist: A.W. Lumkin; Makeup: Roy Ashton; Hair Dresser: Frieda Steiger; Costumes: Rosemary Burrows; Continuity: Pauline Harlow; Fight Arranger: Peter Diamond.

Cast— Ronald Lewis (Lieutenant Robert Case), Oliver Reed (Khan), Duncan Lamont (Colonel Drewe), Yvonne Romain (Ratina), Catherine Woodville (Elsa Connelly), Glyn Houston (Jed Marriott), Ingo Jackson (Captain Boyd), Sean Lynch (Rattu), Walter Brown (Hitala), Jeremy Burnham (Capt. Connelly), Caron Gardner (Maid), Henry Davies (Crowe), John Southworth (Barlow), Jo Powell (Color Sergeant).

A somber voice-over is delivered by Reed: "This film is the story of some young people who chose to become, for want of a better word, beatniks. It is not an attack on beatniks. The film has been made to show the loneliness and unhappiness and the eventual tragedy that can come from a life lived without love for anyone or anything. Merely living for kicks is not enough."

Lt. Case (Ronald Lewis) and Khan (Oliver Reed) plot in *The Brigand of Kandahar* (Columbia, 1965), one of Hammer's rare failures and Reed's last film for the company.

Synopsis

India's Northwest Frontier, late 1800s. At Ft. Kandahar, Lt. Robert Case (Ronald Lewis) awaits court-martial for cowardice, a crime of which he is innocent. The fact that he is mixed race — "half-caste" in the terminology of the day — does not endear him to his fellow officers. Escaping, he joins a band of Gilzhai tribesmen in revolt against British Imperial rule and makes a pact with their leader Khan (Oliver Reed) to train them the way Bengal Lancers of the British Army were trained. Case is driven by thoughts of revenge against Col. Drewe (Duncan Lamont) who had ordered his court-martial.

As he explores the rebel camp, Case finds Capt. Connelly (Jeremy Burnham) a prisoner. Ironically, it was Case's affair with Connelly's wife Elsa (Catherine Woodville) that led to the charges against him. A London journalist, Jed Marriott (Glyn Houston), arrives to cover the fighting and is captured by Khan's men. Case prevents his summary execution and tells Marriott about the trumped-up charges against him. Case, discovering the Gilzhai torturing Connelly, executes a mercy killing, but Marriott misunderstands his motive. In order to prove his integrity, Case allows Marriott to escape. Khan's sister Ratina (Yvonne Romain) despises her brother and tries to arrange for him to be killed on a raid of Ft. Kandahar. Khan, however, returns unharmed, bringing Elsa as a prisoner. Khan accuses Case of leading the plot against him. Case gains control of the Gilzhai after killing Khan in a duel.

A battle with the Lancers ensues and Ratina, Crewe and Case die. Marriott, having learned of Drewe's prejudices against Case and his subsequent victimization of the officer, determines to expose the truth.

Comment

The Brigand of Kandahar was the last of nine pictures that Reed made for Hammer, beginning in 1959. As Johnson and Del Vecchio note, "By 1964, his offbeat personality had attracted the attention of more mainstream producers, and after *Oliver!* (1968), he never looked back. Reed was one of the few actors discovered by the company to move on to bigger things.... He was one of the company's most versatile stars, playing convincing thugs (*Pirates of Blood River*), dashing heroes (*Captain Clegg*), and frightening psychos (*Paranoiac*), in addition to being the screen's best werewolf" (Del Vecchio & Johnson, 254).

Reed told Denis Meikle in 1992, "People loathed [*Brigand* writer-director] Gilling because they said he was a bully, but he got wounded rather savagely in the forehead during the war. He was in the navy. He was the one who tried to get me in a chest wig during *The Brigand of Kandahar*. I liked him; he was brash, gruff. I liked him because once during *Pirates of Blood River* the stuntmen wouldn't jump over a bank so I went charging over the bank with a sword in my mouth and all the stuntmen stopped and he fired them all and he thought I was really quite something. It was only because I was stupid."

Columbia asked Gilling to write a script using action footage that had been taken from *Zarak* (1956), on which Gilling was second unit director. It became the only time that Hammer created a film around another company's stock footage. Roy Ashton had done the makeup on both films in one of those strange coincidences that occur in movies from time to time. Filming started on October 16, 1964, and finished on November 26. It was released on the ABC circuit on August 8, 1965, and the reviews were generally favorable.

Reed did not quite agree and, narrating *The World of Hammer* on the BBC, described it as his worst film. Quite an indictment from its star, and not an evaluation with which the authors agree.

"I regret those Hammer Films, but I gained experience from them. I'm sorry about them because they keep cropping up on television and I can't avoid them," Reed said in *Photoplay Film Monthly* (October 1971). This uncharacteristically snotty remark about the company that made his career was made while riding high with *The Devils* so perhaps it should be taken

Reed as the thoughtful rebel, the mighty Khan, in *The Brigand of Kandahar* (Columbia, 1965).

with the proverbial pinch of salt. On the other hand, one wonders how *The Curse of the Werewolf, Captain Clegg* or *Paranoiac* looked to Reed ten years later while making *Spasms* or twenty years later while in *Severed Ties*?

The Trap (1966)

George H. Brown Productions; released in the U.K. by J. Arthur Rank Film Distributors in 1966 and in the U.S. by Continental Distributing in 1968

Crew—Director: Sidney Hayers; Story and Screenplay: David Osborn; Producer: George H. Brown; Associate Producer: Jan Darnley-Smith; Music: Ron Goodwin; Cinematographer: Robert Krasker; Film Editor: Tristam Cones; Casting: Jack Ammon; Art Director: Harry White; Costume Design: Margaret Furse; Hair Stylist: Ivy Emmerton; Makeup Artist: Richard Mills; Production Managers: Basil Keys, LC Rudkin, Barrie McLean (Canada); First Assistant Director; Bob Gray; Second Unit Directors: Stanley Clish, Tristam Cones;

Oliver Reed on location in Canada for *The Trap* (Continental, 1966).

Assistant Director: David Tringham; Constructors: Ernest Kerr, Peter Prior; Property Master: Carles Torbett; Assistant Props: David M. Robertson; Assistant Art Director: Ken Ryan; Stunts: Brian Lightburn; Stunt Double: George Chapman; Chief Electricians: Bill Newbery, Sid Penner; Wardrobe Supervisor: Cy Cook; Wardrobe Mistress: Salli Bailey; Wardrobe Master: James Smith; Continuity Phyllis Crocker.

Cast— Rita Tushingham (Eve), Oliver Reed (Jean La Bete), Barbara Chilcott (Trader's Wife), Joseph Golland (Baptiste), Blain Fairman (Clerk), Rex Sevenoaks (Trader), Linda Goranson (Trader's Daughter), Jon Granik (No Name), Merv Campone (Yellow Dog), Reg McReynolds (Captain), Walter Marsh (Preacher).

Synopsis

In mid-nineteenth Canada, Jean La Bete, a bearded French-Canadian trapper, huge in build, spirit and strength, makes his living scoping the forests for beautiful furs which he trades every once in a while in what passes for civilization. The rest of the time he lives a solitary existence in the forests, with only the birds and animals for company. When he comes to the trading post, no one has seen him for three years and the Trader, thinking him dead, has "absorbed" Jean's money into the family coffers to pay for his wife and daughter's aspirations to gentility. That same day a boatful of mail order brides arrives from civilization; most of the "brides" have been bought by trappers who purchased them from jails and whorehouses. The going fee is $1,000. Jean craves a young fit wife who will work with him and warm his bed. Such is Eve, an elective mute since seeing her family slaughtered by Indians; she works in the Trader's house and is a general dogsbody, ill-used by the Trader's wife. The trader's wife takes the $1,000 "borrowed" from Jean as payment for Eve and hurries her off in Jean's canoe before her husband hears about it.

When the canoe is beached at Jean's cabin, Eve is trapped; she cannot cry for help, and no one would hear even if she could. Jean has aspirations for a better life and tells Eve his plans, but she shrinks from him. The lonely cabin is made of logs and wood; the walls are covered with pelts and traps. Her new "owner" is tough, untamed and uncivilized, with no manners to speak of, and the annoying habit of bawling the same verse of the same song ad infinitum. Jean tries to teach her about her new world: the deer, the wolf, the bear, the cougar, the lynx, the moose, the fox, the rabbit and the fish. She listens, and listlessly follows him around, but takes no part in the hunting. That is, until Jean is caught in one of his traps as he fights off a cougar attack; then she nurses him, amputates a festering leg, hunts to feed them both and lies with him to break his fever. Slowly they become close and eventually become lovers. But the act of love drives her over the edge and she runs away. Having just escaped drowning in his stolen canoe, she is found by some Indians who care for her until she is well enough to be taken back to the trading post. She has lost the child she was carrying, and everyone agrees that it was probably best that she should. In time she is to marry the Trader's clerk, but on her wedding day she grabs a canoe and heads back to the cabin. Jean touches her face, turns away and smiles covertly and carries on as though nothing has happened.

Comment

The Trap's filming locations were Bowen Island, British Columbia, and Hollyburn Film Studios, West Vancouver, British Columbia. This is probably one of the most beautifully set films ever made. But the beauty of the landscape is used to good effect as an antidote to the brutality of life at that time: Indian massacres, animal attacks, rough amputations, female slavery and villages of corpses, to name just a few of the horrors that become part of Eve's everyday life.

The biggest surprise — after the shock of the opening sequence where Reed is paddling a canoe down the rapids of the river while singing at the top of his lungs in his own inimitable fashion — is that Jean virtually grunts. That beautiful Reed speaking voice vanishes in the barking, grunting roughness of a man who rarely speaks to a living soul. It makes the viewer's throat hurt just to listen to it.

Reed apparently enjoyed the great outdoors; he had a sequence where wolves attack and try to drag him down. In fact, there were just two wolves for close-ups and the rest were guard dogs, crosses between German shepherds and wolves hired for the part. According to the September 18, 1966, *Observer*, "It took seven days to shoot the scene, and after a couple of days the dogs (knowing their Pavlov) attacked the fur-covered Reed as soon as they saw him, not waiting for the handlers to give the word to go. Sometimes they couldn't be called off except with whips, especially when they got to fighting amongst themselves. As the dogs grew more eager, Reed became more reluctant, but he stuck it out to the end, finishing up with wheals all over his body and bites on his arms and legs." According to Reed, "It was the first time I'd ever come into contact with Indians. In actual fact a very drunken Indian once said to me, 'White man taught the Indian to drink so now he must pay the price.' He wanted to scalp me, but he was hit on the back of the head with a stool by a rather large Canadian called Moose. I didn't meet him again until they gave a party and it was there that I saw this same young Indian, with a rather large bruise on his head, pretending to be an eagle. Still pissed" [Sellers, 111–12].

Reed and Rita Tushingham prove a good duo; she acts with her expression and mime, he roars his way through the story. The world premiere at the Leicester Square Theatre attracted the stars, musicians and politicians of the day, watched by an enthusiastic crowd on the pavement outside. The critics were generally enthusiastic.

"Oliver Reed and Rita Tushingham struggle to make their characters more than cardboard cut-outs and some of their scenes together in the log cabin have a certain charm." — *Monthly Film Bulletin*, October 1966; "Oliver Reed, with scraggy beard and guttural French accent, and Rita Tushingham, looking more ox-eyes than ever, struggle in vain against a limp script and flat-footed direction..." — *Guardian*, September 16, 1966; "Mr. Reed grunts quite persuasively in the sort of part we normally associate with Anthony Quinn" — *The London Times*, September 15, 1966; "Oliver Reed has effectively changed his persona from the Chelsea layabout

A GEORGE H. BROWN PRODUCTION

RITA TUSHINGHAM   OLIVER REED

THE TRAP   "A"

Colour Panavision ®   Printed in Italy by "Graphocolor" s.p.a.-Roma

Jean (Oliver Reed), the Trader's Wife (Barbara Chilcott) and the elective mute Eve (Rita Tushingham) meet to seal the bargain — a wife for all his savings — in *The Trap* (Continental, 1966).

of his first appearances to the gross and noble whiskery savage."—*Financial Times*, September 16, 1966; "[Reed] establishes himself as a virile type and the pic could be a turning point of his career. He is larger-than-life as the crude brawling trapper yet also has moments of great sensitivity with his co-star. Here is a hunk of a man that Britain should promote, but fast"— source unknown, September 14, 1966.

This is a great movie and one Oliver Reed could be proud of.

Dante's Inferno (1967)

British Broadcasting Corporation; Popular Arts Entertainment; telecast by the BBC in 1967 in the U.K.

Crew— Producer-Director: Ken Russell; Writers: Austin Frazer, Ken Russell; Dialogue and Com-mentary Writer: Austin Frazer; Cinematographer: Nat Crosby; Film Editors: Michael Bradsell, Roger Crittenden; Production Design: Luciana Arrighi; Costume Design: Shirley Kingdom [Russell]; Makeup Artist: Shirley Boakes; Sound Recordist: Sandy MacRae; Dubbing Mixer: Stanley Morcom; Director's Assistants: Geoffrey Haydon, Sally Jenkins, Rhona Shaw.

Cast— Oliver Reed (Dante Gabriel Rossetti), Judith Paris (Elizabeth Siddal), Andrew Faulds (William Morris), Iza Teller (Christina Rossetti), Christopher Logue (Swinburne), Gala Mitchell (Jane Morris), Pat Ashton (Fanny Cornforth), Clive Goodwin (Ruskin), David Jones (Howell), Norman Dewhurst (Burne-Jones), Tony Gray (William Rossetti), Douglas Gray (Hunt), Derek Boshier (Millais), Caroline Coon (Annie Miller), Jane Deuters (Emma Brown).

Synopsis

As a grave is being robbed, the coffin is opened and a decomposed corpse is pushed aside so that the intruder can retrieve a book.

In 1898 London, a group of young artists have rebelled against conventional notions of beauty in art and poetry. Calling themselves the Pre-Raphaelites, their goal is to overthrow the staid Royal Academy of Art. Among their number is the charismatic Dante Gabriel Rossetti (Oliver Reed). Dante is unable to choose between poetry and painting — whichever is easiest and will make him the richest is his guideline — or between the various women with whom he involves himself. Chief among them is Elizabeth (Judith Paris); they spend their days together playing like children.

They spend their nights apart. Dante leads her to expect marriage, but makes no proposal or overt sexual advances; that will be taken care of elsewhere. The couple is visited, uncomfortably, by Dante's family: Christina (Iza Teller) and William Rossetti (Tony Gray).

Dante has been teaching Elizabeth to draw, but he doesn't take her efforts seriously. After a violent episode during which Elizabeth stabs him with a sewing needle, Dante becomes involved with Fanny (Pat Ashton), a model whom he paints and has sex with. Dante acquires a patron, Hunt (Douglas Gray), whom Dante treats with disdain. Hunt introduces Dante to Ruskin (Clive Goodwin), who is commercially interested in him and sexually interested in Elizabeth; he treats Dante like a schoolboy. When Elizabeth falls ill, Ruskin arranges for her to go to the south of France to recuperate. Dante takes on a new lover, Jane (Gala Mitchell), and alternates between the three women. He eventually marries Elizabeth, who loses their first child. Dante and Elizabeth become drug addicts; when she dies, he places a book of his poems in her coffin which is "returned" to him by Ruskin. He takes up with Fanny but they fall out. Jane offers to bear him a child but he can't commit to her any more than he can to his art. He suffers hallucinations, partly out of guilt, partly from drugs, and he dies alone.

Comment

Dante's Inferno marked Oliver Reed's third BBC production for Ken Russell, following *The Debussy Film* and *Always on Sunday*. The first installment of the new series *Omnibus*, it was telecast on December 22, 1967.

Dante Gabriel Rossetti (1828–1882) was a Pre-Raphaelite poet who had, naturally if he appealed to Ken Russell, a grotesque personal life. Russell had received a letter from the multi-talented Bryan Forbes (a kind of British Orson Welles) who had gotten a script about Dante, oddly enough, just as Russell was contemplating a film about the Pre-Raphaelites. Forbes felt Dante's story was unsuitable for the commercial cinema, but felt it might work on television. According to Russell (Baxter, 132), "Why he thought it wouldn't be commercial I just couldn't understand. A man digging up his wife's remains to get a book he buried with her? It screams commercial!"

Russell began filming in the Keswick Lake District, Cumbria, using 16mm as dictated by the BBC's economics. But after ten days, he realized that the footage was no good, and was forced to start again using 35mm.

Ken Russell recalled, "Oliver Reed had some personal problems which upset him. Also, he was a star by then and knew stars should have a stand-in, but we couldn't afford one" (Baxter, 134).

During the filming, Reed and Russell developed a shorthand for the direction. Russell would ask for Moody One, Two or Three depending on the level of intensity that was needed, usually Moody Three.

Reed wrote in his autobiography, "I think there are all sorts of people who perpetuate the image of Ken as an intellect and as an intellectual director when in fact he plays his players and uses his film with the panache of the great comedian, and this is his magic. Ken is very concerned about his compositions and, because it's necessary for someone to speak, he allows his actors to come into this beautiful picture he has created."

Dante's Inferno is well named; Rossetti's personal hell is a deep one and of his own making. He is depicted as talented, charming and, on the surface, likable, but underneath he is self-absorbed, ruthless and lazy. The film seems like a warm-up for *Women in Love*. Both have as their main characters outwardly attractive people obsessed with art or obscure views of society at the expense of living normal lives. Reed's Dante is similar to Glenda Jackson's Gudrun in the later film. Their cold indifference to their respective lovers is shattering — and fatal.

The film, stunningly photographed in black-and-white by Nat Crosby, opens with a grave being robbed. The coffin is opened, and a man pushes aside the rotting corpse to retrieve a book. The man is Dante; the corpse is that of his late wife. The final shot presents Dante, aged, crippled, drug-addicted and alone, slipping out of the scene. What's in between is a sad story of a talented man with many positive characteristics who failed his art, his friends, and his family.

Reed is brilliant; noticing the parallel here is unavoidable. Dante seems almost like a manic depressive; the Moody Three is certainly in evidence, but it's balanced by many scenes of pure joy. Reed never got enough credit for his ability to portray a character simply having fun. He dances and clowns as believably as he sulks.

Dante's sad relationship with Elizabeth is beautifully explored by Reed and Judith Paris. When they meet, Dante is unsure whether to pursue painting or poetry. Elizabeth is a shop girl and an occasional prostitute.

> ELIZABETH: You're ashamed of me — I'm only a shop girl.
>
> DANTE: I'm jolly fond of you — I'll rescue you.

And he does for a time. He is as indifferent towards Elizabeth as he is towards everyone and everything else. The five-year relationship is going nowhere. Elizabeth, tired of waiting for a marriage proposal, stabs him with a sewing needle. He remains unmoved by her terminal illness, often leaving her for Fanny and Jane, then returning to her. Their eventual marriage hardly solves the problem; she loses both a child and a childlike husband. Dante's so-called mentor Ruskin sums up the artist best of all: "Dante will never be successful until he gets over the habit of doing what pleases him."

In the end, of course, nothing pleases him.

Dante's Inferno is outstanding, better even than the Debussy film; due to its linear structure it's more accessible. Both the director and the star are at the top of their game with a better collaboration still to come.

"The painful distance that can exist between the artist's ideals and his or her own life is a central concern of *Dante's Inferno*. In his approach to Dante Gabriel Rossetti and the Pre-Raphaelite movement, Russell was less concerned with the minute details of history than with the larger philosophical and psychological significance of the movement's failure. For Russell, Rossetti is a paradox of idealism and crude appetites. Rossetti's poetic concept of platonic love is contradicted by his overt sexual desires and his idealized art is increasingly consumed by the dictates of merchandising. As he dissipates himself, Rossetti increasingly realizes how he has failed both his art and those around him. The film's final image, an abrupt cut from a drugged and aging Rossetti to the ending credits played out to a calliope version of the song 'I Just Want to Be Happy,' summarizes the elusive nature of his desires."—film notes from the CMA series, August 13, 2008.

Ken Russell: "After the film, Bryan Forbes had the goodness to write to me and tell me that his wife had watched it and said, 'What a fantastic film! Why don't you do films like this?'" (Baxter, 135).

The Jokers (1967)

Adastra/Gildor Productions/Scimitar Productions; released by J. Arthur Rank Film Distributors in the U.K. in 1966 and by Universal in the U.S. in 1967

Crew—Director and Storyline: Michael Winner; Producers: Maurice Foster, Ben Arberd; Screenplay: Dick Clement, Ian La Frenais; Cinematographer: Kenneth Hodges; Music: Johnny Pearson; Editor: Bernard Gribble; Art Director: John Blezard; Casting: Terry Armstrong.

Cast—Michael Crawford (Michael Tremayne), Oliver Reed (David Tremayne), Harry Andrews (Inspector Marryott), James Donald (Col. Gurney-Simms), Daniel Massey (Riggs), Michael Horden (Sir Matthew), Gabriella Licudi (Eve), Lorre Tarp (Inge), Frank Finlay (Harassed Man), Warren Mitchell (Lennie), Rachel Kempson (Mrs. Tremayne), Peter Graves (Mr. Tremayne), Ingrid Brett (Sarah), Brian Wilde (Sgt. Catchpole), Edward Fox (Lt. Sprague), Michael Goodliffe (Lt. Col. Paling), William Devlin (Brigadier), William Mervyn (Uncle Edward), William Kendle (Maj. Gen. Jeffcock), Kenneth Colley (Chauffeur), Charlotte Curzon (Camilla), Mark Burns (Capt. Browning), Brook Williams (Capt. Green), Freda Jackson (Mrs. Pervis), Nan Munro (Mrs. Jeffcock), Brian Peck (Policeman),

Basil Dingham (Bank Manager), John Kidd, Nicky Henson (Solicitors).

Synopsis

Michael Tremayne (Michael Crawford) and his older brother David (Oliver Reed) are from a wealthy, well-connected family but feel left out because society does not recognize their brilliance. The pair are always up to something; for example, David "helps" his brother win a war game for his regiment by cheating. As usual, Michael is caught — and dismissed from the army — and David escapes unscathed. Michael returns to the home of his embarrassed parents (Peter Graves and Rachel Kempson), his trendy girlfriend Sarah (Ingrid Brett) ... and David. As they celebrate Michael's dismissal, they discuss how their lives went wrong. They agree that they need to make a "grand gesture" by committing an act to outrage the society that has rejected them. The plan: steal the Crown Jewels from the Tower of London. Well, not quite; they will write letters to their solicitors explaining why they did it and expressing their willingness to return the treasures, releasing them, they hope, from criminal charges. They stage a series of bomb threats (with Michael masquerading as "Red George") involving the mad Col. Gurney-Simms (James Donald) of the bomb squad and no-nonsense Scotland Yard Inspector Marryott (Harry Andrews). London is now on edge just as the brothers want it. The robbery is to take place on the night of Sarah's big party. Michael calls in a bomb threat to the Tower, then he and David arrive on the scene dressed as members of the bomb squad. After drugging the colonel, they fake an explosion in the Tower and, covered with fake blood, walk out with the jewels. They hide the treasure under David's floor and wait for the fun to begin. David alerts his solicitor to read his letter and has Michael do the same.

David (Oliver Reed) and Michael (Michael Crawford) joke around in *The Jokers* (Scimitar/ Universal, 1967).

But—when they later lift the floorboards, the jewels are gone. David is arrested. It seems that Michael never wrote or sent the letter. After years of playing the fool under David's leadership, he's had enough. Marryott suspects Michael is just as guilty as David, who is now in prison. As David seethes in his cell, Marryott investigates Michael, but comes up empty.

Michael is having the time of his life, enjoying his victory over David, until Sarah convinces him to come clean. He does, by hanging the treasure in the arms of the statue of Blind Justice on the Old Bailey before alerting Marryott, who then arrests him. The brothers make their peace in David's cell and begin to plot their escape.

Comment

Although Reed has a well-deserved reputation for his brooding, menacing screen persona, he had a gift for comedy that even surfaced in the abovementioned roles. His first, and best, starring role in a comedy came courtesy of director Michael Winner in *The Jokers*.

Even after the success of *The System* in Britain, Winner's career was going nowhere. In April 1966 he had gone nearly a year without making a film. He was surprised then to receive a congratulatory note from writer John Gardner (who would continue the James Bond series after Ian Fleming's death) for the great reviews *The System* had recently received in America. "To my amazement, I was being heralded as the new genius of the English-speaking cinema," said Winner. "*The System*, which I'd made three years earlier, was showing in New York titled *The Girl Getters*. Every New York critic was raving about the film" (Winner, 96). On the strength of these reviews, Winner was able to launch a project he'd had difficulty selling to producers (a comedy about two brothers who steal the Crown Jewels for a laugh) and to prove a point about British society. Winner had written the original story himself. "The only company chief in England who'd not rejected *The Jokers* was Jay Kantner. He'd recently opened an office for Universal Pictures. I took my reviews and put them through his letterbox. On Saturday I'd been unemployable. On Monday I was offered a six-picture deal. Jay Kantner had

seen *The System*. He was a great fan of Oliver Reed and wanted him as one of the brothers. They gave him a six-picture contract" (Winner, 97). *The Jokers* was announced to the press on June 2, 1966. Location filming began in London on June 23 and continued until the end of August.

Michael Crawford, later to play the title role in Andrew Lloyd Webber's *Phantom of the Opera*, had some misgivings. Winner said, "He didn't want Oliver Reed as his brother. He knew I'd made a picture with him and that we were friends. He thought Oliver might get special treatment. He said Oliver didn't look like his brother. Crawford was in a play in the West End. I persuaded Oliver to go see it. Crawford said, 'Don't bring Oliver Reed. I refuse to have him in the part.' The dressing room door opened and Michael Crawford greeted Oliver Reed like an old friend. Within seconds they were like real brothers. Reed had arrived with his real brother and their collective appearance could have been a mirror for the brothers in the film—Crawford was convinced" (Crawford, 114).

Winner's film, along with the Beatles, Carnaby Street and the Mini Cooper, helped to establish "Swinging London." Shooting on locations all over the city, *The Jokers* showed London in a way that had never been seen before on film. Winner said, "We were allowed to shoot a bit in the Tower of London, but soon outstayed our welcome. So I sent in cameramen with hand-held cameras, disguised as tourists. Michael Crawford is the most wonderful comic actor but, although he got on with Oliver Reed well and was deeply professional, he'd never pay for anything. Oliver was very generous and paid for a lot of meals. Oliver kept telling him about his personal meanness. After Michael had not shown up for a meal he'd promised to pay for, we were shooting in Trafalgar Square. Oliver, who normally sits very quietly, got up, rushed over to Michael, picked him up and held him over the pool. He said, 'Michael, unless you pay for the dinner we've just had I'm going to drop you in the fountain.'"

The Jokers was trade shown on June 12, 1967, launched at a festival in Brighton on July 1, and went into release on July 9 to some of the best reviews of Reed's career: "Thoroughly ab-

David (Oliver Reed) makes a life-altering phone call as Michael (Michael Crawford) looks on apprehensively in *The Jokers* (Scimitar/Universal, 1967).

sorbing and constantly amusing. Michael Crawford and Oliver Reed are delightful and convincing" (*Saturday Reviews*, May 20, 1967); "A superior and scintillating instance of the British film comedy" (*San Francisco Examiner*, August 3, 1967); "A fine entertainment; bubbly, tart and surprising too" (*New York Post*, May 16, 1967); "The film is a devilishly sly, witty farce complete with ingenious plot twists, cutting dialogue and excellent performances" (*Los Angeles Herald Examiner*, August 3, 1967); "The film never lets down, never flags, yet never seems to be working hard" (*Los Angeles Times*, July 30, 1967); "It is a brilliant exposition of the London mod set. British comedies never had it so good" (*New York Times*, May 18, 1967); "Two exceedingly funny men, Michael Crawford and Oliver Reed, give adroit comic performances" (*Newsday*, May 16, 1967); "The leading men seem to benefit from the constraints

of their teaming" (*Financial Times*, June 16, 1967); "Quite simply, it is fun. Crawford's amused, faintly effete personality is perfectly contrasted to Reed's dogmatic virility" (*Evening News*, June 15, 1967).

The Jokers is not only Reed's best comedy, it's nearly his best all-round film, accessible to all. He is surrounded by a first-rate cast featuring many of Britain's best character actors: Harry Andrews, Michael Hordern, Frank Finlay (with whom he would later star in the Musketeers movies), and James Donald, who nearly steals the film as deftly as the boys steal the Jewels.

Winner's original story was expanded upon by Dick Clement and Ian La Frenais; the result is a perfect blend of comedy, adventure, social comment and character study. Unlike Winner's *The System* and *I'll Never Forget What's 'Isname*, *The Jokers* remains light, taking its

Michael (Michael Crawford) walks over his brother David (Oliver Reed) — literally and figuratively — in Michael Winner's *The Jokers* (Scimitar/Universal, 1967).

gentle shots at the military, the police, the Royal Family, sex, politics and Swinging London itself. And it all works, held together by Winner's pointed direction.

The Jokers establishes the surface differences between Michael and David early on. After Michael is dismissed from the Army, Mother tells him, "Your brother never found it necessary to do this sort of thing. I've noticed over the last twelve months that you've deteriorated. You're a great disappointment to your father and me ... so unlike your brother. Now, David applies himself...." Cut to David kissing his most recent pick-up!

The plot is hatched in a brilliantly executed running dialogue from flat to pub to London locations:

DAVID: You know, we should do something really big, you and I ... something worthy of our talents.

MICHAEL: Like what?

DAVID: I don't know ... something. I mean, here I am, twenty nine.

MICHAEL: Thirty.

DAVID: ...a qualified architect earning his living as an interior decorator wallpapering randy Chelsea walls ... I'm not even rich, just on a conveyor belt.

MICHAEL: It's a pity the Great Train Robbery's been done. Can't do any better than that.

DAVID: We could try...

DAVID: What we've got to do is find a crime that isn't criminal. It wouldn't be taking for gain. It would be a...

DAVID: Grand gesture? It's got to be something institutional. Somehow, it's got to affect the whole nation.

A visit to the Tower, giving Reed the opportunity to mug outrageously with a Beefeater, solves the problem of what to steal. Then comes a problem.

DAVID: I'm going to sell all the newspaper rights to the highest bidder ... and then, there are film and television.

DAVID: We. This is a joint effort, you know.

DAVID: Yes of course ... but then, as far as the practical side is concerned, I'm in charge.

DAVID: Now listen! I'm perfectly capable...

DAVID: Yes, you're perfectly capable of cocking the whole thing up.

The only real difference, it seems, between the brothers is that David has never been caught and Michael has had enough of playing the fool. David's annoyance prevents him from seeing that, while he is playing the entire City of London, his younger brother is playing him.

James Donald and Harry Andrews play off each other perfectly; one almost insane, the other all business. The robbery is perfectly planned, executed and filmed and would fit nicely in any "straight" thriller. For that matter, the whole film (when looked at in synopsis) doesn't seem much different from any robbery thriller. It hardly seems funny at all. The humor lies in Winner's presentation and in the acting of the two leads.

Reed throws in his usual comic dancing and sarcastic asides, and pulls a few faces. As always, it works. He even takes a cue from W.C. Fields: While he sleeps, completely under his blanket, the phone rings. Both his hands suddenly appear, fingers extended, from under the blanket as he wakes in annoyance. Reed makes David interested in everything, and everything he does is interesting. He never — for example — simply sits, he flings himself onto the furniture, limbs flying. We also get to see David's dark side. When he realizes that Michael has back-stabbed him, he flies into a rage and grabs his brother violently and must be pulled off by several policemen. Given the light-hearted nature of what has preceded this, the scene is fairly shocking.

While lacking the moral significance of the two Winner films that sandwich it, *The Jokers* is easily the most enjoyable of the three. It's clear that Reed and Winner had a good relationship, both on and off camera, and it's easy to see why the films they did together are among the best of their respective careers.

Michael Crawford's take on it all:

Now, I have never been quite sure if Ollie was discovered by Michael Winner or if it was the other way around.... [H]e was what the romance novels call 'broodingly handsome.' There was a tension about Oliver Reed, a certain aura of danger. On the other hand, there was something inside him that rebelled against his background and all authority ... part of him wanted to tear it all down, and perhaps this is what gave him the air of danger that made him stand out among English actors of his generation. Ollie once told a reporter that, for him, going into the acting profession was an involuntary muscular reaction, like going to the bathroom. For all his reputation as a night-owl, Ollie was a thorough professional, and as good as gold to work with. However, depending on how he was cast at the time, I think it is fair to say that there was always a certain amount of physical risk present when you worked with Oliver Reed. The problem was that he tended to live the part he was playing [Crawford, 112].

The Shuttered Room (1967)

Seven Arts Productions; A Troy-Schenck Production; released through Warner Pathé Distributors in the U.K. in 1967 and by Warner Bros/Seven Arts in the U.S. in 1968

Crew— Director: David Greene; Producer: Phillip Hazelton; Associate Producer: Alex Jacobs; Screenplay: D.B. Ledrov, Nathaniel Tanchuck; Based on the xxxxx by H.P. Lovecraft; Music Composed by Basil Kirchin; Conductor: Jack Nathan; Lighting Cameraman: Ken Hodges; Production Manager: David Anderson; First Assistant Director: Stuart Freeman; Second Assistant Director: Alex Carver-Hill; Editor: Brian Smedley-Aston; Assistant Editor: Pepita Fairfax; Camera Operator: Herbert Smith; Art Director; Brian Eatwell; Sound Mixer: Kevin Sutton; Sound Camera Operator: Michael Silverlock; Costume Designer: Caroline Mott; Wardrobe Mistress: Brenda Dobbs; Assistant Art Director: Mark James.

Cast— Gig Young (Mike Kelton), Carol Lynley (Susannah Kelton/Sarah), Oliver Reed (Ethan), Dame Flora Robson (Aunt Agatha), William Devlin (Zebulon Whately), Bernard Kay (Tait), Judith Arthy (Emma), Celia Hewitt (Aunt Sarah).

Synopsis

Through a darkened room in the old millhouse in Dunwich, a tiny island off the New England coast, a shuffling figure creeps towards a sleeping child. In a nearby bedroom, Sarah Whateley and her husband Luther are awakened by the sounds. Luther reaches the child (his four-year-old niece Susannah) and wards off an attack by the shadowy figure. Desperately he drags the thrashing creature back to a shuttered room at the top of the house and bolts the door....

It is years later now and Susannah, grown into a beautiful woman, returns to Dunwich with her husband Mike. She has come to look at the old millhouse which has become hers through inheritance— a house which has been abandoned since her great aunt Sarah dropped out of sight after her husband Luther was found drowned in the millpond forty years before. Quickly the young couple senses antagonism among the closely knit villagers. Ethan, a surly, arrogant young man (and a distant cousin of Susannah's) warns them to stay away from the mill. But Susannah and Mike are determined to look over their inheritance and enter the place, which is dark, cobwebbed and eerie. As she stands there, latent memories begin to rise in Susannah's mind and she feels uneasy.

Ethan comes to the house and tells them that Aunt Agatha, now the oldest surviving member of the family, wants to see them. They meet with the strong-willed old lady, who insists that something evil hangs over the house and the mill, endangering anyone who goes there. Nevertheless the young couple returns to the mill, finding it exactly as it was left by the ill-fated inhabitants a generation before. Susannah begins clearing up while Mike goes for supplies. An abandoned nursery disturbs Susannah as do the shuffling and whispering sounds from the mill where Susannah is convinced she sees a face at the window.

During the night, Emma, Ethan's girlfriend, breaks into the visitors' car and steals silk stockings. She slips into the mill to try them on and is attacked and viciously killed by a strange figure who emerges from the shadows. The next day Susannah enters the shuttered room. There is an old bedstead and a pile of rotting blankets. In a corner, out of sight, a pair of glistening eyes watch.

Mike visits Aunt Agatha again and she tells him the terrible secret of the shuttered room: Susannah's demented sister has been held prisoner there by the family for many years. He races back into the house, where Ethan has been playing cat and mouse with the terrified Susannah. She rushes upstairs to the shuttered room and Ethan follows. In the darkness he picks up a tattered Teddy bear and lights it like a torch. Suddenly from the shadows comes the terrifying figure again, scratching with long claws at Ethan's face. He drops the burning Teddy bear, staggers back and falls to his death below.

Now the attacker is on fire. It is the monstrous figure of a girl, misshapen and de-

Susannah (Carol Lynley) and Ethan (Oliver Reed) try to see eye to eye in *The Shuttered Room* (Seven Arts/Warner Bros., 1967).

mented — Susannah's sister, chained up for many years and bought food only by Aunt Agatha. Mike arrives as the whole house begins to burn fiercely. He races up the stairs and drags the stunned Susannah out. Aunt Agatha rushes into the flames to rescue the strange girl whom she has cared for all these years, only to be trapped. Susannah and Mike watch in horror as the millhouse burns, destroying for all time its terrible secret.

Comment

Suspense-filled, blood-chilling tales set against the background of ordinary small-town life were the stock in trade of H.P. Lovecraft, an American writer of the twenties and thirties and still much appreciated by devotees of creepy tales. Producer Phillip Hazelton felt that with *The Shuttered Room* he had brought to the screen the very best of the moody author's many excellent works. The press release heralding the

production quotes Hazelton thus: "H.P. Lovecraft was a classic writer whom many people still rank as the equal of Edgar Allan Poe in telling tales of terror.... He is reputed to have been an ugly man who shunned the present and was obsessed with the past, and this is reflected in the eerie timelessness of his settings and characters."

Dunwich, the locale of this and many of the author's other tales, is a sinister village with black, weather-board houses, wild, stagnant marshes and the ruined tower on the hill giving it an atmosphere of almost medieval gloom. The production company was fortunate to find appropriate locations within two hours' drive from London. An abandoned lighthouse near Dover's White Cliffs was pressed into service as Aunt Agatha's citadel from which she controls the village nestled below.

An ancient millhouse at Kersey near the Roman town of Colchester in Essex became the property inherited by Susannah and Mike, the

Above: Ethan (Oliver Reed) and Aunt Agatha (Flora Robson) plot together in *The Shuttered Room* (Seven Arts/Warner Bros., 1967). *Below:* Ethan (Oliver Reed) contemplates more mayhem in H.P. Lovecraft's *The Shuttered Room* (Seven Arts/Warner Bros., 1967).

archetypal young married couple, and the place where they discover the grisly truth about their inheritance and the reason the locals shun it. The pretty Kentish town of Faversham, steeped in medieval history, was where the location offices for the company were set up, and where tense dock and boat yard scenes were shot.

Carol Lynley, only in her early twenties, was one of the most well-established dramatic actresses of the day. Some short time later she became Reed's constant companion. Gig Young was attractive and a competent actor. Reed played Ethan with a lurking craziness behind the eyes, and even when being charming, he is quite disturbing. His attempts at stalking Susannah are frightening. His demise is satisfying and his fate well deserved. "Oliver Reed, true to type, is the epitome of evil as Ethan," said the *Kinematograph Weekly* reviewer (June 10, 1967).

"Oliver Reed is his usual screen self as the bullying tearaway, half caveman, half coward."—*The Sun*, June 8, 1967; "[The movie has] a genuine atmosphere of sinister foreboding. But it is a cheat of a film. Once it has you intrigued it starts wantonly piling on the agony in a series of cruel and spooky incidents which are either irrelevant meaningless or just plain daft."—*Morning Star*, June 10, 1967; "Oliver Reed broods with typical intensity as the wild, sex-crazed young man who becomes obsessed with his cousin."—*Total Sci-Fi*, January 12, 2009.

I'll Never Forget What's 'Isname (1967)

Scimitar Productions; Universal Pictures; released by J. Arthur Rank Film Distributors in the U.K. on December 18, 1967, and by Universal Pictures on April 14, 1968, in the U.S.

Crew— Producer-Director: Michael Winner; Writer: Peter Draper; Music: Francis Lai; Cinematographer: Otto Heller; Film Editor: Bernard Gribble; Art Director: Seamus Flannery; Makeup Artist: Richard Mills; Production Manager: R.L.M. Davidson; Assistant Directors: Michael Dryhurst, Michael Guest; Sound Recordist: Charles Poulton; Sound: Chris Paulton, Hugo Strain; Dubbing Editor: Terry Rawlins; Camera Operator: Godfrey A. Godar; Camera Focus: John Shinerock; Musical Director: Christian Gaubert; Assistant Continuity: Pat O'Donnell.

Cast— Orson Welles (Jonathan Lute), Oliver Reed (Andrew Quint), Carol White (Georgina Elben), Harry Andrews (Gerald Slater), Michael Hordern (Headmaster), Wendy Craig (Louise Quint), Norman Rodway (Nicholas), Marianne Faithfull (Josie), Frank Finlay (Chaplain), Ann Lynn (Carla), Harvey Hall (Charles Maccabee), Lyn Ashley (Susannah), Edward Fox (Walter), Mark Burns (Michael Cornwall), Mark Eden (Kellaway), Stuart Cooper (Lewis Force), Veronica Clifford (Anna), Roland Curram (Eldrich), Peter Graves (Bankman), Robert Mill (Galloway), Josephine Ruegg (Marian), Terence Sewards (Pinchin); uncredited: Hugo Keith-Johnston (Young Quint), James Payne (Unruly Student), Anthony Sharp (Mr. Hamper Down).

Synopsis

Andrew Quint (Oliver Reed) is 32, handsome and fed up. He's separated from his wife Louise (Wendy Craig) but they avoid divorce due to their continued sexual attraction. His two mistresses, Jane (Marianne Faithfull) and Susannah (Lyn Ashley), no longer interest him.

Worse, his job at Jonathan Lute's (Orson Welles) advertising agency, as a director of promotional films, disgusts him. He arrives at work with an axe, destroys his desk and resigns. Lute is heartbroken; he was counting on Andrew to win a prize at an upcoming festival. Feeling a need to reconnect to his past, Andrew returns to Nicholas (Norman Rodway), who edits a highbrow but low-profit literary magazine. He is immediately attracted to Nicholas' secretary Georgina (Carol White). They attend an "Old Boys' Reunion" at Andrew's school at the invitation of Maccabee (Harvey Hall) who has come to the office to collect a printing bill. Maccabee is a vicious bully who gave Andrew trouble in school and he remains so. The reunion is a nightmare of senile headmasters (Michael Hordern), mistaken identities, and an unprovoked attack on Eldrich (Roland Curram) led by Maccabee. Andrew intervenes and is severely beaten. Georgina takes him to her home — a houseboat — where she resists his advances. Lute tracks him down and entreats him to direct a film for the festival. Nicholas sends Andrew and Georgina to Cambridge to woo Sater (Harry Andrews), a famous writer, back to the magazine. They are followed by Kellaway (Mark Eden), a PI hired by Louise; Andrew and Georgina quarrel over his ambivalence over the divorce.

Andrew learns that Nicholas has sold the magazine — to Lute! Backed into a corner, Andrew agrees to make the film, and he and Georgina become lovers. While Andrew works on the film, Georgina and Nicholas go for a drink. He gets drunk and has an accident driving her home; she dies in the flaming wreckage. After punching Nicholas, who has confessed his role in her death, Andrew goes to the festival. His film is a pretentious mélange of promotion for a camera, interspersed with snippets of his private life. It somehow wins — to Andrew's disgust. Lute reveals that the jury was bribed, gives him the trophy and dismisses him. Louise picks Andrew up on a bridge and they drive off.

Comment

I'll Never Forget What's 'Isname was the final chapter in an extraordinary trilogy of films starring Oliver Reed and directed by Michael Winner. (The others were *The System* and *The Jokers*.) All three were concerned with attractive young people in attractive settings behaving, mostly, unattractively. They are a fascinating record of England in the sixties, and the last two practically define "Swinging London."

According to Cliff Goodwin, the Tinker character introduced in *The System* was to be continued in a series of films. This didn't happen, per se, but Andrew Quint and Tinker have a lot in common, not surprisingly as both films were written by Peter Draper.

OLIVER REED (*Showguide*, February 1968): I can understand how Quint feels. He's a man who can see his life trapping him, his ideas sold out to a commercial society. It can happen to anyone. But I would certainly like to think it could never happen to me.

MICHAEL WINNER (*Showguide*, February 1968): Andrew Quint makes a gesture most people dream of. He quits the rat race. But he finds the old pressures remain; new pressures arise. But people find these riches less satisfying than they imagined. They want to get out. But can they?

I'll Never Forget What's 'Isname was announced as *The Takers* (which was the provisional title of *The System*) and began filming on location in London on February 25, 1967, concluding in mid–April. Receiving top billing for what amounted to a cameo was the legendary Orson Welles.

Andrew (Oliver Reed) sports a trophy and a bloody lip as Louise (Wendy Craig), accompanied by another partygoer (an unidentified actor), looks on disapprovingly in Michael Winner's *I'll Never Forget What's 'Isname* (Scimitar/Universal, 1967).

Michael Winner explained the unusual billing order. The original line-up was Oliver Reed, Carol White, Harry Andrews, then Orson Welles. "I scribbled that down and Orson signed it. A few days later Orson had gone back to Paris. I still have the telegram he sent. 'Dear Michael. Afraid second thoughts particularly from my own production company make first billing necessity.' Orson did not have a production company insisting on anything. He just changed his mind and wanted to be billed first. So what? I did it" (Winner, 2005, 104).

Orson Welles had had a well-deserved reputation for being "difficult" since revolutionizing the cinema in 1941 with *Citizen Kane*. But on *I'll Never Forget What's 'Isname*, he was on his best behavior. "It was a very jolly film. Orson fitted in wonderfully and everybody loved him," said Winner.

One wonders how much Reed, or at least his uncle, had to do with Welles' spirit of co-operation; Sir Carol Reed had directed him in his most famous role, as Harry Lime in *The Third Man* (1949).

Andrew (Oliver Reed) and Georgina (Carol White) share a rare quiet moment in Michael Winner's controversial *I'll Never Forget What's 'Isname* (Scimitar/Universal, 1967).

I'll Never Forget What's 'Isname was given a trade show on January 2, 1968, and went into general release on February 4. The large gap between the film's completion and release was, in part, caused by what was becoming a common occurrence for an Oliver Reed film: censorship problems. According to *The Daily Mail* (October 17, 1967), "The American censor has banned the £500,000 British film for screening in the U.S. because of frank lovemaking and nude scenes. Mr. Winner said, 'The Americans wanted us to cut this particular scene out. We have refused because it is a vital part of the story. I'm planning to go to America to try to persuade the censor to reconsider his decision.'"

Winner wrote in his autobiography, "The movie has one bizarre distinction. There was a scene where Oliver Reed and Carol White are on a houseboat. After a row, Carol goes on the floor and Oliver disappears off screen between her legs and later she knocks over a pot of white pain in an obvious piece of symbolism. The Catholic Legion of Decency in America which, at that time, held some sway decided this was the first time cunnilingus had ever been seen on the screen and banned the film."

The film (and Reed) got mostly positive reviews. *Kinematograph Weekly* (December 23, 1967): "This is definitely an adult film, uncompromisingly harsh in its comment on one level of civilization. It has wit, brutality, and compulsion. First class fare for intelligent audiences. Much of the credit must go to Oliver Reed for his delicate handling of Andrew's mixed emotions." *Financial Times* (December 29, 1967): "Oliver Reed, who gets better with each movie, surely attains his majority as an actor with this one, even masterfully squaring up to Orson Welles"; *The Observer* (December 24, 1967): "Oliver Reed is quite touching at times"; *The Sun* (December 19, 1967): "Mr. Winner adopts a nervy, restless and commercial coupling of fantasy and swinging London's reality to present us with the startling message that our contemporary beings are wading through a mass of wasted talent and rubbishy ideas. Oliver Reed turns in a performance of dedicated gloominess"; *The Sunday Times* (December 29, 1967): "I don't think Michael Winner is to be overlooked"; *The London Times* (December 21, 1967): "There are odd moments of comedy that work rather well"; *Films and Filming* (December, 1967): "It is beautifully written, savage, yet at times gentle and intimate with expert handling by Michael Winner with good performances from the whole cast, particularly Oliver Reed who handles very well a part which could easily have been devoid of sympathy"; *Cue* (April 11, 1968): "Lovely, smartly made by Michael Winner; offers plenty to look at"; *Look* (May 28, 1968): "It just shows how a good movie can be when it has something to say"; *Los Angeles Times* (August 7, 1968): "Oliver Reed has an unusual and rather impressive charm"; *Variety* (December 27, 1967): "Oliver Reed, an ugly-fascinating thesp of perpetual potential, looks grim and disenchanted."

I'll Never Forget What's 'Isname provided Reed with a first-class showcase, and he knew it, participating in a twelve-theatre personal appearance tour to promote the film. *Kinematograph Weekly* (March 30, 1968): "At each theatre, Oliver made a stage appearance and created an enormous impression among the female coterie. His total professionalism is linked with a casual, laconic appraisal of his success and stardom."

Winner has said of Reed, "He was one of the few actors who went with me right through life — I started with him in his twenties and we went right through to making a film shortly before he died. We did six movies together, all over the world, and a nicer man you couldn't meet. Oliver was a very, very nice man — a very nice, quiet chap who occasionally liked a drink."

I'll Never Forget What's 'Isname presents the "Swinging London" of Carnaby Street, The Beatles and The Rolling Stones — in fact, Mick Jagger's girlfriend of the time (Marianne Faithfull) has a small role. This was very much a transitional period for pop culture and the film captures it all. According to Winner, "There was the new explosion of clothing in the midsixties — people could choose how to dress ... they didn't have to look like their parents. Oliver, of course, is wearing a suit ... he was always rather proud of suits. He would invariably get into some kind of scrap and he and the suit would end up in the water ... in a pond or a fountain ... the number of suits Oliver would ruin in the course of a film ... they were very expensive. They would all shrink!"

Our first glimpse of Quint finds him, immaculately dressed, walking on a crowded London street with a large axe and a nasty expression. After trashing his desk, he confronts his tyrannical ex-employer:

QUINT: I'm going to find an honest job.

LUTE: Silly boy ... there aren't any.

Reed and Orson Welles have several scenes together and they are all wonderful. It's fascinating to see the young upstart on the verge of international stardom going head to head with the film legend on the way down. It's likely that this potentially uncomfortable situation brought out the best in both. They also hit it off personally and remained friendly up until Welles' death in 1985. According to Cliff Goodwin, Welles gave Reed some good advice, "If in doubt, do nothing" [Goodwin, 105].

Andrew Quint, in Reed's hands, is a fascinating character, bursting with paradoxes. He should be happy, but he's not; he seemingly has it all — perhaps he has too much. He's looking for honesty and simplicity yet keeps making his life more complex. Quint is given several telling scenes with the women in his life that reveal his ambivalence towards male-female relationships.

Quint is separated from his wife Louise, but they still occasionally have sex, and he has a fleeting yet real relationship with his young daughter whom he has nicknamed "Thing"(!). He and Louise can't seem to live either together or apart. He fills this hole in his life with Josie and Susannah, an actress who appears in one of his promotional films. Quint decides he needs to discard them both, but how?

SUSANNAH: How's your wife?

QUINT: How's your husband?

SUSANNAH: You and your women...

QUINT: I'm getting rid of you all.

SUSANNAH: Oh darling...

QUINT: You never believe anything that runs counter to your incredible ego. You and I aren't going anywhere and probably don't want to.

SUSANNAH: Oh, Andrew. If you do get rid of all of us, you can always get some more.

And that's exactly what he does, replacing them with Georgina! This hardly helps the situation with Louise.

QUINT: We didn't really work, did we?

LOUISE: Didn't we?

QUINT: Well, not all the time...

LOUISE: Well, like all married couples ... you just got used to me.

QUINT: And you to me.

LOUISE: Maybe ... it's all right for men to go back and try to find the things they think they missed. But women can't ever go back to being nineteen, can they?

Quint's relationship with Georgina is equally problematic; she wants him, but is only too aware of the continuing attachment to Louise. She won't be played for a fool.

Quint and Georgina might have made it as a couple but her shocking death, obviously, put an end to that. He ends up where he probably belonged, with Louise — but not completely by his own choice. After all of Quint's soul-searching and decision-making, his situation ended up dictated by fate. Getting out, it seems, isn't as easy as it looks.

I'll Never Forget What's 'Isname has just about everything one could want in a film, and does it all spectacularly well. The performances are uniformly excellent from the leads to the supporting actors. Special mention should be made of Harry Andrews as the well-named Sater, who gives an incredibly creepy performance, and Harvey Hall as the nasty Maccabee. His fight with Quint at the film's conclusion is extremely brutal; Reed has more blood in his mouth than in *The Curse of the*

Werewolf. "Mr. Reed, dark, chunky and ruggedly handsome, gives the role the masculinity, humor, sadness and reality it deserves. A disturbingly effective picture."—*New York Times*, April 15, 1968.

The film has a lot to say and says it well. Unlike some productions, its many messages don't tread on each other or blunt the entertainment value. Winner and Peter Draper have done what few directors and writers have accomplished — a socially conscious film that's also fun and exciting.

As for Reed, he was at the top of his game. While Andrew Quint may not be his best performance, it's close.

Oliver! (1968)

Romulus Films; Warwick Film Productions; released by Columbia Pictures in the U.K. and the U.S.

Crew— Director: Carol Reed; Screenplay; Vernon Harris; "Book": Lionel Bart; from the novel by Charles Dickens; Producer: John Woolf; Cinematographer: Oswald Morris; Film Editor: Ralph Kemplen: Casting: Jenia Reissar; Production Design: John Box; Art Director: Terence Marsh; Costume Design: Phyllis Dalton; Makeup Supervisor: George Frost; Chief Hair Stylist; Bobbie Smith; Production Supervisor: Denis Johnson; Unit Production Manager: Denis Johnson Jr.; Assistant Directors: Colin Brewer, Ray Corbett, Mike Higgins, Chris Kenny; Assistant Art Directors: Bob Cartwright, Roy Walker; Set Dressers: Vernon Dixon, Ken Muggleton; Sound Recordists: Buster Ambler, Bob Jones; Sound Supervisor: John Cox; ADR and Sound Effects Mixer: Tony Dawe; Stunts: Nosher Powell; Camera Operator: Freddie Cooper; Photographer: Brian West; Wardrobe Supervisor: John Wilson-Apperson; Assistant Film Editor: Marcel Durham; Music Coordinator: Dusty Buck; Choral Arranger: John Green; Associate Music Editor: Robert Hathaway; Music Editor: Ken Runyon; Titles Background Designer: Grahan Barkley; Musical Sequences Stager: Onna White; Assistant Choreographers: George Baron, Tom Panko; Continuity: Pamela Davies.

Cast— Ron Moody (Fagin), Shani Wallis (Nancy), Oliver Reed (Bill Sikes), Harry Secombe (Mr. Bumble), Mark Lester (Oliver Twist), Jack Wild (The Artful Dodger), Hugh Griffith (The Magistrate), Joseph O'Connor (Mr. Brownlow), Peggy Mount (Mrs. Bumble), Leonard Rossiter (Sowerberry), Hylda Baker (Mrs. Sowerberry), Kenneth Cranham (Noah Claypole), Megs Jenkins (Mrs. Bedwin), Sheila White (Bet), Wensley Pithey (Dr.

Grimwig), James Hayter (Mr. Jessop), Elizabeth Knight (Charlotte), Fred Emney (Workhouse Chairman), Edwin Finn, Roy Evans (Paupers), Norman Mitchell (Arresting Policemen), Robert Bartlett, Graham Buttrose, Jeffrey Chandler, Kirk Clugeston, Dempsey Cook, Christopher Duff, Nigel Grice, Ronnie Johnson, Nigel Kingsley, Robert Langley, Brian Lloyd, Peter Lock, Clive Moss, Ian Ramsey, Peter Renn, Billy Smith, Kim Smith, Freddie Stead, Raymond Ward, John Waters (Fagin's Boys).

Synopsis

England in the mid–1800s. Young Oliver Twist (Mark Lester) is an orphan living in misery in a workhouse. The children, who starve while the directors feast, put Oliver up to ask for more gruel. As punishment for his offense, Mr. Bumble (Harry Secombe), the disciplinarian, removes the boy and sells him to the undertaker Mr. Sowerberry (Leonard Rossiter) to work in the funeral parlor. When Sowerberry's assistant Noah (Kenneth Cranham) insults Oliver's mother, the boy goes wild and runs off, alone, to London. While wandering the streets he meets the Artful Dodger (Jack Wild), a young thief who takes Oliver to his master Fagin (Ron Moody). Fagin trains young boys in the art of street thievery, but also feeds, clothes and houses them with some affection. In league with Fagin is the violent Bill Sikes (Oliver Reed), a heartless criminal unaccountably loved by Nancy (Shani Wallis), an "entertainer" in a seedy tavern. Oliver is taught the rudiments of picking pockets, and is soon in trouble; he's taken to court after Dodger botches the robbery of the wealthy Mr. Brownlow (Joseph O'Connor).

Brownlow is touched by the boy's obvious innocence and, with the charges dropped, takes Oliver home with him. Fagin and Sikes fear that Oliver may unwittingly give them away. While Fagin wishes the boy no harm, Sikes has other plans. He forces Nancy to lure Oliver away so that he can be silenced. When Nancy realizes what Sikes' intentions are, she arranges to return the boy to Brownlow but refuses to compromise her lover by revealing his identity.

Nancy manages to get Oliver away from Sikes and his ferocious dog Bullseye and spirits the boy to London Bridge where Brownlow awaits. As she and Oliver weave through the fetid alleyways, Sikes and Bullseye are in pursuit. Before she can hand the boy over, Sikes seizes Oliver. When Nancy fights him, he goes berserk and beats her to death with his walking stick. Sikes tries to kill Bullseye whom he fears will lead to his capture but the dog runs off.

With Oliver in tow, Sikes is pursued by a mob led by Bullseye. When he attempts to cross from one roof to another by swinging on a rope tied by Oliver, Sikes is shot from below by a police officer. Brownlow realizes that Oliver is actually the son of his dead niece and takes him in once again, this time as his son. Fagin, who has lost his fortune in stashed gems, reunites with the Dodger and they plan to continue their life of crime.

Comment

During the late 1940s and early 1950s, Sir Carol Reed (knighted in 1952) was considered to be England's greatest director due to such classics as *Odd Man Out* (1946), *The Fallen Idol* (1947) and *The Third Man* (1949). Despite continuing to make quality films (*Outcast of the Islands,* 1952, *A Kid for Two Farthings*, 1955, and *Our Man in Havana*, 1959), Reed's reputation began to slip due to his lack of self-promotion and being regarded by "film scholars" as lacking "auteur" credentials. Being replaced on *Mutiny on the Bounty* (1962) by Lewis Milestone due to, mainly, Marlon Brando's absurd behavior didn't help much either.

By the 1960s, the idea of a British big-budget musical was almost as dead as Sir Carol Reed's career. But with Lionel Bart's *Oliver!* a West End smash, thoughts of a film were inevitable. Reed had seen the show when it opened in July 1960 and tried — but failed — to secure the film rights. Sir Carol's father, the legendary Victorian actor Sir Herbert Beerbohm Tree, had produced a version of *Oliver Twist* on the London stage which further enhanced Reed's interest.

Oliver! arrived on Broadway in 1963 and Bart was soon besieged with more film offers, finally selling to the British company Romulus run by John and James Woolf. Romulus felt that Carol Reed was the man for *Oliver!* due to his abilities in preparation, concern for detail, success in directing children and the even temperament necessary for such a sprawling

Oliver (Mark Lester) is menaced by Bill Sikes (Oliver Reed) in Sir Carol Reed's Oscar-winning *Oliver!* (Romulus/Columbia, 1968).

production. They also felt he would spend their $8,000,000 investment wisely.

There had been previous film versions of *Oliver Twist*, including silent versions in 1909, 1910, 1912 and 1922 (the latter with Lon Chaney as Fagin). But the prize production was David Lean's classic of 1948 with Alec Guinness (Fagin), Robert Newton (Bill Sikes), Anthony Newley (The Artful Dodger) and John Howard Davies (Oliver). Reed realized that any production of *Oliver Twist*, even a musical, would be compared to Lean's. He also realized that the character of Oliver was far less important than that of Fagin and Sikes and he was very concerned about casting those roles. For a time Peter Sellers was a prime contender for Fagin but Reed wanted the actor who had starred on stage, even though he was not a film box office attraction. Ron Moody was originally dismissed by Columbia, who had secured releasing rights, as not being a bankable star. But Reed held firm, believing correctly that Moody's lack of film recognition was more than balanced by his talent and familiarity with the role. For the two pivotal children's parts, Oliver and the Artful Dodger, Reed found seven-year-old Mark Lester as a result of a two-month casting call, and fifteen-year-old Jack Wild, who was discovered on a football field by a canny agent. Neither boy had any real acting experience, which Reed probably preferred. Shani Wallis, a popular cabaret singer and British TV variety regular, was chosen for Nancy over Reed's favorite Shirley Bassey, who had become an in-

Oliver Reed in the role that made him an international star: Bill Sikes in *Oliver!* (Romulus/Columbia, 1968).

ternational sensation after singing the title theme for *Goldfinger* (1964).

That left the casting of Bill Sikes. In retrospect, one might think, who else but Oliver Reed? After all, he was born to play the part; Beerbohm Tree was his grandfather, Sir Carol Reed was his uncle and his film persona was as nasty as anyone's. But — Reed loathed nepotism and was (overly, pointlessly) concerned that his nephew's casting would be viewed as such. John Woolf set him straight.

Oliver! was announced on December 16, 1965, and planning sessions began on August 18, 1966. Casting commenced on September 1, 1966, and concluded on July 10, 1967.

Production had begun at Shepperton Studios the previous month. Almost 400 carpenters were employed for three months building the massive, fascinating sets. Nothing could be choreographed until the sets were completed. The sets had to be huge; in one scene alone, 400 extras were used. Since most of the children had never acted in a film, Reed's ingenuity was stretched to the limit. According to Andrew Birkin (Reed's nephew and screenwriter), "There's a moment when Fagin opened his box of treasures for Oliver and Carol wanted a reaction shot from Mark, his face lighting up with wonder. But he couldn't get it. Carol went home that night quite bothered about the matter. Then he contacted a friend of his who owned a pet shop and went and collected a white rabbit. When Mark came on the set ... Carol said, 'Oh Mark, I've got something that might rather amuse you' and produced from his jacket the white rabbit. Mark's face lit up and Carol got his shot." In *Carol Reed—A Biography*, Sir Carol said, "The worse thing one can say to a child when aiming a camera at him is 'act naturally.' That will shrivel him on the spot. Children are natural actors, but you must give them something to act" (Wapshott, 324). Mark Lester didn't need any direction to appear to be afraid of Oliver Reed's Bill Sikes—it just came naturally. According to Cliff Goodwin's *Evil Spirits: The Life of Oliver Reed*, "[H]is moody and disturbing performance bought him plaudits and recognition and frightened the kids in the cast half to death.... Jack Wild's abiding memory of Reed was one of total intimidation. 'As kids we were all terrified of him

Oliver Reed as Bill Sikes loses what little self-control he possesses in the Best Picture of 1968, *Oliver!* (Romulus/Columbia, 1968), directed by his uncle Sir Carol Reed.

because he was this giant of a man and the only time we ever saw him was when he was in costume and made up for the part.' Reed didn't truly let his hair down until the end of filming party, as Oliver himself, Mark Lester recalled. Mr. Reed spiked Lester's and Wild's soft drinks with vodka for a lark. Lester recalled, 'Oliver arrived on the set fully made up and mentally into his part. He terrified the living daylights out of me. I think we were all frightened of him. I remember looking into Ron Moody's eyes ... and, even at my age, seeing real fear.'"

Oliver Reed frightened a lot of filmgoers too.

Oliver! is one of the three most important films in his career. *The Curse of the Werewolf* gave Reed his first leading role and steady employment with Hammer in a variety of audience-pleasing roles. *The System* united Reed with Michael Winner who provided films with more mainstream appeal outside the restrictive confines of Hammer. But it was *Oliver!* that made him an international star and opened the door to everything that came next.

Bill Sikes (Oliver Reed) plans his next act of violence in Sir Carol Reed's *Oliver!* (Romulus/Columbia, 1968).

Reed enjoyed working with his uncle and stayed close to him until the director's death. Once, prior to *Oliver!*, Reed arrived at a celebration of his uncle's life at the National Film Theatre and was unprepared to be asked on stage to deliver a tribute. "Bounding upon the stage, standing in front of a packed audience comprising the director's relatives, friends and admirers, Reed dried. He managed to garble some words about how humble he was and then fell off the stage. He was upset at the thought of ruining the evening, but friends said, 'Don't worry, Oliver, they all loved it because that's what they expected you to do'" (Sellers, 129). Interviewed during the making of *Oliver!* by Ian Brown for *Photoplay Film Monthly* (July 1968), Reed said, "I'm a full-time film man. I don't like the theatre or the atmosphere of the theatre. But I'll watch any film you care to show me — even dreadful ones."

Due to the importance of Bill Sikes to Reed's success, his scenes bear close examination. He, Sir Carol and writer Vernon Harris orchestrated Sikes' behavior like a musical piece slowly building from a quiet, barely controlled sullenness that gradually escalates to violent hysteria. Like Harry Lime (Orson Welles), the villain in Sir Carol Reed's *The Third Man*, Bill Sikes gets some negative build-up before appearing on screen: He's first seen (like Lime) as a menacing shadow. Both Lime and Sikes are assigned animals as their "familiars"; Harry a cat, Bill a nasty bull terrier named Bullseye who precedes his master into the film. Both Lime and Sikes will end their lives on the run from a mob.

Sikes makes his entrance after Fagin goes to meet him at the tavern — a real den of iniquity — where Nancy entertains. She's been waiting impatiently for Sikes as Fagin scurries, crab-like, and slides up to a prostitute. Fagin asks, "Is he here ... has he come yet ... Mr. Sikes?" He has. Fagin looks, awestruck, as Bullseye and Sikes approach from the catwalk above.

They exchange the treasures Sikes has recently stolen: Sikes stares at Fagin, saying nothing, then saunters up to Nancy. She sings, ironically, "It's a Fine Life" as her unresponsive lover eats and drinks sulkily, glaring at everything and nothing. He abruptly gets up and leaves, followed by Nancy and Bullseye, his two obedient pets.

It's established quickly and masterfully that Sikes is an angry man: angry at Fagin, Nancy, the boys, life — and, probably, himself. He takes an immediate dislike to Oliver, and why not? The child is Sikes' complete opposite; a positive to his negative.

From their first meeting Sikes seems determined to destroy Oliver in one way or another. He's bent on assaulting the boy's innocence in the hope, perhaps, that Oliver will end up like him. When Oliver is taken home by Mr. Brownlow, Sikes is infuriated and not just because he fears the boy will "peach" on the gang. He can't bear the thought that Oliver will escape the hell in which they exist.

> SIKES: We've got to get him back, you hear? We'll nab him the first time he sets foot out of the door.
>
> NANCY: He never goes out alone — you know that!
>
> SIKES: Don't you talk back to me, my girl.

Fagin rejects out of hand Sikes' typically brutal — and stupid — plan to simply snatch Oliver on his doorstep. Better, he thinks, to have the boy lured away by someone he trusts...

> NANCY: It's no good you trying it on with me.
>
> SIKES: And just exactly what do you mean by that?
>
> NANCY: What I say, I'm not going!
>
> SIKES (getting angry): You'll bring him back here, my girl, unless you want to feel my hand on your throat.

And then, to the horrified surprise of Fagin, the boys and the audience, Sikes viciously backhands Nancy across the face, knocking her to the floor, then says, "She'll go."

Nancy staggers out and watches Sikes and Bullseye stalk off below. She sings, quaveringly, "As Long as He Needs Me." It's an incredibly powerful scene and brings *Oliver!* into an area of darkness that most audience members could hardly have expected.

After capturing Oliver, Sikes and Nancy take him to Fagin.

> OLIVER: Mr. Brownlow will be here after you when he finds out you've got his books and money.

> SIKES (disdainfully): So he'll be out here, will he? After us? What did you tell him about us?
>
> OLIVER: Nothing...
>
> SIKES: Fagin — I'll wager this young rat told him everything. [Screaming at Oliver:] What did you tell him? [Oliver foolishly slaps Sikes, who grabs him and prepares to beat him with his belt.]
>
> NANCY: You'll have to kill me if you lay a hand on that boy.
>
> SIKES: Don't you tempt me.
>
> NANCY: Take care I don't put the finger on all of you and I don't care if I hang for it.
>
> SIKES (sneering): Do you know who you are and where you are?
>
> NANCY: You don't have to tell me...

The scene is actually more devastating than the earlier one in which Sikes hits her; this blow to what's left of her dignity is difficult to watch, and it presents Sikes as even worse than we've come to believe. Sikes then decides to complete his destruction of Oliver by taking him along to burglarize a house.

> NANCY: But why him?
>
> SIKES: 'Cause I need a little one, that's why. And he's nice and thin. And on this particular job, that's what counts.
>
> OLIVER: Must I go?
>
> SIKES: One word out of you while you're out with me and you know what will happen. [Sikes points an empty pistol at the boy and, smiling, pulls the trigger.]

Nancy, horrified, now decides that she must — up to a point — betray Sikes; she goes to Brownlow to arrange the boy's return. Meanwhile Sikes, Oliver and Bullseye go housebreaking. Sikes shoves Oliver through a tiny window and the boy creeps through the dark, silent house toward the door ... and Sir Carol Reed delivers the film's most startling shot. As Oliver approaches the door, a creaking sound is heard as the letter slot slowly opens. Filling the CinemaScope screen are the cold blue eyes of Bill Sikes.

The robbery goes very badly; Oliver knocks a metal plate to the floor that endlessly circles until it falls with a crash, waking the entire house, if not the dead. A servant sets the dogs on the fleeing pair, but Bullseye sees them off. Sikes drags Oliver to the tavern.

FAGIN: Everything all right Bill?

SIKES (hissing): No, it's not, Fagin. The little brat woke them up. We had to run for it.

Nancy is beginning to panic — she must get Oliver to Brownlow, now more than ever. But, while Sikes and Fagin talk, Bullseye guards Oliver. She joins the crowded hall in singing "Oom Pah Pah" and, as she dances by Oliver, snatches him away. Sikes and Bullseye chase the pair through the dark streets leading to London Bridge where Brownlow waits. As Nancy is about to send the boy up the steps to safety, he stops to hug her. It is a fatal mistake. Sikes grabs Oliver, and Nancy leaps on him. She and Sikes disappear behind a wall; we hear her screaming and see Sikes' walking stick rising and falling. Her screams stop. Sikes backs out slowly, staring blankly at his bloody hands. Bullseye glares disapprovingly at his master as Sikes runs off with Oliver. A crowd gathers. Bullseye follows — so Bullseye must die. Sikes whispers, "Come here, Bullseye. They've seen you. So you can't come with me no further. 'Cause if you do, they'll know you, Bullseye. Come here — you ain't afraid of me, are you, Bullseye?" Now he screams: "*Come here, Bullseye!*"

And Sikes' last friend runs off. Brownlow and the growing mob stare, horrified, at Nancy's battered corpse, then grab Bullseye as Sikes heads for Fagin's.

SIKES: Brass. I want some brass. I've got to get away.

FAGIN: What's wrong, Bill?

SIKES (screaming): Did you hear what I said? I want brass! Brass! Money!

FAGIN: There's blood ... blood on your coat. Where's Nancy? Bill! Bill Sikes! What did you do? What did you do?

SIKES: She won't peach on nobody no more.

FAGIN: You shouldn't have done that.

As they argue over money, Sikes is suddenly silent as he hears a dog barking outside. Sikes says, "It's him ... Bullseye! Nancy — I loved you, didn't I? Look what you've done to me!"

There is no doubt that Sikes believes this as he runs out with Oliver, pursued by the *Frankenstein*-like torch-bearing mob. He carries the boy to the top of a building but it's a dead end. Finding a rope, Sikes forces Oliver to inch out onto a beam and loop the rope over the end so that he (Sikes) can swing across to the next building. As Oliver creeps out onto the beam, Sikes — sweating, disheveled, hysterical and terrified — urges him on.

As Sikes, with the rope around him, attempts to swing between the buildings, a policeman shoots him from below. He staggers back and falls from the beam but, caught by the rope, he swings above the streets as if hanged. Few characters ever deserved it more.

Unlike most of Reed's other villainous roles, Bill Sikes has no redeeming qualities. He has no charm, courage, presentability, nothing. He is, simply, evil. We are given no clues as to why he acts this way; we assume he's one of Fagin's boys grown old and very, very bad. (It must be noted though that Bullseye loved Reed so much that he had to have his tail taped down to stop it wagging joyously when they were working together!)

With *Oliver!*, Reed was at the top of his game. He was now an international star in the making. Interviewer Rex Reed found him an easy subject on the *Oliver!* set as he revealed himself to be a bit overcome by his new position and quite unsure how to handle it all:

Everyone told me not to do horror films. But I wanted to act. They knew I looked [like a werewolf] already, so I got it and learned a lot. It's you Americans who did it. Nobody in America remembers a werewolf, but I did *The System* and *The Jokers* for a young director, Michael Winner, and got discovered there. I was picked up by this drunk who was trying to impress his girlfriend because he recognized me as the werewolf. Now, if they tease me, I go ahead and buy them a drink. I've got fifteen scripts on my desk and I'm making more money for *Oliver!* than I've ever made in my life. I could never go back to making horror films now. I don't like starving. When I met my wife she was engaged to someone else and I was so poor I tried to get her to sell her ring. I'm getting good roles now. People want something new. That old mystique of

Bill Sikes (Oliver Reed) and Nancy (Shani Wallis) have a domestic difference in *Oliver!* (Romulus/Columbia, 1968).

movie stars in silk-lined caravans is over. The old marquee names are getting needed American money and they need our talent. I'm being drawn to America now because my expenses are getting bigger. I have an accountant, a personal secretary, a gardener, a handyman, and a maid because movie star's wives don't scrub floors. This country takes everything in taxes. Then everyone wonders where all our British actors have gone? I haven't lived long enough with this much money to know who I am yet. I don't know if it's big cars, or gambling, or fast women I want so I try them all. I don't like swinging London. I went to the Ad Lib once and it was all actors in tweed hats and corduroy pants who dribbled all over my wife's hand and I thought, "Christ, is this a mirror? Am I like that?" Actors are bores. I can only take them in twos or threes — no, three is too many — because then

they start telling you about all the parts they turned down. English actors used to have to go to the Royal Academy and have a very prissy background. Then war came and everyone was employed as full-time murderers and the Noël Cowards with their chiseled noses, and their lavender water, and their Brylcreem hair were out, because the newsreel cameras were shooting men crawling out of trenches. Then, after the war, everyone sighed with relief and escaped for ten years into a world of crinolines and scarlet pimpernels and remakes of old Hollywood Three Musketeer movies. Then the children of the men of war took over and Tony Richardsons were "in." Now after the kitchen sinks and the contraceptives and the rooms at the top, people are crying out for recognition. I've got a face like a dustbin but with the help of the hippies people are learning that if you kick a dustbin over and rhododendrons fall out, it's glorious. I think I'll give it all up when I'm forty for a long think.

Oliver! being a musical, has plenty of songs. They are wonderfully written and performed (in this order) by Oliver ("Food, Glorious Food"), Mr. Bumble and Widow Corney ("Oliver!"), Oliver ("Where Is Love"), Oliver, Fagin, Dodger and Nancy ("I'd Do Anything"), Fagin ("Be Back Soon"), Nancy ("As Long as He Needs Me"), Oliver ("Who Will Buy?"), Nancy ("It's a Fine Life"), Nancy ("Oom Pah Pah"), and Fagin ("Reviewing the Situation").

There is no singing by Bill Sikes. For the reason why, please watch *Tommy*.

Oliver! did very well at the Academy Awards, taking Best Picture, Best Director, Best Set Decoration, Best Score Adaptation and Best Sound. It was also nominated for Best Actor (Ron Moody), Best Supporting Actor (Jack Wild), Best Screenplay, Best Costume Design, Best Editing and Best Cinematography.

Notably absent was Oliver Reed, who could easily have been nominated for Best Actor or Best Supporting Actor. Despite Reed's many outstanding performances, he would never receive a nomination. Bill Sikes may have been his best, but in a career with so many highlights it's difficult to say with any certainty.

Reviews for *Oliver!* were, not surprisingly, overwhelmingly positive: "*Oliver!* has minor faults but its color, humor, familiar but cast-iron storyline plus Bart's catchy ditties provide sparkling standout family entertainment plus. Oliver Reed is a sufficiently menacing and formidable thug" (*Variety*, October 2, 1968); "The 19th century England created for *Oliver!* is never intended to be a literal reconstruction; there is always a touch of stylization in the sets and compositions. The world of *Oliver!* is one of workhouses, funeral parlors, seamy taverns, and thieves' dens, but all seems slightly larger than life through the amazed eyes of a child" (*Film Quarterly*, Spring, 1969); "Oliver Reed is rapidly becoming one of those men you love to hate" (*Life*, April 4, 1969); "Few people will be able to resist this sumptuous mixture of music, comedy, dancing, color and melodrama. Certain big time success. Oliver Reed is a baleful

and menacing Sikes. What this picture may lack in the power of international star names it makes up for in quality of performance. The songs, all pleasantly familiar, are put over with terrific vigor and the dances, mainly quaint in style, have a proper affinity with the sense of period that has been most expressively created by the very striking settings. The star of the show is Ron Moody, repeating his stage characterization as Fagin and commanding in all his scenes" (*Kinematograph Weekly* September 28, 1968).

Perhaps the most perceptive criticism of *Oliver!*'s success comes from Pauline Kael in *The New Yorker*: "Maybe the most revolutionary thing that can be done in movies at the moment is to make them decently again. *Oliver!* has been made by people who know how; it's a civilized motion picture, not only emotionally satisfying but so satisfyingly crafted that we can sit back and enjoy what's going on, serene in the knowledge that the camera isn't going to attack us and the editor isn't going to give us an electric shock. Carol Reed sustains the tone that tells us it's all theatre, and he's a gentleman: he doesn't urge the audience to tears, he always leaves us our pride."

Oliver! received a royal premiere in September 1968 at the Leicester Square Odeon and opened three months later at New York's Loews State Theatre. The film was an instant sensation and put the entire *Oliver!* team in the spotlight. Oliver Reed made the most of his newfound international success. For the next six years or so he was among the top male stars worldwide, and his name on a marquee meant as much as anyone's. But, like most other aspects of Oliver Reed's life, his career did not follow the traditional arc of the successful entertainer or athlete. In most cases there is the initial struggle, the gradual climb to the top, the period of glory, then the slow decline.

In Reed's case, the period of glory was interspersed with lesser efforts like *Blue Blood, ZPG,* and *Days of Fury*. When the slide began — it would take over twenty years — terrible films like *The Great Scout and Cathouse Thursday* were soon followed by good ones like *The Prince and the Pauper*. Just when it looked like his career was over (*Fanny Hill*), Reed would come back with *Captive*. The execrable

House of Usher was quickly followed by the excellent *Hold My Hand, I'm Dying*. And, most mystifying of all, he ended his career (and life) with one of the best films ever made.

His uncle's career after *Oliver!* went straight, inexplicably, downhill. After the incredible success of *Oliver!* Sir Carol Reed could have chosen any project; he picked, of all things, *The Last Warrior* (1970), "a ludicrous ... over-produced American Indian comedy" (*Variety*). The next year brought *Follow Me* and then it was over. He died in 1976.

The final word on *Oliver!* might be the insightful observation made by Jan Dawson: "There is a heightened discrepancy between the romping jollity with which everyone goes about his business and the actual business being gone about. Such narrative elements of the exploitation of child labor, pimping, abduction, prostitution and murder combine to make *Oliver!* the most non–U subject ever to receive a 'U' Certificate."

The Assassination Bureau (1969)

Heathfield; Paramount Pictures; color

Crew— Director: Basil Dearden; Writer: Michael Relph, from a novel by Robert L Fish and an unfinished novel by Jack London; Additional Dialogue: Wolf Mankowitz; Producer: Michael Relph; Associate Producer: Charles Orme; Original Music: Ron Grainer; Cinematographer: Geoffrey Unsworth; Film Editor: Teddy Darvas; Production Design: Michael Relph; Art Directors: Roy Smith, Frank White; Costume Design: Beatrice Dawson; Makeup Artist: Harry Frampton; Hair Stylist: Barbara Ritchie; Production Manager: Barrie Melrose; Assistant Director: John Peverall; Second Assistant Directors: Richard Hoult, Terry Marcel; Set Dresser: Helen Thomas; Roger Cain, Simon Holland; Sound Recordists: Ken Barker, John Dennis, Dudley Messenger; Sound Editor: John Poyner; Special Effects: Les Bowie, Thomas Clark; Stunts: Eddie Stacey, Nosher Powell; Camera Operator: Peter MacDonald; Still Photographer: George Courtney Ward; Wardrobe Supervisors: Rosemary Burrows, John Hilling; Lyricist: Hal Shaper; Continuity: Susan Dyson; Titles Designer: Robert Ellis.

Cast— Oliver Reed (Ivan Dragomiloff), Diana Rigg (Sonya Winter), Telly Savalas (Lord Bostwick), Curt Jurgens (General von Pinck), Philippe Noiret (Monsieur Lucoville), Warren Mitchell (Herr Weiss), Beryl Reid (Mme. Otero), Clive Revill (Cesare Spado), Kenneth Griffith (Monsieur Popescu), Vernon Dobtcheff (Baron Muntzof), Annabella Incontrera (Eleanora Spado), Jess Conrad (Angelo), George Coulouris (Swiss Peasant), Ralph Michael (Editor), Katherine Kath (Mme. Lucoville), Eugene Deckers (La Belle Amie Desk Clerk), Olaf Pooley (Swiss Cashier), George Murcell, Michael Wolf (Zeppelin Officers), Gordon Sterne (Corporal), Peter Bowles, William Kendall (La Belle Amie Patrons), Jeremy Lloyd (English Officer), Roger Delgado, Maurice Browning, Clive Cazes, Gerik Schjelderup (Bureau Members), Milton Reid, Frank Thornton (Elevator Victims); uncredited: Patrick Allen (Narrator).

Synopsis

In 1906 Europe, there is a strange outbreak of highly professional, apparently motiveless killings. A determined young reporter, Sonya Winter (Diana Rigg), decides that the killings are the work of a single organization. She takes her suspicions to Lord Bostwick (Telly Savalas), a cosmopolitan newspaper proprietor, who agrees to back her investigation.

By devious means Sonya contacts the organization and learns from its elegant young chairman, Ivan Dragomiloff (Oliver Reed), that the Assassination Bureau is a group of highly professional international killers, who kill only if they feel the victims deserve to die. Sonya says she has a suitable candidate: Ivan Dragomiloff.

Ivan sees an opportunity to revitalize his flagging organization, which of late has allowed sordid considerations of commercialism and greed to enter its transactions. He accepts the commission and discusses it at a meeting of the Bureau comprised of von Pinck from Germany (Curt Jurgens), Lucoville from France (Philippe Noiret), Weiss from Switzerland (Warren Mitchell), Popescu from Rumania (Kenneth Griffith) and Muntzov from Russia (Vernon Dobtcheff). The British member, astonishingly, turns out to be Lord Bostwick, who sees the bureau as an instrument of his limitless ambitions. Ivan proposes a 24-hour truce, after which he will endeavor to eliminate the members of the Bureau as they try to eliminate him. After Ivan has left, Bostwick encourages his doubtful colleagues with a £10,000 pound prize for the one who kills Ivan.

Sonya follows Ivan to Paris. Ivan tracks Lucoville down to La Belle Amie, the luxurious

Ivan (Oliver Reed) is about to be poisoned by the devious Eleanora (Annabella Incontrera) in *The Assassination Bureau* (Paramount, 1969).

house of pleasure presided over by Madame Otero (Beryl Reid). A hectic chase ensues through the disorderly house of screaming girls and undignified clients, until Lucoville traps them in the linen cupboard and tries to gas

them out. Ivan devises a fuse, and as they reached the street by way of a convenient linen chute, the house of ill repute to goes up in flames.

On the train to Zurich an innocent-looking waiter serves a gun with the brandy and cigar. He turns out to be Popescu and he ends up in flames too. The Swiss member, Weiss, has heard about his colleague and is worried. In his bank he suspects everyone and tries to tug the beard off a genuine customer. An innocent Sonya, sent by Ivan, walks in with a special package for the director. As she and Ivan drive away a mushroom cloud hovers over the bank.

In Vienna they feel they can relax because the Bureau has no man there. They celebrate in a beer cellar, where von Pinck, disguised as a waiter, proffers an explosive, which ends up on the archduke's table with disastrous results for nearly all concerned. On to Venice where Cesare Spado (Clive Revill), Bostwick's most trusted lieutenant, waits eagerly to succeed where the others have failed. Unfortunately for Spado, his beautiful wife Eleanora (Annabella Incontrera) chooses this moment to poison him. She has had her roving eye on a handsome gondolier.

Sonya, left alone in her hotel, has a tricky time with a time bomb Spado has planted, but Ivan saves the day once more. Ivan tells Eleanora he knows she has killed Spado, and pretends to be poisoned when she pours him a drink. The news that Ivan is dead is flashed to Bostwick, who arrives triumphant in Venice with von Pinck. The bureau is his, and just in time. At a castle on the German-Rutherian border all the crowned heads of Europe are assembling for a peace conference and now Bostwick plans the bureau's most stupendous assignment. Confidently they travel to Germany, where they have a zeppelin ready to drop the largest bomb known to man on the castle and the assembled crowned heads. But Ivan is not dead, and he and Sonia see the castle and the bomb. Sonya is dispatched to warn the crowned heads and Ivan climbs aboard the zeppelin when it takes off. A fearsome saber fight develops between Ivan and von Pinck. As the zeppelin zooms over the castle, Ivan corners Bostwick and von Pinck crouching over the bombsight. Bostwick draws a gun and fires. The zeppelin catches fire and plunges earthward in flames, but Ivan escapes.

Sonya arrives at the castle just in time to see Ivan accepting the last of all the highest European decorations for gallantry, chivalry and one-upsmanship. She cries "Ivan!" in relief that he is safe. And he replies smoothly, "Sir Ivan, if you please. Virtue, it seems, has been rewarded." For once she has no reply.

Comment

More the work of one man than most films, *The Assassination Bureau* was produced, designed and scripted by Michael Relph. The film was based on an idea from a Jack London book which Relph had read in San Francisco. Relph had taken on the writing of the screenplay and the colorful Edwardian production design almost out of necessity; other screenwriters' work hadn't worked out and the designer he wanted wasn't available at the right time. In *Kinematograph Weekly* (February 3, 1968), Relph said, "I always think the producer does have a certain amount of time on his hands once the picture has been set up — he has more of a coordinating role. The shooting date was postponed for two or three months and this gave me the extra time I needed."

"It's a sort of in-joke, really, but the various sequences are typical of the countries concerned: in France, it's a sort of French farce; in Italy, an Italianate drama of poison and intrigue; and in Germany it's all rather bucolic and very military, with the Bureau's power-crazed local representative planning to drop a bomb from a zeppelin on Europe's assembled heads of state so he can take over."

Director Basil Dearden was the perfect addition to the mix: an intellectual, quiet, dedicated man whose gentle exterior masked a man who knew exactly what he wanted from his cast and crew and how to get it. Like Sir Carol Reed before him, as Dearden directed, his lips would move silently, repeating the actors' words, so the timing and nuances were correct.

The complexity of the sets and plot didn't faze him at all. "It's all a matter of planning.... I guess the thing that would worry me the most would be a story with only two characters. If you're asked to take a story with just two or three characters and one basic set, that's really a test of your resourcefulness" (Paramount Pictures press release). Not that that would be a problem here; the logistics of the storyline in so many different cities and the need to match the city with the appropriate period must have

PARIS - BASEL - ZUR!

Ivan (Oliver Reed) looking sinister in *The Assassination Bureau* (Paramount, 1969).

been daunting in the extreme but *The Assassination Bureau* pulls it off superbly.

Reed's Ivan is a masterly blend of action, romance and acerbic wit, as witnessed by the exchange between him and Sonya:

> SONYA: With your ideas, I'm surprised you're shocked at the thought of war.

DRAGOMILOFF: Not at all. It's purely a matter of business. How can we charge our sort of prices with everybody happily killing each other for a shilling a day?

Pitted against the wiles of the crafty reporter, admirably played by Diana Rigg, he acquits himself well as the gentleman she doesn't expect him to be. Indeed, Sonya is almost a predecessor of Diana Rigg's most famous character, the original Emma Peel of the legendary *Avengers* series on British TV. Sonya is as witty, stylish and resourceful as ever Mrs. Peel was. Coping wonderfully with the restrictive costumes in an essentially action-packed role, she looks beautiful and elegant at all times. Her sense of comic timing is also a perfect match for Reed's own.

Filmed in Black Park (famous for Hammer exteriors), Paris, Venice and Veneto, Vienna and Zurich, it's as much a travelogue as a historic comedy-thriller. Filming began in January 1968 and the film was released in the U.K. on March 10, 1969, and in the USA on March 23. It rolled out over Europe between April (in Paris!) and December in Finland. And in 1970 it was nominated for a Golden Globe award for Best English-Language Foreign Film.

Business at the box office was brisk and the critics seemed kindly disposed to the film. *The Morning Telegraph* (March 24, 1969): "[The cast makes] *The Assassination Bureau* a lively joy to watch. If, that is, you don't think about it"; *Films in Review* (May 1969): "*The Assassination Bureau* has an asset in Diana Rigg's performance as a feminist newspaper reporter in Edwardian England who tracks down, falls for, and I suppose can be said to redeem, the head of the assassination bureau (adequately played by Oliver Reed)"; *Newark Evening News*: "Miss Rigg looks pretty in a towel and unperturbed when she discovers a time bomb in the canopy over her bed. It's the same expression she has in her love scenes with Reed.... Reed has been getting the big push in movies the past year. It's difficult to understand why, with the abundance of good young film actors in London. He has a very heavy jaw, which supports two big eyes that keep rolling around through all his expressions"; *Filming* (May 1969): "Basil Dearden extracts [Reed's] best performance yet as the sinister, tongue in cheek, daredevil head of an agency whose services are hired to bump off the occasional head of state...."

Hannibal Brooks (1969)

Scimitar Films; released in the U.K. and in the U.S. by United Artists; Thanks to the people and authorities of Munich and Bavaria, Germany, and Tyrol and Vorarlberg, Austria

Crew—Producer-Director: Michael Winner; Screenplay: Dick Clement, Ian Lafrenais, from a story by Michael Winner, adapted from a story by Tom Wright; Original Music: Francis Lai; Cinematographer: Robert Paynter; Film Editors: Peter Austen-Hunt, Lionel Selwyn; Production Design: John Stoll; Art Direction: Jurgen Kiebach; Hair Stylist: Stephanie Kaye; Makeup Artist: Richard Mills; Production Managers: Clifton Brandon, Laci Von Ronay; Assistant Directors: Michael Dryhurst, Udo Graf Lambsdorff; Construction Manager: Harry Arbour; Sound Recordists; John Brommage, Hugh Strain; Dubbing Editor: Russ Hill; Special Effects: Irwin Lange; Camera Operators: Tony Troke, Hans Jura; Music Arranger: Christian Gaubert; Location Managers: James Crayford, Eberhardt Junkersdorf, Timothy Pitt Miller, Wolfgang Von Schiber; Elephant Trainer: Andre Beilfuss.

Cast—Oliver Reed (Stephen "Hannibal" Brooks), Michael J. Pollard (Packy), Wolfgang Preiss (Col. Von Haller), John Alderton (Bernard), Helmut Lohner (Willi), Peter Carsten (Kurt), Karin Baal (Vronia), Ralf Wolter (Dr. Mendel), Jurgen Draeger (Sami), Maria Brockenhoff (Anna), Til Kiwe (Von Haller's Sergeant), Ernst Fritz Furbringer (Elephant Keeper Kellerman), Erik Jelde (Zookeeper), Fred Haltiner (Josef), John Porter-Davison (Geordie), Terence Sewards (Twilight), James Donald (Padre). Aida the Elephant (Lucy).

Synopsis

Stephen Brooks (Oliver Reed) is waiting out the war in a German prisoner of war camp, quite content, with no wish to escape. He understands that the people of each country did not want the war — they are merely the cannon fodder; he is almost a pacifist. He and some of his fellow prisoners go to the Munich Zoo to help care for the animals since many of the zoo employees have been drafted into the army and the camp kommandant is happy to provide free labor. Brooks finds himself in charge of Lucy, the elephant, whose needs he comes to understand with affection. When the RAF bombs the zoo, Brooks is horrified when Lucy's compound takes a hit and her keeper is killed. Some of the prisoners, led by Packy (Michael J. Pollard), a brash American, take the opportunity to escape, but Brooks stays to help the elephant. The High Command agrees with the Minister that Lucy must be taken to safety at Innsbruck, and Brooks, with an antagonistic guard and a gentle one, is detailed to take her. Their transport is

In *Hannibal Brooks* (Scimitar/United Artists, 1969), the title character (Oliver Reed) hides from the Nazis in a deserted shack.

commandeered by Colonel Von Haller (Wolfgang Preiss) and so they must walk.

Brooks is content to amble through the lovely countryside, tolerating his guard, until they stop for the night and the drunken guard tries to rape a young girl. Brooks intervenes and the angry German starts firing his rifle wildly, endangering Lucy. In protecting her, Brooks kills the guard. His other guard, who hated his companion, agrees that they will continue the journey. The girl elects to travel with them; their new destination is neutral Switzerland.

Soon they run into Packy, who has recruited a band of guerrillas to harass the Germans. He's amused that Brooks still has the elephant in tow and asks how they will get to their destination. Brooks indicates a pathway over the Alps and, when Packy scoffs, replies, "Hannibal did it." From then on, "Hannibal" is his nickname. Brooks and Lucy meet Packy and the group on a couple of occasions and inadvertently help in the sabotage until they are cornered by Von Haller near the border. The girl goes to intercede for them and returns with the promise that they can safely pass the checkpoint. But Brooks and Packy have seen the soldiers and reluctantly follow her; Von Haller has her shot on the road and the group scatters. Their only path is blocked by the nest-like checkpoint, partly on the mountain and partly supported by wooden buttresses in the hillside. While Packy keeps the soldiers busy, Brooks slithers down the mountainside and ropes the buttresses; Lucy gets her revenge for the bombing of her home by heaving the supports away and pitching the checkpoint into the valley far below. The group finish their walk to freedom. Packy agrees that they couldn't have succeeded without Lucy and Brooks murmurs, "Why do you think I brought her along?"

Comment

It has been reported that Steve McQueen had been penciled in for the Michael J. Pollard part, which would have been fun, given his *Great Escape* persona. Reed as Stephen Brooks looks to be having a ball, and *why not* ambling through the pretty Austrian scenery full of sunny, flower-strewn fields, blue lakes, forests and villages of prettily painted chalets. Michael Winner's penchant for location filming has never been better served, but filming in Bavaria between May and July 1968 must have been a logistical nightmare.

The story, from Tom Wright's war memoir, was written by Winner. Dick Clements and Ian Lafrenais produced the script; they hadn't Winner's touch and they made Brooks sulky and ineffectual, deliberately awkward at every opportunity.

Aida the elephant had better treatment than most movie stars with her own portable home. She had warm water pumped over her for rainstorm sequences and she got to sleep with Oliver Reed!

Winner was supposed to have begun work on *William the Conqueror* on May 6, 1968, but when it was postponed, he was sufficiently prepared to switch to *Hannibal Brooks*. The logistics would have reduced some directors to nervous collapse; not Winner, who never believes in worrying about future disasters with the result being they rarely occur.

The humor, which was evidently intended to be topmost throughout the film, gets sidetracked by the violence of the resistance fighters and there isn't much humor in the second half of the film. Helmut Löhner as the gentle Austrian guard, who like Brooks, isn't enamored of war makes a splendid contribution — though we see his death coming long before he does. Wolfgang Preiss as the archetypal Nazi officer is most convincing and James Donald as the padre, whose subtly gentle humor is wasted on most of the POWs, is excellent. Reed's other co-star was several tons of elephant whom the actor insisted on sleeping with for three nights in order to build up a relationship, and vice versa one presumes.

Released in the U.K. in May 1969 and in the U.S. on April 30, 1969, the film was well received. *Catholic Film Newsletter* (March 30, 1969): "There is something irresistibly winning about this"; *Morning Telegraph* (May 1, 1969): "Out and out nonsense"; *Sunday News* (April 27, 1969): "Oliver Reed and Michael J. Pollard are good teaming, because Reed is a fine comedian and Pollard is funny just standing there"; *Newark Evening News* (May 1, 1969): "Oliver Reed is sympathetic if a bit of a stuffed shirt"; *The Villager* (May 1, 1969): "Oliver Reed is very very good. Mr. Reed has style and elan in generous amounts"; *Monthly Film Bulletin* (May 1969): "Oliver Reed is unable to bring much conviction to Brooks' curious obsession"; *Sunday Telegraph* (March 16, 1969): "Just because Pollard provides the fireworks, the beautifully quiet, resigned performance of Oliver Reed shouldn't be under-estimated"; *Evening News* (May 13, 1969): "Mr. Reed and the elephant probably speak for the futility of war; Mr. Pollard

Above: Oliver Reed checks out Lucy's toenails in *Hannibal Brooks* (Scimitar/United Artists, 1969). *Left:* Oliver Reed as the prisoner of war turned zookeeper in Michael Winner's comedy-adventure *Hannibal Brooks* (Scimitar/ United Artists, 1969).

for the voice of violence and box office. At the end up comes a sub-title: 'And they all lived happily ever after.' Those incinerated, machine-gunned Germans didn't."

This movie is one of the best whether you like comedy or wartime exploits; it's a good addition to the canon of Oliver Reed's films.

Women in Love (1969)

Brandywine Productions; released by United Artists in the U.K. in 1969 and in the U.S. in 1970

Crew— Director: Ken Russell; Writer-Producer: Larry Kramer; From the novel by D.H. Lawrence;

Gerald (Oliver Reed) and Gudrun (Glenda Jackson) have a rare moment of peace in Ken Russell's groundbreaking film of D.H. Lawrence's *Women in Love* (United Artists, 1969).

Co-Producer: Martin Rosen; Associate Producer: Roy Baird; Original Music: Georges Delerue; Cinematographer: Billy Williams; Film Editing: Michael Bradsell; Art Director: Ken Jones; Set Decoration: Harry Cordwell; Costume Designer: Shirley Russell; Makeup Artist: Charles Parker; Hair Stylist: A.G. Scott; Unit Manager: Neville C. Thompson; Assistant Director: Jonathan Benson; Set Dresser and Designer: Luciana Arrighi; Prop Master: George Ball; Construction Supervisor: Jack Carter; Dubbing Mixer: Maurice Askew; Dubbing Editor: Terry Rawlings; Sound Recordist: Brian Simmons; Assistant Camera: Stephen Claydon; Camera Operator: David Harcourt; Wardrobe Supervisor: Shura Cohen; Continuity: Angela Allen; Production Controller: Harry Benn; Location Manager: Lee Bolon; Assistant to Producers: Tom Erhardt; Choreographer: Terry Gilbert.

Cast— Alan Bates (Rupert Birkin), Oliver Reed (Gerald Crich), Glenda Jackson (Gudrun Brangwen), Jennie Linden (Ursula Brangwen), Eleanor Bron (Hermione Roddice), Alan Webb (Thomas Crich), Vladek Sheybal (Loerke), Catherine Willmer (Mrs. Crich), Sarah Nicholls (Winifred Crich), Sharon Gurney (Laura Crich), Christopher Gable (Tibby Lupton), Michael Gough (Tom Brangwen), Norma Shebbeare (Mrs. Brangwen), Nike Arrighi (Contessa), James Laurenson (Minister), Michael Graham Cox (Palmer), Richard Heffer (Loerke's Friend), Michael Garratt (Maestro), Leslie Anderson (Barber), Charles Workman (Gittens), Barrie Fletcher, Brian Osborne (Miners), Christopher Ferguson (Basis Crich), Richard Fitzgerald (Salsie).

Synopsis

The English Midlands, cradle of the Industrial Revolution, 1920s. Gudrun (Glenda Jackson) and Ursula (Jennie Linden) Brangwen are liberated sisters in the colliery town where Ursula is a teacher. Gudrun, the more extreme of the pair, has just returned from London where she studied art. They attend a wedding; neither feel certain whether they will marry in future. Gudrun is attracted to Gerald Crich (Oliver Reed), the bride's brother and heir to the local mining company. Ursula is drawn to Rupert Birkin (Alan Bates), a school inspector engaged to the bizarre Hermione (Eleanor Bron). When Rupert insults Hermione at her garden party, they break up, leaving the way open for Ursula, no matter that their views on the nature of love differ.

While the sisters are out walking one day, Gerald appears on horseback, racing a train to the crossing. His cruelty to and mastery of his mount excite Gudrun. At a garden party beside a lake, the sisters have an unsettling encounter with some large steers. After that incident, they drift peacefully in a canoe on the lake. The calm is shattered by the drowning of Gerald's sister (Sharon Gurney) and her new husband (Christopher Gable). In an effort to distract Gerald from his grief, Rupert suggests a wrestling match. They fight, which strangely brings them closer together. Rupert proposes a relationship with Gerald as "pure love" without sex but Gerald doesn't understand. As Gerald's father (Alan Webb) lies dying and his mad mother (Catherine Wilmer) adds to the sadness, Rupert and Ursula become lovers. After his father's death, Gerald goes to Gudrun for sex. While Rupert and Ursula's relationship deepens, Gerald and Gudrun circle each other warily. The two couples decide to vacation in Switzerland. Initially idyllic, the trip becomes a nightmare for Gerald as Gudrun becomes repelled by him and is attracted to Loerke (Vladek Sheybal), a homosexual artist traveling with his young lover (Richard Heffer). The situation worsens when Rupert and Ursula leave for Italy. Gudrun questions Gerald's lack of love for her and then initiates sex during which he loses control and attacks her. She moves into Loerke's room the next day. Gerald assaults Loerke and strangles Gudrun, leaving her gasping in the snow. He walks off into the mountains, lies down in the snow and freezes to death. Back in England Rupert and Ursula discuss the difficulty of love. Rupert continues to believe it to be possible for a man to love a woman but also have a nonsexual love for a man.

Comment

It's typical of Oliver Reed's career that, arguably, his best performance in his best film is best remembered as the one in which he ... more about that later.

Women in Love continued his string of controversial films, and came by its reputation honestly; the source novel and its author created quite a stir of their own. D.H. (David Herbert) Lawrence (1885–1930) was one of England's best — and most often banned — novelists, most famously for *Lady Chatterley's Lover* which made the list in 1929. *The Rainbow* (1915) had previously been banned as was its sequel *Women in Love* (1916).

Like many novelists, Lawrence based his works on personal experience. His father had been a coal miner, the character of Birkin was based on himself and Reed's Gerald was, presumably, based on Middleton Murray, Lawrence's best friend.

Lawrence found his ideal interpreter in director Ken Russell, who, like the author, had his own problems with censorship. *Women in Love* was Russell's third feature film. He did, however, have plenty of experience with Reed, having directed him in two outstanding BBC productions, *The Debussy Film* (1965) and *Dante's Inferno* (1965) for the prestigious *Monitor* arts series.

Russell wrote in his 1991 book *Altered States*, "I suppose United Artists initially considered me for the project because they saw it as a high-brow art movie and were mindful of my work on *Monitor*. And when they asked me if I'd be interested in looking at a script based on the Lawrence epic, I naturally said, 'Yes,' thinking they meant Lawrence of Arabia! So, imagine my surprise when I discovered there was another Lawrence besides T.E., who was, in his way, equally famous. Alan Bates was keen to play the role of Birkin and actually grew a beard to convince us of his resemblance to the author. United Artists concurred and also went along with my plan for Oliver Reed as Gerald. In my opinion, Oliver Reed should have received an Oscar." In the book *An Appalling Talent—Ken Russell* he says, "In a roundabout way I owe *Women in Love* to *Billion Dollar Brain*. United Artists liked the Michael Caine film and thought it got a raw deal from right-wing critics, and that I could do better with a more sympathetic subject anyway. One day the two bright sparks of the company, David Chasman, head of the London office, and David Picker, son of the vice-president, got in touch with me. 'We both feel that this is the right subject for you.' Casting was difficult. Because I'd been immersed in television and had mostly used un-

Gerald (Oliver Reed) looks glum as Gudrun (Glenda Jackson) looks on in *Women in Love* (United Artists, 1969).

knowns or actors who didn't look like actors, and since I didn't do films or the theatre much, I was totally out of touch with the real talent to hand. United Artists said Oliver Reed would be suitable as Gerald — I had worked with him before.... [H]e couldn't have played it better."

Filming began in June 1968 with extensive location work, mostly within a twenty-five mile radius of Sheffield including: Sherwood Forest, Bretton Hall (the picnic scene), Newhall School, Thorsley Hall, and Bobbins Mill (Rupert and Ursula's cottage). This continued for three weeks before moving to Derby for six weeks. The wedding scene was shot at St. Giles' Church in Matlock, and the funeral at Belper Urban District Cemetery. Elverston Castle (built in 1633) stood in for Shortlands, preceding ten days at Gateshead (the Crich colliery). Interiors were filmed at Merton Park Studios,

Wimbledon — a triumphant homecoming for Oliver Reed.

The production concluded in Zermatt, Switzerland, near the Matterhorn. As this was a pollution-free zone, no cars (or, for that matter, roads) were permitted. The unit's considerable equipment had to be brought in by train. All told, *Women in Love* required four months of filming.

In *Kinematograph Weekly* (September 7, 1968), Ken Russell said, "I prefer to make films about [people I know], or believe to have lived in reality. This story ... brings an opportunity to dig into the shifting re-assessments of relationships and the ever changing surfaces." In order to achieve this goal, Russell needed cast members willing to bare their souls — and more — to reveal the emotional and sexual torment of their characters. And the most tortured of these was Gerald Crich. Cut to Oliver Reed...

While filming *Hannibal Brooks* for Michael Winner on location in Austria, Reed was approached by Russell on June 6, 1968, to discuss *Women in Love*. Reed was, of course, well acquainted with Russell—a problem he discussed with Winner. According to *Evil Spirits—The Life of Oliver Reed*, the actor told Winner, "Russell wants me to do a film with him. But he's a television director. I'm in movies now. It's a very arty script. I'm trying to be a commercial actor." Fortunately, Winner was able to persuade him to make the film; Reed and Gerald Crich were a match made in Hell. In the novel, Lawrence described Crich as "a fair, suntanned type, rather above middle height, well made, and almost exaggeratedly well dressed. But, about him was the strange, guarded look, the unconscious glisten; as if he did not belong to the same creation of the people around him. His gleaming beauty, maleness; like a young god, a good-humored smiling wolf did not blind her to the significant, sinister stillness in his bearing, the lurking danger of his unsubsided temper." Remove the word "fair" and Oliver Reed stands before us. But Reed had his own take on his appearance; in the *Women in Love* pressbook he is quoted as saying: "I look like a sixties person, like I fell out of a garbage can."

Having secured Reed, Russell next cast Alan Bates who, like Reed, was one of the sixties' biggest stars, and had appeared in several arthouse films including *Georgy Girl* (1966). Russell briefly considered reversing their final casting, but wisely changed his mind. Jennie Linden originally begged off due to the recent birth of her son, but was persuaded to do the film after Russell pursued her to her isolated cottage in Wales. Glenda Jackson of the Royal Shakespeare Company was initially rejected by Russell due to her appearance (varicose veins!) but he was won over by her talent and screen presence. According to Chris Bryant's *Glenda Jackson: The Biography*,

Women in Love had all the marks of a potential box-office success. The cast was impressive.... Despite the fact that Russell had very little money with which to make *Women in Love* (so little that Bates and Reed were persuaded to work for just a share of the profits—an almost unheard-of practice in those days) Glenda had mounted an assiduous campaign for a part in the film.... To get Oliver Reed ... Russell had to clamber up a mountain in the Alps where Reed was filming *Hannibal Brooks* for Michael Winner.... [I]n order to keep Reed on board Russell was forced to accept changes to the screenplay. The four main characters were only able to gather together for the first time for a reading as filming was about to start. Oliver Reed described the scene in Russell's house: "Suddenly this woman sat on a chair on the other side of the room, and this rather plain truck started to make the air move. So I just mumbled my lines, because I had no identity towards Glenda. I didn't know her from Eve; never heard of her. I'd heard of Shakespeare, but not this truck sitting across the room from me. Unlike her I wasn't associated with *art*: I made commercial films. I love motor cars, and you can judge a car by its pitch; suddenly, I'd met a truck, no less, and when its engine started to rev I began to realize it had a different pitch to what I'd expected. Glenda was like a Ford truck with a highly tuned V8 engine in it. If an engine is properly tuned it doesn't care about the road. So, more than making the air move, she began to eat up the road very quickly, because she didn't care about the hypocrisy of the old structure of cinema, the star system and the casting-couch. Glenda didn't take that route. She came straight from the dust of the theatre and she began to growl."

[A]lthough the relationship between Glenda and Reed was sometimes heated, if anything this added piquancy to the onscreen battle of wills. On one notable occasion Glenda refused to accept Russell and Reed's reading of one of the sex scenes. Reed's version of events is shot through with his usual insecurities, but is nevertheless revealing: "Russell and I were trying to convince her that I should rape her and be the dominant factor in that particular love scene. She was so aggressive about it, saying no, *she* would dominate *me*. In the end we had to call in the producers, because this unknown girl was being so headstrong. She thought she had to rape me, had to completely dominate me,

Gerald (Oliver Reed) ponders his few options in Ken Russell's outstanding film of D.H. Lawrence's *Women in Love* (United Artists, 1969).

had to climb on top and be the aggressor. But she wasn't experienced enough to know that to be on top is not the be-all and end-all of the conquest. I don't think she would ever have compromised had she not believed that there was still enough superstition left in male vanity to warrant the leading man, and the director, to think she should be underneath getting fucked for the things that she said."

Two weeks before filming began, Russell brought the quartet together at his house for a read-through ... and that's when the trouble began. Reed and Jackson could not have been further apart on their general views on life, but their main point of departure was sex — and how it related to their characters. According to *Evil Spirits*, Reed asked, "How could a beautiful, feminine girl like you emasculate a tough, rugged character like me?" And that was just

the beginning. *Real* sex also created a potential problem; Jackson felt it was unnecessary to tell Russell that she was pregnant until the production started. Since she had to appear in several nude scenes, this could have been a disaster but Russell took it in his stride and shot them in a way that "nothing showed."

The film's most serious problem, though, involved a scene in which "everything showed." Lawrence's novel included a nude wrestling match — outdoors — between Gerald and Rupert, and Russell was, naturally, keen on filming it. Initially, both Reed and Bates were also keen, but as "the day" grew closer, the pair became less and less keen. The scene would have been the first in film history to show two actors — both major stars — completely nude. While, on paper, this appealed to the two actors, the reality of it actually being on film was something else. According to Russell in *Altered*

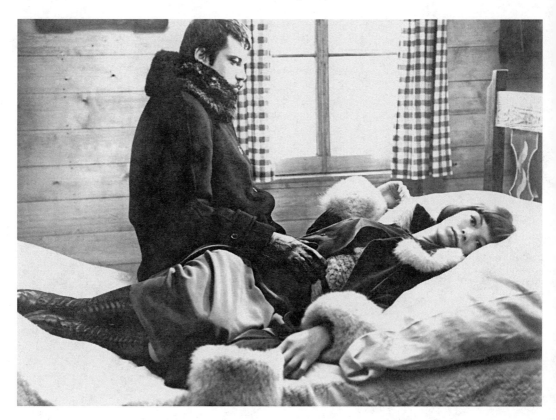

Gerald (Oliver Reed) seeks, but does not find, solace from Gudrun (Glenda Jackson) in *Women in Love* (United Artists, 1969).

States, "[A]s the day scheduled for the big match approached, [Bates] developed a cold. At the same time Oliver hurt his foot and they both had doctor's certificates to prove it. By now the producers had realized the great potential of the scene and were dead scared it might not happen. Two days before the big fight, with Alan blowing his nose every five minutes and Oliver hobbling around like Joseph Goebbels, they were ready to throw in the towel. I ignored their ailments ... because I noticed that during 'takes' Oliver managed not to limp at all and Alan managed not to sniff. Though they more than made up for it directly I said, 'Cut!'"

The reason for their maladies was obvious to Russell; it's one thing to discuss such a scene, but quite another to have the balls to actually do it. *Films in London* (September, 1969) has Reed explaining: "If one isn't very well hung anyway, it's no good having a big paunch as well." He promptly lost weight. Realizing the scene had to be shot, the two stars developed a

friendly rivalry as to which was the "biggest" star — literally! There was some cheating involved; Reed, shall we say, tried to "keep up appearances" between takes by rubbing himself vigorously with a towel — and teasing the continuity lady by saying that she might use her tape measure to ensure the correct proportions!

According to Bilbow and Gau's *Lights, Camera, Action! A Century of the Cinema*, "Reed remained philosophical about that scene, relishing the honor of becoming the legitimate cinema's first full-frontal male nude. 'It will be something to tell my grandchildren, that I was once seen stark naked by millions of women all over the world.' He expected to run the gauntlet of insults and mickey-taking wherever he went after the film opened."

Russell, in a bow to the British Board of Film Classification, moved the scene indoors, to be shot in front of a flickering fireplace in a darkened room rather than in the outdoor setting envisioned by Lawrence. Larry Kramer, producer and scriptwriter, recalls a letter to John Trevelyan, secretary of the BBFC (but the power behind the Board's decisions): "I am sure you will appreciate what an ambitious film this is, and what an extraordinary novel we are tackling. We have been extraordinarily faithful in our adaptation, and nothing appears in the script which does not come from the novel. We feel we are embarking on an extraordinary creative experience which we would like to have you share with us" (Mathews, 179). Trevelyan's reply, according to Tom D. Mathews' book *Censored*: "While we are prepared to accept the wrestling scene, we would like you to remove if possible full length shots in which genitals are clearly visible. The main trouble lies in shots where the two boys are standing still." After this was done, Trevelyan — who had savaged *The Curse of the Werewolf* worse than Reed had his victims — demanded that the scene be further darkened. Russell informed Trevelyan that no more could be done, as there was no material in the cutting room to replace any continuing offensive shots. The censor finally agreed. Russell maintained, "The full nude has a dignity that half a body does not have" (Mathews, 180).

Lawrence believed, well ahead of his time, that adults should have the freedom to feel and express sexual love without guilt or repercussions. Unfortunately, Oliver Reed's Gerald would become a tragic victim of the sexual mores under which he lived. We first encounter Gerald in formal dress at his sister's wedding. Reed and Russell brilliantly capture the character in a few seconds of screen time: tough, in charge, full of himself, but with a soft core. Reed in the pressbook says: "I like everything I'm not. I like gentle people, puppies. I like softness because life is so hard."

Unlike his friend Rupert, Gerald is uncomfortable in expressing himself; he is a man of action, not words. But Rupert is determined to draw him out and draw him in to his philosophy.

GERALD: Have you ever really loved ... anybody?

RUPERT: Yes and no.

GERALD: But not finally.

RUPERT: Finally? No.

GERALD: Nor I.

RUPERT: Do you want to?

GERALD: I don't know.

RUPERT: I do. I want the finality of love.

GERALD: I don't believe a woman, and nothing but a woman, will ever make my life.

RUPERT: What do you live for, Gerald?

GERALD: I suppose I live for my work, and, other than that, I live to go on living.

RUPERT: I find that one needs ... one needs one single pure activity. I would call love a single pure activity, but I don't really love anybody. Not now.

GERALD: You mean that if there isn't a woman, then there's nothing?

RUPERT: More or less. Seeing there is no God.

Rupert, in addition to loving a woman, also wants to love a man, but in a non-sexual way. He is confounded by this belief, which eludes the more pragmatic Gerald, who is, naturally, the object of Rupert's desire for a male-to-male platonic relationship.

RUPERT: The relationship between a man and a woman isn't the last word.... We want something broader. I believe in the additional perfect relationship between man and man additional to marriage.

GERALD: Well, I don't see how they can be the same.

RUPERT: No, not the same. Equally important. Equally creative.

GERALD: I know you believe something like that, only I can't feel it, you see.

In this philosophical exchange, Rupert is upbeat, excited; Gerald, confused and struggling, wanting to understand. But it is just beyond him; poor Gerald is having enough trouble dealing with the equally introspective Gudrun. After their initial coupling following the death of Gerald's father, their relationship begins to unravel while Rupert and Ursula's catches fire. Despite his personal advantages, Gerald is basically a simple man with simple needs. Gudrun, though, needs "something more" than Gerald is capable of providing beyond dazzling beauty of the snowscape is brilliantly contrasted by the ugliness of their affair.

Gerald (Oliver Reed) confronts his lover Gudrun (Glenda Jackson) and his replacement (Vladek Sheybal) in *Women in Love* (United Artists, 1969).

GUDRUN: How much do you love me?

GERALD: How much do you think I love you?

GUDRUN: Very little indeed.

GERALD: Why don't I love you?

GUDRUN: I don't know why you don't. I've been good to you. When you first came to me in that fearful state, I had to take pity on you ... but it was never love.

GERALD: Why do you keep repeating it ... that there was never any love?

GUDRUN: You don't think you love me, do you?

GERALD: No.

GUDRUN: And you will never love me, will you?

GERALD: Why do you torture me?

Reed and Jackson are brilliant in this scene, as they are throughout the entire film.

Her verbal laceration of him is painful to watch, far more so than a vicious physical beating could have been. When Gudrun takes up with the slimy "artist" across the hall, Gerald dies. His suicide in the snow is merely a formality. When Birkin and Ursula review the tragedy in their cottage, the film ends on an even more tragic and completely unexpected note.

URSULA: Did you need Gerald?

BIRKIN: Yes.

URSULA: Aren't I enough for you?

BIRKIN: You are enough for me as far as a woman is concerned. You are all women to me. But I wanted a man friend as eternal as you and I are eternal.

URSULA: You believe it. It is an obstinacy in a theory ... a perversion. You can't have two kinds of love. Why should you?

BIRKIN: It seems as if I can't. Yet I wanted it.

URSULA: You can't have it because it's impossible.

BIRKIN: I don't believe that.

The film ends, with a jarring musical chord, unresolved, leaving the viewer stunned and confused. Despite the film's controversial scenes, over-the-edge plotline and despairing cynicism, *Women in Love* became the biggest hit in London upon its November 1969 release. The film was a hugely popular success in both Britain and America, although perhaps for the wrong reason. One wonders how much the novelty shock appeal of the well-publicized wrestling match outweighed the film's cinematic brilliance in drawing an audience, although it probably mattered very little to United Artists.

Reviews were generally quite positive for both the film and its makers, considering its controversial subject and presentation. "Oliver Reed in his familiar sullen, solitary aspect has a fair shot at Gerald. They have worked wonders with the look of the thing. Visually, it is an exquisite film. And the awkward bits haven't been funked. When Birkin and Gerald ... strip and wrestle naked in the library Mr. Bates and Mr. Reed do, indeed, strip and wrestle naked" (*The Sunday Times,* November 16, 1969); "*Women in Love* is as unlikely a candidate for popular success as *Midnight Cowboy,* but it shows every sign of being another box office smasheroo for United Artists" (*The Sunday Times,* November 23, 1969); "The work of D.H. Lawrence has such a literary style and, in this case, is so imbued with eroticism and despair that it is quite impossible to bring it to the screen and please everyone. The film gives the impression of a brave and intelligent effort that has been defeated (but only just) by the rambling subject.... This is a sombre, introspective look at a collection of unusual people" (*Kinematograph Weekly,* November 15, 1969); "It's a dazzling feat in filmmaking.... [M]ore surprising is Oliver Reed's fine, square, tormented and tormenting Gerald. But, of course, it's Ken Russell's film and its excesses are his" (*The Sunday Telegraph,* November 16, 1969); "Although Alan Bates, Oliver Reed, and Jennie Linden are all remarkably good Glenda Jackson's Gudrun is outstanding. Although there is a great deal of dialogue in the film — all of it faithful to Lawrence — the expressions of passion are entirely physical, balletic. Ken Russell has taken this good work of [producer] Kramer and turned it into a masterpiece of filming" (*The Observer,* November 16, 1969); "[Bates and Reed] bare their bodies and wrestle without inhibition. And as cinema, it works" (*The Sunday Mirror,* November 16, 1969); "*Women in Love* is a film about all-absorbing human passion. It makes other films look wan and underfed by comparison. It re-

Gerald (Oliver Reed) brutalizes Gudrun (Glenda Jackson) in *Women in Love* (United Artists, 1969).

stores the idea of a story to the screen. It is an immensely complex, immensely skillful film. Oliver Reed as the tycoon's son whose love is physical only, looks like he's been hewn from the dark side of one of our mines. At last this actor has a part whose pent-up forcefulness matches his own" (*The Evening Standard*, November 13, 1969); "In terms of filmmaking, this is certainly Ken Russell's most glamorous work to date, mounted with evident care and photographed spectacularly by Billy Williams" (*The Financial Times*, November 14, 1969); "Exceptional and provocative" (*News of the World*, November 16, 1969); "Oliver Reed, in particular, conveys more substantially and credibly the man of blood and iron, the doomed creation of the Industrial Age than the Gerald Crich of Lawrence's original" (*Monthly Film Bulletin*, December, 1969); "A loving intelligent faithful adaptation. Alan Bates, Oliver Reed, Glenda Jackson and Jennie Linden are most attractive and stylish" (*New York Times*, March 26, 1970).

Given *Women in Love*'s success with both audiences and critics, it should be no surprise that the film received more than its share of award nominations. From the British Board of Film and Television Arts came the following nominations (without a winner): Alan Bates (Best Actor), Glenda Jackson (Best Actress), Luciana Arrighi (Art Director), Billy Williams (Cinematography), Shirley Russell (Costume Design), Ken Russell (Director), Larry Kramer (Screenplay), Georges Delerone (Music), Terry Rawlins (Soundtrack), Jennie Linden (Most Promising Newcomer), and the film itself. From the Academy Awards: Glenda Jackson (winner); Billy Williams, Ken Russell and Larry Kramer were nominated. From the Golden Globes: Best English-Language Foreign Film (winner); Glenda Jackson and Ken Russell were nominated. Jackson was also voted Best Actress by the National Board of Review, the National Society of Film Critics and the New York Film Critics.

Reed was not nominated for any award but he certainly was deserving; he would never deliver a more convincing performance. It might be said that no one involved in *Women in Love* would ever do anything better. Given the quality of the cast and the crew, it's no wonder that the film was a masterpiece.

The Lady in the Car with Glasses and a Gun (1970)

Columbia Pictures Corporation; Lira Films; released by Columbia Pictures in the U.S. in 1970; no U.K. release; color

Crew— Director: Anatole Litvak; Screenplay and Dialogue: Sebastien Japrisot, Anatole Litvak; from a novel by Sebastien Japrisot; English version dialogue: Richard Harris, Eleanor Perry; Producers: Raymond Danon, Anatole Litvak; Original Music: Michel Legrand; Cinematographer: Claude Renoir; Editors: Ginou Billo, Peter Thornton; Art Director: Willy Holt; Costume Design: Jean Zay; Production Managers: Claude Ganz, Marc Maurette; Unit Production Manager: Rene Fargeas; Sound Engineer: William Robert Sivel; Title Design: Jean Fouchet; Ms. Eggar and Ms. Audran's Wardrobe: Marc Bohan; Musical Director and Conductor: Michel Legrand.

Cast— Samantha Eggar (Danielle "Dany" Lang), Oliver Reed (Michael Caldwell), John McEnery (Yves-Marie aka Philippe), Stephane Audran (Anita Caldwell), Bullie Dixon (Tall Girl), Bernard Fresson (Jean Yvain), Marcel Bozzuffi (Manuel), Philippe Nicaud (Highway Policeman), Martine Kelly (Kiki), Jacques Fabbri (Doctor), Jacques Legras (Policeman), Lisa Jouvet (Danish Tourist), Andre Oumansky (Bernard Thorr), Yves Pignot (Baptistin), Louise Rioton (American Tourist), Maria Meriko (Mme. Picaud), Robert Deac (Titou — Boy in Cassis), Raoul Delfosse (American Tourist), Paule Noelle (Third Secretary), Philippe Baronnet, Philippe Mareuil (Friends), Jacqueline Porel (Second Secretary), Yves Barsacq (Agent), Edmond Ardisson (Garage Night Man), Gilberte Geniat (Village Storekeeper), Monique Melinand (Barmaid), Fred Fisher (Danish Tourist), Henry Czarniak (Garage Proprietor), Claude Vernier (Psychiatrist), Georges Lycan (Café Customer).

Synopsis

As Bastille Day celebrations approach, the near-sighted Dany (Samantha Eggar) is asked by her boss Michael (Oliver Reed) to stay and type an urgent document that he must take to a meeting in Geneva the next day. He brings her to his home where she is reunited with his wife Anita (Stephane Audran), an old acquaintance who is a former prostitute.

Dany completes the massive assignment and, the following day, drives Michael, Anita and their small daughter to Orly Airport. She is then to drive the huge white convertible back to Michael's house, but somehow she finds herself drawn into the traffic flow heading south to the Cote d'Azur. Elated by the powerful car, Dany simply, irresponsibly, goes with the flow.

Strange things begin to happen; when she stops for lunch, several people claim to have seen her the previous day, and after she is attacked, injuring her hand in a gas station washroom, a man claims to have worked on her car the day before. She next picks up Philippe (John McEnery), a tatty hitch-hiker, and has sex with him in a hotel room. As they take a break in a wooded area by the road, Philippe steals the car. Dany takes a bus heading south and in Marseilles finds the car — with a corpse and a gun in the trunk. She is contacted by Philippe and they agree that the body must have been planted there when they were at the hotel. They dispose of the body in a junkyard, and then Philippe mysteriously vanishes. Helped by a friendly trucker (Bernard Fresson) and his partner, Dany goes to Maurice's — the victim's — home, following information she found in his pocket. She tries to call Michael in Geneva for his help but gets nowhere. At the house, she finds a darkroom with nude photos of Anita. As Dany is about to lose her sanity, the mystery is explained. Anita is a nymphomaniac with a precession of sex partners, one of whom — Maurice — she killed. Michael, despite her proclivities, still loves her and planted false clues — including the car which was Maurice's — to incriminate Dany. When she tells him the police have been called, he meekly surrenders.

Comment

The Lady in the Car with Glasses and a Gun was originally planned by director Anatole Litvak to start production in France in the summer of 1968. However, in May, the political situation was tense and it was decided that it was too risky to start filming there. Since, due to the plot, the film could only be shot in the summer, Litvak moved the production back until July 1969 with interiors being shot at Pinewood.

Although the movie is not without interest, the payoff isn't worth the wait. The plot is as clumsy as the title, and the decision to have Oliver Reed explain the incredible machinations in a voice-over at the conclusion is a poor one. It seems to last as long as the rest of the film. Worse, Reed's character Michael lacks any credible motivation (yes, it's only a movie but...) to go to unbelievable lengths in order to protect his psychotic whore of a wife.

Reed does his best to make it all believable but Michael is just too intelligent, successful and attractive to reasonably take the horrific beating Anita has been handing him with her sexual infidelities. Reed explains it all in a well-delivered, almost convincing speech that's actually quite affecting. (He says, in part, "This might surprise you, Dany ... about the number of times she cheated me. You see, I've always been aware of the needs ... I was incapable of supplying and of the young, dirty trash for whom she would so easily drop her dress.")

That said, it's hard to believe that Michael, who found it so easy to move the corpse of Anita's "lover," frame an insanely elaborate plot to incriminate the entirely sympathetic Dany and threaten to actually kill Dany, can't get up the nerve to kill his horrendous wife.

And speaking of young, dirty trash, it's again hard to accept that a nice girl like Dany would ever speak to Philippe (a splendidly nasty performance by John McEnery) let alone "drop her dress" for him. He's as sleazy a low-life as one could hope to never meet; he treats her like dirt, steals her car, and, incredibly, simply vanishes from the plot just before the climax.

The frame-up is one of the most complex — and absurd — ever presented on screen. The pure luck involved in pulling it off would take more space than is available to explain in any understandable detail. But it really doesn't matter; the whole movie is actually a confidence trick on the audience. But — out of this mess came some genuinely intriguing ideas. The huge white convertible that Michael has Dany drive is naturally accepted by her — and the audience — as belonging to him. It's rather stunning to find out that it actually belonged to the corpse! Dany's decision on the spur of the moment to "borrow" the car for a weekend jaunt completely confounded Michael's well-laid plans and he must now follow her and, in effect, lay his traps in reverse. There are a few Hitchcockian touches of mistaken identity and the fear of police intervention that are quite effective. Perhaps Alfred Hitchcock could have made

Michael (Oliver Reed) instructs his secretary Danielle (Samantha Eggar) in the convoluted *The Lady in the Car with Glasses and the Gun* (Columbia, 1970).

something out of this tangled web. Anatole Litvak had shown a talent for this type of film with *Five Miles to Midnight* (1962), a real nail-biter. The writer of the original novel (and collaborator on the script) Sebastien Japrisot was known for his gripping and atmospheric novels, but what works well on the page doesn't always translate to the screen.

The director was not served well by his composer (Michel Legrand) and cinematographer (Claude Renoir) who delivered totally inappropriate products. Dany is a very likable character and the audience should feel more suspense over her plight than we are allowed to due to, perhaps, the above.

The best aspect of the film is the performance of Samantha Eggar; she's terrific, which is good, since her character is in almost every shot. Reed contributes a good performance but he's off screen for the entire middle of the film and,

as previously mentioned, his motivations are less than believable. He looks great, tough, with a stylish wardrobe and slightly graying hair. The film seems a bit out of place in his filmography; he should have been able to find better roles than this after his recent successes.

"The uncomfortably ponderous Oliver Reed contributes to the uncertainty. The film is effective, well colored but uncertain in line and construction. Samantha Eggar gives what is really a virtuoso performance" (*The New York Times*, December 26, 1970); "I can scarcely credit that such an ingenious tale could have fallen to pieces like this ... partly because of a general lack of pace and frisson" (*Monthly Film Bulletin*, November 1971); "An inflated, foggy, complicated thriller with some surprise and color, but a letdown ending. For undemanding audiences. Samantha Eggar wears a look of puzzlement most of the time that is too likely to be shared by any audience confronted with the tangled tale.... But most perfunctory of all is the way an attempt is made to resolve the mystery in a quick montage of shots in the last few minutes" (*Kinematograph Weekly*, August 28, 1971).

The Lady in the Car with Glasses and a Gun does end on an amusing note. After Michael incredibly and meekly gives it all up (why Dany's threat that she's contacted the police dissuades him from killing her after he's already complicit in another murder is puzzling), Dany finds herself in a train compartment with an acquaintance. Her friend is bitching about the terrible weekend she's had; Dany can only smile.

Take a Girl Like You (1970)

Albion Film Corp.; released by Columbia Pictures in the U.K. and in the U.S.

Crew— Director: Jonathan Miller; Writer: George Melly, from the novel by Kingsley Amis; Producer: Hal E. Chester; Associate Producer: L.C. Rudkin; Original Music: Stanley Myers; Cinematographer: Dick Bush; Film Editors: Jack Harris, Rex Pyke; Art Director: Jack Shampan; Set Decorator: Tim Abadie; Makeup Artist: George Partleton; Production Manager: Denis Johnson Jr.; Assistant Directors: Douglas Hermes, Joe Marks; Assistant Art Director: Richard Rambaut; Wardrobe Supervisor: Bridget Sellers; Conductor: Stanley Myers; Production Secretary: Pat O'Donnell.

Cast— Hayley Mills (Jenny Bunn), Oliver Reed (Patrick Standish), Noel Harrison (Julian Ormerod), John Bird (Dick Thompson), Sheila Hancock (Martha Thompson), Amy MacDonald (Wendy), Geraldine Sherman (Anna La Page), Ronald Lacey (Graham McClintock), John Fortune (Sir Gerald), Imogen Hassell (Samantha), Pippa Steel (Ted), Penelope Keith (Tory Lady), Nicholas Courtney (Panel Chairman), George Woodbridge (Publican), Jimmy Gardner (Voter), Nerys Hughes (Teacher), Jean Marlow (Mother), Howard Goorney (Labor Agent).

Synopsis

Jenny Bunn (Hayley Mills), a beautiful and innocent North Country girl, leaves home to teach Primary School in a Southern redbrick town. After taking lodgings with Martha (Sheila Hancock) and Dick Thompson (John Bird), a Labour Councillor, assaults on her virginity become the local sport. First in the queue is Patrick (Oliver Reed), a charming but overconfident instructor at the local polytechnic college who's been having a desultory affair with Anna (Geraldine Sherman), Jenny's fellow lodger. He makes a move on Jenny when he is to meet Anna for a date. Patrick is stunned when, later, after some heavy kissing, Jenny refuses to go further. She tells him she's a virgin, proud of it, and will remain so until she chooses otherwise — preferably after marriage.

Patrick, who has no shortage of sex partners, becomes obsessed with Jenny because he can't have her. He discusses his plight with his urbane friend Julian (Noel Harrison), a wealthy restaurant owner with a grand country house and a sexy girlfriend Wendy (Ami Macdonald). Julian is also interested in Jenny, as is her landlord and Patrick's nerdy roommate Graham (Ronald Lacey). Jenny loves Patrick, but won't give in easily, especially after his tryst with Wendy. Patrick's verbal assaults on the pointlessness of virginity finally weaken her and she agrees to have sex with him at his flat while Julian throws a party at his house. But — Patrick has foolishly told Julian, who "lets it slip" to Jenny. Disgusted, she goes to bed with him instead. Patrick rushes to Julian's and finds them dressing. He argues with Jenny, who runs out. He follows her down the road in his car.

Comment

Take a Girl Like You sticks out like the proverbial sore thumb on Reed's filmography. Its slight tale of boy chasing girl is in direct contrast with the films that sandwich it: the bitter social commentary of *I'll Never Forget What's 'Isname*, the black comedy of *The Assassination Bureau*, the heavy drama of *Women in Love*, and the brutal violence of *The Hunting Party*, *The Devils*, and *Sitting Target*. It was, probably, a good career move on paper as Reed was becoming typecast as a heavy but the film did nothing to alleviate the situation or to advance his standing. It was simply not the kind of film his fans wanted to see.

The original Kingsley Amis novel was praised by *The Saturday Review* as "his biggest and most ambitious and best novel ... wildly comic yet deadly serious." It was the fourth of his novels to be filmed. The movie version began production on March 1, 1969, at Shep-

The worldly Patrick (Oliver Reed) stalks the innocent Jenny (Hayley Mills) in *Take a Girl Like You* (Columbia, 1970).

perton Studios with location work at Beaconsfield, Slough Station, Kingston Road and Walton. *Kinematograph Weekly* (March 22, 1969) reported, "No justification, after all, for fears that the Albion film version of the Kingsley Amis novel has been over-written into yet another swinging, trendy contemporary comedy. I see from the synopsis of the script that George Melly has remained faithful to the splendid original." Others, including Amis, would later argue that point. On the set, Reed told a *Film in London* interviewer:

> I'm more confident now and I'm financially independent. One does change, of course. I'm a harder person, but I've spent a lot of time getting where I am. It's a pity more people don't have that time to get used to wealth and adulation. I've been "the most promising British actor" for ten years now. As long as we make exciting films in Britain, there is no need to go to Hollywood. I just want to make

movies, and modern actors have to be prepared to sacrifice, because acting is now an international business. We're going back to the old days of strolling players; but they used to have carts, and now we have Boeing 707s. I constantly change my mind. People interview me and they say, "In 1962 you said you like Chinese food." Well, that's fine until you get sick on a prawn budgie. You say something and you're held responsible for it. I always qualify everything by saying "I'll change my mind in five minutes." I suppose actors are always warned that someone else is going to come along but the advantage of getting older is that you can't suddenly find a 31-year-old actor. He has to be 31, and to have been around a while. When I started, I could only play young toughs; now, it's different.

The production wrapped on May 30, 1969, and received a trade show well over a year

Hayley Mills and Oliver Reed star in a not-so-light-hearted light-hearted comedy, *Take a Girl Like You* (Columbia, 1970).

later, on September 23, 1970. Another four months passed before the film's London premiere on January 1, 1971; general release came on January 31 to decidedly mixed reviews. *Variety* (September 29, 1969): "Basically it's not a bad little English kitchen sink drama with some strong but low-key performances but a lack of sense of humor, generally wearisome development, and a downbeat ending. Reed's character as written, directed, and performed, is brooding and quarrelsome rather than randy and charming"; *Long Island Press* (December 17, 1970): "A very British trifle without sherry"; *Kinematograph Weekly* (January 2, 1971): "In spite of its fairly frank love scenes and spattering of four-letter words, this is a somewhat trite novelette, but with some popular humor. Hayley Mills adequately conveys a rather wide-eyed innocence, but Oliver Reed appears unhappy in a role too hesitant for his personality"; *The New York Times* (December 17, 1970): "[Director Jonathan] Miller has obtained excellent performances from his cast, notably Mr. Reed.... [I]t has an essentially comic form but is never very funny"; *Evening News* (December 31, 1970): *Daily Express* (December 30, 1970): "Oliver Reed seems to be under the impression that the rapid extension of his index fingers is a highly dramatic method of self-expression. He is wrong"; *Village Voice* (January 25, 1971): "Box office considerations aside, the pairing of Oliver Reed and Hayley Mills hardly seems ideal on the iconographical level, and yet there's a similarity in the fate of these two performers who seem destined to avoid stardom no matter what. Reed tends to stand out in the memory for his relatively unappealing work in the obnoxious films of Michael Winner rather than for those occasions in which his personality has been successfully integrated with the direction of Carol Reed [*Oliver!*] and Ken Russell [*Women in Love*]"; *Daily Mail* (December 31, 1970): "The film (Jonathan Miller's first as a director) takes the fun more sourly and the girl's emotional dilemma more seriously than the novel"; *The Guardian* (January 31, 1971): "It resembles nothing more than a Doris Day movie. Oliver Reed plays the boy who tries to take a girl like her and in the process proves irredeemably boring."

The unkind *Village Voice* review was, in retrospect, half true. Hayley Mills, after a very successful juvenile career (*Tiger Bay* [1959], *The Parent Trap* [1961]) did not become an adult international star, as she chose having a family over films. Reed was, at the time, by any definition, a star. So there!

Kingsley Amis himself was, according to *The Sunday Telegraph* (January 10, 1971), unimpressed: "Amis saw his film for the first time last week. He will say the acting was good. Otherwise, words, for all intents and purposes, fail him."

Take a Girl Like You is by no means a great film, but it isn't as bad as one might think (with Reed playing a Rock Hudson type). He always had a gift for comedy, and although the film has its serious moments, it is generally light and so is he.

Patrick and Jenny have a running argument about her insistence on remaining a virgin and both the dialogue and acting is excellent. Patrick makes his move soon after meeting her.

> PATRICK: I thought we might have dinner some night alone — to help you escape the councilman.
>
> JENNY: It's out of the question. I don't date other girls' boyfriends.
>
> PATRICK: This may seem like some kind of a line, but I've been waiting years for someone like you to come along.
>
> JENNY: At least you say it nice.

Jenny soon gives in — at least on the dinner — and even goes with Patrick to his flat. Patrick kisses her and she responds — momentarily — then pushes him onto the couch. He continues his groping.

> PATRICK: Please! I promise I'll stop when you say stop.
>
> JENNY: I'm saying it now!
>
> PATRICK: I don't understand you. You see, you don't look like a virgin. Nobody cares about virginity. When Mr. Right comes riding through, he won't care.

After Jenny finally has sex — with the sleazy Julian (effectively played by Noel Harrison) — she and Patrick go at each other.

> PATRICK: You and Julian? Why?
>
> JENNY: I don't know!

PATRICK: I demand an explanation!

JENNY: I don't have one!

PATRICK: Just tell me you were drunk!

JENNY: You sweet-talking bastard! You told him about us!

PATRICK: You did all this just to get even?

And off she (and he) goes, the irony of his re-action entirely escaping him. Let's hope he doesn't catch her — this looks like a match made in Hell.

In addition to taking a frank, and sadly accurate, look at sexual pursuits in the sixties, *Take a Girl Like You* also takes on local politics with its jaundiced view of Dick Thompson's campaigning for office.

Although the film is nothing special, it's well worth tracking down. The two leads are excellent, and Reed deserves special mention for even attempting such a role given his track record and fan base.

The Hunting Party (1971)

Brighton Pictures; Levy-Gardner-Levy; released by United Artists in the U.K. and the U.S.; 108 minutes; color

Crew— Director: Don Medford; Screenplay: William W. Norton, Gilbert Alexander, Lou Morheim; Story: Gilbert Alexander, Lou Morheim; Executive Producers: Arthur Gardner, Jules V. Levy; Producer: Lou Morheim; Original Music: Riz Ortolani; Cinematographer: Cecilio Paniagua; Film Editor: Tom Rolf; Art Director: Enrique Alarcon; Set Decorator: Rafael Salazar; Makeup Artist: Jose Antonio Sanchez; Production Supervisor: Geoffrey Haine; Production Manager: Julio Vallejo; Assistant Directors: Gil Carretero, Jose Maria Ochoa; Sound: Leslie Hammond; Sound Effects Editor: Evelyn Rutledge; Special Effects: Manuel Baquero; Stunt Coordinator: Juan Jose Majan; Focus Puller: Ron Drinkwater; Camera Operator: Alec Mills; Wardrobe Supervisor: Tony Pueo; Conductor: Riz Ortolani; Assistant to Producer: Marilyn Fiebelkorn.

Cast— Oliver Reed (Frank Calder), Gene Hackman (Brandt Ruger), Candice Bergen (Melissa Ruger), Simon Oakland (Matthew Gunn), Ronald Howard (Watt Nelson), L.Q. Jones (Hog Warren), Mitchell Ryan (Doc Harrison), William Watson (Jim Loring), G.D. Spradlin (Sam Bayard), Rayford Barnes (Crimp), Bernard Kay (Buford King), Richard Adams (Owney Clark), Dean Selmier (Collins), Sarah Atkinson (Redhead), Francesca Tu (Chinese Girl), Marian Collier (Teacher), Ralph Browne (Sheriff), Carlos Bravo (Cowboy); uncred-ited: Rafael Escudero Garcia (Mexican), Eugenio Garcia (Mario), Emilio Rodrigues Guiar (Priest), Max Slaten (Telegrapher), Lilibeth Solison (Blonde), Bud Strait (Cowboy), Maria Luisa Tovar (Mexican Girl), Christine Larroude, Stephanie Pieritz.

Synopsis

Texas in the 1880s. Outlaw Frank Calder (Oliver Reed) is warned by the sheriff (Ralph Brown) of Ruger County to take his band of killers elsewhere. Calder is tiring of his criminal lifestyle; he is intelligent but illiterate. As he leads his men out of town, he impulsively kid-naps the local schoolteacher whom he feels could teach him to read. But he has made a deadly mistake; Melissa (Candice Bergen) only helps at the school; she's the wife of Brandt Ruger (Gene Hackman), a wealthy, sadistic cat-tleman for whom the county is named. He treats Melissa as a possession and her kidnap-ping as a game ... and a personal insult. He gives chase on his private train with his millionaire playmates Matthew (Simon Oakland), Watt (Ronald Howard), Bayard (G.D. Spalding) and Buford (Bernard Kay), armed with high-powered rifles mounted with telescopic sights, accurate to half a mile. They hunt Calder and his men as they might hunt buffalo. At first, the outlaws are unaware who's killing them but, when they discover Melissa's identity, rightly blame Calder. As the carnage escalates, Ruger is deserted by all but Matthew. When the dec-imated band of outlaws rests in a small village, Hog (L.Q. Jones) attempts to rape Melissa, but she kills him with a knife. After failing to re-move a bullet from his only friend Doc (Mitch-ell Ryan), Calder is forced to shoot him to re-lieve his agony.

Calder and Melissa — now lovers — at-tempt to cross a desert to reach California and a new life together, but Ruger — now alone — catches them. He shoots both his wife and Calder to pieces before collapsing on the sand.

Comment

Oliver Reed had the uncanny ability to be believable in any role, in any genre, in any time period. Think about it; how many actors have successfully played heroes and villains, comedy and drama, horror and musicals, war and ro-mance, period, contemporary and futuristic

Melissa (Candice Bergen) and Frank (Oliver Reed) die horribly in the ultra-violent *The Hunting Party* (United Artists, 1971).

roles and (with *The Hunting Party*) westerns? In a United Artists press release, Reed said, "I've always wanted to play in a good western. I was delighted to find one I liked."

The Hunting Party was a direct descendant of director Sergio Leone's *A Fistful of Dollars* (1964) starring Clint Eastwood, first of the so-called "spaghetti westerns." Leone's film was initially savaged by the critics but is now looked on as a classic — not unlike *The Curse of the Werewolf* and other Hammer films.

The Hunting Party was originally planned to be filmed in Mexico, but the production was shifted to Spain (Almeria, Andalusia and Colemenor regions) due to the belief that the weather conditions were better. As temperatures soared to 115 degrees, this is debatable!

Filming began on June 22, 1970, and ended on September 5. Specific locations included La Pedriza, the Tajo Reno and the Guadix Plains. These areas duplicated the American

southwest perfectly. *The Hunting Party* was released on October 3, 1971, at the London Pavilion. Most reviews acknowledged the film's quality, but were put off by its extreme violence. "It isn't just a simple bang-bang picture. Mixed up with all that slow action gunfire is an old-fashioned, highly emotional romantic melodrama, good for the heart" (*Morning Star*, September 27, 1971); "Bloodthirsty cowboy exercise" (*News of the World*, September 26, 1971); "Oliver Reed broods away..." (*Monthly Film Bulletin*, October 1971); "Oliver Reed, who is not indigenous to the Old West, gives his role his all" (*The New York Times*, July 17, 1971); "This is a grim, violent and gripping tale ... strong, tough western attraction. The acting of Oliver Reed is an impressive mixture of toughness and tenderness" (*Kinematograph Weekly*, September 25, 1971); "Oliver Reed never ceases to surprise by revealing new facets of his acting.... [He] pulls out a splendid performance as a romantic bandit in the Clark Gable tradition. Don Medford directs with style and is greatly aided by his three chief actors" (*Films and Filming*, January 1972).

The Hunting Party has acquired the reputation of being little more than a bloodbath, which is refuted — at least in part — by the contemporary reviews. Yes, it is violent — very violent — but for all its carnage, the film is really concerned with an impossible relationship. There is as much emotion as killing. But make no mistake: From its opening shot, *The Hunting Party* is a rough ride.

The film opens with Calder and his men butchering a cow interspersed with Melissa being savaged in her bed by her husband, who treats her like a whore. Actually, Ruger treats his whores even worse. His train is stocked with them and he tortures "his" with a lit cigar.

The relationship between Calder and Melissa is reasonably believable. She is initially repulsed by him but had seen worse from Ruger. Calder is far from a saint himself initially; it doesn't take long before he forces himself on Melissa.

Melissa (Candice Bergen) consoles Frank (Oliver Reed) in *The Hunting Party* (United Artists, 1971).

DOC: Frank ain't what other people see on the outside.

FRANK (to Melissa): If you're looking for me to say I'm sorry for last night, I can't. Because I'm not.

Melissa, understandably, tries to stab him and their relationship can only improve from this point! She not only initially refuses to teach Frank to read, she refuses to eat as well. Both refusals are broken down in a funny scene in which Frank and Doc taunt her with a jar of peaches which, eventually, she sloppily devours. The three actors really seem to be enjoying the scene, and it is no wonder that Melissa succumbs to Calder's (or Reed's) charm. Both the

learning process and their growing relationship are put on hold when Ruger and his men attack. The slaughter begins when two outlaws, relieving themselves in some bushes, are shot from half a mile away. The bullet effects are incredibly graphic and no one dies instantly — they lie on the ground screaming and twitching.

Ruger's madness is driven further home when he captures Calder in his telescopic crosshairs but declines to shoot, preferring to prolong Calder's misery. Even worse, after an attack at a waterhole, Ruger lines up the corpses on the ground like trophies on an African safari. This creates a disturbing situation for the viewer; the actions of the (theoretical) law-abiding citizen make the outlaws look like choirboys. Calder's concern, not only for Melissa but also for his men, is evident, as is his horror at creating the situation through his impulsivity.

Melissa (Candice Bergen) and Frank (Oliver Reed) pause while on the run in *The Hunting Party* (United Artists, 1971).

Frank (Oliver Reed) and Melissa (Candice Bergen) in *The Hunting Party* (United Artists, 1971).

The Hunting Party reaches its emotional peak after Calder unsuccessfully tries to remove a bullet from the dying Doc. Propped against a rock, Doc begs Calder to give him a gun so he can kill himself. Calder walks away and suddenly turns and shoots his friend five times while crying hysterically. Reed's intensity is more upsetting than the gore; he is showing us a human being in Hell. He then throws away his guns, renouncing his violent ways, albeit a little too late.

The film ends on a note of nihilism

difficult to match. After Doc's death, Calder and Melissa talk of settling in California, with Frank becoming a farmer or, he jokes, a schoolteacher. They both realize that this is a fantasy as they'll be dead within days. And they are. As they cross the desert, Melissa goes mad from the heat and thirst and Calder is rightfully distraught at her condition and his role in creating it. Ruger appears, shimmering on the horizon, and drops his wife with a shot to the abdomen. He plays with Calder, shooting him half a dozen times; Calder dies, swaying on his knees in the sand, like a bull in the arena.

The entire cast is outstanding with Reed dominating in one of his best performances. He was as believable a westerner as John Wayne or Gary Cooper. According to *Evil Spirits*, "Oliver's contract stipulated a pre-shooting period in Madrid, where he would be taught to ride and handle a gun like a cowboy." Predictably, Reed fell in love with his horse, Archibald, and (echoes of Hannibal Brooks) tried unsuccessfully to buy the animal and ship it to England.

Incredibly, *The Hunting Party*'s extreme violence would shortly be eclipsed by that of *The Devils* and by countless movies since. But it still remains a disturbing experience due to the humanity invested in their characters by Reed and Candice Bergen and by Gene Hackman's cold inhumanity. Unfortunately, Reed's career would soon peak and then begin a long downward spiral.

"I wanted to do a western. I wanted to work with Candice Bergen. It was like a pantomime and I enjoyed it.... I have heard that people think it's too violent. But it's not nearly as violent as pantomime — Hansel and Gretel for instance!" Reed told Susan d'Arcy in *Photoplay Film Monthly* (October 1971).

The Devils (1971)

Russo Productions; released by Warner Bros. in July 1971 in the U.K. and on July 16, 1971, in the U.S.

Crew— Screenplay-Director: Ken Russell; from Aldous Huxley's novel *The Devils of Loudon* and John Whiting's play; Producers: Ken Russell, Robert H. Solo; Associate Producer: Roy Baird; Original Music: Peter Maxwell Davies; Cinematographer: David Watkin; Film Editor: Michael Bradsell; Production Design: Derek Jarman; Art Director: Robert Cartwright; Costume Design: Shirley Russell; Makeup Artist: Charles E. Parker; Hair Stylist: Ramon Gow; Unit Manager: Graham Ford; Production Manager: Neville C. Thompson; Assistant Director: Ted Morley; Construction Manager: Terry Apsey; Property Manager: George Ball; Set Designer; Derek Jarman; Assistant Art Director: Alan Tomkins; Set Dresser: Ian Whittaker; Sound Mixer: Gordon K. McCallum; Dubbing Editor: Terry Rawlings; Sound Recordist: Brian Simmons; Special Effects: John Richardson; Camera Operator: Ronnie Taylor; Assistant Camera: Peter Ewens; Electrical Supervisor: John Swan; Wardrobe Supervisor: Tiny Nicholls; Assistant Editor: Stuart Baird; Conductor: Peter Maxwell Davies; Period Music Arranger and Director: David Munrow; Production Controller: Harry Benn; Choreographer: Terry Gilbert; Continuity: Ann Skinner.

Cast— Vanessa Redgrave (Sister Jeanne), Oliver Reed (Urbain Grandier), Dudley Sutton (Baron De Laubardemont), Max Adrian (Ibert), Gemma Jones (Madeleine), Murray Melvin (Mignon), Michael Gothard (Father Barre), Georgina Hale (Philippe), Brian Murphy (Adam), Christopher Logue (Cardinal Richelieu), Graham Armitage (Louis XIII), John Woodvine (Trincant), Andrew Faulds (Rangier), Kenneth Colley (Legrand), Judith Paris (Sister Judith), Catherine Willmer (Sister Catherine), Iza Teller (Sister Iza); uncredited: Imogen Claire, Selina Gilbert, Doremy Vernon, Alex "Alien" Russell.

Synopsis

This film is based upon historical fact. The principal characters lived and the major events depicted in this film actually took place.

Seventeenth century France. As Father Grandier (Oliver Reed) presides over the funeral of the man responsible for the fortification of Loudin, praising him for his foresight, France is ripped apart by religious controversy. Although Louis XIII (Graham Armitage) theoretically rules, the country is actually governed by Cardinal Richelieu (Christopher Logue) who wishes to divert power from the nobles. Part of his plan involves demolishing the country's town walls to remove their protection. To this end he sends Laubardemont (Dudley Sutton) to Loudin, where he is opposed by Grandier and banished from the city. Grandier is a Royalist, an intellectual and a hypocrite. A dashing figure, the father has not allowed his vow of celibacy to prevent him from having sex with a variety of women. He's fathered a child with Phillippe (Georgina Hale), and performs a blasphemous marriage ceremony between himself and Madeline (Gemma Jones). Sister Jeanne (Vanessa Redgrave) is the Mother Superior who has a deformed body and a grotesque sexual obsession with Grandier. The cardinal and Laubardmont use her sickness to bring down Grandier. They force her — and other nuns equally obsessed with Grandier — under torture administered by the exorcist Father Barre (Michael Gothard) to accuse the father of raping them in demon form. He is arrested, tortured and found guilty of sorcery. Grandier refuses to confess to the charges but admits to vanity and his opposition to the cardinal. As the father is burned at the stake, Laubardemont oversees the demolition of Loudin's walls.

Comment

With *The Party's Over, The System, I'll Never Forget What's 'Isname* and *Women in Love* in his portfolio, Oliver Reed seemed to be making a mini-career out of appearing in controversial films. After his pairing with Ken Russell in *Women in Love*, the cinema world was hold-

Oliver Reed as Father Grandier in *The Devils* (Warner Bros., 1971), one of his greatest and most controversial films.

ing its collective breath when, in April 1970, Warner Bros. announced that the star and director would be reunited in *The Devils*.

Reed and Vanessa Redgrave were presented to the press on June 20 as the film's stars, and shooting was scheduled to begin at Pinewood and various locations on August 17 on a 17-week schedule. Both actors were, fortunately, used to controversy; there would be plenty to come.

Russell's screenplay was based on both Aldous Huxley's 1952 novel and John Whiting's play, produced on the London stage in 1962. Producer Robert H. Solo said in *Kinematograph Weekly* (August 22, 1970): "I think probably in 1961 the climate wasn't quite right to think of it in film terms, but so many attitudes have changed in the last ten years. I think this is now a timely subject, although a very difficult one to make. We have used far more of the Huxley novel than John Whiting. The strange thing is, with a subject like this you might start with a list of about 12 to 20 directors hoping to find one who might be right for it. The first name on my list was Ken Russell." Russell has pretty much made a career out of controversy, both before and after *The Devils*. During the film's production, he declined to comment on charges that he was making pornography — or worse. His position afterwards was that his film was true to both the historical incidents and the literary works that followed.

The Sunday Mirror (December 27, 1970) quoted Russell as saying, "There is nothing pornographic about it. I don't make pornographic films. It is designed to show the wickedness and even the evilness of the Roman Catholic Church in the 17th century. It also shows a man can be regarded as a saint and can really be evil, and a man who is regarded as evil can really be a saint. It is a true story and we have been faithful to the trial. Here was a man who had ordinary weaknesses and was persecuted because of them and under pressure became a stronger and better man. It is a reverent film, not irreverent. There is no pornography. The people who have told these wild stories or written about them are going to feel foolish when the film is released."

The Devils was shot on a closed set, but "wild stories" still managed to escape from

Pinewood. *The Sunday Mirror* (December 27, 1970): "Some people involved have alleged that there are scenes of sexual sadism involving nuns, priests, and children. Equity says they have had more complaints about the sex scenes in this film than any other ever made in this country. A technician who worked on it said, 'I have never seen anything like this before. There were scenes that made us feel ill!'" Russell said, "There have been stories about a scene with a 14-year-old boy. A children's officer was there through his scenes and he made no complaints, and their standards are pretty exacting. We also had a religious advisor who used to be advisor to the Catholic Church and he was satisfied with all religious aspects. There were stories about girls being sexually assaulted during one scene. This was because an extra interfered with a nun, but we did not know anything about it." *The Sunday Mirror*: "Some of the girls who appeared in small parts or crowd scenes say they were asked to do things that were distasteful." *The Evening News* (December 3, 1970): "Some of the rumors are so unprintable and this can only be hinted at in a family newspaper. They include an episode allegedly including an Alsatian dog and a nun and stories that Vanessa Redgrave is given an enema ... that the girl extras were taken to the hospital with shock, and a processing laboratory destroyed the print of two days filming because of its pornography." *Evening News* writer John London had the good sense to go to Pinewood and investigate these horrific accusations and presented the story versus the facts:

STORY: The Alsatian and the nun.

FACT: In one scene a nun keeps an Alsatian in her room. There is no hint of anything else.

STORY: The "enema scene."

FACT: As part of the exorcism Vanessa Redgrave is given an enema, but it is simulated.

STORY: A laboratory deliberately destroyed the print.

FACT: The print was returned because it was scratched.

STORY: Three extras went to hospital.

FACT: In the exorcism scene, one actress fell and cut her head. She was back at work the next day.

Russell reported in *The Evening News* (December 3, 1970): "If each rumor is worth a million tickets at the box office, that's fine." Reed said in *Film Review* (April, 1970), "You would have thought from the critics' hostility that Ken Russell had tried to pull off some obscene hoax. On the contrary, the film is, I think, an utterly serious attempt to understand the nature of religious and political persecution. It is not in any way exaggerated. If anything, the horrors perpetrated in Loudin in the 17th century were worse than Russell has chosen to show."

As *The Devils* lurched towards its September 1971 general release date, both tempers and the controversies continued to flare. *The Daily Mail* (May 14, 1971): "It may be that in his determination to whip up a box office success, Russell has gone too far. Certainly this film will genuinely shock and offend thousands of ordinary people. Maybe Russell has made the most sadomasochistic, sacrilegious flop of all time"; *Variety* (July 7, 1971): "Warner Bros. has cancelled press screenings for the third time in New York due to concern about critical reactions to rumors of graphic rape sequences"; *Variety* (July 14, 1971): "Warmer Bros. has been slapped with an X rating on *The Devils*. In the rare cases of late when a major release has gotten the X, an appeal has been immediate and often successful." Reed is quoted in *The News of the World* (July 18, 1971): "I wondered at first if it should be made. Some of the scenes with nuns pulled me up short. Of course, I don't want to alienate my female fans. But if they can forgive me taking my trousers off in *Women in Love*, then they will look at *The Devils* with respect rather than scorn. People have to understand that the picture came from a famous novel and was a distinguished play in London and New York. It was history. In all humility, I would expect greater and more responsible reactions from British women than for them to have their opinions swayed by small-minded female journalists who walked out of *The Devils*. If there is hypocrisy by the public today they will be behaving exactly like the people in that small French town." And in *Women's Wear*

Father Grandier (Oliver Reed) incites the crowd in *The Devils* (Warner Bros., 1971).

Daily (July 27, 1971) Reed says, "The papers in Los Angeles liked it and it was mixed in London, but I'm prepared to defend the film. My strategy is to fight back. Ken Russell was on TV in London and when he said some naughty words they switched him off. I'm much cooler. If these newspaper critics and interviewers attack the film, I'll ask them if they believe in God."

Variety (September 8, 1971): "Church authorities in Venice succeeded in preventing a screening of the Warner Bros. entry at the Venice Film Festival." The *Centro Cinematografico Cattolico* claimed that the film set a new mark for "hysterical and erotic-sexual sacrilege in motion pictures" and violently attacked Russell for his "scandalous decision to program a film without any validity." *The Daily Mirror* (September 13, 1971): "The Greater London Council subcommittee, who watch over the capital's films, are to be asked to ban Ken Russell's *The Devils*"; *The Evening Standard* (September 13, 1971): "Moves to have the controversial film *The Devils* banned at London

cinemas failed today"; *The London Times* (September 17, 1971): "Ken Russell's powerful new film was totally banned throughout Italy"; *Kinematograph Weekly* (September 18, 1971): "After a stormy two-hour debate at County Hall, it was ruled that the Greater London Council definitely has the power to refuse to allow the showing of a film under its control even if granted a Certificate by the British Board of Film Censorship."

After this — and more — *The Devils* somehow found its way into cinemas and somehow, again, Western Civilization survived. Reviewers responded in various states of shock. "This is the one about the lecherous priest and the hunchbacked nun. Russell's perverse sense of humor may give him claim to being the Hitchcock of the Seventies. It extends even to the choice of studios. *The Devils*, the ultimate bad taste movie, made at that fortress of respectability, Pinewood" (*The Evening News*, August 19, 1971); "Oliver Reed suggests some recognizable humanity..." (*New York Times*, July 17, 1971); "Oliver Reed is left out on a limb, trying to make something coherent and intelligent of Grandier despite the surrounding ensemble encouraged to their worst extravagance" (*Financial Times*, July 23, 1971); "Oliver Reed is a fleshy Grandier sweating through intercourse..." (*Films and Filming*, September 1971); "Oliver Reed better captures the profane rather than the sacred aspects of his role" (*Show*, October 1971); "It is a horror film in the truest sense of the word; horror in the inhumanity of its medieval politics — religious bigotry. The film belongs to Oliver Reed who is immensely impressive. This is a gruesome but powerful historical horror, very well acted and flamboyantly photographed" (*Kinematograph Weekly*, July 24, 1971); "All of Russell's work reveals a terror of physical and mental disintegration. *The Devils* is an incredibly ambitious film" (*New York Times*, August 1971).

The Devils provided Reed with one of his best parts, and he responded with an Academy Award–quality performance. He was clearly at the height of his powers; few actors had the talent, charm and sheer *balls* to take on a part like this. To Reed's credit, the many over-the-top aspects of *The Devils* never intrude upon or diminish his performance.

Russell shows us the many conflicting aspects of Father Grandier's convoluted personality through a series of pointed vignettes. What emerges is a man with as many good qualities as bad; a man who allowed his flaws to give his enemies the power to destroy him.

We first see Grandier in a long shot, speaking from a balcony, presiding over the funeral of the man responsible for preserving the walls of Loudin — a move guaranteed to bring him into disfavor with the authorities. As he walks off with his entourage, the Father and a young woman trade suggestive glances. A group of nuns, piled on top of each other like cheerleaders, struggle to look out of a small window in the convent for a glance at him themselves. "I can see him!" one shouts. "He's the most beautiful man in the world!" After delivering a calm but biting reprimand, Sister Jeanne does the same thing. As she looks longingly at the priest, a voice intones, "There is a man worth going to Hell for."

And there you have it; the Father's desire to protect his city at any risk to himself is un-

done by his sexual desires and others' desires for him. Grandier reveals his hypocrisy in a chilling scene in which he casually dismisses Phillippe, his pregnant mistress; one of many actions he will later regret. (Grandier says, "Go to your father. Tell him the truth. Let him find some good man ... if they exist. How can I help you? Hold my hand. It's like touching the dead.")

Russell brilliantly contrasts the moral decay of France with the physical decay of the Plague; bodies are piling up like garbage. But Grandier, unafraid, ministers to the stricken, revealing the other side of his character. In an extremely ill-advised move again to be regretted, Grandier performs a marriage ceremony between himself and Madeline. He justifies this by pointing out that there is nothing in the Bible that demands that priests remain celibate. He also believes that human love is as important as love for God. He says to Madeline, "I want to tell you ... you know, the lovemaking ... I want to tell you, Madeline, that among the clothes dropped on the floor and the groping and the sweating and the soiled sheets ... amongst all that there is some love."

In what was one of the most outrageous scenes ever put on film, Sister Jeanne is leading a group of nuns in a prayer vigil. As she envisions Christ suffering on the cross, she begins to hallucinate; the figure of Christ becomes Grandier. He leaves the cross to have sex with her, and she shoves her crucifix through her hand.

After softening up the viewer with scenes like this, Russell moved in for the kill with the exorcisms. The cardinal, outraged at Grandier's opposition, dispatches Laubardemont to Loudin, this time not to destroy its walls but its priest. The Father's sexual excesses, both real and imagined, have laid him open to a false charge of sorcery ... of having sex with a nun while in the form of a demon. Under torture disguised as exorcism, the nuns quickly condemn Grandier. Performed by Father Barre (played with loathsome glee by Michael Gothard) they are masterpieces of hysterical horror — unbelievably terrifying and unsettling due to Russell's presentation that reveals less than meets the eye. The viewer believes that he/she has seen something that has not actually

Father Grandier (Oliver Reed) and Philippe (Georgina Hale) have an un-priestly encounter in *The Devils* (Warner Bros., 1971).

been shown other than by implication. While not exactly subtle, the scenes are reasonably restrained. Especially compared to the wild rumors that had escaped from Pinewood, and from the actual events in Loudin.

As the net of conspiracy encloses him, Grandier ponders his fate. When he enters his church he finds the brutal exorcisms have begun for no purpose other than to discredit him for political purposes. He says, "You have turned the House of the Lord into a circus and its servants into clowns. You have seduced the people in order to destroy them. You have perverted the innocent. Call me vain and proud ... call me the greatest sinner ever to walk on God's earth — but Satan's toy I could never be. I know what I have sown and what I shall reap." As Grandier is "questioned" while having his legs broken before the trial, Laubardemont revels in the priest's pain and humiliation. Grandier has now had plenty of time to reflect on his behavior when he addresses the court. He says, "My Lord, I am innocent of the charges, and I am afraid. But I have hope in my heart that be-

fore this day ends, Almighty God will glance aside and my suffering atone for my vain and disordered life."

Grandier now has little about which to be vain. In addition to being crippled, his head has been shaved as well as his beard and his eyebrows. The latter action gave Reed pause. "Oliver was also told to have every hair removed from his head and legs, an order he accepted without a murmur. When Russell demanded the eyebrows also go, the actor decided to make a stand. 'God!' shouted Russell. 'We might as well not make the film at all!' 'Don't be bloody silly,' Oliver countered, 'it can't make all that much of a difference.' 'Of course it's important,' said Russell. 'All right,' said Oliver. 'But I want them insured for half a million pounds in case they don't grow back properly!'" (Goodwin, 146).

Grandier says, "If you wish to destroy me, then destroy me. Accuse me of exposing political chicanery and the evil of the State and I shall plead guilty." But that is not why he is sentenced to death by burning; the court condemns the Father to death for sorcery. And a painful death it is; his legs smashed, Grandier must crawl to the pyre. It was there that Reed nearly shared Grandier's fate. According to Goodwin's *Evil Spirits*, "Russell found himself having to choose between the safety of his leading man and his belief in 'accurate and honest' cinema. The answer, claimed Oliver, was simple. He could act out the execution scene standing on a hidden trap door; when the flames got too close for comfort, Oliver could release the flap and drop to safety. The set was rigged and the pyre torched. As the flames rose, the director and crew watched as Oliver acted out Grandier's death scene. Still he refused to quit with the flames at waist high and 'a very strange smell' coming from his legs. Oliver pressed the hidden release mechanism. Nothing happened. The heat from the fire had swollen the wood and jammed the trap door. Only the rapid intervention of the studio firemen saved Oliver from serious injury."

The Devils is, obviously, not for all tastes and it is impossible to defend the film's excesses to its many protestors. Even its star and director were debilitated. According to Goodwin's *Evil Spirits*, "Oliver and Russell were understandably disturbed by the experience of making *The Devils*. They could no longer look each other in the eye. Sometimes they could not bear to be in the same room. There was an emptiness in the relationship which needed to 'lie fallow' until it recharged." Reed and Russell would not work together again for four years, until they were reunited in *Tommy*. Despite losing his eyebrows (and, nearly, his life), *The Devils* was a triumph for Oliver Reed; in the nearly thirty years of acting that lay ahead, he would find no better showcase for his talent.

The Devils was also well served by Vanessa Redgrave, who submitted to a grotesque makeup and an unsympathetic role, and Michael Gothard and Dudley Sutton, playing as reprehensible a pair as ever seen on film. Not all was doom and gloom though:

Co-star Brian Murphy saw the volatile and often playful nature of Reed's relationship with Russell first hand. "He was a great practical joker, Oliver, and it seemed to me that he and Ken played games with each other. I remember one particular scene: Oliver had done several takes but Ken wanted more and in the end Ollie stormed off the set.

"Everything ground to a halt. Then word was sent to me, Max Adrian and Murray Melvin, who were also appearing in the scene, would we all go to Oliver's dressing room. So we did and we all sat down and Ollie was grinning from ear to ear. 'We'll have a drink in a minute,' he said. 'Have you got something?' I asked. 'No,' he replied, 'but we will have.' There was a knock at the door and this assistant came in with a bottle of champagne and said, 'This is from Mr. Russell and when you feel ready for it, Mr. Reed, we'll see you back on the set.' I think he was up to those kinds of things all the time" [Sellers, 152].

Russell knew how to get performances from his cast. Special mention is also due to the film's stunning set design (Bob Cartwright), costuming (Shirley Russell) and photography (David Watkin). *The Devils* is a one-of-a-kind experience — probably for the best — and should not be missed by anyone with a stomach strong enough to take it.

The Triple Echo (1972)

A Senta Production; released by Hemdale Film Distributore in the U.K. in 1972 and by Altura Films International in the U.S. in 1973

Crew— Director: Michael Apted; Screenplay: Robin Chapman, from the story by H.E. Bates; Producer: Graham Cottle; Associate Producer: Zelda Barron; Original Music: Marc Wilkinson; Cinematographer: John Coquillon; Film Editor: Barrie Vince; Art Director: Edward Marshall; Hairdresser: Ronald Cogan; Makeup Artist: Neville Smallwood; Assistant Directors: Simon Relph, Nigel Wooll, Michael Green; Set Dresser: Simon Holland; Property Master: John Leuenberger; Sound Editor: Alan Bell; Sound Recordist: Derrick Leather; Dubbing Mixer: Doug Turner; Gaffer: Nobby Cross; Camera Operator: Denis Lewiston; Camera Assistant: Michael Rutter; Wardrobe Master: John Brady; Costumes: Emma Porteous; Assistant Editor: Peter Watson; Second Assistant Editor: Jeremy Hume; Location Manager: Grania O'Shannon; Continuity: Connie Willis.

Cast— Glenda Jackson (Alice), Oliver Reed (Sergeant), Brian Deacon (Barton), Anthony May (Subaltern), Gavin Richards (Stan), Jenny Lee Wright (Christine), Kenneth Colley (Provo Corporal), Daphne Heard (Shopkeeper), Zelah Clarke (First Girl), Colin Rix (Compere), Ioan Meredith (Guard).

Synopsis

In the middle of World War II, deep in the wilds of Wiltshire, Alice (Glenda Jackson) is waiting out the war, eking a living on the small farm that she used to work with her husband, a prisoner of war with the Japanese for the last six months. Two Spitfires roaring overhead as Alice goes in search of rabbits to supplement her meager rations only serve to remind her how lonely and tired she is.

During one of her hunting forays she comes across Barton (Brian Deacon), a soldier grabbing a few off-duty hours away from his barracks. She orders him off her land, but eventually offers him a cup of tea. Barton is a farm lad from another county, but they soon discover that they have a lot in common. He begins to drop in during his off-duty hours and starts doing the harder chores that Alice cannot manage, like mending the ancient tractor and chopping lots of wood for the fire.

In a tender moment, Alice kisses him and they eventually become lovers, content to grab what peace and joy they can from each other. Barton decides to spend his leave with Alice on the farm, instead of going home to his family. But at the end of his leave, he is reluctant to return to camp and he tells Alice that he has decided to go AWOL — a dreadful offense in wartime. Alice conspires to hide him, telling the local shopkeeper that she is being visited by a sick sister. To further hide Barton, they decide that he should dress up like her sister, and a bra is duly stuffed and clothes found. Alice buys him makeup with her coupons and they let his hair, already shaggy, grow longer so that it can be styled.

At first Barton enjoys the charade but it soon begins to pall as Alice becomes more strident about him not being seen and not mixing with any strangers. He realizes he's in as much of a prison in her home as he was in the army camp and he becomes very petulant. Into this warped domestic scene comes a tank, manned by a burly, blustering sergeant (Oliver Reed) and his sidekick Stan (Gavin Richards). Stan emulates the sergeant in all things and they have

a competitive streak where women are concerned. Initially lost, having misread their out-of-date map, they make themselves pleasant to Alice. She is cold and unwelcoming, but the Sarge spots another prospect lurking near the barn. Intrigued, he wangles an introduction and promises to come back another time to spend time with the ladies. Alice doesn't encourage him; nonetheless he returns while she is at the shops and chats up her shy "sister," confiding that the Army is planning a dance. Alice refuses to go, but Barton, in a fit of madness, agrees to attend. He even swipes a special gown of Alice's so that he'll look his best!

The Sarge arrives and shepherds Barton into the Jeep. He keeps dropping none-too-subtle hints about the joys of the evening to follow and, for a time, the social niceties of a village hop are played out. Barton feels increasingly at risk and tries to creep out of the hall, but the Sarge grabs him, pulls him into a darkened room (where Stan is happily rutting with a village girl) and begins to kiss and grope him. Instantly realizing that he has padding in his hand rather than a nubile bosom and that his other hand is encountering what should not be there, the Sarge explodes. Barton manages to escape.

Humiliated, Sarge begins to check through the lists of missing soldiers, and soon finds the photo of Barton. A squad of soldiers begins to scour the countryside for Barton, who is too tired and scared to care any more. The Sarge lets Alice know the game is up and, as he picks the photo of her prisoner husband off the mantelpiece, his voice and demeanor drip with contempt for her. Outside, the soldiers shout that Barton has been spotted and the hunt resumes. They flush him towards the farm and as he runs up the path to the house, Alice appears in the window of the bedroom they have shared, aiming her shotgun. Both Barton and the Sarge are in the firing line, but when the smoke clears, it is Barton who lies dead on the muddy ground.

Comment

Shooting mostly on location in the wilds of Wiltshire, Glenda Jackson and Brian Deacon had been working quite a while before Oliver Reed joined them for his scenes.

The sergeant (Oliver Reed) will soon learn a surprising truth about Barton (Brian Deacon) in *The Triple Echo* (Hemdale, 1972).

According to *Glenda Jackson: The Biography*,

Graham Cottle, who had bought the rights [to the original story] and adapted it, had secured Glenda and Oliver Reed before finding a director. Michael Apted, who eventually directed it, had had a long apprenticeship in television but had never made a film before.... Perhaps because she was given the right of refusal over Apted, Glenda was very protective of him, and when it came to filming she behaved, to Apted's mind, impeccably.... Reed was a full-scale movie star with a very dominating personality. He had already proved himself something of a nightmare by demanding changes to the script, and he insisted on a very different style of working. Apted was immensely grateful to Glenda when she decided that since Reed was to be present only for a little over a week there was little point in going "head to head" with him, and that she would not insist on her way of working.

Reed agreed with Glenda that as antagonists they worked together better in *The Triple Echo* for Michael Apted than they did as lovers for Russell. Delighting in his own misogyny, Reed declared that "in the end when she pointed her rifle at me and her lover, there was a gasp of dismay from the bra burners when Brian Deacon dropped." According to *Glenda Jackson, The Triple Echo* (which cost £200,000 to make) "did well enough in Britain, and very well in Continental Europe, especially France, but thanks to a legal bankruptcy wrangle which went on for several years it did not have a proper UA release. When it finally appeared in the States it sank without trace, having been packaged as a sexploitation movie and re-titled *Soldiers in Skirts*."

"*Triple Echo* is tenderly perceptive about such basics as loneliness, love, and some aspects of sex, but as drama, it's disquietingly clouded. Although its sincerity and tragedy are obvious, the character and motivations of the principals [remains] indistinct as a distant echo" (*New York Times,* November 1, 1973); "Oliver Reed contributes a horribly convincing picture of the coarse, brutal, almost sub-human sergeant" (*Monthly Film Bulletin*, December 1972).

Reed's career soldier is a joy to watch; he is master of his squad and his word is their law — particularly Stan, whom we feel is being groomed to rise in the ranks by his mentor. He obviously called on his experiences during National Service, and he certainly had forgotten nothing of drilling and what British soldiers happily refer to as "bullshit." He is obsequious to the officers and a hard but fair taskmaster to his boys. In short, a character Reed must have met on many an occasion in Hong Kong and at the induction camp.

Reed looks to be enjoying his role hugely, and you almost feel sorry for him at his moment of greatest horror — almost.

The setting for the film, a farm as far away from the war as it was possible to get, only brings the pain and loneliness of all the characters into sharp relief. The costumes and hairstyles are "spot on" and some of us are old enough to remember feeling hungry and looking forward to the rabbit stew that supplemented the official rations. In England, rationing of food and other commodities went on until 1954 and some of us have elderly relatives who would still be in jail if they'd been caught trading food on the Black Market! Though Reed's family were reasonably well-off during the war, he would have had such residual memories too.

The Triple Echo is a gem and well worth a look. It's a trip into another time.

ZPG (1972)

Sagittarius Production; U.S. certificate PG; released by Scotia-Barber in the U.K. in 1972 and by Paramount Pictures in the U.S.; color; 95 minutes

Crew— Director: Michael Campus; Writers: Frank De Felitta, Max Erlich; Executive Producer: Frank De Felitta; Associate Producer: Max Erlich; Producer: Tom Madigan; Original Music: Jonathan Hodge; Cinematographers: Michael Reed, Mikael Salomon; Film Editor: Dennis Lanning; Production Design: Anthony Masters; Art Directors: Peter Hajmark, Harry Lange; Set Decorator: Erlong Jorgensen; Costume Design: Margit Brandt; Makeup Artist: Lene Ravn Henriksen; Unit Managers: Geoffrey Haine, H.P. Moeller-Anderson; Assistant Director: Richard F. Dalton; Property Buyer: Anders-Volmer Hansen; Dubbing Editor: Dennis Lanning; Sound: Gert Madsen; Sound Mixer: Hugh Strain; Special Effects: Derek Meddings; Stills Photographers: Norman Gryspardt, Benny Jacobsen; Grip: Jimmy Leavens; Aerial Photography: Jan Weincke; Wardrobe Mistress: Jytte Paby; Conductor: Jonathan Hodge.

Cast— Oliver Reed (Russ McNeil), Geraldine Chaplin (Carol McNeil), Don Gordon (George Borden), Diane Cilento (Edna Borden), Eugene Blau, Bent Christensen (Baby Shop Salesmen), Belinda Donkin (Daughter), Birgitte Federspiel (Psychiatrist), Birgitte Frigast (Nurse), Anne-Lise Gabold (Mother in Baby Shop), Michel Hildesheim (Thief), Peter Hihnen (Edict Boy), Torben Hundal (President's Aide), Theis Ib Husfeldt (Jessie), Wladimir Kandel, Brian Keifer (Edict Examiners), Lone Lindorff (Mother), Victor Lapari (Headwaiter), Carlotta Magnoff (Informer), Sam Aisle (Dad in Baby Shop), Ditte Maria (Telescreen Operator), David Markham

(Dr. Herrick), Bill Nagy (The President), Claus Nissen, Jeff Slocombe (Guards), Sheila Reed (Mary Herrick), Dale Robinson (First Guide), Wayne Rodda (Metromart Salesman), Peter Ronild (Edict Doctor), Paul Secon (Tour Guide), Lotte Tholander (Telescreen Nurse), Birte Tove (Nurse), Lene Vasegaard (Edict Mother), Aubrey Woods (Dr. Mallory).

Synopsis

The time is the not-too-distant future and overpopulation has depleted air, food, water and shelter for the human race. In order to cope with the situation, an edict is issued forbidding the conception of children for a 30-year period. Two couples — Russ (Oliver Reed) and Carole (Geraldine Chaplin) McNeill and Edna (Diane Cilento) and George (Don Gordon) Borden — are authorized personnel of the State Museum of Nature which contains the last living examples of flora and fauna, together with an authentic replica of the "Natural Habitat of 20th Century Man." In two typically 1970 homes, the Bordens and McNeils dwell side by side as living exhibits of the 1970 way of life for the tireless stream of tourists who wait up to four years for admission tickets.

The Bordens have come to terms with the edict, and Edna busies herself to satisfy maternal instincts. Carole, having made up her mind to follow her friend's example, cannot bring herself to accept final delivery of her own doll baby. In spite of a conversation Carole has with her psychiatrist via the McNeils' bedroom telescreen, she is unable to repress her desire to bear a child. That evening she fails to utilize her abortion machine.

Christmas is heralded by the sound of carols emanating from the hovering "Big Mouth Satellite." Russ and Carole celebrate at the Old Vienna Restaurant where they are robbed of a few fresh vegetables by a desperate crowd. On their way home, Russ and Carole visit elderly friends, Mary and Dr. Herrick (Sheila Reid and David Markham), in the Happiness Home. They find there is little real happiness among the elderly people who are waiting to die. Outside in the street they arrive at the Place of Public Execution just in time to see the Transgressors' Bubble lowered over a young couple and a forbidden infant. They were turned in by a woman seeking the promised extra rations of reward.

Hurt and disappointed, Carol asks Russ for a Christmas tree. When Russ returns with a forbidden live tree, she confesses that she is pregnant. They concoct a plan for survival.

Carole, having pretended to leave Russ, will spend her pregnancy in an abandoned atomic bomb shelter beneath the house and bear the child there. Russ will continue to live in the house and allay the suspicions of the Bordens. Baby Jessie is born and Carol returns to Russ, using an artificial baby doll to fool the Bordens. But Edna is not fooled easily. When the child becomes ill and Carol attempts to smuggle him to Dr. Herrick, Edna follows them. With her suspicions confirmed, Edna and George blackmail the McNeils into sharing the child. Daily tensions grow until George insists that he and Edna will take possession of Jessie.

Russ and Carol plot to get to the baby away. During Carole's pregnancy Russ has explored the whole tunnel system beneath the house. George and Edna now decide to denounce the McNeils to the authorities for the extra rations, knowing that the child will be killed with its parents in the Transgressors' Bubble. The couple and their child are placed in the bubble awaiting death by suffocation. Smoke fills the bubble to prevent the crowd assembled from seeing the horrendous death. When the bubble lifts, there are no bodies. Russ and Carole have engineered their capture over a manhole cover to the old underground system and escaped down the hole. Russ takes Carole and Jessie in an inflatable dinghy along the waterways under the city. On reaching daylight they launch themselves onto the open sea. Some time later they end up on a deserted beach where the remains of a great city can be seen in the distance. They have arrived at their new home but the site is badly contaminated by radiation. We do not know what will happen to them but they are together as a family as they wished.

Comment

Depicting the world of tomorrow, a world devoid of animals, vegetation, alcohol and cigarettes, the futuristic sets were cleverly designed by Anthony Masters whose work on *2001: A Space Odyssey* is legendary. They are more *Star*

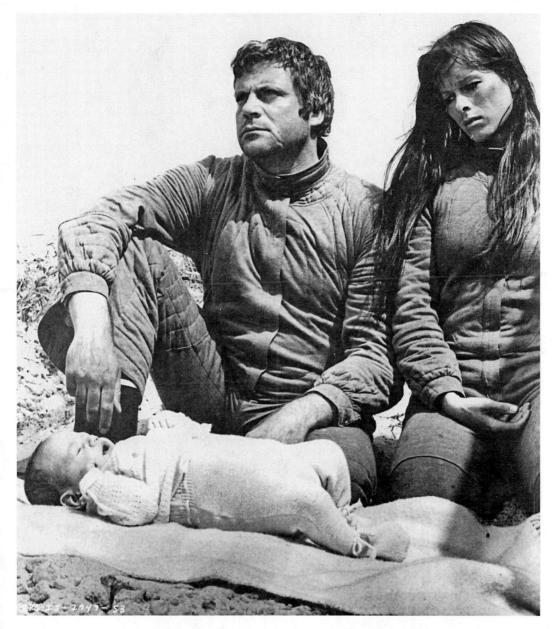

Russ (Oliver Reed) and Carole (Geraldine Chaplin) have serious family problems in *ZPG* (Paramount, 1972).

Trek TV than movie-grade, though. The establishment of the futuristic city, choked with fumes, is quite well handled by director Michael Campus.

Reed, with his current girlfriend Carol Lynley, spoke to Scott MacDonough of *Show* magazine (April 1972) about the company backing *ZPG*, Sagittarius: "I think it's important that film companies like Sagittarius are now taking over. It at least offers an alternative to people to make films. It used to all lie in the laps of Columbia and Universal and MGM, and now they're all realizing that they've either got to sell off their lots for real estate, or they've got to combine their distribution or they've got to share their offices because every-

Carole (Geraldine Chaplin) and Russ (Oliver Reed) with their illegal child plotting to leave the city for a new life in *ZPG* (Paramount, 1972).

thing is way overpriced. It's very refreshing that new companies like Saggitarius are now entering the market." Very astute. According to *Photoplay Film Monthly* (October 1971), "Oliver is venturing into film production, hopefully early next year, with a film about the men who murdered Thomas Beckett. Oliver co-authored the screenplay and will star in the film as well as produce. At the moment he is waiting for the front office to go ahead. He feels, wisely, that 'an actor should have more than one string to his bow' and, having always had a yearning towards farm life, he is considering moving to Ireland. 'I want a farm, a kind of guest house where everything is laid on — hunting, shooting, fishing, riding. I want to surround myself with things I like; I want to be as near England as possible, and maybe for the wrong reasons, I love Ireland and Irishmen. I know farms are expensive to upkeep unless they're very successful so I'd offset that by making films."

Filmed in Copenhagen, Denmark, *ZPG* was released in the USA on May 25, 1972. Geraldine Chaplin won the Medulla Sitges en Plata de Ley for Best Actress in 1972 at the Sitges-Catalonian International Film Festival.

Reviewers were not overly impressed with the movie: "[It] pits Oliver Reed and Geraldine Chaplin against the Orwellian forces of future reason that prescribe an un-pregnant pause in the birthrate.... Interesting idea, chillingly imagined, but tediously handled" (*Sunday Telegraph*, May 28, 1972); "[N]ot all that well made and too slow. But the imaginative ideas about the possible future make up for its faults" (*Sunday Mirror*, May 28, 1972); "Zero Population Growth is the name of an American organization committed to the stabilization of the population by making people have fewer children. Unfortunately, it's also the title of a new film starring Diane Cilento and Oliver Reed.... ZPG in California have already tried to take legal action against Paramount, the film's makers. The only satisfaction they've had so far is to get the cinemas to agree to distribute leaflets explaining the lack of connection between the two ZPGs.... [The film] has scored a notable lack of success even in 'B' feature terms" (*Guardian*, May 18, 1972); "Since the end sees [Reed and Cilento] escaping from a world where offspring aren't allowed into a nuclear devastated wasteland where they can't survive, I fail to see what point about conservation and contraception is being made" (*Evening Standard*, May 25, 1972); "Waste of a talented quartet" (*Morning Star*, May 26, 1972); "*ZPG* is a total waste of a good cast. Abilities of Oliver Reed, Geraldine Chaplin, Diane Cilento and Don Gordon are so thoroughly squandered it's a shame there's no conservationist group for actors' talents" (*Variety*, April 26, 1972).

Sitting Target (1972)

Metro-Goldwyn-Mayer British Studios; Peerford Ltd.; released by MGM-EMI in the U.K. and by MGM in the U.S.; Metrocolor; 93 minutes; U.K. certificate X

Crew — Director: Douglas Hickox; Producer: Barry Kulick; Screenplay: Alexander Jacobs; based on the novel by Laurence Henderson; Associate Producer: Basil Keys; Music: Stanle they Myers; Cinematographer: Edward Scaife; Production Designer: Jonathan Barry; Editor: John Glen; Production Manager: Douglas Twiddy; Special Effects: John Stears; Assistant Director: Ted Sturges; Makeup: Paul Rabiger; Costume Advisor: Emma Porteous; Camera Operator: Stan Mestel; Sound Mixer: Cyril Swern; Dubbing Editor: Alan Sones; Second Unit Cameraman: Alan McCabe; Action Sequence Coordinator: Peter Brayham.

Cast — Oliver Reed (Harry Lomart), Jill St. John (Pat Lomart), Ian McShane (Birdy Williams), Edward Woodward (Inspector Arthur Milton), Frank Finlay (Marty Gold), Freddie Jones (Macneil), Jill Townsend (Maureen), Robert Beatty (Gun Dealer), Tony Beckley (Soapy Tucker), Mike Pratt (Prison Warder Accomplice), Robert Russell, Joe Cahill (Prison Warders), Robert Ramsey (Gun Dealer's Minder), Susan Shaw (Girl in Truck), June Brown (Lomart Neighbor).

Synopsis

Even in the limbo of a one-man maximum security cell, Harry Lomart (Oliver Reed) is like a hair trigger pistol with the safety catch off. There is something obsessive about the way he tunes his body with isometric exercises, his airless cell almost crackling with controlled ferocity. It is now five months since he was convicted of killing a postman, but today marks the occasion of his first visit from his wife Pat (Jill St. John).

In the strained atmosphere of the visiting room it becomes apparent that the prospect of a 15-year separation is too daunting for Pat Lomart and that she is the type who cannot survive without a man. When she tells Harry that she has met someone else, that she wants a divorce and that she is pregnant, he erupts in fury and smashes the glass partition between them in a frenzied attempt to throttle her. He is battered into submission by officers and thrown into solitary confinement. His rage slowly subsides, to be replaced by a deep burning hatred and a desire for revenge.

On his release from solitary, Lomart finds that his former associate Birdy Williams (Ian McShane) and another prisoner, Macneil (Freddie Jones), have a plan for him. The plan

Birdy (Ian McShane) and Harry (Oliver Reed) play tough in *Sitting Target* (MGM, 1972).

is to get to them over the wall and it calls for naked aggression, which is Lomart's department, and a measure of palm and lock greasing. When the scheme is put into practice, Lomart batters two warders. Another warder, who is ready to look the other way for 15 minutes for £1000, gets a nightstick behind his ear — a crude but effective alibi. A trained guard dog is also put away by Lomart before they swarm up some scaffolding, to swing commando-style over the 30-foot spike-topped wall.

Macneil's outside organization is first-rate. A waiting USAAF transporter ticks over, blankets, clothes and whisky are dispensed by Soapy Tucker (Tony Beckley). There is even a blonde in the back for those who feel the need, but Lomart opts out; his only thought is the elimination of his wife. Macneil, Tucker and the transporter head for the Liverpool docks, while Lomart and Williams switch to a stolen Jaguar and drive toward London. They stop at a house in a Riverside boatyard, where a gun dealer (Robert Beatty) a special piece of business equip-

ment for Lomart: a combination 9mm Mauser special, combination rifle and handgun, with a telescopic sight and five clips of ammunition.

CID Inspector Arthur Milton (Edward Woodward) is already checking out Pat Lomart's flat, near the top of a high-rise block in Clapham. He finds the place has been turned over by somebody, though Pat has not been harmed. Even as he inspects the damage, the flat is under surveillance by Lomart and Williams from a passing train. Milton calls up a team of policemen to keep an eye on the glass-and-concrete tower where Pat lives, but before they're in position, Lomart makes his first exploratory assault on his wife's flat. Milton manages to fend him off, and Lomart has to fight his way out through lines of flapping laundry. When two motorcycle policemen pursue him, he is forced to kill them before making his getaway in a van hired by Birdy Williams. Williams drives to a house rented by a former associate of theirs, a bent bookie named Marty Gold (Frank Finlay), who is the only means of

Harry (Oliver Reed) with two thugs (actors unidentified) in *Sitting Target* (EMI/MGM, 1972).

access to ready cash. Gold tips off the police that Lomart wants to meet him, but when he visits his girlfriend, Maureen (Jill Townsend), in the rented house, he finds her entertaining the two people he least wanted to see. Lomart and Williams leave the house, where Gold has had "a fatal accident." Lomart takes possession of $200,000 he heisted in the past.

Lured from Pat's flat by a fire which Williams has started, a figure appears at the window to be struck by a hail of bullets from Lomart's gun. As he stops firing, Williams kicks Lomart in the head and grabs the money. He is just about to shoot Lomart when one of the local residents appears. Williams shoots him and runs, dropping the gun. He joins Pat in her car, and they drive happily away, delighting in the way they have used her poor dupe of a husband. The person at Lomart's flat was a policewoman acting as a decoy.

But their joy at short-lived, for the re-

markably resilient Lomart is right behind them in a stolen car. He pursues them into the Clapham goods yard, viciously ramming their car until it crashes onto the tracks, killing Pat. Williams attempts to escape, but is gunned down by Lomart, who then climbs into the wreck which is smoldering and embraces his wife's lifeless body. As Milton and his policeman arrive, the gas tank ignites and the car bursts into flames.

Comment

"I don't think that any of the characters I've played in films — and I've played some shockers — have been evil all the way through," Oliver Reed told *Film Review* (April 1974). "They wouldn't be believable if they were only one color with no light or shade. I've never tried the part of a credibly evil man before. I say 'credible' because the murderer I play in *Sitting*

All of London is a sitting target for Harry (Oliver Reed)—but is *he* truly the target in *Sitting Target* (EMI/MGM, 1972)?

Target, like most men, also had a sad, pathetic side to him. Evil is not, in my view, an abstraction; it is compounded of some very human flaws. I'm not going to tell anyone that what success I've achieved has happened by accident. I've been through misery and I've worked like mad. There were times in those days when I felt like chucking it all in — but I didn't. The marvelous thing was that when the chance came, I was ready. I knew what to do, what it was all about."

Director Douglas Hickox shot the film on an eight-week schedule; filming took place in Dublin for ten days at the Arbour Hill Prison and Kilmainham jail, the latter infamous in Irish history as the place where the leaders of the Easter Uprising were executed by the British Army in 1916. Eerily, while they were filming the escape sequences, three convicts broke out of Mountjoy Prison using remarkably similar techniques! Filming also used ten major loca-

tions in the London area, primarily around Clapham Junction, one of London's largest railway stations with Europe's busiest marshalling yards. Producer Barry Kulick said, "In this picture audiences will be seeing an entirely different London from the ones they're used to. Clapham Junction isn't exactly Mayfair or Piccadilly. It has a strange netherworld feeling about it. Most of the picture will be filmed there" (*Kinematograph Weekly*, September 11, 1971). If he thought it was like that then, he should see it in 2011!

Reed is fit and healthy, matching the fitness fanatic that he's playing, and well able to participate in the punishing action sequences in this exciting movie. He is almost matched by Ian McShane and they make a crime duo that make Butch and Sundance look like kindergarten kids. Harry's explosive rage when he finds out his faithless wife is also pregnant is truly terrifying to behold, and the casual way he eliminates anyone who crosses him or he thinks is a potential problem mark Harry as a psychopath of the first order. The audience is kept thinking that he's made the jailbreak to punish his wife and whomever is the father of her unborn child; it isn't until the very last moment, when he climbs into the car to cradle her corpse and die in the inferno, that we discover that Harry loves someone other than himself.

With terrific performances from the entire cast, grittily realistic locations, fabulously executed action sequences and a pace that never lets the audience draw a breath, *Sitting Target* is a gem of a thriller. It's also the first movie to get X and R ratings purely on its violent content — another first for Oliver Reed.

"But who is the sitting target? You will find out in the last reel — if, I mean, you can stomach the hideous intervening violence" (*London Sunday Times*, May 14, 1972); "Oliver Reed as a convict ... lumbers through the action with set face and staring eyes" (*Hollywood Reporter*, February 16, 1972); "Reed's portrayal is topflight. For the market which favors such realistic action, this Brit import should hit.... [A] picture of brutish violence" (*Variety*, February 23, 1972); "It also owes immeasurably to Mr. Reed's powerful study of the man of brute strength for whom existence means nothing if he's denied the woman he loves" (*Evening News*, May 10, 1972).

This is Reed at the very top of his game and well worth a viewing if you have a strong stomach.

Blue Blood (1973)

Mallard Productions; released by Impact Quadrant in the U.S. in 1973; color; 86 minutes

Crew— Screenplay-Director: Andrew Sinclair; from the novel by Alexander Thynne; Executive Producers: Peter James, Geoffrey Nethercott; Producers: John Trent, Kent Walwin; Original Music: Brian Gascoigne; Cinematographer: Harry Waxman; Film Editor: Keith Palmer; Casting: Miriam Brickman; Art Director: J. Charrott-Lodwige; Hair Stylist: Betty Glasgow; Makeup Artist: Freddie Williamson; Production Supervisor: Christopher Neame; Assistant Director: Derek Whitehurst; Property: Charles Torbett; Sound Editor: Don Challis; Sound Mixer; Robin Gregory; Dubbing Mixer: Hugh Strain; Camera Operator: Cecil R. Cooney; Camera Grip: Peter Butler; Gaffer: Fred Anderson; Costume Supervisor: Timy Nicholls; Continuity: Penny Daniels.

Cast— Oliver Reed (Tom), Fiona Lewis (Lily), Anna Gael (Carlotta), Derek Jacobi (Gregory), Meg Wyn Owen (Beate), John Rainer (Clurman), Richard Davies (Jones), Gwyneth Owen (Agnes), Patrick Carter (Cocky), Elaine Ives-Cameron (Serena), Tim Wylton (Morrell), Hubert Rees (Dr. Barrett), Dilys Price (Mrs. Barrett), Andrew McCall (Gerrard), Sally Anne Newton (Susannah).

Synopsis

At his country home, Gregory (Derek Jacobi) is master of all he surveys; his lifestyle is perfection and all the responsibilities of running his estate and keeping his family and friends content are handled by his butler Tom (Oliver Reed). The lady of the house spends all her time indulging her passion for singing and cannot really be bothered with the upbringing of her children, like many women of her class; having provided the heir, she has fulfilled her part of the social contract. Gregory is just as content, partying with his friends and copulating with whichever mistress is currently in favor. Tom rules the household with a rigid hierarchy and makes it his business to ensure that no one bothers the master and mistress.

The arrival of a new governess, who really tries to cherish the children and puts their needs before their parents' or the autocratic butler, really complicates matters. Tom is an evil-minded creature who usurps his weak-willed employer's position and belongings whenever he can. He spins an evil web around the family and induces bizarre and terrifying dreams.

As each night passes, the possessions and domination become stronger. The governess discovers that the domestics are bound together as members of a satanic circle with Tom as high priest, leading their ceremonies in a scarlet chapel. She wants to rescue the children, but Tom works to discredit her and get her sacked. The purpose of the children is enigmatic: They are either to "inherit" the coven, or they are being reared to be sacrifices at the ceremonies in days to come.

Comment

This movie is a thinly disguised fantasy representation of the heritage of the English aristocracy and its reliance on other people to perpetuate their comfortable lifestyle. Longleat House, where much of the filming took place, is the country seat of the Marquis of Bath, who co-wrote the script under his family name Alexander Thynne. His father, one of the first of the English peerage to comprehend that the lifestyle of his ancestors didn't sit well with his bank balance, came up with the brilliant idea of opening his lovely home to members of the paying public. And to make sure they got their money's worth he converted part of his extensive grounds into a wildlife park, where the Lions of Longleat became more famous than the family in residence. His son and heir, the aforesaid Alexander, was something of a rebel and outrageous artist — a true English eccentric. He was infamous for populating the house with his wife, actress Anna Gael, numerous concubines that he named "wifelets," and their various children. Nothing changed when he came into his inheritance, scandalizing his social circle, but he did take the opportunity to attend the House of Lords regularly, taking up many social issues, much to the surprise of many. Letting the moviemakers shoot at Longleat brought in necessary money; the fees as co-writer would have helped too — the upkeep of such an estate would make the ordinary man in the street wilt with fright. The scions of these great families are unanimous in the belief that the estate has to be maintained for the future members of the family, however onerous that might be.

So the backdrop was perfect, the surroundings magnificent, and the technical advisor — Alexander has a small part in the party scene — was on the spot for any inquiries. The cast were the cream of English actors; the crew were among the finest of the day. So what the heck went wrong?

It's taken as a given that Oliver Reed and Alexander Thynne got on; their philosophies were so mutually agreeable! And we're sure that the cast had a grand time making the movie, but somewhere the focus of the whole thing got lost. Are the children the future practitioners? Are they future sacrificial lambs? Does anyone care as they battle to make sense of the plotline and lose the will to live? Perhaps some unnamed genius threw all the plotwords into the air—

dream sequences, mansion, child murder, haunted house, nightmare, Satanism, good versus evil, occult — and expected something interesting and creepy to emerge; they succeeded with producing a *Rosemary's Baby* meets *Gosford Park* hybrid.

Reed does his best with a weak script and attempts to create a character that's part Jeeves and part Mephistopheles; he looks the part, ponderous and heavy. But the viewer is left feeling puzzled and mildly irritated. With such superb ingredients, how could the film be so awful?

Dirty Weekend (1973)

Champion; Concordia Compagnia Cinematografica; released by MGM in the U.S. in 1974; no U.K. release; Technicolor; 107 minutes

Crew— Director: Dino Risi; Screenplay: Ruggero Macoari, Bernardino Zapponi, Dino Risi; Producer; Carlo Ponti; Photography: Luciano Tavoli; Art Director: Luciano Recceri; Editor: Alberto Galioti; Music: Carlo Rustichelli.

Cast— Oliver Reed (Fabrizio), Marcello Mastroianni (Giulio), Carol Andre (Danda), Nicoletta Machiavelli (Sylvia), Bruno Cirino (Raoul), Lionel Stander (General), Regina Bissio (General's Wife), Renzo Marigano (Franco), Barbara Pilavin (Giulio's Wife), Luigi Zerbatini (Suocero).

Synopsis

Bank robbers Fabrizio (Oliver Reed), Raoul (Bruno Cirino) and Sylvia (Nicoletta Machiavelli) try kidnapping for a change of pace. Their victims are Giulio (Marcello Mastroianni), a wealthy industrialist, and Danda (Carol Andre), his mistress. Their escape by car becomes a public farce when everything possible goes wrong. Their retreat in a stolen Mercedes is followed by the press, the police, a group of television journalists in a camera car and a truck rented by a lemonade salesman to capitalize on thirsty onlookers! Giulio's father-in-law Suocero (Luigi Zerbatini), who is the real boss of the company, discusses plans to retrieve the pair with the police. But, after reviewing the company's paperwork he decides everyone is better off if Giulio is not returned. When the kidnappers are told that their ransom demand cannot be met by the deadline, Fabrizio grants an extension until the next day. The kidnappers and their captives are spotted by the police helicopter and hide in an old villa where they are reluctantly admitted by the General (Lionel Stander) and his wife (Regina Bissio). The television cameramen record their movements which are watched coldly by Giulio's wife (Barbara Pilavin). Giulio calls her to see when the ransom money is coming but his wife is more interested in Danda, whom he explains away as some girl he gave a lift to. Danda overhears and is not impressed; she turns her attentions to Fabrizio. Giulio is now completely lost; everyone in his life has abandoned him. Fabrizio contacts the police with new plans: he demands an airplane and the money for the following morning ... and frees Danda. Giulio's brother-in-law Franco (Renzo Marigano) and a policeman wearing only underpants and shoes hand over the money. Fabrizio pauses in the transaction to allow a funeral procession to pass; but it is a ruse. The kidnappers and their victim are machine-gunned.

Comment

Dirty Weekend aka *Mordi e Fuggi* was one of the few films on Reed's filmography that the authors were unable to view. A pity; it sounds, from the synopsis, very interesting.

It was shot in October and November 1972 in Italy — mainly Rome and the Viareggio-Geneva superhighway. After completing *Dirty Weekend*, Reed was to return briefly to London, then back to Europe for *Revolver*. This was to be followed by *Technically Sweet* which was to be directed by Michelangelo Antonioni but was never filmed.

Variety (March 28, 1973) was impressed with the movie: "Combination of known names and satiric touch of director Dino Risi should open many markets. Ingredient of suspense action gives the opening half almost frame by frame contrast to satire comedy. Skillful integration of both rarely gives spectator a chance to complete a chuckle or allow tension to undermine comedy. Mastroianni has a difficult task of playing a supine, spoiled, unprincipled bourgeois [and] he somehow infuses a degree of sympathy. Before the film ends, Reed's political motivations for the crime are washed down the drain of unbelievability by

his illogical violences — physical and psychological — that masks deeper doubts in his beliefs and aptitudes."

"Filming *Dirty Weekend* ... Reed showed up on set unshaven, disheveled and fell out of his car and lay motionless, apparently unconscious, on the road. No one noticed, or cared, so he got up and went and had a coffee" (Sellers, 154).

Days of Fury (1973)

Da Ma Produzione; Lowndes Productions Ltd.; released in the U.S. by International Coproductions in 1974 and in the U.K. by Fox-Rank in 1974

Crew Director: Antonio Calenda; Writers: Edward Bond, Antonio Calenda, Ugo Pirro; based on the novel *Vadim* by Lermontov; Producers: Marcello Danon, Harry Saltzman; Production Manager: Marcello Papaleo; Original Music: Riz Ortolani; Cinematography: Alfio Contini; Sound Editor: Ian Crafford; Editor: Sergio Montanari; Production Designer: Franco Ninnis; Set Decoration: Dario Michel; Costumes: Danilo Donati; Sound Recordist: Derek Leather.

Cast— Oliver Reed (Palizyn), Carole Andre (Irene), Claudia Cardinale (Anna), Ray Lovelock (Yuri), John McEnery (Vadim), Zora Valcova (Natalya).

Synopsis

Czarist Russia in 1774. With Pugacev's peasant revolt in the eastern provinces still a distant rumor, Palizyn (Oliver Reed), a rich landowner, spends his days hunting, wenching, ruling his downtrodden serfs with a rod of iron and wondering how to oust his frosty wife Natalya (Zora Valcova) in favor of his adopted daughter Irene (Carole Andre). One day, a stranger with a deformed shoulder, Vadim (John McEnery), arrives and asks for work. Swallowing the humiliations showered on him by Palizyn he soon worms his way into the master's favor while seizing every chance to foment rebellion among his fellow serfs. Irene, disturbed by Palizyn's sexual advances, and much taken by his handsome son Yuri (Ray Lovelock), who has just returned from the capital, is astonished when Vadim tells her she is his sister and that Palizyn killed their father to steal his lands. While Palizyn is hunting, Yuri and

Palizyn (Oliver Reed) in *Days of Fury* aka *One Russian Summer* (Da Ma Produzione/Lowndes/International Co-Productions, 1973).

Palizyn (Oliver Reed) and friend in *Days of Fury* (Da Ma Produzione/Lowndes/International Co-Productions, 1973).

Irene make love in the corn field. Later, as Palizyn relaxes at the buxom Anna's (Claudia Cardinale) inn, Vadim contacts a group of rebels and suggests that they loot Palizyn's estate. Natalya exacerbates the situation when she has one of the women flogged for theft.

The serfs and the rebels attack, killing everyone in the house and burning it; only Irene and Yuri escape. Yuri warns his father and rides for help while Palizyn and Irene are led to safety by Anna's idiot child. Unable to get help, Yuri returns to find his father has raped Irene. Father and son duel to the death while Vadim gloats. As Vadim closes in for his revenge, he is thwarted by the rebels who laughingly kill Palizyn and Irene. Vadim sobs with rage and grief.

Comment

This was Antonio Calenda's first feature film after his "graduation" from TV. The dialogue sounds rather like a cod–Ionesco script and is rather tedious, and the tried and tested TV techniques don't really work for long on the big screen. However, this is received wisdom as the authors were unable to find a print to review. "Oliver Reed indicat[es] the bluff brute by alternately roaring with laughter and sobbing uncontrollably" (unknown source).

Revolver (1973)

(Aka *Blood in the Streets*) Mega Film (Rome); Societe Nouvelle de Cinematographie (Paris); Dieter Geissler Filmprodukion (Germany); made in 1973, released by Independent International Pictures in the U.S. in 1975; no U.K. release; Eastman Color; 118 minutes

Crew—Director: Sergio Sollima; Producer: Hugo Santalveria; Screenplay: Ardinno Ma, Massimo De Rita, Sergio Sollima; Cinematographer: Aldo Scavarda; Editor: Sergio Montariari; Music: Ennio Morricone; Art Director: Cano Sim; Production Manager: Lino Maffei; Assistant Director: Fabrizio Castellani; Set Director: Guy Maugin; Wardrobe: A. Maria Tucci; Camera: Enrico Cortese; Makeup: Amato Garbini; Hair Stylist: Luisa Vanda Plovesar; Sound: Rene Longvet; Special Effects: Gianna D'Andrea; Costumes: Valeria Sponsall

Cast— Oliver Reed (Vito), Fabio Testi (Milo), Paoja Pitagora (Anna), Bernard Giraudeu (Granier), Frederick de Pajaquale (Niko), Gunnar Warner (Harmalochi), Mare Mazza (Carlotta), Peter Berling (Jon).

Synopsis

Milo (Fabio Testi), a small-time Italian criminal, buries his partner Jon (Peter Berling) after he's shot by the police. Jon had previously been the bodyguard of oil minister Harmalochi (Gunnar Warner) who was recently murdered by order of a mass government and police conspiracy. Niko (Frederick de Pajaquale), a singer with mob connections, gives police false information about the hit. Vito (Oliver Reed) is summoned to the prison he administers; while he's gone, his wife Anna (Paoja Pitagora) is kidnapped. Her abductors tell Vito that he must allow Milo to escape or Anna will be killed. Since Milo has only recently been incarcerated, Vito knows little about his background. He beats up Milo so that he must be hospitalized and can escape from the poorly secured infirmary. Vito picks him up outside and learns that Milo has no idea who engineered the plot. Anna is being held by the mysterious Granier (Bernard Giraudeu) who keeps her in Niko's flat. He kills Niko and plants evidence that incriminates Anna for murder and heroin trafficking. Vito and Milo form an uneasy trust — and also realize that they are quite a bit alike. Granier contacts Vito and tells him he must hand over Milo — now — or Anna will be turned over to the police. Vito realizes that Granier, who is tied in with the government corruption, must kill Milo because he has information about Harmalochi's murder. Vito goes to a government minister for help and he's told to resolve it himself. Is Anna's life worth saving Milo? Vito meets Milo in his girlfriend's flat and kills him. Anna is released and joins Vito at the police station. In the morgue is Granier, who was killed to silence him. Anna is stunned when Vito denies knowing him.

Comment

Revolver is a first-class thriller with a first-rate performance by Reed and a plot that's a bit more thought-provoking than one would expect. The plot is, at times, *too* thought-provoking. Many details are vaguely presented, but this adds to the film's interest because the audience is as clueless as Vito as to what exactly is going on. What's going on is a massive corruption of both police and government, and that situation is even more believable now than it was in 1974.

Reed plays Vito at a level of constant tension, and why not? His wife has been kidnapped, he's broken every rule he's ever believed in, and worse, he realizes that he and Milo aren't as different as he'd like. His frequent outbursts of violence, both verbal and physical, are frightening but never over-the-top. Reed delivers a believable performance as a man coming apart as he is in danger of losing everything he values. Fabio Testi, while hardly in Reed's league as an actor, looks good and tries hard, but his performance is diminished due to the dubbing and the fact that most of his scenes are with Reed. The other characters are adequately played, but don't really matter too much; this is a two-actor movie.

The Vito-Milo relationship is constantly shifting; they need each other but can't trust each other because neither one is sure about anything. After Vito realizes that the kidnapping and jailbreak were motivated by a cover-up of the massive corruption, he also realizes that that it doesn't really matter who wants Milo out — his wife's life is at stake and he's going to do whatever is necessary. Milo, naturally, is glad to be out, but he's just as uneasy as Vito — he doesn't know why. Milo is hardly an admirable character, but he has some rules. When he gets an opportunity to kill Vito and vanish, he hesitates.

> VITO: You know, I've seen a lot of murder but I've never seen the moment when a man becomes one.
>
> MILO: How can I let you live?
>
> VITO: Give me my wife and I'll make out I've never seen you.

In this scene, Milo shows that, given what comes later, he's more principled than Vito.

The peripheral characters in *Revolver*'s world of corruption are so shadowy and sleazy, they make Vito and Milo seem positively heroic. Granier, unlike Milo, has no rules or bottom line. He kills Niko who is, presumably, his ally and has no problems framing Anna. He tells Vito that the way to save Anna is to kill Milo himself. That he is subsequently killed by his presumed allies is not surprising. Vito's allies prove no better; he's given the same advice, more or less, by a high-ranking official. (The minister says, "Society has many ways of defending itself; red tape, prison bars, and the revolver.") Vito finally gives in and takes the latter to his final meeting with Milo who, at his girlfriend's flat, says he no longer cares about anything but putting an end to it all.

> MILO: Did you go to the police? Did you report me?
>
> VITO: Yes, I went to the police — not to report you. Jesus Christ! I went for their help and advice. The result of this help and advice was that I should see it through myself.

Milo is of the same mind: He's going to the police himself and blow everything. Vito begs him to stay; if he tells what he knows, Anna will suffer. When Milo opens the door, Vito shoots him in the back ... and then, four times more as he lies on the floor. Claiming self-defense, Vito is exonerated and reunited with Anna. But before they leave the police station, he is asked to identify a corpse. Granier has been killed to silence him, and looking at his corpse on a morgue tray, Vito denies ever having seen him before.

The film closes on a freeze frame of Anna, staring unbelieving at her teary-eyed husband. She knows Vito and Granier have met — is Vito now part of the corruption or does he, like Milo, just want an ending?

Revolver was filmed in Milan and Paris. Unlike similar American-made films of the period shot in "realistic" muddy color, *Revolver* was photographed in brilliant Eastman color. This combined with a typically excellent score by Ennio Morricone makes *Revolver* very easy on the eyes and ears.

Like the film, Reed also looks great, not unlike Gerald in *Women in Love* four years earlier. He gives a confident, convincing performance without a false step. But, behind the scenes, it may have been a different story. On the 2004 Blue Underground DVD release of *Revolver*, director Sergio Sollima and star Fabio Testi recall a man on the edge:

> SOLLIMA: Fabio Testi was not often required to act, but not so here. He was good. He was good even in difficult scenes. Especially when you have to work next to somebody like Oliver Reed.
>
> TESTI: Working with Oliver Reed at that time was very appealing to me. And we liked each other from the beginning even if Oliver was a ... let's just say he liked to drink.
>
> SOLLIMA: Well, Oliver was a very lovely person until two or three in the afternoon. We had to shoot his scenes during the early bottles.
>
> TESTI: The idea of working with somebody like Oliver Reed was exciting on one hand but on the other it was difficult in certain scenes. When he came on the set drunk, he had the tendency to become violent.
>
> SOLLIMA: Oliver Reed belonged to that particular group of actors who needed to be restrained rather than encouraged. He tended to overact a bit. He had to be restrained even though his character needed to be violent.
>
> TESTI: We used to improvise a lot because Oliver, like a good racehorse, was never constrained by a script.

If the above assessment is accurate (and, unfortunately, there's little reason not to think so), Reed's extra-curricular activities were beginning at this early date to intrude into his on-set behavior. *Revolver* afforded Reed a good role in a good movie; he would have very few modern-day parts as good as this one in the future.

The Three Musketeers — The Queen's Diamonds (1973)

Alexander Salkind; Film Trust SA/Este Films; Twentieth Century–Fox Film Corporation; released by Twentieth Century–Fox in the U.S. and U.K. in 1974; Technicolor; Panavision; U.K. Certificate U; 107 minutes

Crew— Director: Richard Lester; Producer: Alexander Salkind; Executive Producer: Ilya Salkind; Executive in Charge of Production: Pierre Spengler; Associate Producer; Wolfdigeter von Stein; Screenplay: George MacDonald Fraser, based on the novel by Alexandre Dumas; Music: Michel Legrande; Cinematographer: David Watkin; Editor: John Victor Smith; Assistant Editor: Peter Boyle; Production Designer: Brian Eatwell; Art Directors: Les Dilley, Fernando Gonzales; Special Effects Supervisor: Pablo Perez; Property, Special Effects: Eddie Fowlie; Fight Director: William Hobbs; Stunt Arranger: Joaquim Parra; Camera Operators: Peter Ewens, Paul Wilson; Camera Assistants: Ronnie Anscombe, Frank Elliott, Luis Pena; Production Assistants: Antonio Del Toro, Luis Diaz Gonzales, Juan Jose Molina, John Ornstein; Continuity: Ann Skinner; Costume Designer: Yvonne Blake; General Production Manager: Francisco Bellot; Production Supervisor: Enrique Esteban; Production Coordinator: Jean-Philippe Merand; First Assistant Director: Clive Reed; Assistant Directors: Francisco Rodriguez, Dusty Symonds, Alain Walker; Makeup Supervisor: Alberto De Rossi; Charlton Heston's Makeup: Cristobal Criado; Raquel Welch's Makeup: Charlene Roberson; Hairdresser Supervisor: Grazia De Rossi; Hairdresser: Carmen Sanchez; Makeup Artist–Wigmaker: Jose Antonio Sanchez; Faye Dunaway's Hairdresser: Susan Germaine; Raquel Welch's Hairdresser: Kaye Pownall; Costume Supervisor: Jean Ray; Raquel Welch's Wardrobe Assistant: Manuela Iglesias; Sound Mixers: Roy J. Charman, Simon Kaye; Sound Editors: Don Challis, Don Sharpe; Dubbing Mixer: Gerry Humphreys; Boom Operators: Tom Buchanan, George B. Rice.

Cast— Oliver Reed (Athos), Raquel Welch (Mme. Constance Bonancieux), Richard Chamberlain (Aramis), Michael York (D'Artagnan), Frank Finlay (Porthos/O'Reilly), Christopher Lee (Rochefort), Geraldine Chaplin (Queen Anne), Jean-Pierre Cassel (Louis XIII, dubbed by Richard Briers), Spike Milligan (M. Bonancieux), Roy Kinnear (Planchet), Georges Wilson (Treville), Simon Ward (Duke of Buckingham), Faye Dunaway (Milady de Winter), Charlton Heston (Cardinal Richelieu), Joss Ackland (D'Artagnan's Father), Nicole Calfan (Kitty), Michael Gothard (Felton), Sybil Danning (Eugenie), Gitty Djamal (Beatrice), Angel del Pozo (Jussac), Rodney Bewes (Spy), Ben Aris (First Musketeer), William Hobbs (Assassin), Gretchen Franklin (D'Artagnan's Mother), Francis De Wolfe (Sea Captain), Frank Thornton (Man in Carriage Ogling Mme. Bonancieux's Bust).

Synopsis

Hoping to become a musketeer in the service of King Louis XIII, young D'Artagnan (Michael York) travels to Paris and befriends musketeers Athos (Oliver Reed), Aramis (Richard Chamberlain) and Porthos (Frank Finlay) after he helps them defeat some guards of the dangerous Cardinal Richelieu (Charlton Heston) who would like to usurp the weak king's power for himself. The cardinal's deadly assassin is Rochefort (Christopher Lee), nicknamed the cardinal's "Living Blade." D'Artagnan falls in love with the queen's dressmaker and confidante, Constance Bonancieux (Raquel Welch), as beautiful as she is clumsy, when he lodges at her husband's house. He also gets into numerous fights alongside his new friends and learns devious ways from them to make ends meet in expensive Paris. Queen Anne (Geraldine Chaplin), ignored by her effete husband, falls in love with the English Duke of Buckingham (Simon Ward) and foolishly gives him a magnificent diamond necklace which had been a present from the king as a love token. She also ends the relationship because discovery would mean disgrace and banishment. The duke returns to England promising to see her again within the year. However, Rochefort has been made aware of the queen's indiscretion and informs the cardinal.

Seizing the opportunity, the cardinal plans a great ball, supposedly to honor the king and queen; he slyly suggests that the queen should wear the king's magnificent gift at the ball. The cardinal also sends word to his agent Milady de Winter (Faye Dunaway) to travel to England and steal the necklace from Buckingham. Milady seduces Buckingham and steals two of the diamonds from the necklace. The queen confides in Constance who in turn tells her lover; he rushes to England with a letter from the queen begging for the return of the necklace. The three musketeers help him escape from the cardinal's forces. Athos' cape is caught on the blades of an irrigation wheel which hoists him into the air and leaves him at the mercy of the cardinal's men. To get to England, D'Artagnan has to defeat Rochefort and steal his travel pass. Just as he's about to lose the fight, D'Artagnan's faithful servant Planchet (Roy Kinnear) smacks Rochefort in the head with an uprooted sapling. It is only when D'Artagnan delivers the letter that Buckingham discovers two of the gems are missing and the race is on to make fake copies and return the completed necklace to the queen. Rushing back to France, D'Artagnan finds himself outnumbered by the cardinal's troops until, bruised, bandaged and limping, the three musketeers arrive to fight beside him. The necklace is returned in time to save the king and queen from the cardinal's plot. D'Artagnan is made a musketeer and his enemies look on unhappily. The cardinal is content to wait for another opportunity to seize power but Milady, Rochefort's lover, swears that she will have revenge on the now four musketeers.

Comment

Michael York, cast as D'Artagnan, noted in his autobiography *Accidentally on Purpose* that director Richard Lester "pioneered an irreverent freewheeling style of screen humor, a cine-cynicism that had exactly caught the essence of the youthful sixties with its brash blowing of raspberries at convention and throwing of banana skins under establishment pomposity."

Lester had already wowed the cinema with *A Hard Day's Night* and *Help!*, both starring the Beatles, and initially he had penned the leading roles in *The Three Musketeers* for them. In choosing George MacDonald Fraser to pen the script he was assured of multiple opportunities to indulge his sense of humor. But this is balanced by his passion for authenticity — in the sets, costumes, weaponry and props — creating a reality where the audience can almost smell the rubbish in the streets. Because of Lester's passion for realism, his stars had to fight with much heavier weapons than had been employed in previous musketeers movies, utilizing all the items around them as *ad hoc* weapons. The fights have a reality missing from the earlier movies. Hardly anyone got off scot free from the fight sequences, with Oliver Reed taking a direct hit, due to a lapse of concentration on his part. It was suggested that Reed was injured by an irked stuntman, hospitalized and given blood transfusions. Of course, these things grow terribly in the re-telling; William Hobbs, the fight choreographer who was on the spot at the time of the incident, tells a completely different story, but it will probably sell fewer books!

Quentin Tarantino is reported as saying, "During the fight training Reed threw himself

Athos (Oliver Reed) in a pensive mood in Richard Lester's spirited version of the Alexander Dumas classic *The Three Musketeers* (Salkind/Film Trust/Este/20th Century–Fox, 1973).

into the fighting so much he made all the other musketeers work twice as hard. They knew if they didn't, Reed was going to own the movie completely. He was that good. You've never seen sword fights the way Reed fights them in this movie." "Oliver Reed was a terrifying presence, an extremely dangerous man," recalled Richard Chamberlain. "He could be very sweet, but if he turned on you, he could make life terrible for you. He was up all night, drinking, then coming to work the next day and being fine" (Sellers, 162).

Reed said of his co-stars, "Faye Dunaway took me into the park and gave me too much wine and told me she respected me but I was a son of a bitch. Well, that summed the women on that film" (*Daily Mail*, September 20, 1972). He continued, "I am much better than I am given credit for. Last year I was third British box office draw. This year I will be the first." In the *Evening News* (November 13, 1973) he said, "The trouble with talking about the birds I act with is that if I say something about them and I've got a twinkle in my eye — the quote goes into print without the twinkle and becomes gospel."

The critics were universally complimentary. "The nature of camp is such that it is aesthetically unassailable, for to criticize it at all one must take it more seriously than the people who created it.... Boisterously. Mr. Lester seems almost exclusively concerned with action, preferably comic, and after a while one gets the impression that he and his fencing masters labored too long in choreographing the elaborate duels. Another of the director's fascinations is period detail, which is sometimes more fun than the comic action scenes" (*New York Times*, April 14, 1974); "The film is what the industry needs. Let's do without water closets and go back to crinolines and lace, eyepatches and feathers" (*Film Review*, April 1974); "[The] Musketeers are played with panache.... Oliver Reed as the gutsy one" (*Variety*, December 26, 1974).

What the outside world didn't know was that the producers had "pulled a fast one." Imagine the surprise and anger of the main cast members at the Paris premiere to watch the final credits roll *halfway* through the movie they had just made. As Christopher Lee told Tom Johnson, his script was entitled *The Three Musketeers* and the contract was for one "project." What was originally planned as a long, roadshow presentation with an intermission had been changed by the wily producers Alexander and Ilya Salkind into two separate movies, and all the principal players could do was complain loudly since the contracts they had signed used the term "project" and not "film." The wrangle went on for some time — and probably meant that anyone else who worked for the Salkinds paid particular attention to every word on the contract from then on. On April 3, 1973, *Variety* reported that the Salkinds had settled their feud with the *Three Musketeers* actors: "Thespians and/or their agents have asked for extra pay while producers insisted no extra chores were involved. The settlement gives actors a percentage share of the profits earned by the follow-up."

Reed probably appreciated the settlement since his home, Broome Hall, was voraciously eating up every penny he earned in its restoration costs. According to the March 21, 1974,

TV Times, "It is by no means complete. The team of builders has been working on the house since he moved in and look like continuing to do so indefinitely. Reed sleeps on the ground floor, in what was once the billiards room. [Reed said,] 'It was in a terrible state when we moved in. There were 25 ceilings down in the first week. All the wiring and plumbing had to be replaced.' Many of the rooms are still without furniture."

Reed's Athos is a masterpiece; he is the overt leader of the musketeers, quick to anger, strong in a fight, a wily tactician and not above using his talents to procure his group food and wine without payment. Perhaps he was Athos in another life! This image of the larger-than-life character has lived on after him; only recently, in an episode of the TV show *NCIS LA* (2009), the diminutive lady who rules the office suggests a Scotch to the returning agents who remark on its excellence. "Oliver Reed thought so too and wanted to make me a 'special musketeer' because of it," she says. "He kept his rapier in his scabbard and I kept the Scotch!"

The Three Musketeers was nominated for four BAFTAs: Best Art Direction, Cinematography, Costume designs and Film Editing. Michel Legrande was awarded a BAFTA for his original music score. Not bad for half a movie.

Ten Little Indians (U.K. Title); And Then There Were None (1974)

Corona Film Produktion (Munich); Comeci Production (Paris); Coralta Cinematografica; Oceania Produzioni Cinematografiche; Talia Films; released by AVCO Embassy Pictures in the U.S. in 1975; no U.K. release; Eastman Color; 105 minutes

Crew— Director: Peter Collinson; Producer: Harry Alan Towers; Screenplay: Peter Welbeck; Cinematographer: Fernando Arribas; Music: Brina Nicolai; Set Design: Jose Maria Tapiador; Editor: John Trumper; Post-Production Supervisor: Nicholas Wentworth; Continuity: Sue Merry; Sound: Mike Le Mape; Assistant Director: Mike Crowley.

Cast— Oliver Reed (Hugh Lombard), Elke Sommer (Vera Clyde), Richard Attenborough (Judge Cannon), Herbert Lom (Dr. Armstrong), Gert Frobe (Blore), Adolfo Celi (General Soule), Charles Az-

Vera (Elke Sommer) and Hugh (Oliver Reed) in Agatha Christie's oft-filmed mystery *Ten Little Indians* (Corona/Comeci, 1974).

navour (Raven), Alberto De Mendoza (Mr. Martino), Maria Rohm (Elsa Martino), Stephane Audran (Ilona), Orson Welles (Voice of Owen).

Synopsis

Eight disparate guests arrive at an isolated Iranian hotel: Hugh Lombard (Oliver Reed), Vera Clyde (Elke Sommer), Judge Cannon (Richard Attenborough), Dr. Armitage (Herbert Lom), Raven (Charles Aznavour), Blore (Gert Frobe), General Soule (Adolfo Celi) and Ilona (Stephane Audran). They are greeted by the staff— Martino (Albert De Mendoza) and his wife Elsa (Maria Rohm)— and the tape recorded voice of Mr. U.N. Owen (Orson Welles). He informs them that he knows they are all murderers who have gone unpunished and that he will rectify that. They have never heard of Mr. Owen, or each other; they worriedly go to their rooms where each one finds a framed version of the nursery rhyme "Ten Little Indians." At dinner they find the table center-

piece to be ten Indian dolls. After dinner, as the rhyme predicted, the deaths begin with Raven, poisoned by his drink. Blore reveals that he is a private detective hired by Mr. Owen and grudgingly the group admits to different levels of guilt. The general suggests they search for Mr. Owen; when that proves to be fruitless, the judge announces that one of *them* must be Owen. Elsa tries to escape and is murdered; her husband dies in the desert; Ilona is bitten in her room by a poisonous snake; the general is stabbed in the cellar; the judge is shot with Lombard's gun; and Blore is pushed from a balcony after spotting the doctor's corpse on the patio. Finally there's only Vera and "Lombard"— who reveals to her that he is actually a friend of Lombard, who recently committed suicide. She fires his gun at him and returns to the hotel to find the judge, who had tricked the doctor into faking his (the judge's) death. He explains his reasons for killing those whom he feels escaped justice and suggests that she hang herself as she'll be the only suspect left after he commits suicide. As he drinks from a bottle of poison, "Lombard"—who along with Vera tricked the judge as he had tricked the others — walks into the room.

Comment

Ten Little Indians was the third official adaptation of British crime queen Agatha Christie's classic, the unfortunately titled *Ten Little Niggers* (1939). Retitled *And Then There Were None* in America, it was first filmed under that title in 1945.

Twenty years later producer Harry Alan Towers had a go with *Ten Little Indians,* which starred Hugh O'Brien as Lombard. Also appearing were Shirley Eaton, the most famous Bond girl, and an uncredited Christopher Lee as the voice of Owen. Towers went back to the subject again in 1974, this time corralling Orson Welles as "The Voice."

Oliver Reed headed an impressive B+ cast of stars, including two of the best James Bond villains: Gert Frobe (*Goldfinger,* 1964) and Adolfo Celi (*Thunderball,* 1965). Also along for the ride were Sir Richard Attenborough in his pre–Gandhi days and the vastly underrated Herbert Lom. Charles Aznavour lets the audience down somewhat as — what else?— a singer, but Elke Sommer was suitably terrified and adorable.

As the eight victims arrive by helicopter at the hotel (the Sha Abbas — a beautiful, magical building), Oliver Reed immediately makes his presence known. As the others walk as a herd towards the hotel, Reed turns to face the helicopter — and the camera — giving the off-screen pilot a smile and a thumbs up. He then helps Attenborough, whose character walks with a cane, up a few stairs. Since none of the others do anything, one wonders whether this was scripted or an example of Oliver Reed's on camera improvisations as Sir Christopher Lee pointed out in his Foreword.

Considering the dire situation, Oliver Reed's "Lombard" (he never reveals his real name) is in pretty good humor throughout the film yet commits the only on-screen act of violence when he viciously slaps Martino for an intemperate outburst. As usual though, there is an undercurrent of menace lurking just beneath the surface.

The main players are pretty much given an equal spotlight which is good, given the limits of Peter Welbeck's (Harry Alan Towers) script and the familiar nature of the plot. Oliver Reed's best scene: he's in bed (but fully clothed) with Elke Sommer, where she reveals that her character is innocent of killing her sister's fiancé— it was actually her sibling that committed the crime, though she did cover it up. Lombard has been accused of killing his pregnant girlfriend.

LOMBARD: But don't you see — that means one thing — our "Mr. Owen" is not infallible. It means you don't belong here — you didn't kill your way into it.

VERA: But the others did. Hugh Lombard did.

LOMBARD: That's another thing our "Mr. Owen" doesn't know. You see, my name is not really Hugh Lombard.

VERA: What do you mean?

LOMBARD: He was my best friend and he committed suicide — I think it was a sense of guilt about the girl. I knew her ... she was ... she was ... anyway, his parents wanted me to clear up some of his affairs. I was looking through his desk and found the invitation from our mysterious Mr. Owen.

The scene is done in two long-take setups and both performances are very low-key in contrast to the high energy acting that preceded it. Both are given the opportunity to inject some humanity into their characters and are successful.

Old pros Herbert Lom and Sir Richard Attenborough are, as expected, wonderful and have a nice scene bulling each other over a game of billiards, forming an uneasy alliance that Lom will soon regret. As they are about to ascend the staircase, neither trusts the other sufficiently to go first; they end up walking up the stairs side by side! Unrevealed to the audience is that Lom agrees to help Attenborough fake his death so that the latter "will be free to find Owen." The trick is turned back on the villain when the two remaining sinners pull it on him.

Reviews, following *Ten Little Indians'* January 18, 1975, release, were generally dismissive. "Oliver Reed, an able English actor, moves through the film like a cruise director on a sinking ship. He pretends to a character that has absolutely nothing to do with the story or the quality of the movie being made. He slaps Attenborough on the back and gives Lom an encouraging squeeze on the arm. Playfully, he slaps Elke Sommer's bottom. Nothing helps. They — and we — know they are in the middle of a disaster" (*New York Times,* April 24, 1975). "They have turned the Christie classic into a soporific, bloodless bore. None of the Christie pleasures are forthcoming in this latest version. Welbeck's screenplay is perfunctory in every aspect.... The one happy inspiration was the decision to move the setting from an island to a hotel in the middle of the Iranian desert" (*Product Digest,* May 14, 1975). "Though it's far less distinguished than its fore-runners, it should do modest-to-Ok business for those new audiences who aren't familiar with the story" (*Variety,* February 26, 1975).

Although *Ten Little Indians* has an interesting cast and a stunning setting going for it, the movie just doesn't make it. At 100 minutes it is too long and despite eight deaths is never very exciting or suspenseful. But a movie that lists its cast "in order of disappearance" can't be all bad.

Mahler (1974)

Goodtimes Enterprises Productions; released by VPS-Goodman in the U.K. in 1974 and by Mayfair Films in the U.S. in 1976; Running Time 115 minutes; Technicolor; U.K. Certificate AA

Crew — Screenplay-Director: Ken Russell; Producer: Roy Baird; Executive Producer: Sandy Lieberson; Executive Producer: David Putnam; Cinematographer: Dick Bush; Film Editor: Michael Bradsell; Art Director: Ian Whittaker; Costume Design: Shirley Russell; Hair Stylist: Joyce James; Makeup Artist: Peter Robb-King; Production Supervisor: John Comfort; Assistant Director: Mike Gowans; Chief Props: Andy Andrews; Associate Art Director: Roger Christian; Original Oil Painting: Paul Dufficey; Props Buyer: Jill Quertier; Construction Manager: Peter Verard; Sound Recordiat: Ian Bruce; Dubbing Editor: Ian Fuller; Sound Recording Mixer: Gerry Humphreys; Boom Operator: Charkie McFadden; Special Effects: John Richardson; Camera Grip: David Cadwallader; Camera Operator: Eddie Collins; Gaffer: Micky Thomas; Assistant Camera: Malcolm Vinson; Wardrobe Master: Richard Pointing; Assistant Costume Designer: Leonard Pollack; Assistant Editor: Stuart Baird; Conductor: Bernard Haitink; Co-conductor: John Forsythe; Music Coordinator: John Forsythe; Composer of "Alma's Song": Dana Gillespie; Piano Music Arranger: Michael Moores; Production Assistant: Clinton Cavers; Producer's Assistant: Brenda Dale; Location Manager: Richard Green; Choreographer: Gillian Gregory; Script Supervisor: Kay Mander.

Cast — Robert Powell (Gustav Mahler), Georgina Hale (Alma Mahler), Lee Montague (Bernhard Mahler), Miriam Karlin (Aunt Rose), Rosalie Crutchley (Marie Mahler), Gary Rich (Young Gustav), Richard Morant (Max), Angela Down (Justine Mahler), Antonia Ellis (Cosima Wagner), Ronald Pickup (Nick), Peter Eyre (Otto Mahler), Dana Gillespie (Anna von Mildenburg), George Coulouris (Dr. Roth), David Collings (Hugo Wolf), Arnold Yarrow (Grandfather), David Trevena (Dr. Richter), Elaine Delmar (Princess), Benny Lee (Uncle Arnold), Andrew Faulds (Doctor on Train), Otto Diamant (Prof. Sladky), Michael Southgate (Alois Mahler), Ken Colley (Krenek), Sarah McClellan (Putzi), Claire McClellan (Glucki), Oliver Reed (Train Conductor).

Synopsis

Europe, 1911. While touring by train with his wife Alma (Georgina Hale), the middle-aged composer Gustav Mahler (Robert Powell) recalls incidents from his past: the early years of his marriage; the death of his daughter; a meeting with Hugo Wolf (David Collings), a deranged composer; his conversion to Christianity from Judaism; and Alma's possible infidelity. Most of the recollections are in the form of fantasy, colored by Mahler's fertile imagination and suppressed longing for his own death. This is nearly realized when he has a heart attack on the train. He is treated by a doctor (Andrew Faulds) and given cause for hope. Mahler leaves the train with Alma, unaware that his next attack will be fatal.

Comment

Ken Russell continued his exploration of music and its creators with his well-made but inaccessible film. Like most of his biographies of composers, *Mahler* is not to be taken literally.

Russell is quoted in the Goodtimes press release: "My film is simply about some of the things I feel when I think of Mahler's life and listen to his music. It is by no means a definitive view. There are as many facets to the mystery of Mahler's music as there are lovers of it." In his autobiography *Altered States* he wrote, "I donned my Sherlock Holmes outfit and searched for the soul of the man in his music, while also keeping the facts of his life in mind. And just as I had with Tchaikovsky, I found a lot of bombast along the way — the sound and fury of a tormented artist. I also found music that was brutal, vulgar, grotesque, macabre — and was inevitably pilloried for reflecting these elements in the film." One of these "pilloried" moments could have involved Cosima Wagner (Antonia Ellis), costumed as a storm trooper, dancing before the Jewish Mahler on an altar as he grovels at her feet.

Robert Powell delivered his typical thoughtful performance in the lead but it's not enough. Mahler was too obscure a personality to the general audience to survive Russell's foray into the "brutal, vulgar and grotesque."

Reed has a tiny role as a stationmaster. Why he was asked — or accepted — we don't know, other than for another Reed-Russell in-joke. Or perhaps it was the bottles of champagne as a fee and the chance to spend time with friends that led him to appear. If so, it really wasn't worth his time. Reed was riding high after *The Three Musketeers* and should have been capitalizing on that; this sort of thing did his career no good at all. The film previewed at the Haymarket Odeon on April 14, 1974, and reviewers (like general audience members) didn't know what to make of it. "I found a great deal loud, even offensive" (*The Guardian*, April 4, 1974); "Russell's film has its eye-catching moments, but they are hardly enough to add up to a whole film" (*Financial Times*, April 5, 1974); "To ride along with it is an extraordinary experience, bruises and all" (*Cinema TV Today*, April 13, 1974).

Mahler is, like all of Russell's films, worth seeing, but don't expect to learn much about the composer or see much of Reed.

The Four Musketeers — Milady's Revenge (1975)

Este Films; Film Trust SA; released by 20th Century–Fox in the U.K. and the U.S. in 1975; color

Crew— Director: Richard Lester; Producer: Alexander Salkind; Executive Producer: Ilya Salkind; Executive in Charge of Production: Pierre Spengler; Associate Producer; Wolfdieter von Stein; Screenplay: George MacDonald Fraser, based on the novel by Alexandre Dumas; Music: Lalo Schifrin; Cinematographer: David Watkin; Editor: John Victor Smith; Assistant Editor: Peter Boyle; Production Designer: Brian Eatwell; Art Directors: Les Dilley, Fernando Gonzales; Special Effects Supervisor: Pablo Perez; Property, Special Effects: Eddie Fowlie; Fight Director: William Hobbs; Stunt Arranger: Joaquim Parra; Camera Operators: Peter Ewens, Paul Wilson; Camera Assistants: Ronnie Anscombe, Frank Elliott, Luis Pena; Production Assistants: Antonio Del Toro, Luis Diaz Gonzales, Juan Jose Molina, John Ornstein; Continuity: Ann Skinner; Costume Designer: Yvonne Blake; General Production Manager: Francisco Bellot; Production Supervisor: Enrique Esteban; Production Coordinator: Jean-Philippe Merand; First Assistant Director: Clive Reed; Assistant Directors: Francisco Rodriguez, Dusty Symonds, Alain Walker; Makeup Supervisor: Alberto De Rossi; Charlton Heston's Makeup: Cristobal Criado; Raquel Welch's Makeup: Charlene Roberson; Hairdresser Supervisor: Grazia De Rossi; Hairdresser: Carmen Sanchez; Makeup Artist–Wigmaker: Jose Antonio Sanchez; Faye Dunaway's Hairdresser: Susan Germaine; Raquel Welch's Hairdresser: Kaye Pownall; Costume Supervisor: Jean Ray; Raquel Welch's Wardrobe Assistant: Manuela Iglesias; Sound Mixers: Roy J. Charman, Simon Kaye; Sound Editors: Don Challis, Don Sharpe; Dubbing Mixer: Gerry Humphreys; Boom Operators: Tom Buchanan, George B Rice.

Cast— Oliver Reed (Athos), Raquel Welch (Mme. Constance Bonancieux), Richard Chamberlain (Aramis), Michael York (D'Artagnan), Frank Finlay (Porthos/O'Reilly), Christopher Lee (Rochefort), Geraldine Chaplin (Queen Anne), Jean-Pierre Cassel (Louis XIII, dubbed by Richard Briers), Spike Milligan (M. Bonancieux), Roy Kinnear (Planchet), Georges Wilson (Treville), Simon Ward (Duke of Buckingham), Faye Dunaway (Milady de Winter), Charlton Heston (Cardinal Richelieu), Joss Ackland (D'Artagnan's Father), Nicole Calfan (Kitty), Michael Gothard (Felton), Sybil Danning (Eugenie), Gitty Djamal (Beatrice), Angel del Pozo (Jussac), Bob Todd (Firing Squad Leader), Tom Buchanan (Firing Squad Sergeant), Leon Greene (Swiss Officer), Lucy Tiller (Mother Superior), Norman Chapell (Submarine Inventor), Tyrone Cassidy (English Officer), Eduardo Fajardo, Jack Watson, Richard Adams (Soldiers).

Synopsis

Cardinal Richlieu (Charlton Heston) endeavors to stop the Duke of Buckingham (Simon Ward) from sending English reinforcements to aid the protestant rebels against the king. There is much political unrest in France, mostly stirred up by the cardinal in his attempts to depose the king and seize his power. The cardinal has Madame Bonancieux (Raquel Welch) kidnapped so that she can no longer act as go-between for the French queen and the English duke. D'Artagnan (Michael York), Athos (Oliver Reed), Porthos (Frank Finlay) and Aramis (Richard Chamberlain) rescue her and hide her in a remote convent. Athos tells D'Artagnan that he once loved a woman who was revealed to be a harlot and a thief after he had married her; it left him a "poor and dishonored man" and drove him to drink where he had stayed ever since. Surprisingly it is Milady de Winter of whom he speaks and to whom he is still married. Milady has been sent to England to assassinate Buckingham. However, she is caught and imprisoned in the Tower where she promptly seduces her jailer, the Puritan Felton (Michael Gothard), and convinces him that the duke is the Antichrist who aims to kill all Protestants so that he might sleep with the French Catholic queen. He frees her and murders the duke on the quayside. Back in France she is congratulated by her lover Rochefort (Christopher Lee) on the success of her mission. He plans that they should race ahead to the convent and kill Madame Bonancieux before the musketeers can arrive. They also plan the deaths of the four musketeers. Milady is delighted with the plan; she strangles Madame Bonancieux with a massive rosary as the musketeers are desperately fighting Rochefort and his men. In a thrilling duel D'Artagnan kills Rochefort. Athos captures Milady as she tries to escape and later she is beheaded on an island as the musketeers watch.

Without the aid of English soldiers the Protestant rebellion collapses and the cardinal must content himself with this victory. The four musketeers gallop off into the sunset as Pothos shouts their motto, "One for all and all for one!"

Comment

This sequel offers, along with the same outstanding acting, a much darker tone and less slapstick comedy than in the first film.... This time the memorable sword fights, while still kinetic and entertaining, seldom mix physical humor with the deaths, otherwise the emotional impact of some events, such as the murders of the Duke and Mme Bonancieux would seem compromised emotionally. Instead, they sting [Johnson and Miller, 267].

The decision of the Salkinds to divide the movie into two films obviously upset the balance of light and dark that Richard Lester had created in the whole; the amazing thing is that it is not too upsetting. The Musketeers, now four, go on in the same rollicking way, fighting, wenching and generally getting into trouble while involved in the politics of the day. Athos (Oliver Reed) is definitely the Number One Musketeer and the others follow his lead. And since Reed made sure that his fight sequences were superb, and he attacked them and his opponents with brio, none could deny it.

Speaking to Tom Johnson, Christopher Lee remarked, "He was a real talent when he wanted to be." At the execution of Milady, the fleeting look of pity and regret that crosses Athos' face is superb — Reed is not just the master of the grand gesture.

Filming in 100°-plus heat with authentic, heavy clothes, the actors found it hard to cope. Certainly they hoped that there wouldn't be more than a couple of takes for the fight scenes, which were exhausting.

This film was originally set to be shot in Hungary; when it was found that the variety of needed locations couldn't be found there, the production shifted to Spain. The film unit, while based in Madrid, travelled hundreds of miles to 55 locations, using 90 vehicles and 200 crew members. Often using multiple cameras, Lester ensured that he had a wealth of interesting angles from which to choose while overseeing the editing of the finished product. Filming lasted from May 10, 1972, until September and ate up a budget of around $7 million, utilizing 110 sets between the two halves of the film.

The Los Angeles premiere at the Vogue

Theatre (March 20, 1975) was graced by the presence of Raquel Welch, Richard Chamberlain, Michael York, Charlton Heston and Christopher Lee. Reviews were as positive as they had been for part one: "A rollicking romp with the cast having as much fun as the audience" (Gene Shalit, NBC); "*The Four Musketeers* is icy and artfully executed without the pretense to lightheartedness that falsified its predecessor" (*Newsweek*); "Visually the film is never less than stunning. It contains a few imaginative ideas and the action sequences are spectacular" (*Daily Express*).

Tommy (1975)

Robert Stigwood Organization; Hemdale Film; released by Hemdale Film Distribution in the U.K. and by Columbia Pictures in the U.S.; 111 minutes; color

Crew— Screenplay-Director: Ken Russell; Producers: Robert Stigwood, Ken Russell; Executive Producers: Beryl Vertue, Christopher Stamp; Associate Producer: Harry Benn; Cinematographers: Dick Bush, Ronnie Taylor; Art Director: John Clark; Set Designer: Paul Dufficey; Film Editor: Stuart Bird; Production Manager: John Cornford; Costume Design: Shirley Russell; Music Director: Pete Townshend; Music Editor: Terry Rowlings; Music Recordist: Ron Nevison; Camera Operator: Eddie Collins; Assistant Director: Jonathan Berson; Continuity: Kay Mander; Sound Recordist: Iain Bruce; Dubbing Mixer: Bill Rowe; Wardrobe Supervisor: Richard Pointing; Makeup: George Blackler, Peter Robb-King; Hairdresser: Joyce James; Location Managers: Lee Bolon, Ricky Green; Choreographer: Gillian Gregory; Set Dresser: Ian Whittaker; Special Effects: Effects Associates; Unit Publicist: Brian Doyle.

Cast—Oliver Reed (Frank), Ann-Margret (Nora), Roger Daltrey (Tommy), Elton John (Pinball Wizard), Eric Clapton (Preacher), Keith Moon (Uncle Ernie), Jack Nicholson (The Specialist), Robert Powell (Group Captain Walker), Paul Nicholas (Cousin Kevin), Tina Turner (Acid Queen), Barry Winch (Young Tommy), Arthur Brown (Priest), Mary Holland (Sally Simpson), and The Who: Pete Townshend, Keith Moon, John Entwhistle.

Frank (Oliver Reed) and Nora (Ann-Margret) before things go wrong in Ken Russell's *Tommy* (Stigwood/Columbia, 1975), based on The Who's rock opera.

Synopsis

In World War II Britain, Nora (Ann-Margret) gives birth to Tommy after learning that her husband, Group Captain Walker (Robert Powell), has been shot down and is presumed dead. Six years later, she meets the flamboyant Frank (Oliver Reed), a Holiday Camp host, and they become lovers. Walker inexplicably returns and finds Nora with Frank; a fight ensues and Walker is killed accidentally. Tommy (Barry Winch) is told, "You didn't see it, you didn't hear it, you won't say nothing to nobody." As a result of this trauma, the child becomes deaf, dumb and blind.

As an adult, Tommy (Roger Daltrey) lives in a sad, solitary world devoid of outside sensations. His guilt-ridden mother tries to cure him by any means possible, including taking him to the bizarre Acid Queen (Tina Turner). She injects him with drugs that enable him to see his reflection but not to interact with the world. Left in the care of his evil cousin Kevin (Paul Nicholas) and his perverted Uncle Ernie (Keith Moon) only adds to Tommy's misery. Tommy finds a pinball machine and, through his extra sensory perception, becomes an expert and then the world champion by defeating the Pinball Wizard (Elton John). A visit to a psychiatrist (Jack Nicholson) accomplishes little; he's more interested in Nora than in her son. While watching Tommy stare at his reflection, the frustrated Nora pushes him through the mirror; miraculously, his senses are restored. Tommy is now proclaimed as the new Messiah. Frank and Nora sense the financial possibilities and begin marketing Tommy and his cure at a series of concerts and at his own Holiday Camp. But, though meaning well, they go too far; their commercialization of Tommy's philosophy turn his followers against them. Distraught at the trinkets being sold to them instead of being allowed to experience Tommy's beliefs, his followers riot and kill Frank and Nora. Tommy is alone again, but free.

Comment

The Who (vocalist Roger Daltrey, guitarist Pete Townshend, bassist John Entwhistle and drummer Keith Moon) spearheaded the second wave of the "British Invasion" of the U.S. in the

Frank (Oliver Reed) living large — for the moment — in The Who's *Tommy* (Stigwood/Columbia, 1975).

wake of the Beatles and the Rolling Stones. More flamboyant — and louder — than their predecessors, The Who specialized in smashing their instruments at the conclusion of concerts.

Townshend began writing the album *Tommy* as *The Amazing Journey* in 1967. Later re-titled *The Deaf, Dumb and Blind Boy*, the "rock opera" was released as a double album in May 1969 as *Tommy*. The Who's concert performances of *Tommy* sold out at every venue and, with the album selling steadily, the band began to contemplate a film version. By 1971 the idea seemed to have died due to a script problem and the incredible success of the new album *Who's Next*. But the following year a new album version of *Tommy* was released, which revived interest in a film.

The problem: Who would have the vision and talent to bring the story, with all its imagery, to the screen? Producer–rock promoter Robert Stigwood entered the scene in 1973 and brought in Ken Russell to direct. Kit Lambert, The Who's manager, drafted a script which was rejected and re-written by Russell. Stigwood wanted cameos to be played by international

Frank (Oliver Reed) competes bravely in the Lovely Legs Contest in *Tommy* (Stigwood/Columbia, 1975).

stars from both the rock and film world, with Roger Daltrey—who else?—as Tommy. Russell wanted Oliver Reed. Since filming Russell's *The Devils*, Reed's star had risen even higher due to the success of *The Three Musketeers*. But one thing hadn't changed; Reed still couldn't sing. Problem number two: All of the dialogue of *Tommy* was to be sung. Unlike Sir Carol Reed, who refused to let his nephew sing in *Oliver!*, Russell felt that the quality (or lack of it) of Reed's voice didn't matter. He was Oliver Reed; no one, Russell reasoned, would care if he could sing or not. That's why Roger Daltrey was in the film—Reed wasn't playing Tommy. The cast met with Russell and Townshend in February 1974 to record their tracks and it was agreed that Reed's lack of singing talent was probably a plus—it helped to define Frank. To be fair, Reed was not the worst singer—not with Jack Nicholson around. Ann-Margret, who claimed that she had no idea who The

Who were, was a professional singer and had learned her lines on the flight to England. Another pro was Tina Turner who, as the Acid Queen, nearly stole the film. Her "treatment" scene with Tommy has to be seen and heard to be believed.

Daltrey, of course, had sung his part countless times and, not surprisingly, turns in a remarkable performance, especially for a first-time actor. Other actual singers included Elton John—perfect as the Pinball Wizard—and Paul Nicholas, excellently repellent as cousin Kevin. Pete Townshend and John Entwhistle appear as, presumably, themselves.

Problem three: Keith Moon. Like Oliver Reed, The Who's incredible drummer could be described charitably as a free spirit. The pairing of these two could have been—and was—a disaster. Their exploits did little to enhance their personal lives and drove Russell to distraction. As Reed remarks (Goodwin, 169), "If Ken

Russell had had his way, Keith wouldn't have been in the film at all." This being Keith Moon's first acting experience (he's effective as the grotesque Uncle Ernie), he was open to any and all help. Moon got it from his partner in hell-raising. He later said, "I learned so much technique from Ollie. More than I can ever repay" (Goodwin, 105).

Filming began in April 1974 at London's Lee International Studios with location work in the Lake District, Weymouth and Hayling Island, which served as Tommy's Holiday Camp. The production wrapped in July and *Tommy* premiered at the Cannes Festival in May 1975.

Reed's singing may have been execrable but his acting was excellent. He makes his first appearance as an employee of Bernie's Holiday Camp, wearing a green coat with orange piping and white trousers. As he combs back his duck-tail haircut, he resembles a psychotic Tony Curtis, singing "Welcome to Bernie's." As Frank courts Nora, he knows no shame, even appearing in a Lovely Legs competition; he is all affability and self-deprecating charm.

Their affair moves quickly; in no time they are living together and planning marriage. Things — including Frank — quickly turn nasty when Tommy's father returns. Reed's facial expression, especially when berating the child to forget the killing, is truly frightening and his intensity literally leaps off the screen.

Frank accepts his unwilling complicity in Tommy's disabled condition and convincingly shows remorse while attempting to find a cure. Like every other character, Frank shrinks into the background as Tommy becomes an adult and Roger Daltrey's dynamic performance takes over the film. He surrenders the dominance only to Tina Turner as the Acid Queen.

Frank's death at the hands of Tommy's ex-disciples is more moving than one would expect in a film as over the top as this one. The audience is left with a feeling of pity for a basically decent character who got in over his head as events simply ran away from his control.

Tommy is not a film — or record — for all tastes. As with most of Russell's work it challenges conventional morality, especially in its mockery of organized religion. The film has something to electrify and/or offend just about everyone!

Although *Tommy* was a highlight of Reed's career, it did little for his personal life. He and The Who's drummer Keith Moon, who was even wilder than Reed, began a series of "adventures" that did neither of them any good. Moon died in September 1977 of a drug overdose.

Tommy marks the approximate halfway point of Reed's career — the good half. He would appear in over fifty more films with only ten or so of any real merit. As for his performance in *Tommy*, Reed stated in the film's pressbook, "I more or less project my lines much as Rex Harrison did in *My Fair Lady*." Mr. Harrison was unavailable for comment.

Previewed at Fox Wilshire Theatre in LA on March 5, 1975, it went into general release on March 12, 1979. "[F]rom pastoral calm to riotous mob scenes, the art direction of John Clark, the sets designed by Paul Dufficey and the set decoration of Ian Whittaker are superior.... Cinematographers Dick Bush and Ronnie Taylor, along with special photographer Robin Lehman, caught the subtleties as well as the sledgehammers of Russell's screen adaptation and conception of the story" (*Variety*, March 12, 1975); "Oliver Reed is correctly almost a cartoon as the opportunistic step-dad. He also sings quite nicely" (*New York Times*, March 20, 1975).

Royal Flash (1975)

20th Century–Fox Film Corporation; Two Roads Productions; A Richard Lester Film; released by Fox Rank in U.K. 1975; no U.S. release; prints by DeLuxe; color by Technicolor; U.K. certificate A; 118 minutes

Crew— Director: Richard Lester; Producers: David V. Picker, Denis O'Dell; Cinematographer: Geoffrey Unsworth; Production Manager: Barrie Melrose; Unit Manager: Brian Burgess; Production Secretary: Vicki Deason; Producer's Secretary: Chrissie Lee-Smith; Continuity: Ann Skinner; First Assistant Director: Vincent Winter; Second Assistant Director: Dusty Symonds; Casting Director: May Selway; Camera Operators: Paul Wilson, Peter Macdonald; Sound: Simon Kaye; Production Designer: Terry Marsh; Art Director: Alan Tomkins; Construction Manager: Peter Dukelow; Supervising Accountant: Arthur Davey; Costume Designer: Alan Barrett; Makeup: Paul Rabiger; Hair: Colin Jamison; Editor: John Victor Smith; Fight Arranger: William Hobbs;

Special Effects: John Richardson; Property Master: Eddie Fowlie; Chief Electrician: Maurice Gillett; Still Photographer: Keith Hamshere; Publicity Director: Gordon Arnell.

Cast—Malcolm McDowell (Capt. Harry Flashman), Alan Bates (Rudi von Starnberg), Florinda Bolkan (Lola Montes), Oliver Reed (Otto von Bismark), Britt Ekland (Duchess Irma), Lionel Jeffries (Kraftstein), Tom Bell (De Gautet), Christopher Cazenove (Hansen), Joss Ackland (Sapten), Leon Greene (Grundwig), Richard Hurndall (Detchard), Alastair Sim (Mr. Greig), Michael Hordern (Headmaster), Roy Kinnear (Old Roue), David Sterne (Policeman), Richard Pearson (Josef), Rula Lenska (Helga), Margaret Courtney (Soprano), Noel Johnson (Lord Chamberlain), Elizabeth Larner (Baroness Pechman), Henry Cooper (John Gully).

Synopsis

Holder of an undeserved Victoria Cross, Captain Harry Flashman (Malcolm McDowell) is given a hero's welcome at Rugby School, where he was a former pupil. Back in London, escaping from the Peelers, he takes refuge in the carriage of Lola Montes (Florinda Bolkan), courtesan and spy, who is accompanied by her arrogant young lover Otto von Bismark (Oliver Reed). Harry becomes Lola's lover and clashes with Bismark again when he goads the German into fighting a bout with ex-champion bare-knuckle fighter John Gully (Henry Cooper). Bismark is furious at losing and makes up his mind that Harry will pay ... eventually. Harry's affair with Lola comes to an end after she fights a duel with an operatic soprano and leaves England to become the king of Bavaria's mistress. Later she invites Harry to visit her and leads him into a trap. A phony rescue by Rudi von Starnberg (Alan Bates) results in Harry becoming Bismark's prisoner. Bismark by now is an important politician and busy building Europe to his own designs. Harry finds himself strong-armed by Bismark into masquerading as Crown Prince Carl Gustav, who is suffering from the clap and unable to attend his dynastic marriage with the Duchess Irma of Strakenz (Britt Ekland), immensely wealthy and influential, if a touch glacial. Harry is dubbed with dueling scars, shown how to open a snuff box with one hand and taught to cheat at billiards. Piqued, he takes a sword swipe at Bismark from behind; he is rewarded with the comment that he is "beginning to behave like royalty already." The impersonation is successful, the marriage takes place and Harry begins to enjoy being royalty and all the perks it brings. One is his bride, "the loveliest piece of tumble" he'd seen all year; in the marriage bed, Harry's skill turn her from practically frigid to a near nymphomaniac. However, now that the wedding has been consummated, Bismark no longer needs Harry. He already has the crown prince imprisoned and plans to dispose of him at leisure. Harry is destined for the same fate, but slightly sooner. After some adventures, Harry comes face to face with the crown prince chained to a dungeon wall and isn't impressed that they are supposed to be doubles. Bismark sends Starnberg to clear up all the loose ends and a wildly acrobatic duel takes place between Harry and Starnberg. He eventually escapes and rides away with Duchess Irma's jewels, small payment for all his inconveniences. A "chance" meeting with Lola deprives him of the gems and leaves him stranded with Starnberg — and a new game, "the Hungarian Roulette."

Comment

With a screenplay by George MacDonald Fraser from his own phenomenally successful series of Flashman novels and Richard Lester's iconoclastic sense of humor, *Royal Flash* had a pedigree that almost assured its success. The dedication to the movie is all-embracing: "To Ronald Colman, Douglas Fairbanks Jr., Errol Flynn, Basil Rathbone, Louis Hayward, Tyrone Power, and all the others." William Hobbs, fight arranger for the *Musketeers* movies, stepped up to the plate and delivered sequences that were breathtaking, exciting and very funny in places. Look carefully and you'll see Hobbs dangling on a hook in the kitchen during a fight! He also made gentle fun of Reed, a man who always led from the front, by choreographing a fight sequence where Reed retreated all the time; this was wryly appreciated by the actor. The *Prisoner of Zenda* homage works very well, with a nod to *The Count of Monte Cristo* en route. History, as you might imagine, gets short shrift; the names are the same, but the history is warped to protect the plot! Lola Montes, the "It" girl of her age, political mover, famous courtesan and avid collector of amazing jewels, is well presented by Florinda Bolkan.

Bismark, courtesy of Reed, is a Machiavellian politician whose plans for the future of Europe were decidedly imperial; he is old and crafty while still a young buck and he grows more devious and dangerous as the film progresses. As usual, Lester sprinkles his galaxy of stars with little treasures such as Margaret Courtenay's indignant soprano, Roy Kinnear scuttling for cover in a brothel raid, and the cleaning lady who goes on smiling and swabbing the floors as the fight rages around her.

Terry Marsh's designs make the Twickenham studio interiors blend with the wonderful Bavarian castles to create a historicity that balances the wildly improbable storyline. Geoffrey Unsworth's photography, as ever, is superb and Ken Thorne's Wagneresque score for the action sequences and his Tchaikovsky pastiche for the romantic theme are very pleasing to the ear, and also instrumental in creating the authentic feel of the setting.

But it would seem that *Royal Flash* came to our screens too soon after *The Four Musketeers*; it was virtually ignored by critics and the paying customers alike. According to the July-August 1976 issue of *Millimeter*, distributor 20th Century–Fox "seemed to brush it aside, not concentrating on the build-up most films require to gain successful velocity. Disappearing from Manhattan within a couple of weeks, the film never acquired the following it so richly deserved.... The historical figures take on a hilarious character: Bismark as an overblown maniac stooping to petty charades to accomplish his aims [and] Lola Montes ... fighting a Zorro-like duel with a soprano."

Royal Flash was shot on a nine-week shooting schedule (October 26 to November 23, 1974) at Twickenham and on location in Germany. For this $3,5000,000 production, Lester employed 300 GIs for crowd scenes while filming near their barracks. He also paid an undisclosed sum — said to run to six figures — to the German authorities to film in historic sites.

Otto von Bismark (Oliver Reed) poses for a portrait in *Royal Flash* (20th Century–Fox, 1975).

"I don't like sadism.... I know, of course, that with Richard Lester in the director's chair what we have here is merely comic sadism. It is, in fact, 'A' certificate sadism. This means that although people fall to their deaths, get stuck in medieval spiked cabinets or have their breasts slashed (this in a nasty fencing duel between two women) they don't appear to mind terribly. I have a feeling that if provoked I could produce quite a good case against the sort of violence that doesn't seem to matter.... There is also a great deal of mock sword fighting in extremely pleasant settings. And the ending is very funny indeed" (*The Spectator*, July 19, 1975); "At moments, it's as if glary-eyed Malcolm McDowell were playing some pusillanimous Fifth Musketeer–Bathos I suppose.... Mr. Lester can do better than this and will again" (*New Statesman*, July 11, 1975); "[T]he performances, confident and knowing, is one of the good things. Another of them is Oliver Reed's Bismark, commanding, the heavy features set in unblinking menace" (*Sunday Times*, July 13, 1975); "[B]ehind Victorian whiskers Mr. Henry Cooper has a neat and funny fight with Mr. Oliver Reed" (*Sunday People*, July 13, 1975); "Actors like Alan Bates, Oliver Reed and Florinda Bolkan give the enterprise heft it might otherwise lack. Mr. Lester throws away more gags in *Royal Flash* than some comedy directors think up in an entire career." *New York Times* (October 11, 1975); "It is left to Oliver Reed to play sheet-anchor and to give weight to the insubstantial material. He combines a little-seen comic talent with a genuine stab at the Junker's Prussian menace and power mania" (*Monthly Film Bulletin*, October 1975); "Swashbuckling is indistinguishable here from slapstick.... Oliver Reed's louring Bismark and Alan Bates' shifty Starnberg are very entertainingly sketched" (*Films and Filming*, September 1975); "The blending of comedy and swashbuckling adventure is better balanced than in either of the two halves of the musketeers' escapades.... Oliver Reed [is] heavily menacing and pompous as Bismark" (*CinemaTV Today*, July 12, 1975).

According to Michael Parkinson's autobiography,

> Oliver Reed was another who felt the need for a drink or two before an interview. Somehow, I always managed to handle him, except for one occasion when, demonstrating his prowess as a boxer, he punched a hole in the set.... [I]n the movie he had to fight a bareknuckle champion played by Henry Cooper. Henry told me that they carefully choreographed the sequence and then broke for lunch, with a view to completing the filming in the afternoon. Henry said that when Oliver reappeared he was wearing a mischievous look and it was obvious he was tiddly. They started filming the fight and straightaway Oliver ignored the choreography and planted an unexpected right hook on Henry's chin. "What happened next?" I asked him. Henry said, "I gently chastised him." A magnificent euphemism for the actor being knocked on his back, a sadder and wiser man.... Oliver Reed was a wonderful screen presence, an actor with a powerful star quality, and it was a pity he allowed drink to dominate his life.

This is a rollicking good movie with Reed giving his all in his villainous role.

Lisztomania (1975)

Goodtimes Enterprises; Warner Bros.; VPS Studios; released by Columbia Warner Distributors in the U.K. and by Warner Bros. Pictures in the U.S.; color; 103 minutes; U.K. Certificate X

Crew— Screenplay-Director: Ken Russell; Producer: Roy Baird; Co-producer: David Putnam; Executive Producer: Sanford Lieberson; Production Manager: Peter Price; Production Secretary: Jean Hall; Assistant Director: Jonathan Benson; Continuity: Ann Skinner; Cinematographer: Peter Suschitzky; Camera Operator: John Harris; Sound: Ian Bruce; Accountant: Paul Cadiou; Art Director: Philip Harrison; Special Effects: Colin Chilvers; Costumes: Shirley Russell; Wardrobe: Richard Pointing; Makeup: Wally Scneiderman; Hair Stylist: Colin Jameson; Editor: Stuart Baird; Stills: Graham Attwood.

Cast— Roger Daltrey (Liszt), Sara Kestelman (Princess Carolyn), Paul Nicholas (Richard Wagner), Fiona Lewis (Countess Marie), Veronica Quilligan (Cosima), Nell Campbell (Olga), Andrew Reilly (Hans von Bulow), Ringo Starr (Pope), John Justin (Count d'Agoult), Anulka Dziubinska (Groupie — Lola Montez), Imogen Claire (Groupie — George Sand), Peter Brayham (First Bodyguard), David English (Captain); uncredited: Oliver Reed (Servant).

Synopsis

Europe, 1830. Franz Liszt (Roger Daltrey) is a charismatic pianist-composer with a legion of maniacal female admirers — including some very powerful ladies in the society of the day. He is approached at a concert by Richard Wagner (Paul Nicholas), a penniless composer who begs Liszt to publish the score of his new opera. Liszt declines and the two become rivals.

Liszt begins an affair with Princess Carolyn (Sara Kestelman), the wife of a wealthy Russian. She persuades him to accept her patronage, promising him success beyond his wildest dreams. Liszt has been slandered by a book written by Marie (Fiona Lewis), a former lover, and Carolyn wants to write a book of her own to vindicate him. Liszt and Wagner meet again during the Hungarian uprising. Wagner, who is the embodiment of evil, wants to write music to inspire Germany to unite and become a superpower. He attempts to create a superman to lead Germany. Liszt tries to exorcise Wagner's evil through music, but Wagner dies and is reincarnated as a combination of himself,

Frankenstein's Monster and Hitler. Liszt also dies, a victim of a curse laid on him by his own daughter Cosima (Veronica Quilligan). In Heaven, Liszt joins forces with the angels and, united, they destroy the monster.

Comment

No synopsis can possibly capture the madness of Ken Russell's *Lisztomania*; it truly must be seen to be believed. The film is so absurd — but entertainingly so — it's beyond criticism or description. As a follow-up to *Tommy*, the film had two wonderful ideas: present Franz Liszt, mid–1800s musical sensation, as a mid–1970s rock star; and cast mid–1970s rock star Roger Daltrey in the lead. Given his outstanding performance for Russell in *Tommy*, Daltrey was the ideal choice.

Unfortunately, *Lisztomania* is so far over the top that it makes *Tommy* look tame. The film manages, somehow, to throw away the above terrific ideas and lose them in a mix of Nazis, the Frankenstein legend and vampirism. Throw in Russell's fantasies — mostly sexual — left over from *The Devils* and you've got quite a concoction. It either works for you or it doesn't; it didn't work for most.

According to Russell's *Altered States*, "This was my first film for Goodtimes Enterprises.... I signed a contract to write and direct five more musical biopics.... I gave [producer] David Puttnam a choice, *The Gershwin Dream* or *Lisztomania*. He went for Liszt, probably because Roger Daltrey, fresh from his success in my rock movie *Tommy*, was keen to play the randy Hungarian. It was typecasting. Franz Liszt was the first pop star of them all — idolized by the fans and chased all over Europe by mobs of aristocratic groupies."

Lisztomania was filmed at Shepperton Studios on an eleven-week schedule starting on February 8, 1975. It was released in November to mostly stunned reviews! "...Ken Russell opens a door on the life of Hungarian pianist and composer Franz Liszt.

"Unfortunately, the door seems to be unhinged" (*The Daily Express*, November 11, 1975); "In concept, the idea of Liszt as Mick Jagger is amusing, but one leaves *Lisztomania* fearing that Russell is a willing passenger on a destructive wheel he can't get off" (*The Daily Mail*, November 11, 1975).

Reed, originally slated for a "guest star" role (which would soon become disturbingly common), was presumably too busy to tackle it and ended up on screen for a few seconds as a servant. His fleeting appearance was certainly intended as joke, but thrown into the cauldron of twelve-foot-long phalluses, a machine-gun–wielding Frankenstein Monster and lines like, "Piss off, Brahms," probably very few viewers noticed, cared or laughed. Opening a door for Daltrey procured a fee of several bottles of Dom Perignon for Reed and a good time with his chums. This was not a good career move, but worse ones were coming.

It was also not a good move for Russell, whose fascination with composers began, with Reed, in the wonderful BBC arts production *Debussy* and ended up with this. To be fair, *Lisztomania* was not intended to be taken seriously — no more than *Mel Brooks' History of the World Part One*. If it's way over the top, get over it. It's a Ken Russell film.

The Sell-Out (1976)

Berkey-Pathé-Humphries; Hemdale Film; distributed by Warner Bros. in the U.K. in 1976 and by Venture in the U.S. in 1977; 101 minutes; color

Crew— Director: Peter Collinson; Screenplay: Murray Smith, Judson Kinberg; Original Story: Murray Smith; Producer: Josef Shaftel; Associate Producer: Tom Sachs; Original Music: Mick Green, Colin Frechter; Cinematographer: Arthur Ibbetson; Film Editor: Raymond Poulton; Casting: Rose Tobias Shaw; Art Director: Tony Pratt; Hair Stylist: Betty Glascow; Makeup Artist: Fred Williamson; Production Manager: Zvi Spielmann; Assistant Director: Scott Wodehouse; Sound Editors: John Beaton, Derek Holding, Colin Miller; Sound Mixer: Ron Barron; Sound Recordist: Trevor Pyke; Stunt Arranger: Miguel Pedregosa; Stunt Driver: Remy Julienne; Camera Operator: Roy Ford; Second Unit Camera Operator: Yehiel Ne'eman; Wardrobe: Elsa Fennell; Conductor: Colin Frechter; Location Managers: Moshe Afryat, David Munro; Continuity: Pamela Davies.

Cast— Oliver Reed (Gabriel Lee), Richard Widmark (Sam Lucas), Gayle Hunnicutt (Deborah), Sam Wanamaker (Harry Sickles), Vladek Sheybal (Dutchman), Ori Levy (Major Benjamin), Peter Frye (Kasyan), Assaf Dayan (Lt. Elan), Shmuel Rodensky

(Zaffron), Fanny Lubitch (Zaffron's Wife), Miguel Pedregosa (Mercedes Man), Yossi Verjansky (Second Mercedes Man), Thelma Ruby (School Teacher), Heinz Bernard (Laboratory Officer), Yossi Graber (Coroner), Yoel Sharr (Senior Police Officer), Dino Gershoni (Young Man in Hotel), Hanna Neeman (Arab Mother), David Biderman (Little Boy).

Synopsis

Former CIA agent Sam Lucas (Richard Widmark) is now living in Jerusalem, selling antiquities, with lover Deborah (Gayle Hunnicutt). He left the CIA when he discovered his friend and partner Gabriel Lee (Oliver Reed) — Deborah's former lover — was a double agent controlled by Moscow. Gabriel is on the run; both the CIA and KGB want him eliminated in Israel. After Kasyar (Peter Frye) and Sickles (Sam Wanamaker), the local CIA chief, fail in an assassination attempt, the Dutchman (Vladek Sheybel) is called in. Gabriel has contacted Sam, who has mixed emotions, but has agreed to help him — and guaranteed that he did not and will not set him up. Israeli Security does not want Gabriel killed under their jurisdiction, and Major Benjamin (Ori Levy) arranges to get both Sam and Gabriel out of the country.

Complicating the situation, Gabriel has made sexual advances on Deborah. The Dutchman learns of a meeting involving the major and Gabriel; Benjamin is killed and Gabriel barely escapes. Gabriel reveals to Sam that Deborah is a double agent and has sold them all out.

When Sam finds it impossible to kill her, Gabriel does it for him. He and Sam kill the Dutchman and force Sickles to help them cross the Jordan. As they near the border, Sam is killed in a hail of bullets. Security officer Elan (Assay Dayan) tells Gabriel and Sickles that Israel will not be used as a location for international executions. As Gabriel leaves the scene, he touches Sam's face and whispers, "I'll see you ... soon."

Comment

Cinema TV Today (February 15, 1975) reported, "After the post–Yom Kippur War slump when few films were made here, it looks like business is picking. In order to persuade more film companies to work here, the Israeli government has raised the premium paid to film makers by 27 percent." The first film to be made under this agreement was *The Sell-Out*, which also received backing from Britain and America. Production began on March 12, 1975, and concluded on May 9; the location work was a highlight of the film.

This was a rough time for Reed to get productions going. According to *Cinema TV Today* (April 5, 1975), "Producer Christopher Miles claims to have the rights to the Robert Bolt screenplay *The Plumed Serpent* and the services of Sarah Miles and Oliver Reed." Production was to begin, presumably, after *The Sellout* was completed. It didn't; *Cinema TV Today* (August 30, 1975) announced that the production was postponed until sometime in 1976. It never happened.

Rider, which was to reunite Reed and Orson Welles, never took off either. *Cinema TV Today* (March 8, 1975): "Olly Reed is still smarting from the ten days he spent in Athens making *Rider* until 'financial problems' closed down the picture and sent them scurrying — and unpaid — back to London. What is really amazing is how many movies do actually get made, world business being in the straits that it is."

A week later, *Cinema TV Today* retracted the statement: "I was misinformed when I stated that Oliver Reed was not paid for his work on the postponed film *Rider* in Greece. In fact, Olly has been paid and *Rider* is to roll with fresh finance later this year with Reed resuming his star role." Wrong again. *Screen International* (November 13, 1976) reported that the film had been "mysteriously halted." No more would be heard of *Rider*.

Then: "*The New Spartans,* to star Oliver Reed, Toshiro Mifune, Fred Williamson, Susan George and Harry Andrews, ended production in November 1975 after nine days as funds ran out" (*Screen International*, December 2, 1975) This sort of thing is not, one supposes, unusual in the career of any star but it seems that Reed was having very little luck in 1975.

Back to *The Sell-Out*. Spy novels and films generally fall within two categories: the Ian Fleming–John Buchan school of romantic adventure and the Graham Greene–John le Carré school of squalid realism. *The Sell-Out* aspired to the latter and, in several instances, realized its goal. But, like too many films, *The Sell-Out* looks better on paper than on screen. Any film starring Oliver Reed, Richard Widmark, Gayle Hunnicutt, Sam Wanamaker and Vladek Sheybal and directed by Peter Collinson should be a winner. *The Sell-Out*, while certainly acceptable, falls a bit short. The main problem may have been in casting Reed as Gabriel. His performance is very good (with a surprisingly accurate American accent — why can't Americans do the reverse?), but for the film to really work we need to feel sorry for Gabriel. Let's face it; it's tough to feel sorry for Oliver Reed. *The Sell-Out* is also about fifteen minutes too long for its plot and its own good.

Most critics were unimpressed; *The Sell-Out* was almost universally panned following its March 24, 1976, release. *The Sunday Telegraph* (March 28, 1976): "Director Peter Collinson's flashy fashion-plating of mayhem reveals a lack of concern with what is, in reality, being depicted." *The Daily Mirror* (March 28, 1976): "It is colorful, noisy, and violent in a predictable manner. Mr. Reed contributes his usual air of Stone Age menace. The image of the American CIA is not improved." *The New Statesman* (March 26, 1976): "Peter Collinson generally manages to insert the odd morsel of sexual ugliness into his films and *The Sell-Out* is no exception." *The Guardian* (March 28, 1976): "*The Sell-Out* [is a] swiftly paced double-agent thriller which intermittently raises moral questions about CIA double dealing and promptly sells out again to the jaded excitement of the script." *The Daily Mail* (March 27, 1976): "The title tells it all. I don't deny it's slickly handled." *Screen International* (April 13, 1976): "Incomprehensible tosh wrapped around a few scenes of exciting action. A sorry waste of a strong cast."

Trashing *The Sell-Out* wasn't enough for some. Next target: Oliver Reed's physical condition. *The Sunday Telegraph*: "Reed's naked torso shows him really to be in need of fighting the flab rather than weightlifting the CIA and the KGB"; *The New Statesman*: "It has Oliver Reed, between whose face and paunch at least one viewer finds it harder and harder to distinguish."

Reed was pushing forty and, yes, he no longer looked as he did at 22. Who does? These were uncalled-for cheap shots, and one speculates on the physiques of the critics. *The Sell-Out* is about the midpoint in Reed's career. He somehow, "flab" and all, managed to make 52 more films.

While not a superior production, *The Sell-Out* does have its moments. The three stars are at the top of their form and have one outstanding scene together that manages to lift the film out of the ordinary and briefly enter Graham Greene–John le Carré country. After Major Benjamin — the film's only decent person — is murdered, Sam returns home to find Gabriel and Deborah sitting quietly.

SAM: Benjamin is dead. I watched a friend get his head blown off because of you. Dead — because of you, you bastard! He trusted me and you screwed up ... what the hell are you doing alive?

GABRIEL: All right — I apologize for living. I screwed up — because I didn't tell you about ... her. I'd hoped she'd changed from a bed-hopping whore.

SAM: Is that why you slept with her last night?

DEBORAH: I didn't, Sam!

SAM: Don't! My orders are to set you up for the Dutchman. The contract comes from both sides.

GABRIEL: Come on, Sam ... let's get out of this together.

SAM: All right — the three of us get out.

GABRIEL: You still don't see it, Sam, do you? How many people knew about the meeting with Benjamin? It was one of us. It wasn't you and it wasn't me ... that leaves the lady.

DEBORAH: All right, why not? You promised me when we came here that it would be over ... and then bloody Gabriel comes here!

GABRIEL: Sam — when you retired, did you think they'd forget you? They sent a walking tape-recorder along with you. Each month a little tape recording report wound up on Sickle's desk...

SAM: You can't know that!

GABRIEL: I can know that ... because a duplicate was sent to Moscow! Sam — she sold you out to both sides!

DEBORAH: Who did I hurt, Sam, except maybe your ego?

SAM: "Benjamin — that's who it hurt ... the little girl blown up in the hotel ... that's who it hurt!

[*Sam points his gun at her as she begs for her life. We see her in close-up as a shot is fired, but it's Gabriel who pulled the trigger.*]

GABRIEL: You would never have done it, and it had to be done.

The scene is perfectly rendered, and, for a few minutes, lifts *The Sell-Out* out of the standard action genre. Gayle Hunnicutt is terrific, ranging from uninterested to sullen defiance and it's a shame that no critic bothered to notice. It takes quite a performance to stand out in a scene with both Oliver Reed and Richard Widmark in top gear.

The Great Scout and Cathouse Thursday (1976)

American International Pictures; released on June 23, 1976, in the U.S. and on June 19, 1977, in the U.K.

Crew — Director: Don Taylor; Screenplay–Associate Producer: Richard Shapiro; Executive Producer: Samuel Z. Arkoff; Producers: Jules Buck, David Korda; Music Composer–Conductor: John Cameron; Cinematographer: Alex Phillips Jr.; Film Editor: Sheldon Kahn; Production Designer: Jack Martin Smith; Set Decorator: Enrique Estevez; Costume Designer: Rene Conley; Makeup Artist: John Inzerella; Post-Production Supervisor: Salvatore Billitteri; First Assistant Director: Brad Aronson; Property Master: Gordon Sumner; Sound Effects Editors: Greg Dillon, Bernard Pincus, Norman Schwartz; Sound Mixer: Manuel Topete; Stunt Coordinator: Jerry Gatlin; Stunt Double: Jesse Wayne; Camera Operator: Carlos Montano; Assistant Editors: Bob Hernandez, Nicholas Korda; Music Editor: Ken Johnson; Transportation Captain: Salvador Gutierrez; Post-Production Executive: Andy Birmingham; Production Executives: Peter Buchanan, Robert A. Kantor; Production Coordinator: Rosalyn Catania; Publicist: Julian Myers; Title Designer: Philip Norman; Script Supervisor: Jose Luis Ortege; Production Accountant: John C. Sargeant; Production Executive for American International Pictures: Harry Templeton; Head Wrangler: "Chema" Hernandez; Wrangler: "Chico" Hernandez.

Cast — Lee Marvin (Sam Longwood), Oliver Reed (Joe Knox), Robert Culp (Jack Colby), Elizabeth Ashley (Nancy Sue), Strother Martin (Billy), Sylvia Miles (Mike), Kay Lenz (Thursday), Phaedra (Friday), Howard Platt (Vishniac), Jac Zacha (Trainer), Leticia Robles (Saturday), Luz Maria Pena (Holidays), Erika Carlsson (Monday), C.C. Charity (Tuesday), Ana Verdugo (Wednesday).

Synopsis

Colorado, 1900. Former scout Sam Longwood (Lee Marvin), now down on his luck, steals the pot in a barroom scam, involving a fangless rattlesnake in a jar, run by his old friend Billy (Strother Martin). Ex-prizefighter Jack Colby (Robert Culp) is not amused at being conned when the pair make off with the money. Meanwhile, half-breed Joe Knox (Oliver Reed), a drunken degenerate, helps a group of prostitutes escape a raid on their cathouse. Joe's goal in life is to infect the "ladies" with his venereal disease in an effort to destroy the white race as payback for the mistreatment of his mother. His plans are put aside when Sam and Billy arrive; Joe has rescued seven girls, one for each day of the week, and releases all of them but one, Thursday (Kay Lenz). The problem: Colby had worked with Joe, Sam and Billy on a gold claim fifteen years previously and took off with the money. He's now a powerful railroad man, fight promoter and candidate for governor. Stealing the pot hardly made up for the $60,000 Colby owes them. The trio kidnap Colby's wife Nancy (Elizabeth Ashley) and hold her for ransom but Colby declines to pay. Their next plan: steal the receipts from Colby's latest fight promotion. Colby strikes back by kidnapping Thursday, and the two women are to be exchanged, much to the miffed Nancy's displeasure. A further complication: A romance has sprung up between the aging Sam and the young Thursday.

Since everything has gone wrong for both sides by this time, Sam and Colby agree to have a fistfight to settle the issue — and the money problems. Colby wins, but Joe and Billy steal the money and take off with the girls from Mike's (Sylvia Miles) cathouse to start one of their own. Sam and Thursday are left alone and couldn't be happier.

Comment

He was an extremely talented and versatile actor known as much for his drinking and hell-

Joe Knox (Oliver Reed) and Sam Longwood (Lee Marvin) in *The Great Scout and Cathouse Thursday* (United Artists, 1976), one of the worst films of each actors' careers.

raising as for his ability before a camera. No, not Oliver Reed — Lee Marvin.

The pairing of these two powerhouse actors should have produced a memorable movie but, instead, resulted in one of the worst of their respective careers.

Having abandoned his position of avoiding Hollywood in favor of appearing in British-made films, Reed arrived in the movie capital of the world in late November 1975. David Reed had contracted his brother to make three films there in late 1975–early 1976: *The Great Scout and Cathouse Thursday, Burnt Offerings* and *Maniac*. None of these would prove to be worth the trip.

From the beginning, Reed and Marvin did not hit it off and it is to their credit that they didn't hit each other. They met at the Beverly Wilshire Hotel when Reed woke up Marvin, who had been napping on a bench. He was not amused and their relationship went downhill from there. Marvin is reported as saying, "I was told I was going to work with Britain's biggest hellraiser. And all I see is this tailor's dummy dressed like a fucking banker" (Goodwin, 177).

An unidentified friend of Marvin's remarked: "Lee Marvin detested Oliver Reed from the moment he first saw him, and it only got worse the more they worked with each other. Lee tried to explain it, but he couldn't. It was not a professional thing — he honestly thought Oliver was a natural and gifted actor."

What probably happened was that for both stars, looking at each other was like looking in a mirror. And they didn't like it. One wonders what they thought when — or if— they looked at the finished film. Marvin appears old and tired beyond his years — a long, long way from *The Dirty Dozen* (1967). Reed simply looks absurd.

We first see Joe Knox sitting on the ground, scowling, drinking whisky from a bottle and smoking a cigar. These are the last four things Reed does convincingly. He's wearing warpaint and, when the prostitutes from Mike's cathouse are brought out by the police, he jumps on the wagon and sets it on fire, dancing all the while. ("Awww! Awww! Woo woo woo woo! Heh! Heh! Heh! Ooh! Wahhh!" And this is some of his best dialogue.) Reed's dancing hasn't improved much since his Michael Winner days ten years before. The whole sad act is embarrassing to see, and is, even sadder, a precursor of Reed's appearances on TV talk shows in years to come.

Remember: This was not an aging former star at the end of the line, desperate to work. In the previous three years, Reed had been on the screen in *The Three Musketeers, The Four Musketeers, Tommy* and *Royal Flash*. It's hard to believe that neither of the Reed brothers could see, after reading the script, that this was a film to be avoided.

Set in Colorado, the film was actually shot in Durango, Mexico, which provided an excellent climate and that Old West atmosphere. The cinema press was gathered waiting, breathlessly, for some joint grotesque behavior from the two stars who let them down by avoiding each other as much as possible off-set. Reed had been told by American-International executives that Marvin was having serious alcohol problems (and Reed wasn't?) and that he should, please, not encourage Marvin's drinking. Film accountant David Ball is reported as saying, "Lee and [wife] Pam would come in and she would let him have a single beer or something very light. And he would chat with Ollie, but Ollie never offered or slipped him a stiffer drink. He respected the man's problem" (Goodwin, 179).

It's unfortunate that American-International wasn't equally concerned about its audience. How does one react to this line? "Give women the vote? You may as well try to teach them to pee standing up — they just can't manage it!" Making things worse, *The Great Scout and Cathouse Thursday* was previewed by the British press on — believe it or not — International Women's Day! If you are interested in seeing an over-the-top, tasteless and offensive comedy-western, try Mel Brooks' *Blazing Saddles* (1974). At least it's funny.

Hazel Court, wife of director Don Taylor, wrote in her autobiography:

It was a nightmare. Life was dangerous when Lee was around. And it was no picnic with Oliver either. They both drank like fish. Finally, Don couldn't stand it any longer. "I've had enough of this," he told them. "You

must take it in turns. One of you can drink one day, the other one can drink the next day." ... At the end we had a big farewell cast party on New Year's Eve. Oliver Reed was always a gentleman. He was dressed in a dinner jacket and he was behaving himself. I danced with him. We were all having fun.... When he wasn't drinking, he was a lovely man, and the same was true of Lee. They were marvelous actors and both very funny.

"The problem with *Great Scout* is the long corrugated road between the beginning and the end. Knox is not so much played as pillaged by Oliver Reed. Rough language and feet sticking out of beds at non-missionary angles." *New York Times* (June 29, 1976); "If played more straight, with the grosser lines and antics cut out, it could have been the basis for a very amiable comedy" (*Monthly Film Bulletin*, November 1976); "For undemanding, uncritical men. Good in popular cinemas until the word gets round. A waste of talent, without charm or wit" (*Screen International*, March 19 1977).

Burnt Offerings (1976)

Produzioni Eruopee Associati. Films Inc. Dan Curtis Productions; released by United Artists in the U.S. in 1976 and in the U.K. in 1977; Color by DeLuxe; Panavision; 116 minutes

Crew— Producer-Director: Dan Curtis; Screenplay: Dan Curtis, William F. Nolan, from a novel by Robert Marasco; Associate Producer: Robert Stringer; Original Music: Bob Cobert; Cinematographer: Jacques Marquette; Film Editor: Dennis Virkler; Casting: Linda Otto; Production Design: Eugene Lourie; Set Decoration: Solomon Brewer; Costume Design: Ann Roth; Makeup Artist: Al Fleming; Hair Stylists: Abraham Meech-Burkestone, Peggy Shannon; Unit Production Manager: Joseph Ellis; Production Supervisor: Ira Loonstein; First Assistant Director: Howard Grace; Second Assistant Director: Stephen Lim; Construction Coordinator: Gerald MacDonald; Sound Recordist: Don J. Bassman: Sound Mixer: David M. Ronne; Special Effects: Cliff Wenger; Stunts: Dar Robinson; Gaffers: Alan Goldenhar, Robert Petzoldt; Still Photographers: Elliott Marks, Wynn Hammer; Camera Operator: Sven Walnum; First Assistant Camera: Bradford May.

Cast— Karen Black (Marian Rolf), Oliver Reed (Ben Rolf), Burgess Meredith (Arnold Allardyce), Eileen Heckart (Roz Allardyce), Lee Montgomery (Davey Rolf), Dub Taylor (Walker), Bette Davis

Ben (Oliver Reed), under the control of his supernatural house, attempts to drown his son David (Lee Montgomery) in *Burnt Offerings* (Curtis/PEA/United Artists, 1976).

(Aunt Elizabeth), Joseph Riley (Ben's Father), Todd Turquand (Young Ben), Orin Cannon (Minister), Jim Myers (Dr. Ross), Anthony James (The Chauffeur).

Synopsis

Ben Rolf (Oliver Reed) and his wife Marian (Karen Black), accompanied by their 12-year-old son Davey (Lee Montgomery), drive to the country to rent the beautiful but neglected Allardyce Mansion for the long summer vacation. Roz Allardyce (Eileen Heckart) and her quirky brother Arnold (Burgess Meredith) make the Rolfs a fantastic offer: the summer rental for a paltry sum providing they agree to look after the aged Mrs. Allardyce who lives in a suite of rooms in the attic and never sees people.

Ben is reluctant to rent the home, fearing a catch, but he gives in as Marian is enthralled with the house and its dusty, neglected contents; she decides, almost as soon as they move in, to take sole care of the old lady. She forbids Ben and Davey to disturb Mrs. Allardyce who

apparently sleeps most of the time. As the summer passes, Marian works wonders in the house: Old carpets are cleaned and re-laid, the furnishings revived and clocks rewound. Ben and Davey tackle the overgrown and neglected garden, responding to Marian's enthusiasm for what the house must have been like in its heyday. They find the Allardyce family burial ground under the shrubbery. Ben even manages to get the swimming pool clean and usable.

Ben is suddenly overcome by a strange force and attempts to drown Davey in said pool; although Davey survives and Ben overflows with apologies and guilt, there is no explanation for his actions. He also begins to suffer from a recurring nightmare from his childhood again: He remembers his mother's funeral and a hearse driver whose sardonic grin terrified then and continues to do so in the nightmare. Ben begins to blame the Allardyce mansion for his unhappiness but Marian seems to neither notice nor care that strange things are happening around her.

Initially Marian is shocked to discover that

the house seems capable of regenerating itself like a living creature but she soon covers up by pretending that she has wrought the changes by working hard. When Davey breaks a crystal bowl, Marian's anger is far too violent; she cares about the house and its contents more than the hurt her anger inflicts on her puzzled son. Marian's hair turns gray and she loses all interest in sex, becoming obsessed with Mrs. Allardyce and spending every available moment in the attic suite. Aunt Elizabeth (Bette Davis), a perky, sharp-witted and articulate old girl who has come to share the summer idyll, becomes weak, tired and drained of vitality while Ben continues his downward slide into depression. Then one night Davey almost dies when his bedroom gas heater malfunctions and he can't get out of the room. Ben, hearing his cries, rescues him. Marian blames Aunt Elizabeth's carelessness since the old lady had been the last adult in Davey's room that night. Shortly afterwards, Aunt Elizabeth's health declines quickly, her back breaks for no apparent reason and she dies. While waiting for the doctor, Ben has a waking vision of the ghoulish hearse chauffeur.

After Aunt Elizabeth's funeral, Ben becomes convinced that the house murdered her. His demand to see Mrs. Allardyce is rebuffed by Marian, so he puts Davey in the car and they attempt to leave. Trees fall in his path, trapping them on the grounds. Ben is hurt and Marian takes him back indoors to recuperate. The house has virtually been reborn, but it still needs more and shortly afterwards a strange occurrence nearly drowns young Davey in the pool. The threat to her son's life is an epiphany for Marian and for a brief while the house's spell is broken as she agrees to leave for good. But before they leave, she feels impelled by good manners to say goodbye to Mrs. Allardyce, going back into the house and into the attic suite. Ben, fretful at the time Marian is taking making her farewells, follows her into the attic where he finds her terribly aged and possessed by the spirit of Mrs. Allardyce. With its strongest enemy at its heart, the house retaliates and a strange force hurls Ben through the attic window and onto the hood of his car, his blood spattering poor shocked Davey who tries to escape only to have a chimney crash down on

him. Imbued with the life-force of all the Rolfs, the house welcomes back Roz and Arnold in the person of the newly revived Mrs. Allardyce/Rolf.

Comment

This is one of the more interesting scary mansion movies. Dan Curtis, who read the novel long before being asked to film it, had always been unhappy with the end and took the opportunity to pen a much more visually satisfying finale. He sets out from the beginning to introduce the house as a character in itself, using unusual low-angled shots and showing the house's point of view at every opportunity.

As usual, the viewer is left wanting to grab the characters by the shoulders and give them a darn good shake — why stay there, for heaven's sake, when such ghastly goings-on take place? The "enchantment" overpowers all reason and sense for the adults, and there isn't even the regulation team of psychic investigators to give their remaining a valid reason. That being said, Curtis provides an interesting take on the vampiric theme.

Karen Black, four months pregnant during the shoot, does a first-rate job with Marian. Lee Montgomery's Davey is well played and totally believable. The restrained madness of Eileen Heckart and Burgess Meredith as the Allardyce "kids" is so well presented that it leaves the viewer feeling rather uncomfortable. Bette Davis' decline from the elderly, sprightly aunt we all know and love to the frightened, drained and sick old lady is a joy. Her best acting? Being believable as affectionate to Ben, since tales of bad relations between her and Oliver Reed were reported. Apparently, the corridor steeplechase on Ms. Davis' supper trolley, which often resulted in her food all over the carpet, carried out with gusto by Reed and stand-in Reg Prince, led to the Hollywood legend referring to Reed as "that man" if she ever needed to speak about him; she never spoke to him if she could avoid it.

Reed seems to have changed his mind about his co-star, the film legend; in the publicity generated during production it was said, "Though he's considered England's top male star, Reed seems genuinely awed to be working

Ben (Oliver Reed) makes amends for nearly drowning his son David (Lee Montgomery) while Aunt Elizabeth (Bette Davis) and Marion (Karen Black) look on in *Burnt Offerings* (Curtis/PEA/ United Artists, 1976).

with the likes of Bette Davis, who plays his aunt" (*San Francisco Sunday Examiner & Chronicle*, August 17, 1975).

Afterwards, having had a run-in with an inebriated Shelley Winters on a TV chat show, his opinion had changed: "While in America Reed filmed *Burnt Offerings* with 67-year-old Bette Davis — who really burned him up. At first, he says, she was very sweet to him — but later blasted him in a magazine article. 'It proved to me that Miss Davis is somewhat two-faced,' he said. But Reed adds that he forgave her because 'she is a bit senile'" (*National Enquirer*, March 23, 1976). One hopes that Miss Davis didn't pursue Reed around the hotel suite as she later did with Hammer's scriptwriter and director Jimmy Sangster — or maybe she did, and got mad at being turned down?

Reed's portrayal of Ben Rolf is quite moving; while he usually has the macho role, Ben Rolf has a gentle, almost feminine side and he is virtually always reactive as opposed to leading

the action. Reed makes Ben someone the viewer could sympathize with. His unhappiness at the way Marian allows the house to overwhelm her feelings for him is palpable and his puzzlement at the change in her is quite painful to watch. We know Ben is the only one who fully understands the evil of Allardyce Mansion and we feel his terror when the ghoulish, grinning hearse driver of his nightmares actually comes to collect Aunt Elizabeth's body. "I've never seen anyone work as rapidly," Reed said of director Curtis. "We did 13 pages of the script this morning. In my country, we sometimes do only three pages a day. There's no advantage, however, in working slowly. If the cast clicks, things can race along. A director is really like a priest. He marries everybody and the rest is up to them" (*San Francisco Sunday Examiner & Chronicle*, August 17, 1975).

Curtis is reported as having said that the hearse nightmare was a memory from his own childhood that he exorcised by putting it in the script. Curtis "does a Hitchcock" and appears in one of the family photographs in Mrs. Allardyce's suite; don't blink or you'll miss it!

Burnt Offerings was filmed entirely on location at Dunsmuir House, Oakland, California; it also appeared in *Little Girl Blue* (1978), *A View to a Kill* (1985), *The Vineyard* (1989), *So I Married an Axe Murderer* (1993), and *True Crime* (1999).

Burnt Offerings was chosen as the Best Horror Film of 1976 by the Academy of SF and Horror Films at a ceremony held at the Directors Guild Theatre in Hollywood on 15 January 1977.

The Prince and the Pauper (1977)

International Film Production; Prince and the Pauper Film Export AG; Released in the U.K. on August 21, 1977, and by Warne Bros. in the U.S. in 1978; color; 121 minutes; U.K. Certificate A

Crew— Director: Richard Fleischer; Producer: Pierre Spengler; Executive Producer: Ilya Salkind; Final Screenplay: George MacDonald Fraser; Original Screenplay: Berta Dominguez, Pierre Spengler; Based on the Novel by Mark Twain; Music Composer: Maurice Jarre; Cinematographer: Jack Cardiff; Film Editor: Ernest Walter; Production Supervisor: Basil Keys; Production Manager–First Assistant: Nigel Wooll; Costume Designers: Judy Moorcroft, Ulla Britt Soderland; Production Designer: Tony Pratt; Sound Mixer: Roy Charman; Camera Operator: Alec Mills; Dubbing Editor: Colin Miller; Choreographer: Sally Gilpin; Fight Arranger: B.H. Barry; Makeup: Jose Antonio Sanchez; Hair Stylist: Pepita Rubio.

Cast— Oliver Reed (Miles Hendon), Raquel Welch (Edith), Mark Lester (Tom Canty/Prince Edward), Ernest Borgnine (John Canty), George C. Scott (The Ruffler), Rex Harrison (Duke of Norfolk), David Hemmings (Hugh Hendon), Charlton Heston (Henry VIII), Harry Andrews (Hertford), Murray Melvin (De Brie), Sybil Danning (Mother Canty), Felicity Dean (Lady Jane), Lalla Ward (Princess Elizabeth), Julian Orchard (St. John), Graham Stark (Jester), Michael Ripper (Ruffian).

Synopsis

Tom Canty (Mark Lester) is a teenage pauper who lives in Offal Court, the London underworld slum, in the year 1547: his parents are John Canty (Ernest Borgnine), a brutal ruffian, and the long-suffering Mother Canty (Sybil Danning). Tom has daydreams about royalty, in which he figures as a fairy tale prince; the daydreams are shattered when his father drives him out to steal for the family.

In the marketplace, Tom is detected stealing a purse. To escape from his pursuers he's driven to seek refuge in Westminster Palace where by accident he blunders into the presence of Henry VIII (Charlton Heston) and court members Norfolk (Rex Harrison), St. John (Julian Orchard), Hertford (Harry Andrews) and the Jester (Graham Stark). Prince Edward (also played by Mark Lester) and Tom encounter each other in the prince's chambers when Tom is found hiding from punishment in the fireplace. Almost at once they realize they are doubles, and Prince Edward conceives the idea of attending that evening's masked ball dressed in Tom's pauper rags, with Tom going along dressed as the prince. Tom is scared and reluctant, but at the prince's insistence they switch clothes. Edward, eager to try out his joke, goes out into the corridor looking like a ragged beggar. The first person he meets is Norfolk, who naturally assumes that he is the pauper who invaded the king's garden earlier; Norfolk summons the guard and, before he can protest, Edward finds himself flung into the street.

He protests that he is the prince of Wales but the guards, and also the beggars and ruffians who hang around the palace gates, simply mock and jeer at him. In desperation, Edward produces the prince of Wales' seal, which he wears around his neck, but this merely incites the beggars to attack him. In the nick of time he is rescued by Miles Hendon (Oliver Reed), a soldier of fortune.

At Hendon's lodging house, Edward still insists that he is the prince; Miles, a practical man, treats him tolerantly, listens to his tale and the next morning takes him to Offal Court on the assumption that he is Tom Canty. There John Canty, furious at his son's absence, starts to horsewhip Edward; Miles intervenes, but is set on by Canty and his ruffians and left for dead. Canty, fearful of being hanged for murder, decides to leave London, taking with him the still-protesting Edward whom he believes is Tom.

Back at the palace, Tom has been left in

the prince's clothes and discovers that everyone is prepared to accept him as Edward. He protests that he is just a pauper, but at the masque the king and his courtiers think that he is playing a practical joke. The next day, when he still insists he's Tom Canty, they decide that he is the prince gone mad.

The king maintains that it is only a temporary insanity, and forbids anyone to talk about it. He is especially troubled because he knows that his own death is approaching but he is determined that, mad or not, his son shall succeed him to the throne. In the meantime, the king has ordered the arrest of Norfolk whom he suspects of treason. The Duke is imprisoned in the Tower, awaiting execution.

Tom allows himself to be treated as the prince and even regains his spirits sufficiently to become attracted to (Felicity Dean) Lady Jane. They and Princess Elizabeth (Lalla Ward) go that night to a guildhall banquet, and just for a moment their path crosses that of Edward, who, in a bewildered state, is being taken out of London by John Canty. During the guildhall banquet the king's death is announced, and Tom finds himself hailed as the new king. His first act is to pardon Norfolk, which immediately establishes his popularity.

Canty, with Edward, has fled to the country and sought refuge from the law with an eccentric outlaw called the Ruffler (George C. Scott), leader of a gang of beggars and outcasts. In their camp, Edward sees for the first time some of the horrors and injustices suffered by the ordinary people of England; many of the Ruffler's followers are dispossessed peasants or people persecuted for religious reasons. When he hears of his father's death, and announces himself as king, the beggars naturally conclude that he is mad and taunt him by holding a mock coronation. Edward is obsessed with the notion that he must get back to London and claim his throne before Tom Canty is crowned in his place; John Canty tries to prevent his leaving the gang but Edward escapes. Canty is killed by one of the Ruffler's gang.

Miles reappears; he had not been killed by Canty but merely badly beaten. He rescues Edward and, although he still regards him as a lunatic, humors Edward, promising to see him safely back to London. First, however, Miles insists on visiting his ancestral home, Hendon Hall, which he has not seen in 20 years, and claiming his own little inheritance. At the Hall, his evil younger brother Hugh (David Hemmings), who has usurped the inheritance in Miles' absence, pretends not to recognize him; his servants and even Miles' childhood sweetheart Lady Edith (Raquel Welch) whom Hugh has married, are terrified of the powerful Hugh and join in treating Miles as an imposter.

Miles now finds himself in exactly the position that Edward has been in; when he announces who he is, no one will believe him. Gradually the growing doubts that he has had about Edward vanish; for the first time he believes that Edward is the king and agrees to help him. Tom is enjoying royalty thoroughly. He is not a very good king, since he neglects the affairs of state to spend time with Lady Jane, thereby incurring the anger of his sister Elizabeth. When the wicked Hugh, accompanied by Edith, sets off for London by coach, Edward and Miles ambush him. Miles dons Hugh's clothes and, with Hugh bound and gagged under the seat, they drive at high speed to London. They reach the Abbey where the coronation ceremony has begun, and make their way past the Abbey guards. Edward's appearance in pauper's rags creates a sensation. At first the nobles are prepared to have Edward flung out as an imposter, even when Tom announces who is truly the king and who is the pauper. Only when Miles appears, wounded, and urges Edward to produce the prince's seal, are they convinced. Edward, having forgiven Tom and learned what life is like at the bottom of the ladder, regains his throne, not only for himself but for the subjects whom he began to understand only when he was a pauper.

Comment

Shooting in Hungary during the Communist-led times was always an adventure. Paid in local currency, the cast spent most of it eating out in the restaurants of Buda and the bars that were on every street corner. Michael Ripper told the authors how much he enjoyed the trip; he had a particularly bittersweet memory of a night celebrating Mark Lester's birthday. Michael and Reed were pals and drinking

Oliver Reed as Miles in Mark Twain's *The Prince and the Pauper* (Salkind/Warner Bros., 1977).

buddies from way back, so when Reed suggested a special birthday gift for Lester, Michael was happy to go along (fueled, no doubt by beer); poor Lester was presented with a fetching "lady of the night" by the two older men and almost died of embarrassment. Older and wiser

now, Lester looks back on the night with amusement and says it was certainly unforgettable!

The Prince and the Pauper had a convoluted journey to the screen. Seven years before production began, Berta Dominguez and Pierre

Spengler collaborated on a long, very faithful *Prince and the Pauper* script. They had good reason to think that the script would be filmed for Berta's husband was Alexander Salkind who had a production company, and Spengler, then 22, was a boyhood pal of Ilya Salkind, son of the abovementioned.

George Cukor had agreed to direct it, but he wanted a child star — Mark Lester, from *Oliver!*— while the Salkinds preferred the adolescent Leonard Wintin. The disagreement and other problems, such as the fact that the Salkinds had not yet produced the hugely successful Musketeers movies, caused the Dominguez-Spengler project to be shelved. A couple of years passed; Berta wrote a completely different script for a movie to be called *The Prince Melagre* and now that they were successful, there was no problem getting finance. Reed and Peter O'Toole were to play the leads and Reed signed his contract. But at the last moment O'Toole became unavailable and other difficulties arose. A lot of additional commitments had been made in order to shoot the picture in the summer of 1976 and the Salkinds were in the uncomfortable position of spending a fortune dismantling a half-set-up film. Berta, attending a crisis meeting, reminded them of the *Prince and the Pauper* script gathering dust on the shelf. This was the answer to their prayers: They could honor all the commitments that they had made, just with another movie!

Reed remarked that it was all the same to him, whichever movie they settled on. The revived script went to Richard Fleischer who agreed to direct the film — but not with that script. So George MacDonald Fraser was parachuted in to save the day, writing the complete thing in a few weeks. Fleischer also disliked the meager production values envisaged; Fleischer convinced the Salkinds to commit $7 million to make "the kind of lavish production I do once in a while. I never think of them as costume pictures. When I put the actors in period dress, they look like they're wearing everyday clothes. That's what I mean by realism" (*The Guardian*, August 29, 1976). In agreeing, the Salkinds left themselves with no money for promotion of their movie — they had already committed millions to *Superman*.

Reed plays Miles Hendon with sensitivity

Miles (Oliver Reed) in a portrait from *The Prince and the Pauper* (Salkind/Warner Bros., 1977).

and brio. The weary mercenary only wants to get home after twenty years, collect his inheritance and marry his long-suffering betrothed. The look of puzzlement and anger on his face when denied by his evil young brother (David Hemmings) and his lady (Raquel Welch) is a joy. The duel-brawl between the brothers seems to have had an added dimension by some sort of falling-out between Reed and Hemmings, centered on Welch. Or as remembered by Hemmings decades later, "[Reed] grinned at me, laughed in recognition, and we lapsed into tales of old, of lovers we'd shared and, in particular, *The Prince and the Pauper* when he'd beaten me to a pulp in a horse-drawn carriage on the pretext of making it look 'real.' And when Raquel Welch, smitten by Ollie's mischievous eyes and aggressive wit, had to be rescued from despair on the banks of the Danube" (Hemmings, 400). To pass the time, Reed and Welch also fabricated a feud for the press; it gave them free publicity and kept their names at the forefront of people's minds while they were in exile behind the Iron Curtain.

It's sad that its creators expended so little post-production energy on their product, which is easy on the eye and great fun to watch. The critics were mostly complimentary. "Oliver Reed injects some vitality into his role…" (*Daily Express*, June 4, 1977); "[F]lamboyant Reed attacks his role … with such conviction that he helps you forget Richard Fleischer's direction and the appalling 'original' screenplay" (*Sunday Express*, June 5, 1977); "Reed, whose stock in trade is debonair thuggery, lends a heroic role a welcome touch of the sardonic" (*Financial Times*, June 3, 1977); "Oliver Reed makes every attempt to overwhelm the part and the movie. There is no sense of fun in his performance" (*New York Times*, March 2, 1978); "Oliver Reed has never been better in a film made for a mass audience; a strong but gentle performance" (*Screen International*, June 11, 1977).

Ransom (1977)

(Aka *Maniac, Assault on Paradise* and *The Town That Cried Terror*) New World Pictures; A Sunset Project; Inter-Ocean Film Ltd.; released by New World pictures; Panavision; Metrocolor

Crew—Director: Richard Compton; Executive Producer: Patrick Fennell; Producers: Patrick Fennell, Jim Hart; Associate Producers: Bond Denson Fennell, John M. Hawn; Co-Producer: Peter MacGregor-Scott; Screenplay: Roger Sikosky; Story: John C. Broderick; Camera Operator: Charles Mills; Special Effects: Roger George; Stunts: Conrad Palmisano; Assistant Director: Gary Credle; Gaffer: Norman Glasser; Key Grip: John Linden; Property Master: Robert Visciglia; Wardrobe: Llandys Williams; Makeup: Del Acevedo; Script Supervisor: Doris Grau; Music: Don Ellis; Music Supervisor: Ronald Stein; Pilot: R. Ross; Sound Effects: Mayflower Films.

Cast—Oliver Reed (Nick), Deborah Raffin (Cindy Simmons), Jim Mitchum (Tracker), Stuart Whitman (William Whitaker), John Ireland (Chief Halburton), Paul Koslo ("Victor"), Arch Archambault (Inspector Davey), Robert Lussier (Wolf), Dennis Redfield (Jackson), Kipp Whitman (Officer Steiner), Bill Allen (Carson), Shatka Bear-Step (Red Sky), Chard M. Alexander (Larry Owens), Richard E. Kennedy (Texas), Julian Wells (Floozy), Thomas J. Conlan (Mayor), Paul Roland (Barney), Wendy Donahue (Miss Davis), John Hirohata (Tommy), Judith Nugent-Hart (Miss Paradise), Gilda McCabe (Girl on Tennis Court), Ramon Chavez (Officer Garelo), Charles Fearn (Man on Tennis Court).

Synopsis

In Paradise, Arizona, an upscale resort community, Philip McCall (Paul Koslo), a failed Olympic-class swimmer, has become psychotic. Calling himself "Victor," he disguises himself as a Native American and shoots several police officers with a crossbow. He leaves a message on the station chalkboard: "The rich must pay or the rich will die—$1 million by 3.00 PM tomorrow." Chief Halburton (John Ireland) calls his friend Whitaker (Stuart Whitman), a wealthy land developer, to warn him. Whitaker calls in Nick McCormick (Oliver Reed), a soldier of fortune, to sort things out. Nick arrives with Wolf (Robert Lussier) and is told by Whitaker to kill "Victor"—no trial, no publicity to drive down land values. Nick steals reporter Cindy Simmons' (Deborah Raffin) microphone during an attempted interview; she follows him to a bar and they leave for her apartment for sex. She tells Nick that Whitaker is little more than a white collar Mafia thug. After "Victor" attacks a tennis club, Mick arranges for Tracker (Jim Mitchum) to be released from jail to help in the search. A money drop is set for Devil's Mountain, but "Victor" escapes on a motorbike after setting off smoke bombs. Whitaker, against Nick's order, had filled the bag with slips of paper. "Victor" next attacks Whitaker's estate, killing Wolf who is stationed there to guard him. While Nick and Tracker make a new plan, "Victor" kills the mayor (Thomas J. Conlan) during a parade. Whitaker tries to make amends by staging another drop—this time with $4 million in cash—and takes on "Victor" himself. They kill each other during the exchange, and Nick and Tracker take the money. Nick flies off with his share—and Cindy.

Comment

Ransom/Maniac/Assault on Paradise/The Town That Cried Terror is as much of a mess as its title situation. The film is just about watchable despite okay performances from Reed (sporting his dead-on American accent) and Stuart Whitman (another old pro trying, unsuccessfully to rise above his material).

Reed plays hardass Nick McCormick, accurately described as a "typical soldier of fortune"—at least the movie version. He's called in (how do you find these guys?) to solve the sticky ransom situation and says little, orders everyone about, has sex with a cute reporter, flies around in a helicopter, rides a motorbike ... well, you get the idea — "typical soldier of fortune" stuff.

He plays everything very, very low-key, which is refreshing because just about everyone else is very, very over the top. Reed even manages, as he always did, to bring life to the pretty much dead dialogue he's been handed; like this:

> FRIGHTENED RICH GUY: What guarantees do we have he'll succeed?
>
> NICK: No guarantees.
>
> FRIGHTENED RICH GUY: I thought as much.
>
> NICK: Gentlemen — if that's what I call you: On behalf of Wolf and myself, thanks for the plane ride.

If you think that's bad, try this: After Cindy comments on Nick's handgun, Nick says, "Never point a weapon [*smirk*] unless you mean it." They then head to her place for sex. Get it? Sadly, the dialogue isn't the worst part of the film. What's worse is that we have no idea what "Victor" is really up to or why. We are given no sensible reason why he dresses like a Native American or where and how he developed his skill with a bow and arrow.

At least Paul Koslo tries to invest some life into his character, which is more than can be said for the sleepwalking Jim Mitchum, whose character is even more sketchily drawn than "Victor." Actually, Tracker does so little in the film, one wonders why Mitchum was even cast, unless the producers hoped audiences would think it was Robert.

Screen International (October 20, 1976) reported that Reed left the U.K. on October 16 for filming what was to be called *Maniac* in Arizona. Filming was set for a six-week schedule in and around Scottsdale, Mesa and the Salt River–Roosevelt Dam area. Richard Widmark was set to co-star but (wisely) dropped out and was replaced by Stuart Whitman.

The authors could find no reviews of *Ransom* (or whatever) at the Lincoln Centre for Performing Arts or the British Film Institute. Our guess is that, unlike the authors, no critic had the guts to sit through it.

The Class of Miss MacMichael (1978)

Brut Pictures Inc.; Kettledrum Films; released by Gala Film Distributors in the U.K. in 1978; U.S. release in 1979; color

Crew— Director: Silvio Narizzano; Screenplay-Producer: Judd Bernard; from a novel by Sandy Hutson; Executive Producer: George Barrie; Associate Producer: Patricia Casey; Music: Stanley Myers; Cinematographer: Alex Thomson; Film Editor: Max Benedict; Casting: Esta Charkham; Art Director: Hazel Peiser; Makeup Artist: Colin Arthur; Hair Stylist: Patti Smith; Production Supervisor: Christopher Sutton; First Assistant Director: Jake Wright; Second Assistant Director: Terry Pearce; Third Assistant Director: Peter Kohn; Production Buyer: Jeanne Vertigen; Sound Recordist: Kevin Sutton; Sound Editor: Tony Sloman; Dubbing Mixer: Paul Carr; Camera Operator: Ray Andrew; Electrician: Dave Clark; Camera Focus: Peter Versey; Still Photographer: John Jay; Wardrobe Supervisor: Joyce Stoneman; Assistant Editors: Chris Ackland, Geoff Hogg; Special Music Arrangements: Francis Monkman; Titles: Robert Ellis.

Cast— Glenda Jackson (Conor MacMichael), Oliver Reed (Terence Sutton), Michael Murphy (Martin), Rosalind Cash (Una Ferrar), John Standing (Charles Fairbrother), Sylvia O'Donnell (Marie), Phil Daniels (Stewart), Patrick Murray (Boysie), Sharon Fussey (Belinda), Riba Akabusi (Gaylord), Perry Benson (Timmy), Herbert Norville (Ronnie), Owen Whittaker (Victor), Danielle Corgan (Tina), Angela Brogan (Frieda), Dayton Brown (John), Paul Daly (Nick), Victor Evans (Abel), Deidre Forrest (Deidre), Simon Howe (Rob), Tony Longdon (Adam), Stephanie Patterson (Pattie), Peta Bernard (Mabel), Judy Wiles (Ms. Eccles), Patsy Byrne (Mrs. Green), Christopher Guinee (Mr. Drake), Ian Thompson (Mr. Bowden), Mavis Pugh (Mrs. Barnett), Constantin de Goguel (Major Brady), Sylvia Marriott (Mrs. Wickens), Sally Nesbitt (Mrs. Brady), Marianne Stone (Mrs. Lee), Pamela Manson (Mrs. Bellrind), Thomas Baptiste (Visitor), John Prior (Philip), Ian Donnelly (Brian), David Elmon (Boris), Graham Kennedy-Smith (Allen), Beverly Martin (Bernice), Debbie Morton (Debbie), John Wreford (Minister), Honoria Burke (Mrs. Wyles), Alma Yang Tuk (Visitor), Christopher Driscoll, Ken MacDonald, Nigel Humphreys (Basketball Fans), Josh Medak (Raspberry Blower), Adrianna Bernard (Girl with Dog), Boliver (Dog).

Synopsis

In the East End of London, in an almost derelict school, Terence Sutton (Oliver Reed) oversees an establishment for the dregs and drop-outs of the school system — and that in-

Oliver Reed as the principal, Mr. Sutton, in *The Class of Miss MacMichael* (Brut/Kettledrum/Gala, 1978).

cludes his staff too. Conor MacMichael (Glenda Jackson) spends her days fighting him for some care and leniency for her class of social misfits and her nights trying to convince her lover that their affair really does mean more than her job.

Her class invades her private life, to the disquiet of her lover. Sutton becomes more demented each day, having to keep the lid on his school while showing an avuncular face to the visitors who view his social experiment each day.

Things can only get worse, and they do. The visitors having spent some time there, can safely go away — this snapshot of the academic hell continues. The school disintegrates around the staff. Sutton blames everyone but himself and launches an attack on Ms. MacMichael that should have seen him arrested.

Comment

Producer Judd Bernard waited for the chance to make this black comedy, based on the actual experiences of American teacher-novelist Sandy Hutson. He wrote his own screenplay, selected Silvio Narizzano as director and persuaded Glenda Jackson and Oliver Reed to accept a percentage rather than a salary so that he could stay on budget; he ruled out all the normal "perks": no parties, no expensive lunches, and he used the subway to come to work. He economized in the props and costume department by using his wife's clothes and some spare furniture from his basement. He even cast his own dog in a part.

Reed's Terence Sutton is a gem; both the authors are retired teachers and, when viewing the movie, had recollections that made Sutton less a caricature than you might think. Mark Brennan of *Blitz* magazine (March 1987) was present during some of the shooting: "I peered over Silvio Narizzano's shoulder to watch headmaster Reed in action. Clad in a dark blue suit, he was pacing the large room where over 100 defiant children were seated cross-legged on the hard wooden floor. It was assembly time in the great hall where Glenda Jackson, wearing a navy track-suit as non-conformist schoolteacher Conor MacMichael, was leading her pupils in a lusty piano accompaniment of 'Onward Christian Soldiers' before Reed dismissed the class."

"This headmaster, Sutton, is such a hypocrite," said Reed. "He's all things to all people. The audience will be wondering what he's going to do next. The kids are slightly wary of him. During rehearsals I was talking to a group of them, mostly recruited from London acting schools, and their interest in filmmaking is amazing.... I went to about thirteen different schools but I never encountered a headmaster like the one I play in this film. He wouldn't have been allowed to behave this way in real life. The authorities wouldn't have put up with him. He's a tyrant who shouts at the other teachers as well as the kids, then he's very smarmy to school authorities when he wants a grant or to raise money from them. The army sergeant I played in *Triple Echo*, which I did with Glenda four years ago, was just a bully but Sutton ... is a hypocrite, egocentric and totally different. I don't like rehearsals. I came in cold and did my scene with Glenda. Out of the corner of my eye, I could see all the kids sitting there staring at me and wondering what I was going to do next. Glenda plays a teacher who cares, maybe a little too much, about her charges. She's constantly in conflict with Sutton. We have a lot of heavy dialogue together — and that means a lot of shouting!" (*Blitz*, March 1987).

Reed's role means he's frequently surrounded by large groups of tough Cockney schoolchildren. Look carefully and you'll see Sutton's name on the board outside the school — Terence Sutton MA (Cantab). It's an in-joke, since his friend Michael Winner always describes himself as an MA (Cantab).

Jackson got hurt in a sequence where Reed pulls a bookcase down on her in his fury; perhaps a bookcase from the basement wasn't such a good idea, as it didn't have safety glass. Jackson, however, took it in her stride.

Filmed at locations in Kensal Town, various streets in London, around the National Film Theatre, South Bank Centre and at Lee International Studios, the film had a gritty realism, for all the supposed comedy.

Conor MacMichael is a trendy, lefty schoolteacher with the kind of agenda that makes some educationalists weep. She wants the best for her class of reprobates and outcasts, but prefers being matey to being any kind of disciplinarian. The kids need love, but they also need structure. Pretty soon they're invading her personal life and she's letting them.

Terence Sutton, on the other hand, is a dyed-in-the-wool traditionalist — if he could have the birch in his office, and use it, he'd be a happy man. While Conor's students have an affectionate toleration for her, they fear and despise Sutton since they frequently see the other side of him. Sutton, to all intents and purposes, runs a "beacon" school which reforms the kids and puts them back on the academic straight and narrow; his eclectic staff members range from liberationists like Conor to old-fashioned plodders and they all, with the possible exception of Conor, fear him and his roaring temper. Since his school is so special, a great many visitors are shown around by preening councilors, keen to get the kudos for whatever good the school does. When it goes wrong, it goes horribly wrong, and Sutton implodes. All of which Reed does superbly. His Sutton is just a smidgen on the right side of caricature to be acceptable.

With a budget of $1 million, the company returned a slick, slightly disjointed movie which didn't impress the critics. "Oliver Reed plays Sutton, the headmaster, as though he was a music hall character" (*Monthly Film Bulletin*, May 1979); "Oliver Reed is quite grotesque and absurd as the overbearing headmaster. The result is a mess" (*Daily Express*, May 5, 1979); "Oliver Reed as the headmaster is an enjoyable joke" (*Daily Mail*, May 11, 1979).

Tomorrow Never Comes (1978)

Classic; Montreal Trust; Neffbourne; released by J. Arthur Rank Film Distributors in the U.K.; color

Crew— Director: Peter Collinson; Screenplay: David Pursall, Jack Seddon; Associate Producers: Denis Heroux, Robert Sterne; Producers: Michael Klinger, Julian Melzack; Original Music: Roy Budd; Cinematography: Francois Protat; Film Editor: John

Shirley; Art Director: Michel Prolux; Makeup Artist: Marie-Angele Protat; Unit Manager: Ginette Hardy; Production Manager: Robert Menard; Assistant Director: Peter Price; Property Master: Jacques Chamberland; Sound Editor: Peter Best; Sound Recordist: Gerry Humphries; Sound: Brian Simmons; Stunts: Jerome Tiberghien; Key Grip: Serge Grenier; Chief Electrician: Kevin O'Connell; Still Photographer: Barry Peake; Camera Operator: Alan Smith; Wardrobe: Shura Cohen; Fight Arranger: Craig R. Baxley; Production Accountants: Len Cave, Lucie Drolet; Publicists: Prudence Emery, Fred Hift; Supervising Production Accountant: Denton Scott.

Cast— Oliver Reed (Jim Wilson), Susan George (Janie), Raymond Burr (Burke), John Ireland (Captain), Stephen McHattie (Frank), Donald Pleasence (Dr. Todd), Paul Koslo (Willy), Cec Linder (Milton), Richard Donat (Ray), Delores Etienne (Hilda), Sammy Snyders (Joey), Jayne Eastwood (Girl in Bar), Mario Di Iorio (Second Man in Bar), Stephen Mendel (Vic), Ian De Voy (TV Commentator), Norris Dominique (Bellhop), Jack Fisher (Hotel Manager), Robert King (Young Cop), Jefferson Mappin (First Man in Bar), Walter Massey (Sergeant), Julian Melzack (Drunk in Bar), John Osborne (Lyne), Earl Pennington (First Waiter), Pierre Tetrault (Man in Apartment).

Synopsis

Frank (Stephen McHattie), an amiable loser, returns to his busy resort town after being away on a job for three months. He goes to the apartment he shared with his girlfriend Jane (Susan George) and finds her gone. Frank is told by his bartender friend Ray (Richard Donat) that she's working — and living — at the Barbizon Hotel. A patron suggests that Jane is also sexually involved with Lyne (John Osborne) who owns the hotel and most of the town. A nasty fight ensues, and Frank sustains a serious head injury. He goes to Jane's cabana to confront her and is challenged by a police officer as the couple argue. Frank takes the officer's gun, accidentally shoots him, and holds Jane hostage. Among those at the scene is Lt. Wilson (Oliver Reed) who is leaving the force the following day. Wilson is disgusted with the town in general, and specifically with his corrupt chief Burke (Raymond Burr) and the overly enthusiastic Willy (Paul Koslo), a fellow officer. Frank is becoming more dangerous due to his injuries — Dr. Todd (Donald Pleasence) tells Wilson they could prove fatal — and is determined to kill Lyne. Wilson, a decent man, wants to talk Frank down, but Burke has a dif-

ferent plan. He wants to keep Lyne's name out of the situation due to his planned infusion of millions of dollars into the town — and the chief's pockets. After failing with several attempts to extract Frank from the cabana, Wilson walks Lyne to the scene to talk to him. As Lyne cowers on the ground, Wilson and Frank reach an agreement and he hands his gun to the policemen. Burke gives Willy the order to fire and Frank is shot to death by a dozen marksmen. Wilson, horrified, walks away.

Comment

Tomorrow Never Comes plays like an overlong, slightly above average TV police procedural — with bad language. Watching it is a somewhat disturbing experience, but not so much for its corrupt cops and its nasty violence. What makes *Tomorrow Never Comes* so disturbing is that, as undistinguished as it is, the film might contain one of Oliver Reed's best performances between *Royal Flash* and *Castaway*— a period of twelve years.

Tomorrow Never Comes certainly afforded Reed a decent role and he gave a performance to match; nothing special, but a long, long way from *The Great Scout and Cathouse Thursday*. We first meet Lt. Wilson as his career is winding down; he's had his fill of the town and its corruption and is going home to start over. He's harassed by Willy — a good, annoying performance by Paul Koslo — who revels in the excitement of the job. (Wilson: "Look at you. It's all rotten. Even the biggies are on the take. I used to think like you, Willy boy. I did. Until my wife was killed — hit and run. That gave me a jolt.")

Reed plays this scene — and most of his scenes — with a low-key detachment. He never resorts to violence and rarely raises his voice. *The Monthly Film Bulletin* (May 1978) noted, "Although saddled with an impossibly clichéd role, Oliver Reed plays with an uncharacteristic, banked down authority which at least makes his scenes watchable especially in the final confrontation." *Variety* (March 1, 1978) felt that Reed's character "is unremittingly grim, the result of losing his wife and too many years on a brutish force.... Actor plays it to the hilt."

Reed does his best, and it's plenty good enough, but the film's best performance was given by McHattie as Frank. He begins the film as a nice guy who, after being dumped by his girl and beaten in a brawl, realistically begins to lose it. After he accidentally shoots the police officer, there's only one way to go — down — and McHattie is up to the job. He has a just-right, slightly crazed look and is in bloody makeup for all but the first few minutes of the film.

Tomorrow Never Comes is difficult to praise or condemn; it's just *there*. Most reviewers were unmoved. *Variety* (March 1, 1978): "What we have here, along with a lot of nasty people and rough albeit credible language, is one of those hunks of overripe pulp with stock characterizations to match. [Ireland, George, Pleasence and Koslo] all acquit in seasoned fashion. But nobody's gonna win any honors"; *The Western Mail* (June 17, 1978): "An unusually strong cast fails to raise *Tomorrow Never Comes* above the level of the mundane." *The Guardian* (March 2, 1978): "Oliver Reed trying to do a Raymond Burr and Raymond Burr trying to be Orson Welles"; *The Sunday Times* (March 5, 1978): "It looks like it had been made by someone who once studied the stills from *Dog Day Afternoon.*"

Tomorrow Never Comes was filmed entirely in Canada — probably for financial reasons — but it could have taken place anywhere, which is a sobering thought.

The Big Sleep (1978)

Incorporated Television Company; Winkast Film Productions; released by United Artists in the U.S. and U.K.; color

Crew— Screenplay-Director: Michael Winner; from the novel by Raymond Chandler; Producers: Jerry Bick, Elliott Kastner, Michael Winner; Executive Producer: Lew Grade; Associate Producer: Bernard Williams; Original Music: Jerry Fielding; Cinematographer: Robert Painter; Casting: Maude Spector; Production Design: Harry Pottle; Art Director: John Graysmark; Costume Design: Ron Beck; Hair Stylist: Stephanie Kaye; Makeup Artist: Richard Mills; Production Managers: Clifton Brandon, David Middlemas: Property Master: Barry Wilkinson; Sound Editors: Russ Hill, Mike Le Mare, John Poyner; Sound Recordist: Brian Marshall; Sound Re-recordist: Hugh Strain; Camera Focus: Eddie Collins; Camera Operator: Ronnie Taylor;

Still Photographer: Keith Hamshere; Continuity: Pamela Carlton; Production Executive: Denis Holt.

Cast— Robert Mitchum (Philip Marlowe), Sarah Miles (Charlotte), Richard Boone (Lash Canino), Candy Clark (Camilla), Joan Collins (Agnes Lozelle), Edward Fox (Joe Brody), John Mills (Inspector Carson), Oliver Reed (Eddie Mars), James Stewart (General Sternwood), Harry Andrews (Norris), Colin Blakely (Harry Jones), James Donald (Gregory), Diana Quick (Mona), Richard Todd (Commander Barker), John Justin (Geiger), Martin Potter (Owen Taylor), Simon Turner (Karl Lundgren), Patrick Durkin (Reg), David Saville (Rusty Regan), Don Henderson (Lou), Roy Evans (Man in Overalls), Mike Lewin (Detective Waring), David Jackson (Inspector Willis), Dudley Sutton (Lanny), Derek Deadman (Big Nose), David Millett (Detective), Clifford Earl (Police Doctor), Joe Ritchie (Taxi Driver), Michael Segal (Barman), Norman Lumsden (Lord Smethurst), Nik Forster (Croupier), Judy Buxton (Cheval Club Receptionist).

Synopsis

London-based American P.I. Philip Marlowe (Robert Mitchum) is hired by crippled millionaire General Sternwood (James Stewart) to investigate the blackmail of his nymphomaniac daughter Camilla (Candy Clark). Sternwood's older daughter Charlotte (Sarah Miles) thinks Marlowe has actually been hired to find her missing husband Rusty (David Saville). Marlowe is given a blackmail note from Geiger (John Justin), a pornographer who has nude pictures of Camilla. When he stakes out Geiger's house he sees Camilla enter — then he hears gunshots. He finds Geiger dead and Camilla nude and in a stupor. During the course of his investigation he encounters Agnes (Joan Collins) who works in Geiger's bookshop; Joe Brody (Edward Fox) who is involved in the blackmail plot; and Eddie Mars (Oliver Reed), a smooth but dangerous casino owner. Mars' wife Mona (Diane Quick) is missing — presumably she has run off with Rusty. Marlowe goes to Brody's flat and finds Agnes there — and soon after his arrival, Camilla comes to demand the return of her photos. When Brody answers the doorbell, he is shot through the door. Marlowe gives chase and apprehends Karl (Simon Turner), Geiger's lover, who believed that Brody killed Geiger. At Mars' casino, Charlotte wins a large sum of money and is held up in the car park but Marlowe intervenes. Marlowe then catches Harry (Colin

Blakely) who has been tailing him. Harry is working with Agnes and gives Marlowe a tip on where to find Mona — and is killed by Canino (Richard Boone).

Mars has hidden Mona away to prevent his being suspected of killing Rusty. Sternwood makes it clear he wants Rusty found; Marlowe traces Mona to a secluded house but is overpowered by Canino. Mona frees Marlowe who kills Canino. He gives Camilla a gun loaded with blanks and she confirms his suspicions by shooting at him. She had killed Rusty when he turned her advances down.

Comment

Raymond Chandler was, hands down, the greatest writer of hard-boiled private detective thrillers. Dashiell Hammett may have been the first; *The Maltese Falcon* (1930), which introduced Sam Spade, set the template. But Chandler's Philip Marlowe ate guys like Spade for breakfast.

Chandler began his writing career relatively late at 45, having spent some time as a journalist and oil company executive. After losing his job due to the Great Depression, he turned to writing mystery short stories for pulp magazines, beginning with "Blackmailers Don't Shoot" (1933) for *Black Mask*. Chandler spent the next six years exploring the works of the tough but honest man who "walked the mean streets alone." In 1939 he combined several plot points from these stories and expanded upon several character types to produce his first — and breakthrough — novel *The Big Sleep*. He referred to this process as "cannibalization" which resulted in his novels having odd, disjointed plots which he somehow managed to tie together. Chandler's specialty was a jaundiced view of morality in general and Los Angeles in particular.

Chandler turned to screenwriting in 1944, adapting the equally hard-boiled James M. Cain's classic *Double Indemnity* for director Billy Wilder. When Warner Bros. turned to *The Big Sleep* in 1946 they ignored Chandler. Director Howard Hawks wasn't above contacting the author about an obscure plot point when stuck for an answer. According to legend, Chandler, too, was stuck for an answer! Starring Hum-

phrey Bogart as Marlowe, *The Big Sleep* was a huge hit, epitomizing the concept of film noir. It was one of those instant and enduring classics that no one would dream of remaking. Who would have the nerve?

Michael Winner remarks in his autobiography, "Producer Elliott Kastner showed me the book and asked me to write a script. I'd never read Raymond Chandler before. I was struck with the poetry of his rhythms and choice of language. I'd always thought he was a street writer dealing with the seamy side of life in LA. But he did it with a cadence that was almost like Oscar Wilde."

Kastner had scored big with Chandler's *Farewell My Lovely* in 1975, itself a remake of *Murder My Sweet* (1944) with Dick Powell. Set in period and starring film noir icon Robert Mitchum, the film was a good approximation of the 1940s-type mysteries that no one was making any more. This time round though, the plot was to be set in present-day London — which drove Chandler purists mad.

According to Michael Winner, "It came about because it seemed to me that the original film was so immensely well known that to ape it in any way would be ridiculous. Furthermore, Raymond Chandler was a great Anglophile" (Server, 479). Kastner secured Mitchum for a second go as Marlowe and populated the film with a cast to die for (which many actually did). Listed last in the opening credits with special billing was "Oliver Reed as Eddie Mars." Reed's role was, as they say, small but showy; he was certainly not lost in the bevy of stars who surrounded him.

In the ITC Entertainment press release, Winner said, "It's nice to work with Oliver Reed again. I first worked with him fifteen years ago when he was unemployable. At that time I had to beg and beat people to give him anything at all." Some of the press felt that Reed was getting too many roles lately, and had become over-employed. Reed responded in the ITC Entertainment press release, "When one is given the opportunity of acting, one should do it. If James Hunt didn't drive a car he wouldn't be a champion, but people don't say, 'James Hunt's driving too many cars — he's making too many appearances at Grand Prix.' That's his job. You can't tell me I'm making too

Charlotte (Sarah Miles) and Eddie Mars (Oliver Reed) are up to no good in Michael Winner's re-make of the Raymond Chandler classic *The Big Sleep* (United Artists, 1978).

many films. That's my job. I'm a professional actor. I get paid for it, so I do it. In the sense of what I am, people must accept the way I am. I'm quite versatile. When people started offering me work in Europe and America, I de-cided I'd rather do that than sit around not working. I never thought about doing guest spots in films. But you have to change."

The Big Sleep began production on August 1, 1977, with an eight-week schedule. Typical of Winner, there was extensive location work in and around London. Winner was careful to avoid too many tourist-friendly spots, which gave the film a fresh look. It was not Los Angeles, but it is not quite London either.

The film opens and closes with Mitchum's world-weary reading of Chandler's original dialogue. Unfortunately, the presentation of Marlowe immediately departs from Chandler's conception. As envisioned by the author — and as played by Dick Powell and Humphrey Bogart — Marlowe is a bit seedy, a bit down-and-out. Mitchum's Marlowe drives a Mercedes roadster and is better dressed than the incredibly well-dressed Eddie Mars. His flat is a bit opulent — far from Marlowe's rented houses.

This quibbling aside, Mitchum is fine, if a bit old at 61. This becomes embarrassing when Camilla — admittedly a nympho — drools after first seeing him. Mitchum brought a lot of history to the part, and his laid-back style is perfect, more than making up for the aforementioned lapses. Reed enters a complex plot through the door of Geiger's house and finds Marlowe and Camilla — much to everyone's surprise. Reed/Mars and Mitchum/Marlowe immediately size each other up. It seems that Mars had been the late Geiger's landlord. Mars says, "Marlowe — stop believing you're so amusing. And stay away from this house. And [whispers] stay further away from me." The two characters don't seem to scare each other much, and even develop a live-and-let-live philosophy. Mars' part in the goings-on is kept vague; we're never sure how guilty he is of anything. Reed makes him sinister yet somehow likable, a difficult job at best. They next meet when Marlowe finds Mars, uninvited, in his flat.

> MARS: "May I tell you something soldier? I'm nice to be nice to. But I'm not nice not to be nice to."
>
> MARLOWE: "If you listen real hard, you'll hear my teeth chattering."

The two hard guys stop trying to scare each other and settle into an uneasy truce; neither one trusts the other or has any idea what the other is up to. Reed and Mitchum effortlessly get across the idea that their two characters are more alike than they want to be. Mars isn't as bad as he seems, but Marlowe isn't as good either. Reed's Eddie Mars, though, is far from an angel. What he won't lower himself to do personally, he directs the psychotic Canino to do. Richard Boone plays him, effectively, as way over the edge and very nastily so.

Mars' motivation is to avoid being suspected of Rusty's death, which is fair enough since Camilla actually killed him. Under different circumstances he and Marlowe might have been friends. His character, as the excellent John Ridgely played him in the original, is just ambiguous enough to keep Marlowe — and the audience — guessing. The two Marses, however, meet entirely different ends. Ridgely is shot through a door by his own men — engineered by Marlowe — while Reed walks away with his wife and a smirk.

Like the film, Reed was pretty much dismissed by the critics, but his performance was a good one. He has three main scenes, all with Mitchum, and more than holds his own as does Mitchum. Reed showed again that all he needed to do to steal a scene was to enter it.

"Remaking a film classic is dangerous business under even optimum conditions. The effort here seems a mixture of dedication and canned elements. So-so but handsome" (*Variety*, March 15, 1978); "Primarily for fans of Mitchum who come fresh to the story. The trouble is that everything updates and transplants very neatly except the attitudes. Most of the naughty goings-on would rate little more than a few lines in a gossip column" (*Screen International*, October 7, 1978); "Oliver Reed is hilariously foppish" (*New York Times*, March 13, 1978); "I'm afraid *The Big Sleep* is just that" (*The Daily Mirror*, August 8, 1978); "Usefully employed is Oliver Reed. Plenty of people, plenty of plot" (*The Sunday Times*, September 28, 1978); "A lot of distinguished actors and a lot of British technicians were employed in making this film which is compensation if not justification" (*The Morning Star*, September 29, 1978).

This *Big Sleep* simply can't compete with the original, which is hardly an indictment, and it is more or less forgotten, apart from being a free DVD giveaway in one of the British Sunday papers. It's not that bad — really — and is worth a look if only for its all-star cast. Michael Winner deserves credit for trying to bring something new to the old (and very confusing) story. It's a quality production that, unfortunately, would soon be a rarity for Oliver Reed.

A Touch of the Sun (1979)

No production or distribution credits could be unearthed by the authors.

Crew— Film Editor–Director: Peter Curran; Writers: Peter Curran, George Fowler; Producer: Elizabeth Curran; Executive Producers: Oliver I. Irwin, Jerry Kingsley; Cinematographer: David Mason; Assistant Director: David Curran; Camera Operator: Bob Jordan.

Cast— Oliver Reed (Capt. Daniel Nelson), Sylvaine Charlet (Natasha), Keenan Wynne (General Spellman), Peter Cushing (Commissioner Potts), Wilfred Hyde-White (M-1), Hilary Pritchard (Miss Funnypenny), Bruce Boa (Jim Coburn), Melvyn Hayes (Ginger Rogers), Edwin Manda (Emperor Sumumba),Ted Spain (Boatman), Fred Carter (President P. Nuts), Mike Cross (Fred Astaire), Kristi Anne Farrow (Nurse), Benjamin Shawa, Friday Nyamba, (Emperor's Aides), Dave Kallimore, Jim Kenny (U.S. Operators), A.M. Phiri (Chief Zawie), Roland Kuard (Doorman).

Synopsis

Captain Nelson (Oliver Reed) is hopelessly out of place as the general's (Keenan Wynn) factotum. He is clumsy, inept, giggly and totally without experience in the world. He is targeted by Natasha (Sylvaine Charlet) when the general details him to take care of the landing of a very expensive space capsule. He makes a complete mess of it and the landing is interrupted by an unknown force. The space capsule lands unexpectedly in Central Africa.

Emperor Sumumba (Edwin Manda) captures the spacecraft and demands a huge ransom for its return. Lieutenant Nelson, the general and CIA agent Coburn (Bruce Boa) are sent to retrieve it. They learn that the capsule was downed by a laser powered by the sunlight in a plot engineered by Sumumba and his aide, Russian agent Natasha. Complicating the situation are a diminutive, slightly feminine Tarzan type (Melvyn Hayes) and the British Commissioner Potts (Peter Cushing). Potts is a somewhat confused but very crafty ex-colonial official who was left behind at his post when World War II ended. He is apparently unaware

that all the African states have achieved independence and he carries on as if the Great British Empire still existed. He is extraordinarily good at extracting money from all around him. The tribesmen who act as his police force are busy looking for their women, stolen by the emperor. During the final battle, Potts' soldiers get into the building where the laser is kept and find their women, who are the emperor's technicians.

Comment

Filmed in Zambia, Africa, the movie began production on June 19, 1978, and was scheduled for an eight-week shoot. A screening of a rough cut was held at the Cannes Film Festival in May 1979 and there was to be a premiere in Lusaka, Zambia, on October 24 to celebrate the nation's fourteenth anniversary of independence. The actual African premiere was September's 13. The film was released through 20th Century–Fox in Africa but apparently no one else in the world wanted it, and the film seems not to have been shown in either the U.K. or the U.S. As the first international film to be shot in Zambia it received a good deal of coverage in the press. The *Zambia Daily Mail* (August 5) noted that Reed and Keenan Wynn had taken part in a charity walk to raise money for the poorest Zambian children. The wonderful Peter Cushing was a last minute replacement for an actor who dropped out, fortunately for us as Cushing's performance is, as ever, a gem. Edwin Manda, who starred as the emperor, was a local actor and a gifted singer. Many of the minor parts and extra roles were played by local Zambian actors. Location shooting took place at the Victoria Falls, the Kafue River and the countryside around Lusaka.

The film apparently never had a proper release, though why remains a mystery since it had a budget of £1.5 million, a good cast and a quirky story. It should have done better — perhaps someone needed a tax write-off?

Reed's Nelson is played for laughs; it is a little heavy-handed and gets to be tiresome. The great unspoken joke is that Nelson is the flip side of Reed: He doesn't drink, is a clumsy oaf and is absolutely terrible with women. He must have been enormous fun to play, with slapstick being the order of the day. It is perhaps not surprising that the authors could find no reference to the movie at either the British Film Institute or Lincoln Center and are very grateful to their friend Mark Walter for loaning them a copy to view; there are worse ways to spend an hour or so.

The Brood (1979)

Canadian Film Development Corporation; Elgin International Films Ltd.; Mutual Productions Ltd.; Victor Solnicki Productions; released by New World Pictures in the U.S. in 1979; no U.K. release; color

Crew— Screenplay-Director: David Cronenberg; Executive Producers: Pierre David, Victor Solnicki; Producer: Claire Heroux; Cinematographer: Mark Irwin; Art Director: Carol Spier; Editor: Allan Collins; First Assistant Director: John Board; Production Manager: Gwen Iveson; Second Assistant Director: Libby Bowden; Continuity: Nancy Eagles; Gaffer: Jock Brandis; Best Boy: Bob Gallant; Property Master: Peter Lauterman; Props Assistant: Tom Reid; Set Dresser: Angelo Stea; Wardrobe Mistress: Delphine White; Assistant Wardrobe: Granada Venne; Makeup: Shonagh Jabour; Hair Stylist: Jimmy Brown; Sound: Bryan Day; Boom: Tom Mather; Focus: Robin Miller; Clapper/Loader: Greg Villeneuve; Key Grip: Maris Jansons; Grip: Carlo Campana; Production Secretary: Trudy Work; Production Accountant: Wayne Aaron; Location Manager: David Coatsworth; Production Assistants: Maureen Fitzgerald, Bob Wertheimer; Assistant Editor: Carolyn Zeifman; Casting: Canadian Casting Association; Stills: Rick Porter.

Cast— Oliver Reed (Dr. Hal Raglan), Samantha Eggar (Nola Carveth), Art Hindle (Frank Carveth), Cindy Hinds (Candy Carveth), Nuala Fitzgerald (Juliana), Henry Beckman (Barton Kelly), Susan Hogan (Ruth), Michael McGhee (Inspector Mrazek), Gary McKeehan (Mike Trellan), Bob Silverman (Dr. Jan Hartog), Joseph Shaw (Dr. Desborough), Felix Silla (The Child), Larry Solway (Resnikoff), Rainer Schwartz (Birkin), Nicholas Campbell (Chris).

Synopsis

Frank (Art Hindle) and Nola Carveth (Samantha Eggar) have separated due to her abuse of their five-year-old daughter Candy (Cindy Hinds); Nola has been admitted to Dr. Hal Raglan's (Oliver Reed) Somerfree Institute. Raglan is secretive about his methods, called Psychoplasmics, in which he uses intense role play to treat his patients' rage. Frank finds bruises on Candy's back after a weekend visit to her mother and confronts Raglan. He dismisses Frank's accusations and insists that ending the child's visits would be devastating to Nola. Frank is advised that he doesn't have enough evidence to go against Raglan's decision. After picking up Candy from school where he flirts with her teacher Ruth (Susan Hogan), Frank takes his daughter to visit her grandmother Juliana (Nuala Fitzgerald).

As Raglan role-plays with Nola, during which she condemns her mother, Juliana is murdered in her kitchen by a small deformed creature (Felix Silla). Frank is notified by Inspector Mrazek (Michael McGhee), who has taken Candy to headquarters where she is examined by a psychologist who is convinced that she (Candy) witnessed the murder. Frank, seeking evidence against Raglan, visits the insane Dr. Hartog (Bob Silverman) who claims he developed huge cancerous tumors through Psychoplasmics. Nola's father Barton (Henry Beckman) after hearing of his wife's murder, goes to Somerfree to see Nola, but is turned away. He and Raglan quarrel, then Barton goes to Juliana's house where, after begging Frank to go with him to Somerfree, he passes out drunk on the bed and is murdered by the deformed creature, which is subsequently killed by Frank. An autopsy reveals that the creature isn't human.

Raglan closes Somerfree so that he can be alone with Nola, who now believes that Frank and Ruth are having an affair. The next day Ruth is killed in front of her class by two of the creatures, who abduct Candy and take her to Somerfree. Frank accosts Raglan who, surprisingly, agrees to help him save Candy. He explains that the creatures are Nola's brood — physical manifestations of her all-consuming rage. Candy is in the attic with the brood; Raglan tells Frank to keep Nola calm to neutralize the brood's actions. As Raglan tries to free Candy, Nola goes berserk at Frank's disgust of her, causing her creatures to attack. Frank strangles her, which kills those of the brood that Raglan hasn't killed in his death throes. Seeing Raglan's corpse, Frank spirits Candy away. In the car, Frank notices small tumors on her arm.

Dr. Raglan (Oliver Reed) is attacked by the strange children of his patient in *The Brood* (New World Pictures, 1979).

Comment

While watching *The Brood*, one can't help wondering if writer-director David Cronenberg was having marital and/or custody problems during the production. If one was, one would be right. *Cineart Biography* reported that *The Brood* was written by Cronenberg while he was "undergoing a divorce and bitter custody battle for his daughter"—he called the film his *Kramer vs. Kramer*.

Cronenberg said in *Fangoria* #3, "For me it's a very different film from my earlier two. It's less of an action film — it has fewer characters that you get to know better; it's more interior and quiet. It's also autobiographical in a way. I was writing with that as a starting point. It then became the nightmare version of the situation."

His earlier films — *They Came from Within*

(1976) and *Rabid* (1977)—and those following *The Brood*—*Scanners* (1981) and *Videodrome* (1983)—established his interest in what has been called "body horror." These films and, especially, *The Fly* (1986) reveled in the revulsion of the disintegration, disfigurement and mutilating of the body, often in a vaguely and very off-putting sexual manner. No other director managed to present such disturbing images and concepts so well; *The Brood* is near the top of the list.

Variety (January 28, 1981) reported, "Despite the critical attention and consistent financial success, the director had difficulty obtaining a bigger budget from Cinepix for his next project, *The Brood*. Unable to make a deal with Cinepix, Cronenberg turned to Toronto lawyer Victor Solnicks who, in turn, pacted with distributor Pierre David to put [this] shocker together."

The demand by Cronenberg for more money was almost connected to the hiring of the two stars; Reed and Samantha Eggar probably cost ten times as much as the entire cast of *They Came from Within* and *Rabid*. And they were worth it; both are excellent and elevate *The Brood* to a higher level. After the budgetary problems were solved, *The Brood* was shot between January and April 1979.

Reed has vaguely been associated with horror films since beginning his career with Hammer, but this is not really the case. Of his nine films for Hammer, five were costume adventures. Only *The Curse of the Werewolf* was an all-out horror movie, *Paranoiac* more of a mystery, and his role in *The Two Faces of Dr. Jekyll* (more of a sex film than horror) was a small one. Giving a broad definition to "horror movie," Reed only appeared in a dozen out of his one hundred films — not a large number. *The Brood* was definitely one of them — it's as horrific as horror movies get.

Cronenberg and Reed pulled an interesting bit of audience manipulation with the character of Dr. Raglan. We assume, before the film begins, that Reed is the villain because, well, he's Oliver Reed. The opening scene seems to confirm this as Raglan brutally role-plays with the pathetic Mike (Gary McKeehan).

> RAGLAN (nastily): You're not looking at me, Mike. You're not looking at me in the eye. Only weak people do that.

Raglan's behavior shouts "bastard!" He's curt, rude, vain and imperious. We should dislike him, and initially we do. But as *The Brood* unspools, we come to realize that he cares about his patients and believes in himself and his theories. Gradually, some of his negative characteristics turn into positive ones, especially when compared to Frank, the nominal — but ineffectual — hero.

Reed was a master at making characters whom we should dislike (including Calder in *The Hunting Party*, Frank in *Tommy*, Gerald in *Castaway* and Proximo in *Gladiator*) strangely appealing, against our better judgment. We have no trouble accepting Raglan's heroism at the film's conclusion even though we've labeled him "no good" at the beginning.

Eggar accomplishes this in reverse in an equally excellent performance. We're prepared to like her from the beginning because she's, well, Samantha Eggar. She quickly divests us of that notion in a role-playing scene with Raglan, during which he presents himself as her mother.

> RAGLAN: Mommy never hurt her children.
>
> NOLA: You beat me, and scratched me [*hissing*], and threw me down the stairs. [Then she glares at Raglan with a psychotic intensity that's too painful to watch.]

Juliana's murder in the next scene is horrific, as are many of the images to come, but none are more disturbing than Nola's piercing rage. In a later role-playing scene, Raglan takes Frank's side, telling Nola that he's simply doing what any good father would do. Nola is reminded that her own father stood by and allowed Juliana to abuse her. Her pathetic vulnerability is as upsetting as her anger. She says, "You didn't protect me! You didn't. You shouldn't have looked away when she hit me. You should have stopped her." And suddenly she explodes and hits Raglan. "God! I love you, but you pretended it didn't happen! Didn't you love me?"

At this moment, *The Brood* becomes too real, becomes more than a horror movie. One wonders what emotions may have been triggered for filmgoers who had been victims of abuse themselves. Although *The Brood* is filled with outrageously graphic images, the film's real power stems from its wider implications.

The creepiest moment in *The Brood* is a non-visual one. When the creature that killed Nola's father is given an autopsy, we see it in a long shot on an operating table. As the observers discuss the thing, it's described as having incredible deformities: no sex organs, no navel ... and a camel-like hump on its back filled with energizing fluid. In short, it's not human, has not been born in any way human. Cronenberg's offhand presentation of this information is more chilling than the bloody killings.

After Ruth is killed, brutally, in front of her class, Cronenberg treats us to an inexplicably unsettling visual. Two of the creatures walk hand in hand with Candy along a snowy road. It's perhaps the film's most nightmarish shot, but why? It defies explanation — it just *is*.

Nola apparently doesn't realize what her "children" are doing — they are bidden by her unconscious thoughts. This is reminiscent of Dr. Morbius' "Monsters from the Id" in *Forbidden Planet* (1956)—monsters created from unspoken thoughts and desires. When Frank realizes that Candy has been taken to Somerfree by the creatures, he goes there himself and confronts Raglan, who reveals the truth.

RAGLAN: If they brought her back here, she'll be in the attic. That's where they live. They'll kill you if you try to take her.

FRANK: Why?

RAGLAN: Because, in a sense, she's one of them.

FRANK: Nola is their surrogate mother? She must love them.

RAGLAN: She's not their surrogate mother ... she's their real mother ... their only mother. They are the children of her rage.

Reed plays the scene so convincingly that he makes the absurd situation real. This is a talent, denied to many, necessary to put across a horror movie. It makes persuasively acting in a film like this more difficult than in a "straight" one. This ability could well be traced to Reed's experiences at Hammer, where the masters of the talent, Peter Cushing and Christopher Lee, routinely worked their magic.

Raglan has now become a classic hero; he will risk his life to save a child he hardly knows, the child of a psychotic mother and a father who despises him. The plan hinges on Frank's being able to keep Nola calm, to hide his fear and disgust. But we know he isn't up to it—who would be?

NOLA: What's happening to me is so strange—too strange to share with anyone from my old life. Are you ready for me, Frank?

FRANK: I want to be with you...

Until, that is, Nola lifts her gown and reveals one of Cronenberg's most nauseating images. Her body is horribly deformed and on her thigh is a huge tumor.

Upstairs, Raglan has Candy in hand and is walking her past the docile—for the moment—creatures. Downstairs, Nola bites into the tumor, releasing the newborn creature, and licks blood and fluid off it. Nola senses Frank's considerable horror and goes berserk.

The brood has sensed her rage and attacks Raglan, who just manages to get Candy out of the room to safety before dying a hideous death. Downstairs—equally enraged—Frank strangles Nola. As she dies, so does the brood.

The shock ending was typical of the period but more low-key than most. It also set up a sequel, which fortunately didn't develop. *The Brood* succeeds brilliantly on two levels; as a no-holds-barred horror movie and as a metaphor for generational child abuse. The real horror is that Candy will become another Nola.

Unfortunately most critics dismissed *The Brood* as nothing more than a well-done splatter movie. An exception: "Whatever its failings, *The Brood* is a fascinating and pretty daring film that truly went where no film had gone before, or wanted to" (*Chicago Sun Times*, June 13, 1986).

Reed would return to horror movies a half dozen times to no positive effect whatsoever, but that hardly diminishes his excellent performance in this engrossingly gross film.

Dr. Heckyl and Mr. Hype (1980)

Golan-Globus Productions; released by Cannon Film Distributors; no U.K. release; color; 99 minutes

Crew— Director: Charles B. Griffith; Writers: Charles B. Griffith, Roger Corman (uncredited); Producers: Yoram Globus, Menahem Golan; Associate Producer–Production Manager: Jill Griffith; Original Music: Richard Brand; Cinematographers: Robert Carras, Robert Primes (uncredited); Film Editor: Skip Schoolnik; Casting: Ann Bell; Production Design: Maxwell Mendes; Art Director: Bob Ziembiki; Set Decorator: Maria Delia Javier; Makeup Artist: Karen Kubek; Special Effects Makeup for Oliver Reed: Steve Neill; First Assistant Director: Peter Manoogian; Second Assistant Director: Darryl Michelson; Art Department Assistant: Alan Toomayan; Supervising Sound Editor: Richard L. Anderson; Special Prosthetic Effects: J.C. Buechler; Special Mechanical Effects and Construction: Tim Doughten; Stunts: Ken Fritz; Camera Operator: Eric Anderson; Gaffer: Larry Pogolar; Additional Photographer: Hal Trussell; Electrician: Vance Trussell; Electronic Orchestrator: Joel Goldsmith; Production Assistant: Kent Adamson.

Cast— Oliver Reed (Dr. Henry Heckyl/Mr. Hype), Sunny Johnson (Coral Careen), Maia Danziger (Miss Finebum), Virgil Frye (Lt. Mack

Druck — Il Topo), Mel Welles (Dr. Vince Hinkle), Kedric Wolf (Dr. Lew Hoo), Jackie Coogan (Sgt. Fleacollar), Corinne Calvert (Pizelle Puree), Sharon Compton (Mrs. Quivel), Denise Hayes (Liza Rowne), Charles Howerton (Clutch Cooger), Dick Miller (Irsil/Orson), Jack Warford (Herringbone Flynn), Lucretia Love (Debra Kate), Ben Frommer (Sgt. Gurnisht Hilfn), Mickey Fax (Mrs. Fritz L. Pitzle), Catalaine Knell (Mrs. Fritz L. Pitzle), Jacque Lynn Colton (Mrs. Fran Van Crisco), Lisa Zebro (Mrs. Fran van Thomas — Bad William's Ideal), Michael Ciccone (Hollowpoint — Twin Officer), Steve Ciccone (DumDum–Twin Officer), Candi Brough (Teri — Tailspin Twin), Randi Brough (Toni — Tailspin Twin), Dan Sturkie (Naso Rubico, the Wino), Yehuda Efroni (Bull Quivel), Herta Ware (Old Lady on Bus), Samuel Livneh (Acuticklic Patient), Dana Feller (Nurse Pertbottom), Katherine Kirkpatrick (Nurse Neetkiester), Carin Berger (Nurse Lushtush), Cindy Riegel (Nurse Rosenrump), Merle Ann Taylor (Nurse Talltale), Jessica Griffith (Policeman's Daughter), Christina Ann Saul (Blinkin'), Ed Randolph (Midnight Eaglehead).

Synopsis

Podiatrist Dr. Henry Heckyl (Oliver Reed) is a lovable guy desperately searching for love, but his grotesque physical appearance prevents him from approaching any pretty girls, who either laugh or run away scared. Henry is particularly attracted to a young secretary, Coral (Sunny Johnson), who travels on his bus to work each day. Hardly believing his luck, she accepts Henry as her podiatrist, convinced she had ugly feet. Henry's colleague Dr. Hinkle (Mel Welles) has invented a wonder slimming drug that he expects will make millions and he gives a batch to Henry for safekeeping, warning that an overdose would result in bodily disintegration. Henry, disconsolate over his inability to find love, decides to use the drug to commit suicide. However, instead of ending his life, it transforms him into a slim, handsome man. Overjoyed, he disturbs his neighbor; she is willingly seduced by the brash young man but on seeing a reflection of ugliness in his eyes starts to scream. The next day, bewildering the clinic staff, "Hype" (as he now calls himself) arrives to take over his "cousin" Henry's practice. Cancelling all appointments except the lovely Coral's, Hype is surprised that she isn't interested in him but tells him how much she likes Henry! Hype passes the time with a prostitute who also comments on the ugliness in his eyes

and is murdered for her candor. Returning to the clinic, he is horrified to discover that his transformation is only temporary; at the same time, Hinkle's successful slimmers all revert to their original obese forms as Henry grabs another megadose of the formula to bring Hype back. Though horrified by Hype's actions, Henry is seduced by the drug. He runs amok in the community and is pursued by the police. Finally, after multiple transformations, he realizes that Coral loves him for himself — physically ugly, maybe, but spiritually beautiful.

Comment

This is another take on Robert Louis Stevenson's *Dr. Jekyll and Mr. Hyde*, this time played for laughs. A good-looking Hyde had beaten Oliver Reed nearly to death in Hammer's *The Two Faces of Dr. Jekyll*; now he was playing the man himself — and more good-looking than Paul Massie had been.

"Reed is actually somewhat touching as his monster half, and has a field day playing a parody of a macho leading man as Mr. Hype" (*Variety*, July 2, 1980) says it all. According to the Ciccone twins, they were the only ones Reed allowed in his trailer and they shared lots of fun and adventures together. With a face that "looks like a moldy melon with a half-eaten carrot for a nose and topped by a used Brillo pad," the grotesque Dr. Heckyl yearns for love. When in desperation he drinks a potion with a view to ending his desperately unhappy life, he morphs into the dishy movie-star Oliver Reed and murmurs in the mirror with mock seriousness, "My God, I'm beautiful!" While the movie is enormous fun to watch, the underlying theme is more "Beauty and the Beast" than the Stevenson original; Heckyl is sweet, loving and kind with an outer self that frightens the people in the bus queue, while Hype is drop dead gorgeous on the outside and murderous selfish and cruel on the inside. Like all good comedies, it all comes out right in the end in a finale that owes much to Mack Sennett.

Writer-director Charles B. Griffith, previous creator of scripts for Roger Corman's *A Bucket of Blood* and *The Little Shop of Horrors*, produces a good modern take on the old tale. Max Mendes' great production design is photographed well by Robert Carras. "Against all odds *Dr. Heckyl and Mr. Hype* has emerged as a real rib-tickler, a massively perverse comedy which pumps new life into an overworn basic premise" (*Variety* July 2, 1980). If anyone still doubts the comedic talent of Oliver Reed, they could do worse than check out this quirky movie.

Lion of the Desert (1981)

Falcon International Pictures; released by United Film Distribution Company in the U.S. and by Enterprise Pictures Limited in the U.K.; color; U.K. Certificate AA; 163 minutes*

Crew— Producer-Director: Moustapha Akkad; Writer: H.A.L. Craig; Assistant Producers: Nahila May Al-Jabri, June Bordcosh; Executive Producer: Geoffrey Helman; Original Music: Maurice Jarre; Music Played by the London Symphony Orchestra; Cinematographer: Jack Hildyard; Film Editor: John Shirley; Production Designers: Syd Cain, Mario Garbuglia; Art Directors: Bob Bell, Maurice Cain, Giorgio Desideri; Costume Designers: Piero Cicoletti, Hassan Ben Dardaf, Annalisa Nasalli-Rocca; Production Manager: Ray Frift; Unit Manager: John Oldknow; First Assistant Directors: Miguel Gil, Carlos Gil; Second Unit Director–Stunt Coordinator: Glenn Randall, Jr.; Music Editor: Robin Clarke; Sound Recordists: Norman Bolland, Lionel Strutt; Sound Editor: Chris Greenham; Special Effects: Kit West; Special Effects Technician: Dino Galiano; Stunts: Sergio Mioni, Roy Alon; Camera Operators: James Bawden, James Turrell; Assistant Cameraman: Adolfo Bartoli; Gaffer: John Fenner; Production Coordinator: Reyad Akkad; Technical Advisor: Franco Fantasia; Location Managers: Claude Gresset, Frank Sherwin Green, Moustapha Hijaouy, Umberto Sambucco, Mohammed Bufana; Script Supervisor: Sally Jones; Production Controller: Maurice Landsberger; Production Accountant: Stanley Burridge; Production Assistant: Corrado Sofia; Maurice Jarre's Assistant: Christopher Palmer.

Cast— Anthony Quinn (Omar Mukhtar), Oliver Reed (Gen. Rodolfo Graziani), Irene Papas (Mabrouka), Raf Vallone (Colonel Diodiece), Rod Steiger (Benito Mussolini), John Gielgud (Sharif El Gariani), Andrew Keir (Salem), Gastone Mischin (Major Tomelli), Stefano Patrizi (Lt. Sandrini), Adolfo Lastretti (Colonel Sarsani), Sky Dumont (Prince Amadeo), Takis Emmanuel (Bu-Matari), Rodolfo Bigotti (Ismail), Robert Brown (Al Fadeel), Eleonora Stathopoulou (Ali's Mother), Luciano Bartoli (Capt. Lontano), Claudio Gora (President of Court), Giordano Falzoni (Judge at Camp), Franco Fantasia (Graziani's Aide), Ihab Werfali (Ali), George Sweeney (Capt. Biagi), Luciano Catenacci (Italian Soldier), Pietro Brambilla (Young Soldier), Pietro Tordi (Field Marshal), Massimiliano Baratta (Capture Captain), Mario Feliciani (Lobitto), Gianfranco Barra (Sentry), Piero Gerlini (Barillo), Lino Capolicchio (Capt. Bedendo); uncredited: Claudio Cassinelli (Escort Guard), Mark Colleano (Infantry Corporal), Tom Felleghy (Italian General), Scott Fensome (Machine Gun Sergeant), Angelo Ragusa (Italian Soldier), Ewan Solon (Fascist Major), Alec Mango (Tank Commander), Victor Baring (Infantry Colonel), Mario Adorf.

Synopsis

In 1929, Benito Mussolini (Rod Steiger), furious at a twenty-year insurrection by patriots in Libya resisting Italian colonization, appoints a new military governor, General Rudolfo Graziani (Oliver Reed), to deal with the situation. Learning of his arrival, Omar Mukhtar (Anthony Quinn), the 72-year-old leader of the Bedouin resistance movement, arranges a "welcome" which leaves twenty Italian soldiers dead and fifty more wounded. Reprisals come swiftly; Major Tomelli's (Gastone Moschin) troops raids a village. Mabrouka (Irene Papas) watches the death of her first-born son; the abduction of her daughter by the Italian soldiers; and her husband Salem (Andrew Keir) being struck to the ground. The attack convinces Salem to join the rebels. Mukhtar and the rebels lure Tomelli's troops into a brilliant desert ambush, barely survived by Lt. Sandrini (Stefano Patrizi) who surrenders to Omar Mukhtar. Furious, Graziani declares open war on the rebels, and the people are herded into barbed-wire-fenced concentration camps, arousing the sympathy of Colonel Diodiece (Raf Vallone). Graziani dispatches Diodiece to Omar Mukhtar to sue for peace but the conditions are not acceptable to the rebel leader. Advancing with all the might of the Italian war machine, Graziani attacks Kutra and, despite its ferocious defense, takes the town.

Among the massacred is Omar Mukhtar's second-in-command Bu-Matari (Takis Emmanuel). Graziani again attempts to make Mukhtar capitulate and sends a childhood

---

*The U.S. home video VHS release of the '80s runs 160 minutes. Footage has been added in the Director's Cut released by Anchor Bay Video. This version, released in 1998, runs 206 minutes.

friend of Mukhtar's, Sharif El Gariani (John Gielgud), as his emissary but the collaborator is firmly rejected by the rebel leader. The failed attempt is followed by a brilliant piece of Bedouin military strategy in the Wadi El Kuf where the Italian army is trounced. Graziani, summoned to Mussolini's presence to explain his lack of success, returns infuriated at the humiliation meted out to him by the Italian dictator and determined to make the people pay. He lays siege to the people by erecting a barbed wire fence cutting them off from their supplies.

While continuing to raid from the mountain hideouts, the rebels are eventually flushed out and surrounded. Mukhtar is captured and brought by Graziani to a military tribunal in Benghazi where he is judged guilty and sentenced to death. To hammer home his victory,

Graziani has the hanging performed in public before the sorrowful crowds. But the very act strengthens the people's resolve to pursue the revolt; Mukhtar achieves a martyr's status and the Italians leave the scene in a retreat that foreshadows the final outcome of the war.

Comment

Lion of the Desert depicts Mussolini's egomaniacal desire to revive the Roman Empire in Africa. In the attempt to carry out his decree, Italian forces killed very nearly half of the population. The film faithfully recreates the horrors of war and attempted genocide. *The New Statesman* (August 28, 1981): "The film opens with Mussolini, hammed by Rod Steiger, dispatching General Graziani as his proconsul for the final solution. The brutish features of Oliver Reed (softer mind you than they were in *Triple Echo*) make their appearance.... In British war films it is conventional to portray the Italians as comic stereotypes, devoid of courage or character and almost unfit to play the role of enemy. Here we see them as debauched by fascism and capable of any atrocity. (Graziani was one of the pioneers of the concentration camp).... At one or two points Akkad inserts newsreel clips of the period into the film — this is especially effective in giving an idea of the scale of the camps. It's a device that doesn't jar the attention at all, and it does serve to remind the audience that all this wretched story actually took place in living memory."

The movie was shot entirely on locations in Libya, with the blessings of Colonel Gaddifi, his country's money and the loan of Libyan infantry as extras. *The New York Times* (April 17, 1981): "Money may not be able to buy happiness, but [this movie] demonstrates that money, at least a

General Graziani (Oliver Reed) emulates the statue of his leader Mussolini in *Lion of the Desert* (Falcon-International, 1981).

very great deal of it — reportedly more than $30 million — can buy enough talent, know-how and extras to make a big historical movie that is at least technically respectable and occasionally spectacular in its geography.... [T]he biggest piece of movie partisanship to come out of the Middle East or North Africa since Otto Preminger's *Exodus*." Gaddafi, at the time a political pariah to the west and seeing himself very much in the line of succession from Omar Mukhtar, could not have been more helpful to the filmmakers. Government ministers and hordes of sightseers, Gaddafi included, visited the sets.

The movie effectively portrayed the horrors of the campaign, the courage and spiritual beliefs of the rebels and the occasional softer side of the Italians. Critics found themselves vacillating between approval of the film and ire at Gaddafi's attempt to manipulate the audience. The recreations of the battles (counterpoised with scenes of the Italian and rebel planning meetings, the skillful use of newsreels for authenticity and the splendid cast) provided Gaddafi with the platform he craved; the $35 million movie only recouped $1 million worldwide, making it one of the largest financial disasters in movie history, but this did not appear to move him unduly. A village was created at Aujulah, in the desert some 600 miles from Benghazi, and another in Shahat, a mountain area thirty-five minutes from the sea, to house the entire production throughout the shoot. A replica of the Italian concentration camp where Bedouin women, children and animals were herded (and where more than 250,000 Bedouins starved to death) was constructed using photographs and a military documentary film of the time. Logistics problems included catering, food being freighted in as cold-storage was non-existent. And the desert sand clogged cameras, film canisters and the firearm props necessitating cleaning every hour or so, illustrating the not-so-glamorous side of moviemaking.

Three months of filming in the desert culminated in a move to the Libyan mountains for the final scenes employing Gaddafi's troops. "'At least for those few weeks,' joked one of the crew returning to Rome for a home visit after 90 days of 85–127 degree heat in the Sahara, 'we can be sure there will be no war in the area'" (*Variety*, July 7, 1979).

Surprisingly the film only contains one scene where Omar Mukhtar and General Graziani meet face to face "[T]he concluding confrontation between Mukhtar and Graziani (with Oliver Reed finally reining in his stentorian mannerisms) has a low-key conviction which is unexpectedly moving" (*Monthly Film Bulletin*, August 1981); "*Lion of the Desert* is too long for the simplistic insights it offers. Oliver Reed is a plausible Graziani" (*Newsday*, April 17, 1981) .

Reed's portrayal of Graziani is a masterpiece; he would also have made a great Mussolini. The arrogance, the strut and the mixture of intellect, charm and viciousness make his portrayal memorable. Critics at the time who castigated both Reed and Steiger as being over-the-top had obviously not watched film of the real characters in this story; neither performer over-acts. The plot is uncomfortably close to many current war theatres so that it is difficult to be objective. The ponderous unfolding of the story belies the bloody battles and the clash of wills between Graziani, a trained military tactician with a love of his country's past military glories, and Mukhtar, a teacher and scholar whose military expertise is entirely intuitive. They bring the conflicts in present-day Afghanistan and Iraq to mind.

> "There's just no alcohol at all in Libya. I'm sure some of the people on the oil rigs boil up some hooch, but you can get yourself killed with that. So I just gave up drink for a while. It makes a change from my regular routine and it certainly is much cheaper than a health farm. By the time I'd got to Iraq I'd worked up a good thirst which stopped me worrying about the war going on, even if there were people all around getting killed for real." Reed did have another source of sustenance for *Lion of the Desert*: his 19-year-old girlfriend, Josephine Burge, who acted as his personal assistant and Girl Friday throughout filming. "She at least made me forget about the lack of drink," the incorrigible Reed says.—*Daily Mail* (August 31, 1981).

"A tired, tedious, lumbering historical spectacle that's entirely predictable right down to the casting" (*Los Angeles Times*, April 17, 1981); "The singularly British Oliver Reed is impressively believable as an Italian general, adopting an intimating, quiet authority uncannily like actor Raf Vallone. Oddly enough, Vallone himself is in the picture, as Diodiece, a career military man with a lot more respect for Mukhtar's bravery than Graziani is for a long time willing to give" (Stuart Galbraith IV, December 7, 2005, IMDb DVD review).

Given the opportunity to watch this movie, the reader is urged to give it a viewing to watch a master (Reed) at work.

Condorman (1981)

Walt Disney Productions; released by Buena Vista in the U.S. and in the U.K.; color

Crew— Director: Charles Jarrot; Writers: Mickey Rose, Marc Sturdivant; from the novel *The Game of X* by Robert Sheckley; Executive Producer: Ron Miller; Producer: Jan Williams; Associate Producer: Hugh Attwooll; Original Music: Henry Mancini; Cinematographer: Charles C. Wheeler; Film Editor: Gordon D. Brenner; Production Design: Albert Witherick; Costume Designers: Kent James, Jean Zay; Makeup Artist: Dan Striepeke; Makeup Supervisor: Robert J. Schiffer; Production Managers: John D. Bloss, Antoine Compin, Charles Horton, Philippe Modave; Assistant Director: Richard Learman; Sound Editor: Ben F. Hendricks; Sound: William Sivel; Sound Supervisor: Herb Taylor; Special Effects Supervisor: Colin Chilvers; Special Effects Technician: Art Cruickshanks; Stunt Coordinator: Remy Julienne; Stunt Pilot: Marc Wolff; Stunts: Dominique Julienne, Michel Julienne, Remy Julienne, Jean-Claud Lagniez, Colin Skeaping; Camera Operator: Jacques Mironneau; Assistant Camera: Pierre Boffety, Philippe Houdart; Second Unit Photography: Godfrey Godar; Second Assistant Camera: Michel Abramowicz.

Cast— Michael Crawford (Woody Wilkins), Oliver Reed (Krokov), Barbara Carrera (Natalia), James Hampton (Harry Oslo), Jean-Pierre Kalfon (Morovich), Dana Elcar (Russ Devlin), Vernon Dobtcheff (Russian Agent), Robert Arden (CIA Chief).

Synopsis

In Paris, Woody (Michael Crawford), creator of the comic-book hero Condorman, has a rule that his creation does not do what his creator cannot. He "flies" from the Eiffel Tower but the costume fails and he's dumped in the Seine. His friend Harry (James Hampton) is a CIA filing clerk. Harry's boss Russ (Dana Elcar) leaves Harry in charge of the Paris office and

instructs him to find an outsider to go to Istanbul to deliver some secret documents to a Russian contact — no CIA operative is to be involved. Harry, in desperation, recruits Woody, who assumes a spy alter ego, much to Harry's disquiet. In Istanbul, Woody is hardly inconspicuous, handcuffed to the briefcase containing the documents. He creates havoc in the restaurant where the handover is scheduled. The Russian agent Natalia (Barbara Carrera) asks for his code name; "Condorman," replies Woody. Overacting his spy role, Woody takes on three Turkish thugs, and Natalia is impressed. She reports to her boss and former lover Krakov (Oliver Reed) about the new agent. Shortly afterwards, the CIA office hears of a major defection: The spy wishes to have Condorman collect her. Woody refuses until he discovers that it is Natalia who is defecting.

He asks for, and gets, all kinds of equipment to carry out the mission. In Yugoslavia, Woody rescues Natalia from Krakov's henchmen with the aid of a cane-rifle he can barely handle. In Italy, Woody and Natalia are chased by Krakov's team until Woody slides into a Condormobile built into the ancient truck that they are traveling in. Eventually all the pursuit cars are destroyed and the runaways hope to find shelter in Switzerland. Harry arrives to accompany them on the last part of the journey and Natalia discovers Woody's true identity. Using another of Woody's inventions, they attempt to cross the frontier going uphill on a cable. Krakov, observing from a distance, orders Harry and Woody shot and snatches Natalia from the cable; he then deliberately flies her over the spot where the holes in the snow mark their fallen bodies. In Monte Carlo, Krakov expects Natalia to return to all her former duties in his service; he prepares a story about her being used as bait to catch Condorman which will prevent her execution as a defector but gives him complete power over her. Believing Woody dead, she agrees. But Woody and Harry have escaped and, hearing that Natalia is in Monte Carlo, they plot to get her back. The CIA declares the case closed and forbids any attempt at a rescue, but Woody talks Harry into the attempt which includes more of Woody's inventions. In Monte Carlo, Krakov sees an oil sheik win $5 million at the casino and tells Morovich

(Jean-Pierre Kalfon), his chief henchman, to ensure that the sheik is at the party in his villa the following day. The sheik, of course, is Woody in another of his disguises, accompanied by Harry disguised as his aide. Harry has explosives secreted in the folds of his robes at the party; he sets the charges while Woody endeavors to get close to Natalia. Finding her on the grounds, away from Krakov, he tries to get her to leave with him; she pretends she doesn't care about him but a chance remark as she walks away with an insistent Krakov reveals the opposite. As Harry explodes the devices, Woody grabs Natalia and heads into the house and up to the roof, hotly pursues by Krakov and his minions. Natalia believes they are trapped, but Woody is wearing his Condorman costume under his robes and they literally fly away. Harry loses Krakov's men and meets them at the quayside where they escape in a jet-powered Condorboat. In Los Angeles, Natalia is enjoying being Americanized at Dodgers Stadium, and we close with Harry offering Woody another Condorman adventure.

Comment

When we last saw Oliver Reed and Michael Crawford (as the Tremayne brothers in *The Jokers*), they were behind bars, planning their escape. In 1966 the two young actors were on fairly even footing, both on the way up. After *The Jokers*, Reed's career took off like a rocket; by the beginning of the next decade, he was among the world's top stars.

Crawford's star was rising too, mixing films and theatre. He hit the big time in 1968 with *Hello Dolly!* and returned to Michael Winner in *The Games* in 1969. He continued to mix films, plays, and television throughout the 1970s, avoiding superstar status but doing very well. Then on May 19, 1986, Crawford signed to star in Andrew Lloyd Webber's *The Phantom of the Opera*, arguably the most successful theatrical production of all time.

Reed's career had leveled off when he and Crawford were reunited in the autumn of 1980 for *Condorman*, and Crawford approached the reunion with caution. Crawford said:

Even when the script was a little thin, Ollie was bound to give it his all. In this one he

played the enemy, a murderous Russian agent, and remembering his penchant for living roles, I feared for my life. For the first few weeks of production, he remembered the good old days when we were "brothers" and every now and then, for old times' sake, he'd give me one of his crushing bear hugs on the set. Our leading lady had a slightly rougher time of it, and Ollie clearly felt her talent was (unfortunately for her) below Ollie's high standards. I recall they had a scene in a helicopter where she was supposed to be terrified by him, but in take after take, she was unable to project enough fear for Ollie's taste. So while they were in flight for a final shot, Ollie actually opened the door and threatened to throw her out. She had no doubt that he meant every word, and the glance of fear that crossed her face at that moment was very real [Crawford, 228].

On *Condorman*, Reed's practical jokes included turning all the beds (with the exception of Crawford's for some reason) in a Monte Carlo hotel upside down, locking his co-star in his dressing room while leading a search party to find him, and ordering caviar and smoked salmon at a five star restaurant in Crawford's name. Oh yes, and: "Ollie had a few late evenings on location with *Condorman*. I recall the night he threw his tuxedo into the sea from the window of his Monte Carlo hotel room. (Our cost-conscious company manager rowed out at dawn in a little boat to catch it before it floated away and disappeared entirely into the Mediterranean.) [Crawford, 228]. Apparently, Crawford didn't mind too much; it was just "Ollie being Ollie."

At first thought, Reed starring in a Walt Disney movie seems like a practical joke in itself. Five films earlier he had appeared in *The Brood*, which is about as far from Disney as one can get. But then, *Condorman* is just about as far from a Disney film as *The Brood*. It's unimaginative, looks cheap, lacks charm and fails to entertain. The best things about *Condorman* are its beautiful locations; Paris (many of the major tourist sites), Switzerland and the Riviera. Mostly everything else is subpar.

Condorman begins somewhat promisingly as Woody, in his engagingly goofy supersuit, attempts to fly off the Eiffel Tower and naturally

In *Condorman* (Buena Vista, 1981), Oliver Reed was reunited with his *The Jokers* co-star Michael Crawford to much less effect.

fails. This scene was more of a disaster for Crawford than for Woody as he was dragged underwater by the Seine's strong current. He bravely offered to do the shot again but director Charles Jarrot wisely substituted a stuntman.

The special effects in the scene are not terribly special, setting the stage for the remaining 88 minutes. Crawford, who has been, at the very least, good in everything else he has ever done, is not good here. He never seems able to hit the right note for Woody. Crawford is described by *Science Fiction, Horror and Fantasy Film Review* on the Moria site as "still stuck in Frank Spencer mode, playing with a whiny introverted effeminacy that more than gives the impression that either he or the character are in the closet. Certainly as a hero, he is a complete wet blanket ... while Oliver Reed glowers thuggishly as the villain." Compare *Condorman* to another superhero spoof from the same period, *The Return of Captain Invincible* (1983), with a wonderful performance by Alan Arkin as an alcoholic superhero on the skids and an even more wonderful performance by Christopher Lee as his nemesis (Lee's "Drink, Drink, Drink" is marvelous). *Captain Invincible* manages to make fun of the genre while being fun itself.

The novel on which *Condorman* was based, *The Game of X* by Robert Sheckley, had nothing to do with comic-book heroes; it's simply about a "regular guy" masquerading as a secret agent. The Disney Company overplayed its hand at a time when its creative hand was practically empty.

Reed appears in a half-dozen scenes, spending most of his time ordering his minions to do rather than doing anything himself— a very non–Reed thing to do. But he does it well. We first see Krakov as he flicks on a light in Natalia's Moscow flat, looking elegant in a dark three-piece suit and holding a drink. He's not happy to hear from her that the agent she encountered in Istanbul is good ... perhaps as good as he is. Krakov whispers, "What was his name? Surely when you were finding out how good he is, you found out his name? Condorman? How quaint."

Reed's Russian accent, like all his cinematic accents, is excellent; not so heavy as to be a caricature, but just enough to be convincing. According to Crawford, "As time went by, Ollie grew deeper into his character. He always spoke with a Russian accent."

After numerous attempts to kill Condorman have failed and, worse, after discovering Natalia has betrayed him, Krakov becomes less happy. His top killer Morovich (Jean-Pierre Kalfon) provides some well-needed action as he leads a team of black Porsches after the fugitives who are trundling through a beautiful village in an old truck. Under the truck, however,

is a Batmobile-like supercar that quickly dispatches (Aston Martin–*Goldfinger* style) the Porsches. The scene is naturally derivative but fun, if one enjoys the destruction of beautiful, expensive cars. If Krakov was angry before, he goes off the chart when he hears about Condorman. He screams at Morovich, "Have you seen the report on Condorman? He is an amateur ... he's a writer of comic-books!"

Natalia discovers Woody's secret in a clever scene during which she is recognized by the village children reading *Laser Lady* comics featuring her likeness — another of Woody's creations. After snatching her off in a helicopter, Krakov lets her have it verbally as only Reed can do: "You don't know how tempted I was to kill you. Remember — what happens in the future is better than a slow death in Siberia. Any more trouble from you and I will, personally, kill you!"

Perhaps the director and the screenwriters must not have seen *The Jokers* and were unaware of the great chemistry between Reed and Crawford. Because, up until the final scene at the casino, the two actors have not been close to being in the same shot! This is rectified at the casino when they *almost* appear in the same shot. Reed looks dashing in a white suit, and Crawford looks (purposely) absurd dressed as an oil sheik. The hero and villain never get close to having it on, which is indicative of how poorly *Condorman* is constructed. One wonders why they weren't given the opportunity to fight it out like real heroes and villains do. The elegantly dressed Krakov versus the superhero-suited Woody would have been good for a well-needed laugh.

Condorman does contain a moment of sheer horror. At the Dodger Stadium finale there is a hint of a sequel (probably why all the expensive props were given the go-ahead).

The film wastes every opportunity to expand on any of its good ideas. The opening credits suggest a *Pink Panther*–like approach that never materializes. Crawford dons several Inspector Clousseau-ish disguises and tumbles about a bit, but that, too, goes nowhere. Perhaps if Woody had been played more like Clousseau rather than the embarrassingly overearnest reading he got the film might have moved up a few notches. Barbara Carrera and

James Hampton are likable enough but not enough to make much of a difference.

Reed hands in an okay performance that, if given in a decent Disney production, might have pumped some life into his career. Instead, *Condorman* was followed by *Venom*, *Deathbite*, and a half-dozen more forgettable films before the excellent *Captive* came along, in the same year that Michael Crawford played *The Phantom*.

Condorman was released in the U.K. on July 2, 1981, and in America on August 7, and was quickly forgotten in both countries. Reviews were dismissive. Typical was *Variety* (August 5, 1981): "*Condorman* does everything in its power to perpetuate the bland, benign image Walt Disney Productions has lately been trying to get away from. There might be a small audience of kids amused by the shenanigans, but overall pic is a silly rehash of an overused theme. [The director and writers] seem to have called in their work, and Henry Mancini's music is probably among the most unimaginative in his career." Other critiques: "Oliver Reed does his standard menacing turn. *Condorman* is so dull and has been done so many times before — and so much better — that it defies you to watch it" (*Los Angeles Times*, August 14, 1981); "As one chase follows another, *Condorman*, both film and character, is left with little to do but mimic the smug self-satisfaction of James Bond" (*Monthly Film Bulletin*, August 1981); "Oliver Reed, the Soviet agent, menaces more like Papa Bear than a clever spy" (*Newsday*, August 29, 1981).

Venom (1981)

Morison Film Group; Venom Productions Ltd.; released by HandMade Films in the U.K. in 1981 and by Paramount Pictures in the U.S. in 1982; color; 93 minutes

Crew— Director: Piers Haggard; Producer: Martin Bregman; Executive Producer: Richard R. St. Johns; Production Executive: Louis A. Stroller; Associate Producer: Harry Benn; Production Manager: Ron Fry; Cinematographer: Gil Taylor; Camera Operator: Malcolm Vinson; Assistant Director: Dominic Fulford; Second Assistant Director: Nick Daubeny; Third Assistant Director: Simon Manley; Continuity: Ceri Evans; Production Assistant: Pauline Stevenson; Sound Recordist: Simon Kaye;

Boom Operator: Keith Batten; Sound Assistant: Des Edwards; Art Director: Tony Curtis; Assistant Art Director: Fred Carter; Set Decorator: Tessa Davies; Focus Puller: David Wynn-Jones; Makeup Artist: Basil Newall; Hairdresser: Meinir Brook; Wardrobe Mistress: Eileen Sullivan; Wardrobe Assistant: Cindy Bishop; Casting Director: Maude Spector; Editor: Michael Bradsell; First Assistant Editor: Tim Jordan; Second Assistant Editor: Jim Howe; Property Master: Terry Wells; Property Buyer: Dennis Maddison; Construction Manager: Bill Waldron; Special Snake Effects: Richard Dean; Reptile Consultant: David Bell.

Cast— Sterling Hayden (Howard), Klaus Kinski (Jacmel), Sarah Miles (Dr. Marion Stowe), Oliver Reed (Dave Averconnelly), Cornelia Sharpe (Ruth), Nicol Williamson (Commander Bulloch), Susan George (Louise), Lance Holcomb (Philip), Mike Gwilym (D/C Rich Edwards), Rita Webb (Mrs. Loewenthal), John Cater (Lord Dunning), John Forbes-Robertson (Sergeant Nash), Hugh Lloyd (Taxi Driver).

Synopsis

Howard (Sterling Hayden), a former big game hunter, is staying with his daughter Ruth (Cornelia Sharpe) in her London mansion to help care for her asthmatic son Philip (Lance Holcomb) while her husband is away. A precocious ten-year-old, Philip is an animal fancier and has a small zoo in his room. Louise (Susan George) the maid and Dave the chauffeur (Oliver Reed) are planning — with the mysterious Jacmel (Klaus Kinski) — to kidnap the boy.

Their plan is thwarted when Philip and Howard go to an exotic animal store to pick up a harmless African house-snake. Meanwhile, Dr. Stowe (Sarah Miles), at the Institute of Toxicology, is stunned to take delivery of that very snake; she'd ordered a deadly black mamba. She deduces that the order was switched and frantically contacts the police, who trace the mamba to Philip. Jacmel arrives at the house and takes the family hostage, ordering Dave and Louise around like children. Louise inadvertently releases the mamba and is fatally bitten. When Sergeant Nash (John Forbes-Robertson) arrives, Dave shoots him. Commander Bulloch (Nicol Williamson) blocks off the entire neighborhood and begins a testy negotiation with Jacmel to free the hostages.

Dr. Stowe arrives on the scene and is tricked into the house. Bulloch enters through

Top: Jacmel (Klaus Kinski) and *bottom:* Louise (Susan George) confront the cowardly Dave (Oliver Reed) in *Venom* (Paramount, 1981).

a hidden rear door and shoots Dave, who is then bitten by the mamba. It then attacks Jacmel, who kills it before being shot by the police. The hostages are released, but an egg has hatched in an air conditioning duct....

Comment

Venom was an "all-star cast horror movie" and was no better — or worse — than one would expect of this subgenre. The problem in general with this type of film: There aren't enough good parts to warrant the weight of the stars playing the roles (see *House of Frankenstein*, 1944). Since the main attraction is the cast, the viewer is often left a bit wanting.

The cast of *Venom* is certainly attractive; the villains are Reed and Klaus Kinski, the heroes are Nicol Williamson and Sterling Hayden (in his final film) and the women are Susan

George and Sarah Miles. Any one of these performers could carry a film on his/her own. Throw in Michael Gough and Edward Hardwicke in bit parts, and you've got quite a group. Despite the mostly underwritten roles, the performances are all good. Incredibly, the best performance may have been given by young Lance Holcomb.

The specific problem with *Venom* is that of the five people originally trapped in the house with the mamba, three of them deserve to be bitten ... and they are. It's difficult to sympathize with a group of kidnappers. *Venom* was originally to be directed by horror master Tobe (*The Texas Chain Saw Massacre*) Hooper, who left the film after shooting several scenes. He was replaced by Piers Haggard who had previously directed a pretty good horror movie himself, *The Blood on Satan's Claw* (1971).

According to Haggard, "Oliver was one of the finest film actors that we had ... and he would test you all the time. When I met Oliver for the first time in the canteen at Elstree studios he played a trick on me, pretending that he was going to walk out and leave the film because I had insulted him by saying something completely spurious. But it was just a hoax. He was just testing me" (Sellers, 214). Haggard, interviewed by Jonathan Sothcott on the *Venom* DVD, said, "There were a lot of personalities involved.... Klaus Kimski, an experienced actor and a tricky man, Oliver Reed ... *extremely* experienced, quite a powerful personality, quite a naughty boy really. Liked to have a laugh. He and Klaus didn't get on very well, which was a bit hard since they had most of their scenes together. Oliver was one of the finest film actors we had — he could do something with the flick of an eyelid. An enormous power and enormous capacity to use his power. But he was a handful."

Kinski, incidentally, had reputedly given up a role in *Raiders of the Lost Ark* because the producers of *Venom* had offered him more money! Reed and Kinski allegedly hated each other during the production with Reed constantly provoking Kinski into losing his temper. The pair made as nasty a pair of villains as one could possibly want. In addition to their usual proclivities for on-screen violence, the fact that they actually disliked one another off-camera added to the tension. Neither actor was given much of an opportunity to develop a character but, as Haggard pointed out, their extreme personalities easily punched the point across.

Dave is a bully and a coward; he is unnecessarily harsh to young Philip, but takes a lot of guff from Jacmel — including a good slapping. This is Dave's first (and last) foray over the line, and his nervous fear causes him to act irrationally in direct contrast to Jacmel's cool deliberation. Reed conveys this perfectly — he's constantly sweating and looks ready to throw up at any moment.

A potentially interesting situation is introduced when Louise begins playing Dave and Jacmel against each other for her sexual favors. Her early, shocking and unexpected death at the fangs of the mamba, however, put an end to that. Susan George's performance in her death scene is the acting highlight of the film. It must rank near the top of unpleasant deaths and is incredibly believable.

Nicol Williamson is calmly — and amusingly — in charge of the melee and is given more of an opportunity than the rest of the cast to create his character. Michael Gough, in a very brief role, played a "real" character — David Bell, curator of poisonous snakes at the London Zoo. Bell — the real one — served as 'reptile consultant' on the film. All technical aspects of the film were above average.

Venom was released in the U.K. on January 19, 1982, and in the U.S. ten days later. Reviews were mixed: "*Venom* is an engrossing traditional suspense thriller ... boasting an unusually uppercase cast.... [The] combo of Kinski's quiet dominant menace and Reed's explosive brutish violence make for a memorable ensemble of villains" (*Variety*, January 27, 1982); " The all-star cast of *Venom* seems strangely to have had their eyes and minds on something other than their deadly, upstaging reptilian co-star. In the end, a curiously inept attempt" (*Films and Filming*, February 1982).

Venom is perfectly acceptable entertainment for those looking for a few thrills. In fact, it's difficult to find anything really wrong with the movie other than wondering what better film could have been made with that wonderful cast. Reed did okay, but there was a time when he was far more than that; *Venom* took him another large step away from that period.

The Sting II (1983)

Universal Pictures; released by Universal Pictures in the U.S. and the U.K.; color

Crew— Director: Jeremy Paul Kagan; Producer: Jennings Lang; Writer: David S. Ward; Cinematographer: Bill Butler; Production Designer: Edward C. Carfagno; Editor: David Garfield; Original Music and Adaptation: Lalo Schifrin; Costume Designer: Burton Miller; Casting: Penny Perry; Unit Production Manager: Don Zepfel; First Assistant Director: L. Andrew Stone; Second Assistant Directors: Ross Brown, Robert Engelman; Special Visual Effects: Albert Whitlock; Boxing Choreographer & Stunt Coordinator: Ron Stein; Set Decorator: Hal Gausman; Sound: Ronald G. Cogswell; Sound Rerecording: Robert L. Hoyt, John J. Stephens, Stanley H. Polinsky; Supervising Sound Editor: Richard Oswald; Sound Effects Editor: Michael Redborn; Music Editor: Kenneth Hall; ADR Editor: Jack Gosden; Camera Operator: Jim Connell; Panaglide Operator: Ronald Vidor; First Assistant Camera: John M. Walker; Second Assistant Camera: Ron Frantzvog; Additional Editing: Gina Brown; Assistant Editor: Cari Coughlin; Negative Cutter: Wally Weber; Negative Timer: Bob Raring; Matte Photography: Bill Taylor; Script Supervisor: Cynnie Troup; DGA Intern: Mike Henry; Recordist: Neil Stone; Production Secretary: Amy McElhenney; Assistant to Producer: Jane Nunez; Choreographer: Alton Ruff; Makeup: Bob Ostermann, Ken Chase; Costume Supervisors: Robert E. Ellsworth, Norma Brown.

Cast— Jackie Gleason (Gondorff), Mac Davis (Hooker), Teri Garr (Veronica), Karl Malden (Macalinski), Oliver Reed (Doyle Lonnegan), Bert Remsen (Kid Colors), Kathalina Veniero (Kid's Girlfriend), Jose Perez (Carlos — Lonnegan's Bodyguard), Larry Bishop (Gellecher — Lonnegan's Second Guard), Frank McCarthy, Richard C. Adams (Lonnegan's Thugs), Ron Rifkin (Eddie), Harry James (Bandleader), Frances Bergen (Lady Dorsett), Monica Lewis (Band Singer), Danie-Wade Dalton (Messenger), Val Avery (O'Malley), Jill Jaress (Gertie), Paul Willson (Man in Ticket Line), Sidney Clute (Ticket Clerk), Al Robertson (Redcap), Hank Garrett (Cab Driver), Bob O'Connell (Clancy), John Hancock (Doc Brown), Larry Hankin (Handicap), Jerry Whitney (Page Boy), Michael D. Alldredge (Big Ohio), Danny Dayton (Ring Announcer), Corey Eubanks, Mike Raden (Fighters), Tim Rossovich (Typhoon Taylor), Fred Dennis (Card Player), Sam Thead (Old Second), Marty Denkin (Referee), Rex Pierson (Healy), Angela Robinson (Doc Brown's Girl), Elaine Goren, Iva Rifkin, Lise Kristen Gerard (Macalinski's Girls), Joe Monte (Bandleader), Carl Gottlieb (Maitre D'), David Ankrum (Waiter), Tony Giorgio (Rossevich), T. Max Graham (Bartender Tom), Melodie Bovee, Cynthia Cypert, Lesa Weiss, Jacqui Evans (Girls in Club).

Synopsis

New York, 1940. Banker–con man Doyle Lonnegan (Oliver Reed) is out for revenge for being out-conned and begins by having the Kid (Bert Remsen) killed. Next on his list: Gondorff (Jackie Gleason) and Hooker (Mac Davis). Hooker attempts to run a con on Veronica (Teri Garr) but she outsmarts him. Hooker and his friend Eddie (Ron Rifkin) get a telegram from Gondorff inviting them to Florida. Short of cash, they lift a wallet from O'Malley (Val Avery) in the train station — a bad move, since he's a cop. When they arrive in Florida, they find that Gondorff is in prison but will be out in a week. He tells Hooker about the Kid and his plans to get even. The problem: He dismisses Lonnegan as the killer and suspects Macalinski (Karl Malden), a millionaire gambler. Gondorff begins to recruit grifters for the big con. Hooker runs into the slippery Veronica and hires her for the con (Macalinski has a weakness for women). Gondorff accepts her and turns her loose on Macalinski. The two men check each other out at a club, then Gondorff beats Macalinski at billiards. The scam will involve a fixed boxing match. Hooker, an ex-boxer, approaches Macalinski for protection from Gondorff, who he claims wants him to throw his next fight. Lonnegan has heard of the scam and, with his henchman Carlos (Jose Perez), plans to make a killing — in all possible ways. O'Malley has spotted Hooker but Lonnegan bribes him to back off until after the fight with Torres. Macalinski bets a million on Hooker to win but, ringside, Lonnegan tells him that Hooker is taking a dive. After reversing his bet, he is stunned when Hooker wins. Macalinski shoots Lonnegan outside the arena. At the train station, Gondorff reveals to Hooker that he paid off Torres. And a further surprise: Veronica is Gondorff's daughter.

Comment

Generally speaking, it's probably not a good idea to make a sequel to the Oscar winner for Best Picture. Yes, there was *The Godfather, Part II* (1974) which was at least as good as the original, but thoughts of *Return to Casablanca* or *Son of the Bridge on the River Kwai* leave one with a queasy stomach.

Carlos (Jose Perez) plots revenge with his boss Lonnegan (Oliver Reed) in *The Sting II* (Universal, 1983).

That said, Universal decided to do a follow-up to *The Sting* (1973). If that wasn't enough of a bad idea in itself, the studio didn't bring back one single original cast member and replaced Paul Newman and Robert Redford with ... Jackie Gleason and Mac Davis! Not that Gleason wasn't a terrific actor — watch him eat Newman's lunch in *The Hustler* (1961) for verification. And Mac Davis was certainly an affable performer — but still!

Stepping into the Robert Shaw part as the villainous Doyle Lonnegan was Oliver Reed. According to Cliff Godwin, Reed's biographer, Reed had originally been offered Shaw's roles in *The Sting* and *Jaws* (1975) by producer Richard Zanuck. Simon Reed said "he was the biggest star in Europe and he needed another step to be among the top five actors in the world. In Oliver's eyes, moving to Hollywood would have been like tarting himself around and he wasn't prepared to do that." The actor said, "It seemed probable that I could make Europe my stomping ground. Ultimately, I ended up making obscure European films that paid

well but did nothing to further my reputation" (Goodwin, 273).

Eventually Reed went to Hollywood — when it was too late. Production on *The Sting II* began on November 10, 1981, at Universal City, using over fifty sets and various Los Angeles locations including the Main Street Gym, Union Station, the Olympic Auditorium, the Variety Arts Theatre and the Santa Monica Pier. All stood in well for New York. Director Jeremy Paul Kagan came to the set each day dressed in period clothing and played tapes of 1940s music to inspire the cast. He even took the trouble to fly Reed in a few days early to get acquainted with the cast. In the Universal press release Reed says, "Lonnegan is a man who will take opportunity of a lady, of a man, of a situation, any situation. He doesn't like to be out-conned and the one thing that someone tried to do to him in the old days was to take him for half a million. Anybody who takes Lonnegan for half a million has to put it back, one way or another."

Reed was easily Robert Shaw's equal as an

actor but he doesn't get much of an opportunity to show it here. Like the rest of the movie, Reed's part is just a little too thin. He doesn't have much to do, but does it well, creating a sense of menace without using anything but his voice which is seldom raised above his trademark whisper. He keeps his adversaries — and the viewer — off-guard with the occasional winning smile or, at times, a giggle. Reed also looks good in the vintage clothes.

Most of his scenes are played with Jose Perez as his henchman Carlos; Perez is very good. Carlos doesn't understand much about his boss (or anything else, actually). They provide the film with most of its funny moments as Reed's deadpan contrasts nicely with Perez's earnest bewilderment as they discuss, in this case, their next wrong move.

> CARLOS: Let me kill them now. What are we waiting for?
>
> LONNEGAN: First, they pay me back, then you can have them, okay?
>
> CARLOS: I don't get it.
>
> LONNEGAN: Revenge is a luscious fruit that needs a little time to ripen. Give these fools a little time and they'll be so trapped in my web, dear boy, that they will regret they've ever heard of me. For revenge, I shall be as sure as guts are made of pudding.
>
> CARLOS: Guts are made of pudding?
>
> LONNEGAN: Yes. That's Shakespeare. But don't let it bother you.

Both actors are perfect; Perez in his contrition, Reed in his certainty. He's like a large spider, waiting for the helpless flies. Later, Lonnegan sits resplendent in red dressing gown and white scarf, looking like he was born in them, and interviews O'Malley (an exasperated Val Avery), who is a crooked as Carlos is confused.

> LONNEGAN: I know you're a cop, and I know what kind of cop you are. Okay? I'm not asking you to look the other way. You're going to get your man because I'm going to give him to you.
>
> O'MALLEY: Why not now?
>
> LONNEGAN: Because he's running a little con that's going to backfire on him and I

don't want anything to interfere with that. See?

> O'MALLEY: No — I'm sorry. I can't turn my back on crime.
>
> LONNEGAN: Try.

Lonnegan makes it easy for O'Malley by offering a large bribe, willingly and quickly taken. Reed plays these — and all his scenes — quietly, with good humor just beneath the menace.

The reviews that followed *The Sting II*'s January 1983 release were stinging. The authors do not wish to be apologists for Reed; we sat through more than a few poor performances and films. But in this case, the attacks are, in our opinion, unjustified. No, *The Sting II* is not as good as the original. So what? *The Sting* set a very high standard, out of the reach of most productions, and its sequel fell short. This is hardly a condemnation in itself.

"Part two is mostly just a chore to watch.... [T]he overriding feeling is how much better it was all done before. Oliver Reed does a less than distinguished turn.... [T]echnical elements all work quite well" (*Variety*, January 26, 1983); "[T]he Robert Shaw character [is] played dreadfully here by Oliver Reed..." (*New York Times*, February 18, 1983); "Now interpreted as an epicene, Shakespeare-quoting smoothie, Reed's Lonnegan qualifies as one of the most innocuous villains in screen history" (*New Musical Express*, June 4, 1983); "Reed talks as if Noël Coward were giving him lessons in diction" (*The Standard*, May 26, 1983); "[I]t is a highly entertaining, stylish reworking.... [T]he flaw of the film is that the casting definitely has an aura of being second rank" (*What's On*, May 26, 1983).

The Sting II is clever and well acted throughout. Unlike many actors who have played boxers, Mac Davis actually looks like he knows what he's doing, in addition to giving a very appealing performance. Karl Malden is suitably sleazy, and Teri Garr does her expected quality turn. There are a lot of worse ways to spend 100 minutes than by watching this movie.

Fanny Hill (1983)

(Aka *Sex, Lies and Renaissance*) FH Filmproduction Ltd.; Playboy Productions; color

Cast— Director: Gerry O'Hara; Writer: Stephen Chesley; from John Cleland's novel *Fanny Hill or Memoirs of a Woman of Pleasure*; Producer: Harry Benn; Executive Producer: Harry Alan Towers; Original Music: Paul Hoffert; Cinematography: Tony Spratling; Film Editor: Peter Boyle; Casting: Sue Whatmough; Art Director; Geoffrey Tozer; Set Decorator: Denise Exshaw; Makeup Artist: Hajera Coovadia; Hair Stylist: Ross Carver; Production Manager: John Oldknow; Assistant Director: Tony Hopkins; Construction Manager: Bob Cross; Buyer: Dennis Griffith; Property Master: Ernie Lille; Sound Recordist: Laurie Clarkson; Dubbing Editor: Michael Crouch; Dialogue Editor: Peter Elliott; ADR Mixer: Peter Maxwell; Still Photographer: Douglas Dawson; Gaffer: Maurice Gillett; Second Assistant Camera: Martin Kenzie; Camera Operator: Herbert Smith; Focus Puller: Tony Woodcock; Wardrobe Master: James Smith; Wardrobe Supervisor: Joyce Stoneman; Assistant Editor: Brian Mann; Continuity: Juliet Clarke; Choreographer: Kim Kinne; Location Manager: Derek Whitehurst.

Crew— Lisa Raines (Fanny Hill), Oliver Reed (Mr. Edward Widdlecome), Wilfred Hyde White (Mr. Barville), Shelley Winters (Mrs. Cole), Alfred Marks (Lecher), Paddy O'Neil (Mrs. Brown), Jonathan York (Charles), Maria Harper (Phoebe).

Synopsis

In 18th-century England, Francis "Fanny" Hill (Lisa Raines), a young, beautiful but naive country girl, is on the way to London to seek her fortune. She is falsely accused of theft by an aging roué (Alfred Marks) and is then herself robbed of her meager possessions.

Fanny is hired by Mrs. Brown (Paddy O'Neil) as a servant, but actually to be a prostitute. In the course of her new profession she meets Charles (Harry Fowler) and they fall in love. With the help of attorney Mr. Widdlecome (Oliver Reed), Mrs. Brown is forced to release Fanny from her servitude and is paid off with fifty guineas. To end their affair, Charles is kidnapped by his own family and sent to the West Indies. On her own again, Fanny connects with Phoebe (Marion Harper), one of Mrs. Brown's "girls," and is soon in the service of a new madam, Mrs. Cole (Shelley Winters). She arouses the interest of wealthy, elderly Mr. Barville (Wilfred Hyde-White), who, upon his death, leaves her his considerable fortune. The

newly rich Fanny returns home and, while stopping at a country inn, is reunited with the now penniless Charles.

Comment

John Cleland's 1749 novel *Fanny Hill* was banned for over 200 years in Britain; it wasn't till 1963 that the unexpurgated version was published. If the novel was anything like the film version, it wasn't worth the wait!

Producer Harry Alan Towers had a long and successful career making exploitation films with horror-erotic themes, ranging from the excellent (*The Face of Fu Manchu*, 1965) to the okay (*Count Dracula,* 1970) to the execrable (this one). Often featuring top-notch actors like Christopher Lee, Dan Duryea, Klaus Kinski and Herbert Lom, Towers' movies, even the bad ones, usually have some interest.

But not always. *Fanny Hill*, with its graphic softcore sex scenes, might have been a sensation in the sixties, but by the eighties it had all been done before — and often by Harry Alan Towers. He continued his tradition of employing interesting performers, in this case Shelley Winters, Wilfred Hyde-White and Reed. None of them has much to do, and Reed is awful in what little he does.

We first see Reed, as lawyer Mr. Widdlecome, decked out in a gray curled wig, black robe and white neckwear. So far, so good; and then he speaks. Reed uses a ludicrous, fruity delivery, replete with popping eyes and flapping hands as he confronts the madam, Mrs. Brown.

> MR. WIDDLECOME: I am very pleased that you were wise enough to accept my invitation to pay me a visit.
>
> MRS. BROWN: It wasn't so much an invitation. The gentleman who delivered the message made it very clear that if I didn't come to you, the bailiff would come to me.
>
> MR. WIDDLECOME: I'm afraid my clerk can be very tactless. However, I daresay you got the general drift of the affair. My client, you see, contacted me about a very private and personal matter regarding you and your establishment.
>
> MRS. BROWN: To be sure, most matters conducted in my house are personal and usu-

ally extremely private ... as you ought to know.

Oh! This was supposed to be funny; Reed was going for comedy. Unfortunately, he was trying too hard. He was very funny — effortlessly so — in *The System, The Jokers* and *I'll Never Forget What's 'Isname.* But then, they were real movies.

His next scene is even sadder. Reed discusses with an elderly actor that man's likelihood of consummating a relationship with Fanny. Unfortunately, that actor was Wilfred Hyde-White who appeared in *The Third Man.* One wonders if the two talented actors were thinking back to their work with Sir Carol Reed in two of the best movies ever made ... and now this. One hopes not.

Lisa Raines, as Fanny, is no better or worse than the audience should have expected, or deserved. She finds herself involved in just about every possible sex act one can imagine. In between the above is something of a plot involving the old rags-to-riches chestnut; she is much less effective in these scenes.

The few critics who reviewed *Fanny Hill* were mostly, surprisingly, lenient. "With Shelley Winters, Wilfred Hyde-White and Oliver Reed playing cameo roles, it's more than likely that this first legitimate production of *Fanny Hill* [will] have certain decorum" (*The Daily Mirror*, December 12, 1982); "Although clearly not a big will budget picture, it makes appealing use of country locations and authentic looking sets with quite attractive costumes and decorations" (*What's On*, March 21, 1983); "[There's] remorseless mugging from the cast, notably Oliver Reed" (*The Monthly Film Bulletin*, May 1983).

It's bad enough that *Fanny Hill* is pretty bad; Reed is even worse, further reinforcing the steadily growing opinion that he was no longer an "A" list actor. With a punchier script and better acting, this could have been a half decent indecent film.

Al Mas' Ala Al-Kubra (1983)

(Aka *Clash of Loyalties*) A Disa Al Bayali Film Production, Baghdad; released in Moscow in 1983 at the International Film Festival

Credits— Director: Mohammed Shukri Jameel; Screenplay: Latif Jorephani, Mohamed Jameel, Ramadan Gatea, Roger Smith; Original Music: Ron Goodwin; Cinematography: Jack Hildyard, Malid Kamel; Film Editor: Bill Blunden; Sound: Feisal al-Abbasy, Norman Bolland.

Cast— Oliver Reed (Colonel Leachman), Yousef al-Any (Blind Leader), Ghari al-Takriti (Dhari al-Mahmood), Bernard Archer (Sir Percy Cox), John Barron (General Haldane), James Bolam (A.T. Watson), Helen Cherry (Lady Cox), Barrie Cookson (Colonel Hardcastle), Sami Abdul Hameed (Nationalist Leader), Helen Ryan (Gertrude Bell), Marc Sinden (Captain).

Synopsis

A fascinating chapter in modern Iraqi history, this is a tale of the Liberation Movement of the 1920s, when Iraqi revolutionaries struggled to throw off the British yoke. One of the leading characters is Dhari al-Mahmood, one of the leaders of the uprising who gave his life for the cause.

Comment

This movie was filmed during the Iran-Iraq War at the Baghdad Studios and Kut, Iraq, and only seen (as far as we can ascertain) at the 1983 Moscow Film Festival where the director was nominated for the Golden Prize. The authors were unable to find a print to view, which is disappointing as the premise seems to intriguingly mirror *Lion of the Desert.*

Variety (July 12, 1983) was in Moscow to review the film and said, "As an historical chronicle, *Clash of Loyalties* will find an appreciative audience, for there is little in the way of feature films made on this period in the Middle East and Iraq in particular. The presence of Oliver Reed in the film lends an authenticity to the proceedings. Lastly, the action scenes are well handled. What's missing is a tighter dramatic unity and sharply penned dialogue scenes. Still, Iraqi cinema is maturing year by year, and this film offers a strong prognosis of things to come at the well-geared Baghdad studios. British thesps in Iraqi pics assure a universal appeal for historical themes; just as much care should be given to all-round top-quality production credits."

Spasms (1983)

Cinequity; Hyperion Pictures; released by Producers Distributing Corporation in the U.S. in 1984; no U.K. release

Crew—Director: William Fruet; Writers: Don Enright, William Fruet; from the novel *Death Bite* by Michael Maryk and Brent Monahan's; Executive Producer: Martin Erlichman; Co-Producers: John Newton, Gordon Robinson; Producers: John G. Pazhke, Maurice Smith; Original Music: Christopher Franke, Edgar Froese, Johannes Schmolling as "Tangerine Dream"; Cinematography: Mark Irwin; Film Editor: Ralph Brunjes; Casting: Deirdre Bowen, Clare Walker; Art Directors: Carmi Gallo, Gavin Mitchell; Set Decorators: Patricia Gruben, Melanie Johnson; Key Makeup: Sandi Duncan; Special Makeup Effects: Stephan Dupuis, Carl Fullerton; Assistant Makeup: Linda Preston, Dick Smith; Unit Manager: Keith Large; Production Manager: Gordon Robinson; First Assistant Director: David A. Shepherd; Second Assistant Directors: Richard Flower, John Rainey; Property Master: Andrew Deskin; Assistant Art Director: Rolf Harvey; Sound Re-recording Mixers: David Appleby, Don White; Production Sound Mixer: Stuart French; Boom Operator: Cory Siddall; Stunt Coordinator: Robert Hannah; Stunts: Roy T. Anderson; Grip: Christopher Dean; Extras Casting: Peter Lavender; Wardrobe: Gina Kiellerman; Wardrobe Assistant: Mary Partridge-Raynor; Location Manager: David Coatsworth; Script Supervisor: Gillian Richardson.

Cast—Peter Fonda (Dr. Tom Brasilian), Oliver Reed (Jason Kincaid), Kerrie Keane (Suzanne Cavadon), Al Waxman (Warren Crowley), Miguel Fernandez (Mendes/Tasaki), Marilyn Lightstone (Dr. Claire Rothman), Angus MacInnes (Duncan Tyrone), Laurie Brown (Allison), Gerard Parkes (Capt. Novak), William Needles (Dean Franklin), Denis Simpson (Abo Shaman), Patrick Brymer (Sailor/Agent), George Bloomfield (Rev. Thomas Thanner), Al Maini (Abo Interpreter), Denise Fergusson (Psycho Patient), John Bayliss (Chauffeur), Barry Flatman (Reporter), David Bolt (Customs Officer), Les Rubie (Janitor), Walker Boone (Sgt. Brody), Don Buchsbaum (Policeman #1), Harvey Chow (Coroner), Peter McConnell (Policeman #2), Julie Khaner (Marcie), Sandra Await (Sharon), Moira Stone (Girl in Bikini), Scotty Allan (Country Boy).

Synopsis

Wealthy adventurer Jason Kincaid (Oliver Reed) is awakened from a nightmare by a phone call from Mendez (Miguel Fernandez) who has captured a monster snake in New Guinea. Kincaid has formed a telepathic link with the creature since it killed his brother. Kincaid bribes Dr. Tom Brasilian (Peter Fonda), an ESP researcher at the university, to free him from the curse when the snake arrives in Toronto. His niece Suzanne (Kerrie Keane) has misgivings, but warms to Dr. Brasilian. Also interested in the monster is the Rev. Thanner (George Bloomfield), a Satanist who believes it is the guardian of the gate to Hell. He hires sleazy operative Crawley (Al Waxman) to acquire the snake as an object of worship. After killing Crawley's henchman on the ship, the monster is taken to Dr. Brasilian's lab from which it escapes during Crawley's attempt to steal it. Dr. Brasilian and Suzanne track it to a greenhouse and barely escape with their lives. Kincaid is questioned by Captain Novak (Gerard Parkes) and explains what they are up against. Crawley is killed after tracking the creature to Kincaid's estate. While Brasilian studies Kincaid's brainwaves, Kincaid has a seizure as Crawley is being torn to pieces. Through the ESP connection, Kincaid now knows the creature's location and flees the lab with Brasilian and Suzanne in pursuit. Kincaid confronts the monster and is killed, but Brasilian quickly destroys the snake with a machine-gun.

Comment

Most actors are lucky enough not to appear in any movies about killer snakes, but Oliver Reed found himself in two. *Venom* was clearly the superior one, but *Spasms* isn't as terrible as one might expect.

Filmed in Toronto by Cinequity Corporation with financial aid from the Canadian Film Development Corporation in 1981 (as *Death Bite*), the film failed to acquire a countrywide distributor and appeared in America in 1982 on Thorn/EMI video as *Spasms*. It was also shown under that title on Canadian cable TV.

Why two upper level stars (albeit on the way down) would agree to appear in a monster animal movie is anyone's guess. At least Peter Fonda came by it naturally; his father, Henry, went slumming with other A-list stars in *Tentacles* (1977) which featured a giant octopus. It is also true that both Reed's *Women in Love* and Fonda's *Easy Rider* were made a long time (1969) before. Fonda was also enticed by the opportunity to work with Reed. Reed said of the movie, "I accepted at once. There was no way I was going to pass up the chance of working with this legendary actor" (Reed, 217).

Spasms gets off to a good start as Mendes spies on a worship ceremony as the New Guinea tribesmen pay homage to the snake monster. His later phone call to Kincaid kicks the plot into high gear; Reed is very intense.

> MENDES: I believe the legends are true. I think I should do us both a favor and kill this creature right now.
>
> KINCAID: No! No, don't do that. You take good care of it and put it on the ship as arranged, all right?
>
> MENDES: I would have killed it on the island had I been able to.
>
> KINCAID: You don't kill things that are one of a kind.

Spasms looks good for a low-budget movie. It's well photographed in interesting places with no stinting on props — Kincaid owns, among other things, a vintage Rolls-Royce and a Jaguar XK140. We get to see something of Toronto, and whatever was used for New Guinea looks convincing.

What we don't get to see is the snake.

There's a tradition in horror movies dating back to producer Val Lewton's *Cat People* (1942) in which the audience is only given fleeting glimpses of the monster to heighten surprise and not strain credulity. This can work very well in psychologically oriented horrors, but in, say, a Frankenstein (or a giant snake) movie, we've got to see the thing. Another reason to refrain from showing the monster is that it looks unconvincing, and that's what we've got here.

Although we don't get to see much of the snake, we do get to see what it sees. Director William Fruet gives us blue-tinted, speeded-up ground level shots to simulate the snake's vision as it attacks its victims who, it must be said, look very convincingly terrified. This becomes slightly annoying — there are a lot of victims — but it's better than seeing too much of a bad thing. The snake attacks are very well staged and brutal, especially in a girls' dorm (some gratuitous nudity) and in Crawley's car.

Fonda looks and plays his part well with his customary laid-back style. Reed goes slightly over the top once or twice (when having a seizure, though, how else do you play it?), but is mostly his low-key, whispering self. Both actors are better than the movie requires them to be: two old pros getting the job done, two old pros a long way from 1969.

Variety (a May 28, 1984, review of the cassette) was unimpressed: "Unconvincing fantasy film is mainly a tease.... [A]cting is poor."

Spasms was nothing special and certainly did little to enhance Reed's career. But, there is a market for this type of film, and they've usually done a lot worse than *Spasms*.

Two of a Kind (1983)

A 20th Century–Fox–Joe Wizan–Roger M. Rothstein Production; released in the U.S. by 20th Century–Fox on December 15, 1983; 87 minutes; color

Credits— Director-Screenplay: John Herzfeld; Producers: Joe Wizan, Roger M. Rothstein; Associate Producers: Michele Panelli, Joan Edwards, Kate Edwards; Cinematographer: Fred Koenekamp; Editor: Jack Hofstra; Music Adaptation: Patrick Williams; Production Design: Albert Brenner; Art Director: Spencer Deverell; Set Design: Kandy Stern, Diane Wager; Set Decorator: Marvin March; Costume Design: Thomas Bronson; Sound: Bud Alper; Second Unit Director; Johm Moio; Assistant Director: Frederic Blankfein.

Cast— John Travolta (Zack), Olivia Newton-John (Debbie), Charles Durning (Charlie), Beatrice Straight (Ruth), Scatman Crothers (Earl), Castulo Guerra (Gonzales), Oliver Reed (Beazley), Richard Bright (Stuart), Vincent Bufano (Oscar), Gene Hackman (Voice of God), Toni Kalem (Terri), James Stevens (Ron), Jack Kehoe (Mr. Chotiner), Ernie Hudson (Detective Stagg).

Synopsis

God (voice of Gene Hackman) has been on vacation, leaving angels Charlie (Charles Durning), Earl (Scatman Crothers) and Ruth (Beatrice Straight) in charge. When He returns, God decides that mankind is so worthless that it would be best to start over; perhaps another flood? The angels object and ask for a chance to save Earth. God will reconsider —*if* they can find one decent person. Cut to one completely worthless person — Zack (John Travolta), a failed inventor in debt to the mob. When threatened by Stuart (Richard Bright), Zack decides to rob a bank. Debbie (Olivia Newton-John), a failed actress working as a teller, manages to steal the money herself and is fired for flirting with the robber. She and Zack become reacquainted when pursued by Stuart he falls from a building and both are killed. Charles intervenes and begs God for one more chance. He agrees — if both are willing to sacrifice for the other. Beazley (Oliver Reed) — actually Lucifer/Beelzebub, get it? — enters the fray and literally rewinds reality to the point of their deaths, betting on the unlikelihood of their redemption. Zack discovers that Debbie has "his" money and demands its return. They realize they are attracted to each other and go to the Plaza Hotel where they are accosted by Beazley and Stuart but are saved by Charlie. They escape to her apartment where they become lovers. Debbie has missed a call-back for a big role on Broadway and they quarrel. Beazley arranges for their arrest. Detective Staggs (Ernie Hudson) tricks Zack into informing on Debbie, but they are released when Charlie destroys the evidence. Beazley realizes that if he wins, he loses; God will depopulate the world and he'll have no one to corrupt. He masquerades as a psycho gunman and holds Debbie hostage, giving Zack the opportunity to sacrifice himself and save mankind. God restores Zack to life, and Beazley and Charlie part as friends.

Comment

Two of a Kind is a one-of-a-kind movie; it's hard to think of another one with so many talented people used to so little effect. Consider: the film boasts Gene Hackman (or at least his voice), who won an Oscar for *The French Connection* (1971). Beatrice Straight won an Oscar for *Network* (1976) and Charles Durning was nominated for *The Best Little Whorehouse In Texas* (1982). The two leads certainly had their moments too; *Grease* (1978) remains one of the top-grossing musicals of all time, and John Travolta, despite reviewers predicting that *Two of a Kind* would end his career, has scored again and again in dramatic roles. Add to the mix Scatman Crothers (*The Shining*, 1980) and Ernie Hudson (*Ghostbusters*, 1984) and this is one talented cast. And then there's Oliver Reed for good measure.

Two of a Kind — really — isn't as bad as the reviews which follow would indicate. The problem is that all of the above performers have each done twenty things that are better than this, which makes the film seem far worse than it is. Not, of course, that it's very good in itself. What little life *Two of a Kind* possesses is supplied by Reed, who hams it up delightfully as Beazley/Lucifer. Resplendent in a series of outrageous suits, slicked-back jet black hair and curled moustache, Reed is a joy, more or less, to behold. He and Charles Durning have an amusingly adversarial yet genial relationship representing the opposite ends of good and evil. In fact, their relationship is more plausible than the one shared by John Travolta and Olivia Newton-John.

Two of a Kind's best bits are those involving Reed and Durning as they argue the film's questionable theology.

CHARLIE: There's something you should know. If there is a flood, He's bringing everyone up here. Well, laugh — it's true. You'll be reduced to teaching evil to animals.

BEAZLEY: Well, *He's* the one who's going to flood the world. You see, mankind is basically selfish, rotten and evil and I want to rub it right in His face.

Two of a Kind might have benefitted from more special special effects. As they stand, they consist of Beazley and Charlie stopping the action and rewinding events to the point where they choose to intervene. The first time this happens it's amusing, but it gets old quickly. The film is not a musical, but does manage to feature three songs by Newton-John plus a duet with Travolta to, presumably, sell the soundtrack album. Reed even gets to sing a few lines of the Beatles' "Rain" when the fire sprinklers let loose during a fight at the Plaza.

Although *Two of a Kind* was nothing to be proud of, Reed escapes relatively unscathed. He delivers his lines lightly but with understated menace, giving Beazley a bit more weight than the script provided. He looks agreeably funny in over-the-top costumes and doesn't seem to be the least bit embarrassed, which is something.

Reviews were brutal. *Variety* (December 17, 1983): "*Two of a Kind* is an embarrassment of the first order. Aside from the presence of the two stars, confection has all the earmarks of a bargain basement job. Oliver Reed oozes through the proceedings as a Lucifer figure"; *The Daily Mirror* (December 30, 1983): "It's five years since Travolta starred in *Grease,* but he's never repeated this success. [*Two of a Kind*] looks like just another nail in his career's coffin. Within hours of its release, some of America's top critics had labeled the £16 million film the worst of 1983"; *New York Post* (December 16, 1983): "...Reed, is dressed like a Times Square three-card-monte dealer. The film is a monument to ineptitude and incompetence that makes *Staying Alive* look like *Citizen Kane* and *Singin' in the Rain* together."

It's difficult to defend *Two of a Kind* but it's not quite as bad as the reviews make it sound. Not quite.

Captive (1986)

Les Productions Belles Rives; Union Generale Cinematographique; Virgin Films; World Audio Visual Entertainment; released to video in the U.S. by Continental Video in 1987, U.K. release Virgin; Lawson Colegrave Productions (London) 1987; color; 98 minutes

Crew— Screenplay-Director: Paul Mayersberg; Executive Producers: Al Clark, Stanley Sopel; Producer: Don Boyd; Co-Producer: Christian Ardan; Associate Producer: David A. Barber; Production Coordinators: Jacques Ristori, Diana Sprot; Location Manager: Christopher Webster; Assistant Directors: Jakes Wright, Paul Frift, Carol Brock; Cinematographer: Mike Southon; Camera Operator: Philip Sindall; Editor: Marie-Therese Boiche; Production Designer: Voytek; Assistant Designer: George Djurkovic; Set Design: Jennifer Williams; Special Effects Supervisor: Derek Langley; Music: (The Edge) The Edge, Michael Brook; Song "Heroine" by The Edge, performed by Sinead O'Connor; Costume Design: Sheelagh Killeen; Wardrobe Mistress: Katie Birell; Makeup: Norma Hill; Sound Editor: Juliette Welfling; Special Sound Effects: Jerome Levy, Alain Levy; Consultant on Body Alignment: Dreas Reyneke.

Cast— Oliver Reed (Gregory Le Vay), Irina Brook (Rowena), Xavier Deluc ("D"), Corinne Dacla (Bryony), Hiro Arai (Hiro), Nick Reding (Leo), Annie Leon (Pine), Michael Cronin (McPherson), Marissa Dunlop (Little Rowena), Choyling-Man (Kim), Mark Tandy (Hammond), Sarah Cam (Sister), Lucien Morgan (Marksman), Benny Young (Psychologist), Sidney Livingstone (Reporter), Geoff Harding (American), Arturo Venegas (Second Man), Alan Turner (Security Guard).

Synopsis

Awaiting a visit to her castle-like home from her wealthy father Gregory Le Vay (Oliver Reed), Rowena (Irina Brook) sends her lover away while Hiro (Hiro Arai) lurks outside. Gregory brings her a birthday gift, her late mother's gown, then leaves to join his mistress.

Rowena is kidnapped by Hiro, Bryony (Corinne Dacla) and "D" (Xavier Deluc). They drug her, take her to a warehouse and begin to psychologically torture her. The kidnappers, like Rowena, are from wealthy families and force her to see the hypocrisy of her life. Under this assault, Rowena comes to believe that she doesn't love her father, and that he has used her as an emotional surrogate for her mother (who died in childbirth). Rowena gradually falls in with her captors, especially Hiro; she reminds him of his dead lover.

Gregory has called the police but, when they fail to find a lead, burns his yacht as he has been instructed to secure her release. Although free to go, Rowena elects to stay and help with a terrorist attack on an art gallery which involves pretending to execute the patrons and destroying a valuable painting donated by Gregory. They escape to a farm where "D" has sex with Rowena. When she is found to be pregnant, "D" is disgusted with his behavior and realizes that he has hurt everyone. In desperation, Gregory has contacted a clairvoyant who alerts the police to the group's hiding place at a private airfield. Hiro makes his escape in a small plane. "D" and Bryony commit suicide. Rowena is taken into custody, refuses Gregory's attorney, and serves two years in prison where she miscarries. She is visited by both Gregory and Hiro but dismisses them both, realizing that she is to them only a replacement for the women they really love. Devastated by her attitude, Hiro cuts his throat. Now completely alone, Rowena is free.

Comment

The authors were expecting very little from *Captive*, sandwiched as it was between some of the worst movies of Oliver Reed's career. We could not have been more wrong.

Captive is an excellent film — exciting, disturbing, thought-provoking. In short, it's everything most of Reed's movies from this period are not, and it provided him with one of his best supporting roles. Since it's relatively difficult to obtain a copy of the film, we feel it's necessary to examine his scenes in some detail.

Instead of opening with the low comedy or high violence we've come to expect, the movie begins with the strains of "Tosca." A fairy-tale castle looms in the background darkness. Cut to a screen-filling sleeping eye — cut to a stalker hiding in the woods. The sleeper wakes; it is Rowena (Irina Brooks, daughter of director Richard Brooks) and she's in bed with her lover whom she curtly dismisses. Her father is coming to celebrate her birthday. He arrives after midnight. Reed makes an entrance worthy of Orson Welles: top hat, opera cloak and a halo of cigarette smoke. Huge and bearded, Gregory has brought a gift for Rowena, a gown worn by her mother. She strips in front of him and slips it on. It's a perfect fit. Dining together, they are unaware their conversation is being taped.

GREGORY: You know — I miss her terribly.

ROWENA: Dad, I'm ... I'm sorry.

GREGORY: You can't blame yourself ... I have you now. Well, I'm late. It's going on two. I've got a business meeting.

ROWENA: At two in the morning? Daddy, please don't go.

GREGORY: What do you want to do with your life Rowena?

She wants what her mother wanted (to be a singer), but Gregory has put an end to both of their dreams. As for his "business meeting," he's off to see his Asian mistress. And Rowena is about to meet her grotesquely costumed abductors who drug her and take her to a warehouse where she's blindfolded and shoved into a packing case.

But these are no ordinary kidnappers. They resent all of the Gregorys in this world and want to turn Rowena against him. It doesn't take long for her to question whether she loves her father and vice versa. After her mother died

in childbirth, Rowena's growth was stifled by her father who, presumably, wanted her to remain a child. While imprisoned in the packing case, Rowena flashes back to a disturbing incident from her childhood. She hides under a table while Gregory, in a white suit, prances about madly as a fairy-tale ogre. "I'm going to eat you up," he intones. He behaves as though his little daughter should be having fun. She isn't. His reassuring hug does little to reassure her.

Reed brilliantly gets across that Gregory has feelings for his daughter, but what exactly are they? He shows no overt sexual interest in her but it's lurking on the edges, just like his well-controlled anger that is always on the edge of eruption. After some harrowing torture ranging from the physical to the psychological, Rowena is placed blindfolded in front of a television showing an interview with Gregory.

INTERVIEWER: We understand, Mr. Le Vay, that you've received a demand from the kidnappers.

GREGORY: It's not a ransom. I don't wish to talk about it. What I can say is that I have no intention of giving in to these people.

INTERVIEWER: By rejecting them, are you not in danger of jeopardizing your daughter's life?

GREGORY: My daughter ... she would not want it any other way. If she was in my position, she would do just the same as I am doing.

Upon hearing this, Rowena breaks down, sobbing, "I don't love him. I hate him." Gregory eventually gives in to the unspecified demand: that he prove his love for Rowena by burning his most valued possession, his yacht. He sits alone, drinking and listening to "Tosca." He takes a candle and sets fire to the boat; his expression, seen through the flames, is devastating.

But despite her father's sacrifice, Rowena has thrown in with her captors and they raid the art gallery. When she is identified, Gregory addresses the media and claims, reasonably enough, that she was forced to join the gang. After she is captured at the airfield, Gregory visits her in her cell and learns that she is pregnant.

GREGORY: That thing ... that you did ... did you do it to hurt me?

ROWENA: Yes, I did.

She miscarries while in prison. After her release she returns, against Gregory's wish, to the castle. He wants to take her to New York; she flatly refuses.

GREGORY: The other day I was ... I was talking to a psychologist. He said that maybe somewhere in your past the seeds were sown. I told him you had a happy childhood, despite everything. Don't you remember all the fun we had ... on the yacht? Don't you remember how you used to play hide and seek ... on the yacht?

ROWENA: I did what?

Gregory flashes back to the incident that Rowena revisited while a captive but he remembers it in an entirely different way. From his perspective, it was all innocent, childish fun, not the nightmare of Rowena's memory. This version ends with Gregory hugging his happy, smiling child; but she's not happy and smiling now.

ROWENA: It's not true.

GREGORY: That's how it was. [*They quarrel bitterly but Rowena refuses to budge.*]

GREGORY: I burned my yacht for you.

ROWENA: You gave something up just once in your life. It's not so terrible. I've given a few things up.

Gregory leaves with their relationship unresolved, and unlikely ever to be. The scene is among the best of his career as he pleads quietly for his daughter's love, but with violence about to explode. Reed showed that he still had what it took, and it did not go unnoticed by the critics.

"The most astonishing thing about the film is the persuasiveness with which it demonstrates Rowena's escape from family environment and social convention to become not just her real, but another, self. The magical opening sequence and the first appearance of Gregory, part Mephistopheles and part pantomime demon.... [T]he stunning images of *Captive* owe much to Voytek's design, Mike Southon's cam-

era work, and an excellent cast (Oliver Reed is literally a revelation), but the magical spell they cast is entirely Mayersberg's" (*Monthly Film Bulletin*, September 1986); "*Captive* looks like it's going to be yet another retelling of the ordeal of Patty Hearst, but, thankfully, writer-director Paul Mayersberg has other ideas in mind. He catches you as much by surprise as does the erotic trio who abduct a young British heiress. Reed, in what could be the most restrained and understated performance of his career, is just fine, as is Brook. *Captive* is a dazzling directorial debut" (*Los Angeles Times*, April 30, 1987); "At least Oliver Reed is interesting as the gothically romantic man with a painful past and a spoiled princess as a daughter" (*New York Post*, April 13, 1987); "*Captive* is a good deal like the Patty Hearst story without the politics with more than a whiff of psychic incest" (*Newsday*, April 3, 1987); "What detracts a little from the achievement of Mayersberg's film is the uncertain playing of all but the experienced Oliver Reed" (*Sight and Sound*, Summer 1986); "I suspect that the real story isn't the spoiled princess but the wounded father — a giant played with delicious ambivalence by Oliver Reed. His brief scenes are the most powerful; we sense the erotic dimensions of his need to control his daughter" (*The Village Voice*, March 24, 1987).

Captive is one of the few films from the latter stages of Reed's career that should not be missed; both the movie and its star are excellent. It is a first-rate effort all round, especially from the first-time director Mayersberg and director of photography Southon.

Of Reed's next and last twenty-seven movies, only a handful would have any merit. It's unfortunate — and puzzling — that *Captive* didn't re-boot Reed's career.

Castaway (1986)

Cannon Screen Group; United British Artists; United Artists; released by Cannon Film Distributors in the U.S. in 1986 and in the U.K. in 1987; Technicolor; 120 minutes

Credits— Director: Nicolas Roeg; Executive Producers: Peter Shaw, Richard Johnson; Producer: Rick McCallum; Associate Producer: Selwyn Roberts; Production Design: Andrew Sanders;

Music: Stanley Myers; Cinematographer: Harvey Harrison; Editor: Tony Lawson; Screenplay: Allan Scott; Based on a book by Lucy Irvine; Assistant Director: Michael Zimbrich; Location Managers: Charles Salmon, Paul Turcotte; Researcher: Ruth Halliday; Camera: Gordon Hayman; Underwater Camera: Mike Valentine; Clapper: Dean Morrison; Grip: Kenny Atherford; Sound: Paul Le Mare; Art Directors: George Galifzine, Stuart Rose; Props: John Mills; Makeup: Christine Beveridge; Hair Stylist: Carol Hemming; Costumes: Nic Edge; Construction: Geoff Kingsley; Special Effects: Alan Whibley; Gaffer: Dennis Brook; Best Boy: Tommy Finch; Stand-in for Oliver Reed: Reg Prince.

Cast— Oliver Reed (Gerald Kingsland), Amanda Donohoe (Lucy Irvine), Georgina Hale (Sister St. Margaret), Frances Barber (Sister St. Winifred), Tony Richards (Jason), Todd Rippon (Rod), John Sessions (Man in Pub), Virginia Hey (Janice), Sorrell Johnson (Lara), Len Peihopa (Ronnie), Paul Reynolds (Mike Kingsland), Sean Hamilton (Geoffrey Kingsland), Sarah Harper (Swimming Teacher), Stephen Jenn (Shop Manager), Joseph Blatchley (Registrar).

Synopsis

Gerald Kingsland (Oliver Reed) is a middle-aged, divorced London businessman with a dream: to spend a year on a deserted tropical island with a beautiful woman. He places an advertisement in *Time Out* magazine and is surprised to receive a reply from the stunning Lucy Irvine (Amanda Donohoe). They have two tentative, embarrassing meetings discussing the project, then Lucy, unexpectedly, takes Gerald to bed — presumably to seal the deal. Gerald survives an encounter with Laura (Sorrell Johnson), Lucy's roommate, and a more problematic situation: an official (an unbilled Richard Johnson, also the movie's executive producer) tells them that their island, an Australian protectorate, requires them to be married before they can live there. They reluctantly marry and when they move onto the island realize that they have an even worse dilemma. Gerald wants nothing but sex, and Lucy, despite her earlier behavior, wants nothing to do with him on that level. They swim, fish, make pointless conversation, build a shelter and keep diaries. Gerald seethes while Lucy grouses about his lack of ambition. He spends his days sulking while she shouts at him. The deteriorating situation goes quickly downhill with the arrival of two young Australians (Tod Rippon, Tony Richards) to, unbelievably, take a census. They

flirt with Lucy, who responds, sending the cuckolded Gerald into a rage. Gerald and Lucy begin to suffer malnutrition, despite his attempts at gardening, and infection. They are saved by the arrival of two nuns (Georgina Hale, Frances Barber) who cure their physical, but not emotional, distress. Gerald finds a measure of peace when Ronnie (Len Peihopa) from a neighboring island takes him there to mend machinery. After their island is hit by a violent storm, Gerald and Lucy have sex, but neither is any happier. The year finishes, and she returns to London while Gerald moves to Ronnie's island.

Comment

By the mid–1980s it seemed as though Oliver Reed was finished as a serious actor in quality films. His last prestigious roles were a decade earlier (*The Three Musketeers, Tommy*); his recent appearances were in *Fanny Hill* and *Two of a Kind*. Then, as Reed was pondering retirement, came *Castaway*.

His personal life was in the upswing too; at the time he was offered *Castaway*, Reed married for the second time. His marriage to Josephine Burge would last for the remainder of his life.

Castaway was based on the real-life adventures of Lucy Irvine and Gerald Kingsland and the books each had written about them. As one might expect, each had a different perspective on the year on the island and were not altogether complimentary to each other. Irvine portrayed Kingsland as an "ill-tempered old lecher" (*LAM Magazine,* November 12, 1985); he found her to be "neurotic and foul-mouthed."

In the film and both of the books, Lucy — who admittedly has sex with Gerald in London before embarking — decided against continuing in that direction when on the island, which caused most of their problems. Question: exactly what did she think the purpose of the trip was for Gerald? According to Amanda Donohoe (*The London Standard*, November 12, 1988), Lucy "knew her life needed a violent change both in its externals and emotionally, and she was determined it would be her that Gerald took with him. So she used her charms to see off the competition."

Gerald (Oliver Reed) carries a stricken Lucy (Amanda Donohoe) in *Castaway* (Cannon/United Artists, 1986), which should have been his comeback role.

Donohoe went to great lengths to understand both Lucy's and Gerald's motivation and personalities, which resulted in an incredible performance. She easily gives one of the best performances as a female lead in an Oliver Reed film, certainly the equal of even Glenda Jackson in *Women in Love*.

Lucy and Gerald, in both the film and reality, spent most of their time naked, or nearly so, sex or no sex. According to *The London Standard* (November 13, 1988), Irvine told Donohoe after seeing her screen test, "You were the only one who wasn't embarrassed or body conscious."

Reed, of course, had already appeared nude on screen (and according to the tabloids, plenty of other places as well) so *Castaway* presented little difficulty for him either.

Several reviews, as in *The London Standard* (February 19, 1987), quite unreasonably went out of their way to trash his physique: "It boasts the smallest cast as well as possibly the largest paunch." This is absurd; Reed was in excellent condition, especially for a man pushing fifty.

He'd worked hard getting into shape for the role, both physically and emotionally, and it shows, resulting in one of his greatest performances. Reed said in a Cannon press release,

Gerald? I'm very much like him. He is a bit of an eccentric and so am I. He will do things — not always completely sane — on an impulse and so will I. Also, if I get in a spot of trouble, people will always think the worse. There will be no explanations. Gerald is a bit like that — you have to understand the full story before you can understand why he does what he does. Before he became a castaway he was making a good living. We all talk about 'getting away from it all' and going off to some distant, tropical island — but how many of us are actually brave enough to go off and do it? When Gerald got to his island, he didn't want to be pushed. He wanted to grow his vegetables, build a shelter, fish — but in his own time. Like most men, he wanted to call the tune. Perhaps that was one of the major differences between him and Lucy. She wanted immediate action, no delay. Lucy loses respect for Gerald because he "won't get things done." On the other hand, she's always calling on him. I think that at times Lucy is very self-centered and self-opinionated. It is that which contributes to the drama and makes the relationship such a fascinating one. Lucy may think she is brighter than Gerald but I believe you'll find that in the film it comes out the other way.

Director Nicolas Roeg first encountered Reed as they both were breaking into the big time, Roeg having photographed *The System*. His most notable work as director of photography was probably *The Masque of the Red Death* (1964), Roger Corman's stylish take on the Edgar Allan Poe tale starring Vincent Price. By 1968 he was co-directing (with Donald Cammell) the notorious (and shelved until 1970) *Performance* starring Mick Jagger and James Fox. Roeg scored a huge hit with *Don't Look Now* (1973) with Donald Sutherland and Jane Fonda and never looked back. Although *Castaway* was a critical success and one of his best efforts, Roeg had mixed emotions about it. He said in *Women's Wear Daily* (June 18, 1987): "It will take me some time to figure out why I did *Castaway*. I still don't know, except it was like twenty years of life in one year." Roeg's odyssey began in the spring of 1985 at Elstree Studios and London locations (including Kensington) and the outlying areas of Harrow, Middlesex. Finding a proper island was as difficult for Roeg as it was for his two protagonists, finally settling for an island in the Seychelles group in October.

Reed was clearly inspired not only by the excellence of his role but also by the director, who drew a quality performance from an actor who had basically been sleepwalking for a decade. Reed said in the Cannon press release, "It was a wonderful experience. Roeg has an extraordinarily artistic eye and a way of communicating with his crew that is magic. Also, he doesn't believe in long rehearsals, which is a joy for me. Nicolas believes that what doesn't come naturally shouldn't come at all — and I agree."

He was a bit less charitable towards his co-star, however. He told *The New York Post* (February 11, 1988): "Amanda, like a lot of beautiful women, is preoccupied with her own beauty.

She was preoccupied with her toast for breakfast! Amanda brought her good-looking, handsome fellow along on the set.... [W]hen we were filming a love scene her guy was so close to us he was ... never mind." But he was also impressed with her performance: "She is incredible. She *is* Lucy. It would be difficult to imagine any other actress playing the part better."

Both Reed and Donohoe deliver Academy Award–level performances but neither received as much as a mention. For ninety minutes they are the only actors on screen and they both devour the camera. It's difficult to understand how powerhouse performances like these went unnoticed by the industry's various awards committees. It could easily be argued that Reed warranted four or five nominations throughout his career, but perhaps his personal life stood in the way.

Castaway had a showing at the London Film Festival on November 13, 1986, and officially opened on February 20, 1987, at the Shaftesbury Avenue Cannon. *The Guardian* sponsored a series of twelve free showings around the U.K. beginning five days earlier. The American premiere came on September 11, 1986.

Oddly, *Castaway* was denied a New York showing until May 26, 1989; the *New York Post* called it "an overlooked gem." The film had actually been given a video release a year earlier.

We first meet Gerald as he lies about his age while filling out his advertisement for *Time Out*. He's clearly fascinated by water and fish, but with his red bushy hair and beard and bulky build he actually resembles a lumberjack. He shares a bantering relationship with his two sons as they watch Peter Finch in *The Pumpkin Eater* on TV. Cleverly, when the scene cuts to Lucy's flat, she's watching the same film.

The pair have an awkwardly funny first meeting at a hotel. Both are naturally quite nervous and afraid to make a false move and both actors play the scene perfectly. There's enough of a connection to warrant a second meeting, this time for dinner. As they are eating pasta...

GERALD: It's the preparation of these kind of things that's important.

LUCY: The pasta?

GERALD: No, I mean real life — I mean the island. And some asshole like Robinson Crusoe who suddenly finds he has the whole ship's stores at his disposal...

LUCY: And a manservant sort of slave.

GERALD: I beg your pardon?

LUCY: He had a Friday as well.

As they discuss the logistics of the trip, she takes his hand and he reveals his innate chauvinism by guessing her profession as being either a secretary or a nurse — the only jobs he believes a woman can hold. She's actually a top-level Inland Revenue agent. It should have been obvious to both of them at this point that they were making a huge mistake. Lucy compounds this by having sex with Gerald at her flat, convincing him that the island will be his (limited) idea of paradise. Her decision to marry him — after initially throwing a fit at the news — is even less informed, showing that Lucy's desire to "get away" for a year is just as intense as Gerald's desire for unlimited sex.

The island is achingly beautiful and Harry Harrison's photography is beyond description. It soon, however, becomes a personal hell for the couple as their isolation and lack of real preparation magnify their innate differences. Gerald plans to lay back as often as possible, waiting for the uninhibited sex that never comes. Lucy sees the island as a challenge to her personal resourcefulness; sex with Gerald has become out of the question. Denied sex, Gerald turns his attention to creating a garden (of Eden?), not just for nutrition. He says, "It's something I've always wanted to do — grow my own food on my own island. Now, I'll make sure we don't starve, Lucy, and I'll make sure that you learn to fish but I want to do this first because I owe it to myself and to prove to myself that I believe in our future here. Understand — our lives may depend on these vegetables."

Lucy vacillates between verbally attacking Gerald, then apologizing for it. But the problem between them remains the lack of sex, and Lucy is only too aware of her position.

LUCY: It makes you angry, doesn't it? God! It frightens me. I mean your anger. I mean, we're here on this island alone ... it makes me feel so guilty...!

GERALD (*hovering menacingly over her*): Nothing's changed here. I didn't get fat or bald or forget to wash behind my ears. Nothing's changed here, girl — nothing's changed except you! You changed! You welched on the deal, do you understand? You lied, didn't you? You lied your way down here. Well, we've got nine months to go. Let's see if we can both last that long, shall we?

The scene is shattering, and leaves the viewer torn between supporting either Lucy or Gerald. Both, ultimately, are right and wrong. Later Lucy has her own back on Gerald's lack of honesty. She tells him, "You're such a liar — your whole character is a lie. You pretend you don't read, don't think, don't listen. You pretend you're just a 'give me a good lay and a good beer and I'm happy' sort of chap."

Their lives get immeasurably worse when two Aussie beach-boy census-takers (Todd Rippon, Tony Richards) arrive and *Castaway* suddenly becomes very suspenseful. There were a lot of directions this situation could have taken, and none of them good. The lads are immediately attracted to Lucy and, unfortunately, vice versa. Gerald immediately, and quite naively, hastens to point out that he and Lucy are married — as if that would make any difference if the boys decided to go after her. Reed makes Gerald quite vulnerable here, in contrast to his previous bombastic over-confidence, and gains, for the first time, audience empathy if not sympathy. Lucy goes off with Jason (Richards) and in her own inimitable way undermines Gerald even further. She says, "He just lives there, doing nothing. No imagination. I suppose it's because he's so much older than me." This is the signal for Jason to make his move and he doesn't miss it.

Gerald senses something has happened and Reed explodes his character in a frightening verbal — but not physical — attack. He rants, "You're like a randy little bitch on heat. Do you know that if you behave like this tomorrow I'm going to beat the shit out of you? Did we have them both? Did we — one at each end?" He then goes berserk, pointing out all he's done for her, and all that he's been denied. This is Reed at his most intense, which is as intense as it gets. It's doubtful that he's ever been angrier on screen. Lucy, pointlessly, excuses her behavior by trashing Gerald's: "Look. I wanted to be proud of you, that's all! I wanted to say, 'Look what we've done here! Look how we've survived!' But I couldn't even say that! Look at what you've done! Nothing!"

The Aussies leave but the strain between Gerald and Lucy remains and we find ourselves torn over which one to support. This is perhaps the most interesting aspect of this interesting film and Roeg exploits it brilliantly. In addition to their emotional distress, the couple are also becoming physically debilitated. The arrival of the nuns (Georgina Hale, Frances Barber) seems too contrived for words until one realizes that what one is seeing is factual.

Castaway continually shows us that no behavior or incident is beyond belief. Gerald, after having his physical problems tended to by the nuns, finds his emotional ones helped by Ronnie (Len Peihopa) who gives Gerald the opportunity to use his mechanical skills. More importantly, Ronnie and his fellow islanders truly appreciate Gerald and don't mind showing it — something Lucy can't and won't do. Intriguingly, Lucy only appreciates Gerald when he's on the other island but, predictably, can't resist berating him when he returns.

> LUCY: But, Gerald — one thing I am not is a mechanic's wife — and that's what you're making me! You're not even here any more! You're on Bardu getting pissed or laid!
>
> GERALD: Maybe if there were some sex here, I wouldn't have to go buggering off! What I'd like to see right now is you lying flat on your back with your hands behind your head being given one!

When Lucy finally, inevitably, gives in, neither one is happy. Gerald feels that she's sold herself to keep him on the island. So, it finally comes to this — all Gerald wanted was sex, but when he got it, it wasn't enough; or for the right reason; or — take your pick. After a storm almost as violent as Gerald's temper, their little world is virtually destroyed and it's just as well. Their time is up in more ways than one.

The great lesson of *Castaway*: Be careful what you wish for, especially in a relationship. What initially attracted them to each other in London became what separated them on the is-

land. Everything happened so quickly that they never saw aspects of each other beyond the obviously attractive ones. When they failed to bring them together, there was nothing left. Throughout the film, Lucy is the one seemingly in control of her life but by its conclusion, Gerald is the one who has found himself.

Reviews were uniformly positive. "Reed gives the performance of his career ... and is admirably complimented by Amanda Donohue, the determined but fickle object of his lust" (*Variety*, December 10, 1986); "Stunning! Reed gives an extraordinarily fine performance. I liked Roeg's film very much" (*The Guardian*, February 2, 1987); "*Castaway* is at its best when it shies away big Man-Woman statements. Oliver Reed has a peach of a part, and newcomer Amanda Donohoe does a remarkable job" (*The Independent*, February 19, 1987); "Languorous, moody, intricate. In one year these two learn to hate each other as if they'd been married for twenty" (*The New York Post*, February 11, 1988); "Oliver Reed does Gerald a kind of gentle justice" (*The Observer*, February 15, 1987); "Gerald is played by Oliver Reed as an aging lovable clown with a fondness for magic tricks" (*Monthly Film Bulletin*, February 1987).

Castaway is a superior film in every possible area. It boasts an intriguing — and true — story, beautiful photography, pointed direction and two incredible performances. Reed has never been better; Gerald sits at the same table as Bill Sikes, Gerald Crich, Father Grandier and Proximo.

But, incredibly, *Castaway* did nothing for his career. It appears that, despite this superb offering, producers were only able to focus on the Reed of the bottle and fights even though that aspect of his life seemed to have passed. His next film was the mediocre *Rage to Kill* and three films later the pathetic *The House of Usher*. He was right back on the treadmill he'd been on before *Castaway*. With the exception of *Hold My Hand, I'm Dying* (which went nowhere), Reed's next exemplary film would be his final one.

Skeleton Coast (1987)

A Silvertree/Gerald Milton/Michelle Marshall Production; The Walamar Group; Breton Film

Productions Ltd.; released to video in the U.S. in 1987; no U.K. release; color; 90 minutes

Crew—Director: John "Bud" Cardos; Producer: Harry Alan Towers; Executive Producers: Gerald Milton, Michelle Martin, Barry Wood; Associate Producers: Keith Rosenbaum, John Stodel; Executive in Charge of Production: Dina Stroppa; Screenplay: Nacha Caillou; Story: Peter Welbeck; Cinematographer: Hand Mohr; Editors: Allan Morrison, Mac Errington; Continuity: Marlow De Mardt; Sound: Conrad Kuhne; Makeup: Betty Church; Wardrobe: Elaine Downing; Grip: Leonard Nitsandeam; Best Boy: Bruce Thomas; Gaffer: Don Reid; Special Effects: Freddy Unger.

Cast—Ernest Borgnine (Col. Smith), Robert Vaughn (Col. Schneider), Oliver Reed (Capt. Simpson), Herbert Lom (Elia), Simon Sabela (Sckarsi), Daniel Greene (Rick), Leon Isaac Kennedy (Chuck), Nancy Mulford (Sam), Peter Wong (Tasmiro), Robert Townshend (Opal), Arnold Vosloo (Blade), Tullio Moneta (Armand), Larry Taylor (Robbins), Jonathan Rands (Michael Smith), Rudi De Jager (Dr. Schmidt), Anthony Wilson (Malko), Joe Ribiero (Manuel), Nigel Kane (Marcus).

Synopsis

In Angola, loyalist troops kidnap CIA agent Michael Smith (Jonathan Rands), a rebel supporter, and take him to a fortress commanded by Col. Schneider (Robert Vaughn). Michael's father, ex–Marine Col. Smith (Ernest Borgnine), arrives at the Hotel Nambib to meet with Elia (Herbert Lom), an information broker, to find where his son is held. Col. Smith and his mercenary recruit Rick (Daniel Greene) kill a man trailing them, assuming—wrongly—that he is a loyalist agent. They then assemble the rescue team: Chuck (Leon Isaac Kennedy), Sam (Nancy Mulford), Tasmiro (Peter Wong), Blade (Arnold Vosloo), Armand (Tullio Moneta), and Robbins (Larry Taylor). Elia's African wife Opal (Robin Townshend) secretly meets with Capt. Simpson (Oliver Reed), head of Diamond Mine Security, reporting that Col. Smith is responsible for the death of Simpson's agent. Simpson suspects that Col. Smith is planning to steal diamonds, and is surprised to learn the reason for his being in the country.

The team crosses the desert for the fortress as Col. Schneider checks with Dr. Schmidt (Rudi De Jager) on Michael's condition after brutal—and fruitless—interrogations as to the location of rebel leader Sckarsi's (Simon Sabela) troops. The team is followed and attacked by Capt. Simpson's officers who destroy their vehicles. The team members kill a group of diamond smugglers and steal their plane—together with a cache of gems. The team join with Sckarsi who agrees to help free Michael, and is paid with Col. Smith's share of the diamonds. The colonel bluffs his way into the fortress posing as a Cuban mercenary and finds Michael in the cells. Col. Schneider discovers the ruse and takes the team prisoner. Sckarsi attacks from the outside; Schneider is killed and the colonel takes Michael to safety in Sckarsi's vintage Rolls-Royce.

Comment

Skeleton Coast was so far below the cinematic radar that it eluded general media coverage. The British Film Institute and the Lincoln Center for Performing Arts yielded no information whatsoever. It's likely that *Skeleton Coast* went directly to video; the print viewed by the authors was a 2004 Troma DVD.

The movie is a typical Harry Alan Towers production—competently (and cheaply) made with a watchable (but clichéd) storyline enacted by interesting stars. Any movie with Ernest Borgnine, Robert Vaughn, Oliver Reed and Herbert Lom can't be all bad, and *Skeleton Coast* isn't. But how actors of this quality end up in a film like this is hard to fathom.

The four stars play their stereotypical personas: Ernest Borgnine is boisterous and bullying, Robert Vaughn is sophisticated and sarcastic and Herbert Lom is suave and sinister.

And then, there's Oliver Reed...

His character, Capt. Simpson, has no real place in this movie. It seems as though Reed was vacationing in South Africa, heard a film was being made, dropped by to watch and got recruited for a day's work. Simpson is in the plot only to destroy the team's vehicles so that they can move onto the next scene stealing an airplane.

We first see Simpson, head of Diamond Security, as a suspected thief is handcuffed to a Jeep in the rising surf. He won't tell Simpson what he wants to know and will pay for it by drowning. Worse, he used a dog in the theft and Simpson loves dogs.

THIEF: Give me a chance!

SIMPSON (*angry*): You've had your chance, you foolish fellow! You screwed it up, didn't you? You made me kill that sweet little puppy, you fucking bastard! I love animals. I should cut *your* belly open!

Opal, Elia's wife, arrives to inform Simpson that Col. Smith and Rick killed his agent. Simpson was having Smith followed because he suspected Smith of being a diamond thief. He's amused to learn that Smith is in Africa to rescue his rebel-supporting son. Opal and Simpson then have sex. Simpson, fortunately for the viewer, is fully clothed — we're a long, long way from *Women in Love*. He tracks the team to the desert, blows up their vehicles, laughs, and vanishes from the plot.

Reed plays the part as well as anyone could play such a part, but almost any hardass could have done as well. At least he seems to have enjoyed himself. Most audiences will, too; *Skeleton Coast* isn't hard to watch. At 90 minutes the plot isn't stretched too thin and there are plenty of convincing action scenes. The problem is trying not to remember that the stars appeared in *Marty, Bullitt, Oliver!* and *Night and the City*.

Rage to Kill (1987)

An Action International Picture; released by Action International Pictures in the U.S. in 1987; no U.K. release; color; 94 minutes

Crew— Screenplay-Producer-Director: David Winters; Executive Producer: Hope Holiday; Associate Producer: Jonathan Vanger; Cinematographer: Vincent Cox; Music: Tim James, Syeve McClintock, Mark Macina; Editor: Bill Archer; Production Manager: Debi Netherslade; Location Manager: Trevor Fish; Continuity: Bev Wilbraham; Key Grip: Tony Slotar; Sound: Neil Thain; Wardrobe: Diana Cillers, Yvonne De Neder; Makeup: Anni Taylor; Props: Dicky Classins; Special Effects: Rick Crisswell; Stunts: J. Attean.

Cast— James Ryan (Blaine Stryker), Oliver Reed (Gen. Turner), Cameron Mitchell (Sgt Miller), Henry Cele (Wally Ahn), Maxine John (Trish Baker), Ian Yule (Slade), Sydney Champ (Webster), Liam Cundill (Glen), Lionel Newton (Delaney), Michelle Clark (Lisa), Beverly McLash (Gina), Tapee Motoking (Secretary of Information), Jill Kirkland (Cynthia), Richard Cox (Capt. Martin), John Harvey (President), Brian O'Shaunessay.

Synopsis

On the Caribbean island of St. Heron, a coup is led by American mercenary Gen. Turner (Oliver Reed). His troops attacks a luxury compound for government officials, killing everyone in sight. The president of the United States (John Harvey) is concerned about the situation, especially because American students attend a medical college there. Race driver Blaine Stryker (James Ryan) promises his mother that he will check up on his brother Glen (Lian Cundill), a student at the college. Stryker is captured soon after arrival, tortured and placed under arrest at the college where he finds Glen. Stryker learns that an opposition force, pro-west, is led by Willy Ahn (Henry Cele), who is marked for death by the general. Glen's friend Delaney (Lionel Newton) steals a Jeep to scout the area and finds an abandoned nuclear power plant housing Soviet missiles. Trish Baker (Maxine John), a reporter, confronts the general about the ban he's placed on the press. To placate her, he takes her to the college to see a friend. Stryker is being interrogated and is spared death by Sgt. Miller (Cameron Mitchell), who says he doesn't want the additional problem of a murdered prominent American. Miller later reveals himself to Stryker as a CIA agent in league with Willy Ahn. The general plans to decimate the college and blame it on Ahn as Miller informs Washington that Soviet missiles are being assembled. When Washington stalls, Miller demands that Ahn attack the power plant; Stryker is concerned about loss of lives. A combined force of Ahn's men and students move on the missiles as the president sends in the Marines. As Ahn's men converge on the general's headquarters, he commits suicide.

Comment

The misleadingly titled *Rage to Kill* begins with an intriguing and topical premise: The military takeover of a small island does not strain our credibility, and the plight of the college students caught up in the events adds to our interest.

So does the first scene. A heavily guarded luxury compound is raided by terrorists led by a camouflage-suited Reed as the general. He cold-bloodedly fires with a machine-gun at swimmers and tennis players from a helicopter. A government official, who knows he's going to die, begs for the lives of his wife and child. The general, smiling, kills him and then his wife. The child runs screaming across the lawn and is shot by one of the general's minions. The general is not pleased.

> SOLDIER: General — the revolution has started!
>
> GENERAL: It's finished for you, soldier — we don't kill children, see? We don't kill children!

But we do, apparently, kill those who disobey; the general shoots out the soldier's kneecaps, then swings the helicopter blades into the wounded man.

Reed looks perfect as the rogue general and, as expected, his American accent is dead-on. Unfortunately *Rage to Kill* goes downhill — quickly — after the effective opening despite Reed's good performance. It's not James Ryan's fault either. He plays Blaine as a mini–Rambo and does it pretty well. If we stop to wonder how a racing driver has the necessary skills to take on an army — well, it's only a movie — and not a very good one.

What kills *Rage to Kill* is the inclusion of several ludicrous scenes that lower the film into the realm of an exploitation flick, like a T&A scene of college girls in cut-off leotards at an exercise class, the general and his girlfriend lounging in the hot tub with another couple, and the finally aroused students taking on the mercenaries with automatic weapons. We can buy the hero doing this, but...

Perhaps the worst scene might be a phone ringing next to a bed. A hand reaches out to answer it from under a quilt, revealing two naked girls as the guy shouts into the phone. Yes, the hand belongs to Oliver Reed.

Fortunately, he gets to make up for this in the final scene. As Ahn's forces overrun his compound, the general knows the end has come and addresses his troops: "It's all over. And he's won. Take your leave and make the best deal you can for yourselves." The lines are delivered calmly, rationally, without emotion. He then shoots himself in the head. The scene is so effective, it seems to belong in another movie.

Rage to Kill delivers pretty much what one would expect. The action scenes are well staged, the effects are okay, the sex scenes are predictable, reasonably tasteful, and don't intrude too much on the minimal plot. Location filming adds a touch of realism.

Other than the two male leads (who are much better than the film required), most of the remaining cast members are pretty much indistinguishable. Two exceptions: old pro Cameron Mitchell, who has been wonderful, is not, and Henry Cele, who is very convincing.

Rage to Kill took its star yet another step away from the days of *The System* and *Women in Love*, but his performance was nothing to be ashamed of, even if the film was.

"A mishmash politically somewhere to the right of Clint Eastwood's *Heartbreak Ridge*, but typical of today's home video fare. Filmmaker David Winters manages to mix in several genres what with torture and sadism scenes, sexy co-eds in the shower and his trademark aerobics class footage. Unfortunately most of the excitement is in the opening reels" (*Variety*, February 8, 1989).

Gor (1987)

Cannon Films; Cannon International; released by Cannon Film Distributors in the U.S. in 1988; no U.K. release

Crew— Director: Fritz Kiersch; Screenplay: Rick Marx, Harry Alan Towers; from the novel *Tarnsman of Gor* by John Norman; Producers: Avi Lerner, Harry Alan Towers; Cinematographer: Hans Kuhle Jr.; Film Editors: Ken Borstein, Max Lemon; Casting: Don Pemrick; Production Design: Hans Nol; Key Makeup Artist: Colin Polson; Makeup: Debbie Christiani, Ann Dempsey, Tessa Scott; Executive in Charge of Production: Rony Yacov; Production Supervisor: John Stodel; Post-Production Supervisors: Michael Alden, Alain Jakubowicz; Assistant Director: Cedric Sundstrom; Second Assistant Director: Marc Roper; Third Assistant Director: Sally Ann Caro; Set Dresser: Cecily Chase; Assistant Set Dressers: Jeffrey Bezuidenhout, June Martens; Production Buyer: Brandon Bergman; Property Master: Patrick Willis; Assistant Property Master: Ben Horowitz; Draughtsman: Geoffrey Hill; Construction Coordinator: Ian Mulder; Sound Editor: Bill Asher; Assistant Sound Editor: Jeanne Fourie; Stunt Coordinator: Reo Ruiters; Camera Operator: Nick Heroldt; Continuity: Marlow De Mardt.

Cast— Urbano Barberini (Tarl Cabot), Rebecca Ferratti (Talena), Jack Palance (Xenos), Paul L. Smith (Surbus), Oliver Reed (Sarm), Larry Taylor (King Marlenus), Graham Clarke (Drusus), Janine Denison (Brandy), Donna Denton (Queen Lara), Jennifer Oltmann (Tafa), Martina Brockschmidt (Doma), Ann Power (Beverly), Arnold Vosloo (Norman), Chris du Plessis (Sarsam), Ivan Kruger (Sarm's Rider), Joe Ribeiro (Auctioneer), Visser di Plessis (Compound Guard), Philip Van der Byl (Whipman), George Magnussen (Old Man), Nigel Chipps (Hup), Fred Potgieter (Brand Master), Etty Orgad, Amanda Haramis (Hooded Women), Eve Joss (Auction Slave), Bobby Lovegreen (Sarsam's Rider), Rick Skidmore (Prisoner), Vic Tearnan, Andre du Plessis (Bodyguards), Fred Swart (Feast Master), Nobby Clarke (Merchant), Alex Heyns (The Elder), Rufus Swart (Torm).

Synopsis

In the present, on a New Hampshire college campus, Tarl Cabot (Urbano Barberini), a young Italian exchange professor of physical science, has trouble with women. His beautiful physics assistant Beverly (Ann Power) isn't interested in pursuing their work during the vacation and so he sets off alone, in an electric storm. On his finger is a strange ring, treasured by all his ancestors. The professor is suddenly blinded by a flash of lightning that sends him on an inter-dimensional journey to the past.

On the planet of Gor, Tarl becomes aware of a bloody massacre of the villagers Ko-Ro-Ba by the forces of the priest-king Sarm (Oliver Reed). Forced to witness the murder of hundreds of villagers and the capture of their precious mystic Home Stone, Tarl is horrified. He is accidentally drawn into the battle when he kills Sarsam (Steffan Erikh), the king's son, following which he is hailed as the savior of the people. He promises to retrieve their Home Stone and those of the other villages Sarm has pillaged in his drive to create a huge empire. It's not an altruistic promise: Tarl realizes that he needs the Stone to get himself home to Earth and the present when he sees the stone glow in the same way as his ring.

He joins Talena (Rebecca Ferratti), daughter of the Ko-Ro-Ban King Marlenus (Larry Taylor), the Elder (Alex Heyns) and young warrior Torm (Rufus Swart). Torm, Tarl's peer, is chosen to teach Tarl how to fight in the manner of Gor with ancient weapons. The two also both have a great interest in Talena, and Torm becomes jealous as Talena admires Tarl's growing aptitude with the sword. They set off across the deserts of Gor, travelling on a prehistoric creature to facilitate their journey. They meet all kinds of hazards: outlaws, deserts, mountains and bad weather. They encounter Sarm's warriors and travel through a barbarian town populated with nomads, traders and slavers. Although Tarl is shocked by the slave market and bound women, the others accept it as the norm and even bind Talena so as not to be conspicuous. They meet Hup (Nigel Chipps), a blonde midget who offers to guide them to the realm of Sarm. Often more a hindrance than a help, he cheers them all up when they become discouraged.

Eventually reaching Sarm's fortress, they release Marlenus and the slaves. Sarm is killed in the thick of the fighting and his forces defeated. The Home Stones are retrieved and returned to their villages as freedom returns to Gor. Tarl has a dilemma: Should he go home to Earth or stay and enjoy his increasingly close relationship with Talena? It would seem that he is at home on Gor, since his ring fits perfectly into a chip in the Home Stone of Ko-Ro-Ba. Perhaps there are more adventures to come...

Comment

When we first see Sarm the priest-king (Reed), he is astride his horse, directing a battle from a ridge. The costumes are all Conan-Lite; the interesting thing is that Reed wears his with dignity and a show of strength. He has that wonderful ability, like his friend Christopher Lee, to wear any period or genre costume without looking out of place or uncomfortable. He plays the Sarm with a mixture of majesty, craftiness, cruelty and downright villainy, stealing the mystical stones from all the "kingdoms" around him to make his empire stronger. If he was wearing Norse gear, he'd make a good Beowulf. He rules a kingdom where the court runs according to his whims, slave girls fight for his pleasure, he drinks and eats to excess and brawls when he thinks it's necessary. The Reed signature whisper-and-roar are used to good effect and one can't help but be a little sad when he gets his comeuppance.

Gor really does appear to be Conan-Lite. Menahem Golan and Yoram Globus filmed it along with several other sword-and-sorcery pictures to milk the market at the time. According to *Moria: The SF, Horror and Fantasy Film Review* (September 6, 2008): "A clearly impoverished Oliver Reed has been employed as the bad warlord and seems to be having fun. Jack Palance has been given top billing along with Reed, but only turns up a cameo of less than a minute at the end." This is probably because the sequel, shot back to back to save money, was *Outlaw of Gor sans* Reed but with a larger Palance presence.

Gor was based on the highly controversial series of fantasy–SF novels of John Norman, the *nom de plume* of John Lange Jr., an associate philosophy professor at Queens College in New York. *Gor* has its roots in Edgar Rice Burroughs' John Carter, Warlord of Mars by way of Robert E. Howard's barbarian fantasies. The first half-dozen were fairly routine heroic-human-versus-various-adversaries on the planet Gor. The controversy erupted when, as the series progressed, Gor's society of slavery began to focus on female, submissive, sexual slavery and became more overtly pornographic in content. Norman allegedly came to believe that his writings mirrored the natural status of things; he frequently engaged in philosophical discussions on "women's naturally submissive position to men and how an increasing awareness of this subservient role and the enjoyment of the infliction of pain by the master increased sexual desire." Naturally there was a feminist backlash in the '80s and many bookstores withdrew the books. Interestingly, there are reported to be any number of Gorean groups, in real life as well as online, which continue to thrive. This philosophy is even more antediluvian than Reed's own avowed belief that he was the provider and his woman was lover-helpmate-mother and that he was (or should be) the focus of her universe.

"John Norman's popular series of pulpy adventure novels might have made good movie material a few years back but the sword and sorcery genre has been tapped out for some time now and *Gor* doesn't bring anything new to the party. The movie is competent enough though and the kids may enjoy it" (*Video Reviews*, January 1989); "*Gor* is a sword and sorcery vehicle that seems geared to under 16 audiences despite some pastiche erotica" (*Variety*, May 13, 1987).

Shot in Italy, as all Golan and Globus' sword-and-sorcery movies were, it was poorly dubbed; several Italian actors took leading roles including the pedestrian Urbano Barberini whose name is more interesting than his performance. While adapting the novel well, the movie leans towards the adventure rather than the bondage genre — fortunately. With luck, Reed got a good salary and enjoyed the Italian sunshine; he acquitted himself as well as his role allowed and seemed to be enjoying himself.

The Misfit Brigade (1987)

Panorama; released by Trans World Entertainment in the U.S. in 1988; no U.K. release; filmed at Avala Film Studios, Belgrade; Technicolor; 100 minutes

Crew— Director: Gordon Hessler; Producers: Just Betzer, Benni Korzen, Milos Antic; Screenplay: Nelson Gidding; Photography; George n Nikolic; Editor: Bob Gordon; Music: Ole Hoyer; Production Design: Vladislav Lasic; Camera: Milija Zivotic; Costumes; Mirjana Ostojic; Makeup: Rafko Rustic; Special Effects: Baban Zivkovic; Fights: Jay O. Sanders.

Cast— Bruce Davison (Porta), David Patrick Kelly (The Legionnaire), Don W. Moffett (Captain von Barring), Jay O. Sanders (Tiny), Keith Szarabajka ("Old Man"), Oliver Reed (The General), David Carradine (Colonel von Weisshagen), Branko Vidak (Stege), Stravko Stimac (Sven), Bons Kommenic (Baver), Andrija Maricic (Muller), Anton Sosic (Freckles), Sveltislav Gome (Siegfried), Gordon Bjelica (Russian Officer), Irene Prosen (Madame), Lidija Pletl (Irma).

Synopsis

It's 1943 and Germany is losing the war; desperate measures are required. One of them is to use criminals to replace the depleted ranks of the regular troops. A group of misfits, more or less led by Porta (Bruce Davison), is first placed in charge of a funeral detail which they solve by using a tank to bury the SS brigade under a pile of rubble. The Legionnaire (David Patrick Kelly) is accepted into the group after he survives a savage beating by the gigantic Tiny (Jay O. Sanders). Colonel von Weisshagen (David Carradine) places the reluctant Captain von Barring (Don W. Moffett) in charge of the

Misfits, who are detailed to the Russian Front to blow up a train. On their way to the deployment, the Misfits engage in a fierce tank battle and prove that they have skills and courage far in excess of their superiors' expectations. Their mission is accomplished and they return to base where they are to receive the Iron Cross and, they hope, clemency for their previous criminal behavior.

Despite their less than sterling backgrounds, the Misfits are disgusted by the killing they were forced to do and have no belief in the Nazi cause. When the general (Oliver Reed) is about to present their medals, the Misfits infuriate him with their lack of respect and decorum. He explodes, threatening them with prison or a return to the Front. The Misfits, led by Porta, place the general and the colonel in front of an airplane and shoot them.

Comment

The Misfit Brigade aka *Wheels of Terror* was based on a series of novels by Sven Hassel based on his experiences in World War II ... with hopefully a nod to the fiction of *The Dirty Dozen* (1967). The twist: The Misfit heroes of the story are Nazis!

The film was a U.S.-British production filmed in and around Belgrade and it looks great. The costumes, sets, military equipment and scenery are first-rate and beautifully photographed.

Not that *The Misfit Brigade* was intended to be an instructional manual, but one of its pleasures is that it gives the viewer a sense of how the weapons — especially the tanks — actually work. Another plus for the viewer is that the decision was made to forgo German accents for the characters. They're *all* German — there's not an Englishman to be seen or heard — so it's not necessary to differentiate between them.

The story of a group of derelicts being given one last chance for redemption is an old and familiar one, but is very well presented by director Gordon Hessler, who keeps the 100 minutes moving quickly. The acting is good, too, with Bruce Davison a standout as the nominal hero. Jay O. Sanders (who also ably supervised the fight scenes) is effective as a brutal psycho giant (named Tiny) with some

feelings — a part that the young Reed might well have played.

David Carradine and Reed were thrown into the mix to class the film up a bit, which they do with ease. Carradine plays the "Lee Marvin role" and appears sparingly throughout the movie, but Reed appears only in the final minutes. Both make the most of their limited screen time.

Reed makes quite an entrance, arriving by plane to decorate the Misfits who, he discovers, are more misfit than he ever could have imagined. He, as the general, is not impressed by the louts before him, and makes that quite clear to Carradine's colonel.

> THE GENERAL (*snarling*): Are these the cutthroats you expected me to decorate? I suppose this fellow is wearing the latest in military millinery?
>
> TINY: No, it's a Russian douche-bag.
>
> THE GENERAL (*snarling and twitching*): I want this man ... court-martialed and I want the rest of these rats on the Eastern Front!

It's difficult to imagine anyone looking angrier than he does in this scene; he literally quivers with disgust and barely seems able to avoid personally shooting the Misfits.

They take care of that by shooting both him and the colonel.

As the general and the colonel realize what's happening, they exchange glances that range from incredulity to shock to resignation as the shots wind down into ultra-slow motion. It's a well-played, effective, unexpected scene that caps off an unexpectedly pretty good movie.

Although Reed could hardly have spent more than a day or two on the set, he made the most of his time to indulge his love of animals by adopting a scruffy, half-starved hound. "He first fed it from his own plate and then ordered a daily bowl of food for the stray. By the end of the shoot he was so attached to the animal that he paid for it to be flown back to Britain and quarantined.... Oliver named the dog 'The General' after his part in the film" (Goodwin, 235).

The Misfit Brigade was not widely reviewed. *Variety* (February 11, 1987) caught the film in Copenhagen: "Devoid of high-minded artistic ambition, it is likely to do fast theatrical playoff business wherever it is picked up before heading for near-immortality as a surefire video item." Fair enough.

The Misfit Brigade is well worth a look. Its action scenes are exciting, the ensemble acting is all that one could want, and there's just enough comedy and pathos. Just don't expect to see much of Reed. But what little there is — is terrific.

Hold My Hand, I'm Dying (1988)

(Aka *Blind Justice*) A Lars International Picture; A Burlington Enterprises/Mark Cassidy Production; released on DVD in the U.S. by Platinum Disc; no U.K. release; 111 minutes; color

Crew— Director: Terence Ryan; Producer: Mark Cassidy; Co-producer: Christopher Coy; Executive Producers: Pamela Sherlin, Patricia Rowley; Screenplay: Mark Ezra; based on the Novel *Hold My Hand, I'm Dying* by John Gordon Davis; Cinematographer: Hanro Mohr; Music: Julian Laxton, Patricia Blerk; Production Design: Jon-Jon Lambon; Editors: David Heitner, Max Lemor; Location Manager: Pete Ball; Assistant Director; Mark Roper; Sound: Phillip Rey, Moley De Beer; Gaffer: Robbie Wilter; Best Boy: Elliot Sewpe; Key Grip: Juni Geldenboys; Sets: Garry Meilatith; Armorer: Paul Meyers; Wardrobe: Lisa Perry; Hair Stylist: Wendy White; Stunts; Reo Ruites; Special Effects; Dawe Van Heerden.

Cast— Christopher Cazenove (Joe Mahoney), Edita Brychta (Suzanne), Patrick Shai (Sampson), Oliver Reed (Ian Ballinger), Henry Cele (Kamisu), Sigfried Mynhardt (Mr. de Villiers), Robin Smith (Max), Fats Dibetso (Eddie), Thapelo Mofukeng (Police Sergeant), Clive Scott (Auctioneer), Margaret Heale (Mrs. Smedley).

Synopsis

Rhodesia, 1958. Deputy Commissioner Joe Mahoney (Christopher Cazenove) is a decent man doing his best to be fair in his administration of blacks in the British Colony. A huge area is to be flooded to create a dam to produce hydro-electric power and thousands must be displaced. Factions within the colony want independence, and terrorism is rife. Joe's servant (and friend) Sampson (Patrick Shai) disagrees with the government position, but is loyal to Joe. While trekking to facilitate the migration, they meet Suzie (Edita Brychta), whose car has broken down. She, too, is offended by the political situation, but believes in Joe's honesty and commitment. They soon develop a bond as he returns her to the family farm. When tribal leader Max (Robin Smith) objects to the move, Joe sends Sampson with him for protection. After Max commits suicide, Joe becomes disillusioned and returns to England for five years. One rainy night he's hit by a car and helped by a black man to whom he tells his troubles. Encouraged by the stranger, Joe returns to Rhodesia, where he finds everything has changed. When he arrives at his old club he confronts a group of whites beating a black man. He is saved from the mob by Ballinger (Oliver Reed), who feigns anger at him and, in the confusion, spirits him away. Joe and Sampson, who now works for Suzie, are reunited and attend an auction of a farm. Presiding over the auction is Ballinger, who is actually a minister of religion. Joe outbids Kamisu (Henry Cele), a local terrorist, for the land. When a white racist, Mrs. Smedley (Margaret Heale), provokes a riot, Ballinger is killed while breaking it up. Kamisu forces Sampson to set fire to Suzy's farm and, despite her intervention with Joe, Sampson is hanged. The local police sergeant (Thapelo Mofukeng) is set ablaze and says to Joe, "Hold my hand, I'm dying."

Comment

There is no mention of this movie at the Lincoln Center for Performing Arts or the British Film Institute. The Internet Movie Database passes it off with a few desultory comments by subscribers — which is more reviewing than *Variety* did. Yet, in the opinion of the authors, it is an excellent film in every possible way, with a standout supporting performance from Oliver Reed — possibly his best until *Gladiator* a decade later.

Filmed in South Africa in 1988 and based on John Gordon Davis' 1967 novel *Hold My Hand, I'm Dying*, the movie does not seem to have been theatrically released in the United Kingdom or the United States. The print viewed by the authors was titled *Blind Justice* and was released on DVD in 2005.

The film boasts no superstars; Reed is the only generally recognized name. Most of the roles are played, not surprisingly, by Africans. Both Patrick Shai, as the loyal Sampson, and Henry Cele, as the terrorist Kamisu, are excellent. Cele has little to say but gets the job done with a most chilling smile — the complete antithesis of his only other well-known major performance in the TV series *Chaka Zulu*.

Christopher Cazenove is perfect as the conflicted Joe. He never allows his high-minded ideals to appear sanctimonious, and his relationship with Sampson comes across as genuine friendship despite the racial and political barriers placed between them. His well-justified anger at the treatment of blacks comes to a boil when he intervenes in a beating in his old club. Just before the mob turns its fury on him, a huge presence enters the bar from the backroom, face contorted with rage. Ballinger bellows, "We've been looking for you all fucking day. Now you get out of here. As far as I'm concerned, the very sight of you makes me want to puke!" Reed's "anger" is terrifying. Ballinger explains that terrorist groups are forming and burning white-owned farms as he drives the thankful Joe to Suzie's farm.

When a nearby farmer, fearing a terrorist attack, puts his farm up for auction, Joe, Suzie and Sampson attend. Joe is stunned to see the "Reverend" Ian Ballinger, calm and dignified in a white suit, presiding over the auction.

JOE: You're full of surprises.

BALLINGER: You should know that I go where the people are. I find I get a bigger flock here than in church.

The Reverend Ballinger recites a prayer and closes by saying, "In God we trust; the rest of us pay cash." And he smiles; a rare thing for an Oliver Reed character during this period of his career. It's a shock, actually; Reed loses, instantly, 25 years of age. He looks like the young man who starred in *The Curse of the Werewolf* and *Captain Clegg*. It's both gratifying and sad at the same time.

The Reverend Ballinger's smile is to be short-lived. A nasty racial incident is sparked when the vile Mrs. Smedley (played quite chillingly by Margaret Heale) foolishly berates the local terrorist leader Kamisu, telling him he has no place at the whites-only auction. A fight erupts, and Ballinger is stabbed and dies in Joe's arms.

The relationship between Joe and Sampson is complex but well and realistically presented by both excellent actors. It never tips over into sugary sentiment. Sampson burns Suzie's farm because he must; his family will be killed by the terrorists if he refuses. Joe and Suzie, although far from happy about it, do not blame Sampson, and their empathy for his situation rings true. They visit him in his cell in a very emotional scene to beg him to explain his actions to the judge. He refuses; he'd rather die than have his family killed.

As Sampson stands on the gallows, the rope around his neck, he fantasizes about standing on a veranda at sunset with Joe and Suzie. They are laughing and hugging. Then — the trap door opens and he falls to his death. The scene on the veranda is shown again, but minus Sampson. It is a brilliant moment and packs quite a punch.

Hold My Hand, I'm Dying is a wonderful film that somehow fell between the cracks. It succeeds on every level; its acting, script, photography, costumes, sets, music and direction are all first-class. If it had received a proper release, it might have restored Reed's reputation before *Gladiator* did, albeit too late.

Producer-director Terence Ryan, who excelled at both roles, was born in London and was a founding member of the Irish Academy of Film. He began his career in 1972 and promptly won a BAFTA award for the best short feature. In 1980 he and Ray Marshall formed Opix Films and produced 120 movies and television features over the following twelve years. In 1988, the year in which *Hold My Hand, I'm Dying* was shot, he won the gold medal at the Houston Film Festival for producing and directing *Going Home*, a World War II drama. All this makes the obscurity of *Hold My Hand, I'm Dying* even harder to understand.

The Adventures of Baron Munchausen (1988)

Allied Filmmakers; Columbia Pictures Corporation; Laura Film; Prominent Features;

released by Columbia Pictures in the U.K. in 1989 and in the U.S. in 1989

Crew—Director: Terry Gilliam; Writers: Rudolph Erich Raspe, Gottfiried August Burger (both uncredited); Screenplay: Charles McKeown, Terry Gilliam; Producer: Thomas Schuhly; Co-Producer: Ray Cooper; Executive Producer: Jake Eberts; Supervising Producer: Stratton Leopold; Line Producer: David Tomblin; Original Music: Eric Idle, Michael Kamen; Cinematographer: Giuseppe Rotunno; Film Editor: Peter Hollywood; Casting: Francesco Cinieri, Irene Lambe, Margery Simkin; Production Design: Dante Ferretti; Art Directors: Teresa Barbasso, Giorgio Giovannini, Nazzareno Piana, Massimo Razzi; Set Decorator: Francesco Lo Schiavo; Costume Design: Gabriella Pescucci; Makeup and Hair Designer: Maggie Weston; Production Supervisor: Mario Pisani; Property Masters: Charles Torbett, Gianni Fiumi; Sculptor: Gianni Gianese; Supervising Sound Editor: Peter Pennell; Special Effects: Richard Conway; Camera Operator: Franco Bruni; Unit Publicist: Eugene Rizzo.

Cast—John Neville (Hieronymus Karl Frederick Baron von Munchausen), Eric Idle (Desmond/Berthold), Sarah Polley (Sally Salt), Oliver Reed (Vulcan), Charles McKeown (Rupert/Adolphus), Winston Dennis (Bill/Albrecht), Jack Purvis (Jeremy/Gustavus), Valentina Cortese (Queen Ariadne/Violet), Jonathan Pryce (The Right Ordinary Horatio Jackson), Bill Peterson (Henry Salt), Peter Jeffrey (Sultan), Uma Thurman (Venus/Rose), Alison Steadman (Daisy), Ray Cooper (Functionary), Don Henderson (Commander), Robin Williams as Ray D Tutto! (King of the Moon), Sting (Herois Officer), Andrew Maclachlan (Colonel), Mohamed Badrasalem (Executioner), Kiran Shah (Assistant), Franco Adduci (Treasurer), Jose Lifante (Dr. Death), Ettore Martini (First General), Antonio Pistollo (Second General), Michael Polley, Tony Smart (Gunners).

Synopsis

In a walled city at the end of the 18th century under siege from the Turkish Army, the Henry Salt Theatre Company is staging a re-enactment of the baron's exploits. When the real baron stands up in the audience and shouts that the play is based on falsehoods, only young Sally Salt (Sarah Polley) believes him. The baron promises Sally that if he could only find his four friends — Albrecht, stronger than a giant, Berthold, who runs faster than the wind, Adolphus, who sees further than a telescope, and Gustavus, who can blow harder than a hurricane — the town's sultan would be outwitted and the siege would be lifted. As the creaky old play takes on a new and vivid life, the duo relive

the past while fighting the present, taking off in a hot-air balloon made of silk underwear to find the four missing friends. The siege is the baron's fault because he beat the sultan in a bet and angered him. The journey takes the pair to unlikely places: the moon, ruled by a nutty queen and king whose heads and bodies are detachable, and the underworld, domain of Vulcan (Oliver Reed), shouting with a Sheffield accent, a beast whose impossibly lovely wife becomes enamored of the baron. The enraged Vulcan throws the old soldier and his band into a forbidding vortex through which they pass into a sea and the mouth of a sea monster where they are all reunited. They arrive home in the midst of a huge battle and liberate the town from the Turks. But the specter of death that has been pursuing the baron comes to pay a final visit.

Comment

This is a physically opulent film with scenery and costumes that ravish the eyes. The number of sets seems countless and every one, conceived on a grand scale, bristles with endlessly clever details. "Special effects man Richard Conway's ingenuity has been tested every step of the way, and the film's hallmark may well be its incredibly elaborate fantastical set-pieces, which include the baron shooting through the night over Turkish troops clinging to a cannonball.... The effects are generally so successful that these events nearly appear normal" (*Variety*, January 18, 1989). Director-co-writer Terry Gilliam tried to get Marlon Brando for Vulcan and had a happy afternoon discussing the project until the producer and Brando's agent turned up! Reed was then cast and had a whale of a time with the part. "Weighing in at around 49 million dollars, Terry Gilliam's free-falling fantasy lands with a dull thud" (*Sunday Express*, March 19, 1989); "Oliver Reed is a sturdy Vulcan, facing trooble (sic) at t'dark Satanic mill" (*Mail on Sunday*, March 19, 1989); "Oliver Reed brings proceedings to life as a splendidly irascible King of the Underworld who takes exception to Munchausen chatting up his wife" (*Today*, March 17, 1989); "Oliver Reed as Vulcan in his best role for many years" (*Daily Mirror*, March 17, 1989); "Oliver Reed makes a roistering Vulcan" (*Village Voice*, March 19, 1989).

The film was nominated for Oscars for Best Art Direction–Set Decoration, Best Costume Design, Best Effects Visual Effects and Best Makeup. It won BAFTA Film Awards for Best Costume Design, Best Makeup Artist, Best Production Design and was nominated for Best Special Effects.

When Gilliam saw the rushes from Reed's Vulcan, he was impressed when the actor said he'd reined in his performance. Gilliam suggested that he should go for it, so the following day, Reed did. The result is pure pantomime, and as such, adds another genre to the Reed canon.

Captive Rage (1988)

The Movie Group; Oka Film Productions Ltd.; released in the U.S. on video by Forum Home Video in 1988 and in the U.K. on DVD by ILC Ltd. in 2002

Crew— Director: Cedric Sundstrom; Writers: Rick Marx, Cedric Sundstom, Peter Welbeck (aka Harry Alan Towers); Executive Producer: Avi Lerner; Producer: Harry Alan Towers; Co-Producers: Keith Rosenbaum, Barry Wood; Original Music: Mick Hope Bailie, Mark Mitchell; Cinematography: George Bartels; Film Editor: Allan Morrison; Production Design: George Canes; Special Effects Makeup: Adam Behr; Second Unit Director: Ed Anders: Property Master: David Glasscoe; Animatronic Fabricator: Adam Behr; Special Effects: Greg Pitts; Stunt Coordinator: Ed Anders; Stunt Arranger: Paul Siebert; Stunt Team: Angel Castignani, Maureen Lahoud, Isaac Mavimbella, Gavin Mey, Graham Press, Guy Pringle, Raymond Sammel, Tyrone Stevenson, Edgar Texera, Melony Walker.

Cast— Oliver Reed (General Belmondo), Robert Vaughn (Eduard Delacorte), Claudia Udy (Chiga), Lisa Rinna (Lucy Delacorte), Maureen Kedes (Jan), Sharon Schaffer (Cindy), Diana Tilden-Davis (Dori), Deon Stewardson (Claude Belmondo), Frank Notaro (Romero), Rufus Swart (Eddie), Greg Latter (Bud), Trish Downing (Maria), Adrian Waldron (Miguel), Lynne White (Ms. Renay), Carrie Glyn (Kate), Cissy Thompson (Laurie), Martin Dewee (Andre), Richard Loring (Coke Dealer), Grant Preston, Warren Batchelor (DEA Officials), Leon Capon (Martinez), Nick Collis (Airline Captain), Bob Haber (TV Newscaster).

Synopsis

Innocent college girls become the pawns in a deadly game of revenge when a South American cocaine baron, Gen. Belmondo (Oliver Reed), retaliates against the chief of the American Intelligence Agency Eduard Delacorte (Robert Vaughn) by kidnapping Delacorte's daughter Lucy (Lisa Rinna) for jailing his son Claude (Deon Stewardson) on drug charges. Belmondo keeps his abductees imprisoned in the jungle but four girls manage to steal some machine-guns and use them to escape. The general tracks them down until they finally find a radio and expose his location.

Comment

This is bottom-of-the-barrel girls-and-guns nonsense. The girls are brave, defiant and athletic, and very easy on the eye — well, it *is* a Harry Alan Towers offering, after all. However, for college girls, their expertise with knives, explosives and guns never gets explained; even the geologists they later meet could be on vacation from the CIA.

We hope Reed had a good payday and enjoyed a holiday while on location — after all, with his work ethic, there doesn't seem to be much time left in any year in his career for a holiday.

This is direct-to-video B movie fodder, with nudity and rape. The authors could find no copy of the film to review.

The Revenger (1989)

Take Two Films; released by Action International Pictures in the U.S.; no U.K. release

Crew— Director: Cedric Sundstron; Writer: John Cianetti; Producers: Gregory Vanger, Jonathan Vanger; Executive Producer: Lynne Widgrow: Original Music: Garm Beall, Tim James, Steve McClintock; Cinematographer: George Bartels; Film Editors: Mark Baard, Paul O'Bryan; Art Director: Ruth Strimling; Costume Design: Dianna Cilliers; Hair Stylist: Jennifer Elson; Makeup: Debbie Nicoll; Assistant Makeup: Beverly House; Production Manager: Trevor Fish; First Assistant Director: Sally Ann Caro; Second Assistant Director: Sheila Hall; Third Assistant Director: Daron Chatz; Property Master: Dirk Buchanan; Scenic Artist: Roland Hunter; Construction Manager: John Tooley; Set Dresser: Claire Walker; Sound Editors: Kami Asgar, Jason Coleman;

Special Effects Coordinator: Nick Creswell; Stunt Coordinator: Roland Jansen; Wardrobe Mistress: Sylvia Vanden; Location Manager; Martin Jaconson.

Cast— Oliver Reed (Jack Fisher), Frank Zagarino (Mike Keller), Jeff Weston (Harry Crawford), Nancy Mulford (Lisa), Sean Taylor (Tyron Richardson), Norman Anstey (Detective Marsh), John Cianetti (Willie Testa), John Pasternack (Big John Barron), Robin Smith (Chuck), Frank Notaro (Freddie), Al Taraki (Stoke), Jamie Bartlett (Haber), Arnold Vosloo (Mackie), John Maythem (Eliot Russell), Michael Brunner (Mel), Debra, Nico (Couple Making Love), Candy-Lee, Kenny (Couple Making Love, Murder Scene), Fats Bookhalane (Frank Price), Nobby Clark, Guy Pringle (Guards), Musetta Vander (Marissa), Dan Roberts, Sean Higgs, Reon Botha (Policemen), Cathy Vinacombe (News Reporter), Elizabeth Giordano (Carol), Jennifer (Kimberley Stark), Bill Olmstead (Chopper Pilot).

Synopsis

Mike Keller (Frank Zagarino), mean sax player, gets jailed while helping his acquaintance Mackie (Arnold Vosloo) by being his driver. Mackie's car happens to have a dead body in the trunk, so naturally he needs another car.

The police chase them and, after Mackie stashes a mysterious bundle which contains half a million dollars belonging to psychotic mob boss Jack Fisher (Oliver Reed), they are caught and Mackie dies in a gun battle. Guilty by association, Mike goes to jail. On his release three years down the line, he painfully tries to rebuild his relationship with his wife Lisa (Nancy Mulford). Fisher kidnaps Lisa and demands his money back; Mike retrieves the bundle and, with the help of his old friend Harry (Jeff Watson), goes to get Lisa back. But not before Fisher has raped her just because he can. They rescue Lisa, killing Fisher's current girlfriend in the process, and he goes after them as they try to escape. They run to Harry's cabin (equipped like something out of *Rambo*) where they make a stand against Fisher, his mob and his friendly, paid-for policemen. All comes right in the end, with all the bad guys dead and the good guys (and girl) in the Caribbean with the half-million dollars for compensation.

Comment

Mixed with quality films like *Hold My Hand, I'm Dying, The Adventures of Baron Munchausen* and *The Return of the Musketeers, The Revenger* was a return for Oliver Reed to mindless villainy, the type of role he could play in his sleep ... and often did.

Starring as Keller, the "basically decent guy who gets screwed over by the system," was Frank Zagarino. He had the physical skills to be convincing in the film's many violent scenes and was a good enough actor to get by in the scenes that weren't. We can only sympathize with Keller; he got into trouble for helping a friend — who hasn't? And, once he's in, it's like being stuck in quicksand.

The set-up with his criminal friend Mackie (Arnold Vosloo) works well, and when Keller gets released from prison we know that the mysterious bundle left by the roadside is going to come back to haunt him. We just know something very bad is going to happen.

What happens is Mr. Jack Fisher (Oliver Reed).

We first see Fisher in shadows in the back seat of a car — huge, dressed in black, sporting a large moustache, taking enough coke to kill a horse. Fisher is into just about every nasty thing you can think of, and some that you can't. He has, however, one good quality: He's patient. But after waiting for three years for Keller's release — and the money — his patience has worn thin.

When Keller reunites with Lisa (Nancy Mulford), the scene is played with a believable awkwardness, as one would expect in such a situation. In a clever shot, while the couple are making love, the scene morphs into two porno actors being "directed" by Richardson (Sean Taylor, in a wonderfully sleazy performance), Fisher's main man. It looks like this might be worse than "just" a porno; the "actor" in bed reaches under it for a knife just as the police burst in. A snuff film, perhaps?

When Fisher decides to resort to kidnapping Lisa to get leverage on Keller, we're not surprised, as there doesn't seem to be much he won't do; his message to Keller gets right to the point and is chillingly delivered: "By now you've got a good understanding of the situation. If you fuck with me, you're going to force me to turn your girlfriend into a moving picture star."

A fairly interesting subplot involving

crooked cops on Fisher's payroll is introduced, as is Keller's recruit Harry (Jeff Weston), a regulation Vietnam vet character — and an enjoyably quirky one at that. But these aren't enough to divert us from the standard plotline. Reed has the odd line, "You're pissing me off — why don't you go shopping?" to his whiny girlfriend to add to the amusement; but it isn't enough. The pace picks up a bit when Fisher finds his whore-girlfriend dead in his bed after Keller and Harry have liberated Lisa. Fisher is already on the edge, but now he's way over it; his rage is actually frightening compared with the banality of the rest of the proceedings. For a moment, Fisher stops being simply a very bad man and becomes an animal.

The final, not unexpected shootout at the cabin is adequately staged with Fisher back in control, ordering everyone about — including one of his dirty cops: "I'm asking you to go up to that house, knock on the door, and see if anyone is home. You're a policeman — do what a policeman does. Should I send someone along to hold your hand? I'm not asking you, I'm telling you — before I put an end to your career right now."

When Keller confronts him about Lisa's kidnapping and assault, Fisher is blithely offhand; it was simply business ... no big deal.

KELLER: Was rape part of the deal?

FISHER: Just call it a fringe benefit — no extra charge.

Reed delivers his lines with his usual casual menace, making them seem — almost — to be a part of a better movie. Speaking of casual, Fisher shoots Richardson in the back with all the concern of a man swatting a fly when his lieutenant tries to run off. Fisher then asks, "Does anybody *else* want to leave?"

Fisher gets his after Lisa, in the foolish way of heroines in this type of film, leaves her relatively safe hiding place and runs right into his grasp; Harry shoots him in the back while he uses her as a bargaining chip. With Fisher and Richardson dead, all the bad guys are gone — but wait a minute! Detective Marsh (Norman Anstey) decides to fill the vacuum and make off with the money himself. This comes as a surprise to both the audience and Keller, but he is able to do something about it. After killing Marsh, Keller, Lisa and Harry (whom we thought was dead — another surprise) take off for the Caribbean.

The Revenger isn't Reed's worst movie — it is beyond the scope of the authors to pick the one that is — and he's not terrible in it. But there would be worse to come.

The Revenger does not seem to have had a general theatrical release; no reviews could be found at Lincoln Center or the British Film Institute. The authors viewed a DVD of the movie.

The House of Usher (1989)

A 21st Century Production; Breton Films Ltd.; released by 21st Century Film Corporation and to video by RCA/Columbia Home Pictures in the U.S.; no U.K. release; color; 92 minutes

Crew— Director: Alan Birkinshaw; Producer: Harry Alan Towers; Screenplay: Michael J. Murray; Executive Producer: Ari Lerner; Associate Producer: John Stodel; Cinematographer: Jossi Wein; Editor: Michael J. Duthrie; Production Design: Leonardo Coen Cagli; Special Prosthetic Effects: Scott Wheeler; Production Supervisor: Danny Lerner; Unit Production Manager: Stefan Abendroth; Music: George S. Clinton; Associate Director: K.C. Jones; Art Director: Leith Ridney; Sets: Lisa Hart; Wardrobe: Dianna Cilliers.

Cast— Oliver Reed (Roderick Usher), Donald Pleasence (Walter Usher), Romy Windsor (Molly), Rufus Swart (Ryan), Norman Coombes (Mr. Derek), Anne Stradi (Mrs. Derek), Carole Farquhar (Gwendolyn), Philip Godewa (Dr. Bailey), Leonorah Ince, Jonathan Fairbin (Children).

Synopsis

Molly (Romy Windsor) and Ryan (Rufus Swart), newly engaged, are driving to visit his Uncle Roderick's (Oliver Reed) isolated estate in England. Ryan swerves to avoid hitting two children (Leonorah Ince, Jonathan Fairbin) and slams into a tree. Molly finds her way to the estate and help is sent to get Ryan to the hospital. Roderick and Molly dine. He is suffering from terribly acute senses — he can only eat the blandest foods, must avoid pungent smells and must have near silence. Molly sees portraits of the children but is stunned to learn that they've been dead for 100 years. Roderick is served by Mr. and Mrs. Derek (Norman Coombes and

Anne Stradi) and a mute child, Gwendolyn (Carole Farquhar); all concerned are vague about Ryan's condition. Roderick appears to be overly familiar with Molly and asks very personal questions about her family and general health. Roderick explains that the Usher mansion is crumbling as is the Usher line — he is the last.

Molly's requests to be taken to see Ryan are ignored until Roderick admits that her fiancé bled to death in the car. Dr. Bailey (Philip Godewa) tells Molly that the Ushers have long suffered from a rare blood disorder caused by inbreeding. She tries to get him to take her from the house, but he turns her in to Roderick, then subjects her to a physical exam. Roderick's plan: He will impregnate Molly to continue the line. When Dr. Bailey offers himself as a stand-in, Roderick has Derek kill him. At the funeral service for Ryan, Molly sees his finger move.

But Roderick closes the coffin and inters it in a wall. While following the ghostly children, Molly finds Walter (Donald Pleasence), Roderick's brother, a physical and mental wreck with an electric drill attached to his arm. He has been kept a prisoner for decades and wants the Usher line to end. Molly is drugged and raped by Roderick, followed by a grotesque wedding ceremony. Walter escapes and kills Mrs. Derek (cutting off her head) and Gwendolyn (penetrating her head with the drill). Roderick tells Molly he has impregnated her and is attacked by Walter. The two seemingly die in a fire, as does the just-revived Ryan. Molly suddenly finds herself in the car with Ryan, approaching the estate.

Comment

The House of Usher is a standout in Oliver Reed's filmography. In a career with so many highs and lows, this is one of the lowest. The film is terrible, and so, for the most part, is Reed. And Donald Pleasence is even worse. It's not, of course, entirely their fault; the film was ineptly produced, written and directed. But they signed on; that's their fault.

What makes this even worse is stealing the title from one of Edgar Allan Poe's best stories and one of the best Vincent Price–Roger Cor-

man films. There is practically nothing of the original tale; it's far more Harry Alan Towers than Poe. It's unfortunate that the author, actor and director were unable to sue for defamation of reputation.

The House of Usher was filmed in South Africa, but the exteriors of the Usher estate (also featured in 1973's *The Legend of Hell House*) were shot in England. These images are the best the movie has to offer. The interiors are incredibly unconvincing; the stone looks exactly like the Styrofoam it really is. (One is reminded of Ed Wood productions like *Bride of the Monster*.) The only thing worse than the look of the production is everything else.

We first see Roderick (who, unlike Vincent Price's character, looks nothing like Poe's description), formal in dress and manners, but a bit overly familiar with Molly as he greets her at dinner. He alternates coming on to her with lying about Ryan and bitching about his heightened senses and the terrible food.

It soon becomes reasonably clear that Roderick has engineered their visit and Ryan's "accidental" death. Why? So that he can have sex with Molly to continue the Usher line without resorting to the traditional inbreeding. Why, one wonders, didn't he pay a hooker? In one of the film's most embarrassing scenes (there are so many from which to choose), Roderick delights in Dr. Bailey's examination of Molly.

RODERICK: Well?

DR. BAILEY: Everything is in working order; she's even ovulating.

Molly, not surprisingly, is not flattered.

RODERICK: Molly, I'm so very sorry it had to be done like this, but there's so little time. My family is dying out. Now that Ryan is gone, I'm the last of the line. I have to find a bride. That's why I've chosen you.

MOLLY: Don't touch me! You make me sick!

DR. BAILEY: Women!

Walter Usher is a mess; he makes Roderick look like David Niven. Walter is filthy, cackling and has an electric drill permanently attached to his arm. And he's played, quite badly, by Donald Pleasence. Yes, the same Donald

Pleasence who, like Reed, had been so effective in so many real movies. It's sad and embarrassing to see a real actor like Pleasence in a film like this but he provides one valuable service: He makes Reed's performance seem subtle by comparison.

There's little subtlety in Walter's behavior when he escapes from his room. After promising to help Molly, he promptly cuts off Mrs. Derek's head, puts an apple in her mouth and puts this obscenity on a serving tray. What he does to poor Gwendolyn's face with his arm-mounted electric drill need not be discussed here. As the house begins to (unconvincingly) crumble, Roderick grabs Molly's arm and her attention when he informs her that she is carrying his child. As for Ryan...

> RODERICK: A slow, painful death seemed to be in order. We drugged him and buried him alive. You come flouncing into this house here, seeking your proper English fortune. Here it is! Savor it! You little bitch — do you know what you are? You're nothing!

Ouch! The final scene of this debacle, in addition to not coming soon enough, makes little more sense than what preceded it. Roderick and Walter appear to kill each other — several times, actually — and Ryan (who is not really, really dead) is revived by Molly only to be killed (maybe) by Roderick who then (possibly) dies. Molly escapes from the crumbling, burning mansion only to be attacked by Roderick as he leaps through a window.

And then, believe it or not, we're back in the car with Molly and Ryan, approaching the Usher estate. Could this have all been a dream? And ... who are the children? And who cares?

Although this looks like the work of a first-time filmmaker (if not a junior high school play), Alan Birkinshaw had previously directed *The Man Who Couldn't Get Enough* (1974), *Killer Moon* (1978), *Dead End* (1980) and *Horror Satan* (1982). Producer Towers was involved in countless low-budget productions, and most of them — including several with Reed — were far better than this one. In fact, most of them were, at worst watchable. But not this one.

Reed has a few moments — mostly while

ranting — that qualify as acceptable acting, but not nearly enough. *The House of Usher*, to be perfectly clear, is bad. It's not endearingly bad or so bad it's good. It's simply bad. It's so bad that it could have ended a lesser actor's career. But Oliver Reed was no one's lesser actor.

The Return of the Musketeers (1989)

Cine 5; Fildebroc; An Iberoamericana Film Produccion; Timothy Burrill Productions; released by Entertainment Film Distributors in the U.K. and by Universal Pictures in the U.S.; color; 102 minutes

Crew— Director: Richard Lester; Producer: Pierre Spengler; Executive Producers: Mario Sotela, Wayne Drizin; Screenplay: George MacDonald Frazer; from the Alexandre Dumas novel *Twenty Years After*; Music: Jean Claude Petit with the London Symphony Orchestra and the Academy of Ancient Music; Cinematographer: Bernard Lutic; Editor: John Victor Smith; Production Designer: Gil Parrondo; Art Director: Raul Paton; Set Decorator: Michael Seirton; Costume Designer: Yvonne Blake; Production Supervisor: Francisco Molero; Production Managers: Fernando Marquerie, Christian Fuin; First Assistant Director: Clive Reed; Makeup: Jose Antonio Sanchez; Kim Cattrall's Makeup: Cynthia K. Cruz; Hairdresser: Paquita Nunez; Supervising Sound Editor: Les Wiggins; Sound Editors: Colin Miller, Stan Fiferman; Sound Mixer: Jean Louis Ducarme; Sound Re-recording Mixer: Robin O'Donoghue; Dialogue Editor: Archie Ludski; Camera Operators: Freddie Cooper, Alfredo F. Mayo; Location Managers: Vicente Ortega, Alejandro Ruiz, Manolo Garcia; Fight Arranger: William Hobbs; Continuity: Ceri Evans Cooper; Stunt Arranger: Joaquim Parra; Special Effects: Reyes Abades; Models Effects: Meddings Magic Camera Co.

Cast— Michael York (D'Artagnan), Oliver Reed (Athos), Frank Finlay (Porthos), Richard Chamberlain (Aramis), C. Thomas Howell (Raoul), Kim Cattrall (Justine de Winter), Geraldine Chaplin (Queen Anne), Roy Kinnear (Planchet), Christopher Lee (Rochefort), Philippe Noiret (Cardinal Mazarin), Eusebio Lazaro (Beaufort), Alan Howard (Oliver Cromwell), David Birkin (King Louis XIV), Bill Paterson (King Charles I), Jean Pierre Cassel (Cyrano de Bergerac), Servane Ducorps (Olympe), William J. Fletcher (De Guiche), Laure Sabardin (Chevreuse), Marcelline Collard (Lamballe), Pat Roach (French Executioner), Jesus Uryman (Henchman), Fernando de Juan (Breton), Barry Burgess (Young Clerk), Leon Greene (Capt. Groslow), Agata Lys (Duchesse de Longueville), Bob Todd (High Bailiff), Lucy Harwick (Lady in Waiting), Aldo Sambrell (Burly Demonstrator), Jack Taylor (Gentleman on Horseback), Ricardo Palacios (Big Lackey), Luciano Federico (Tall Lackey), Teatro de Camera de Madrid, Carmen Fernandez, Rafael de la Cruz, German Estebas, Jesus Garcia, Fernando Simon (Comedia dell'Arte players).

Synopsis

In 1649, 20 years after the musketeers' last adventure, Oliver Cromwell (Alan Howard) is overthrowing the English King Charles I (Bill Paterson) in England. In France the boy King Louis XIV (David Birkin) sits on the throne while his mother Queen Anne (Geraldine Chaplin) and her lover Cardinal Mazarin (Philippe Noiret) act as regents. They have imprisoned the people's party leader the Duke of Beaufort (Eusebio Lazaro); the cardinal releases Rochefort (Christopher Lee) from the Bastille to guard the duke personally. He also hires D'Artagnan (Michael York) and asks him to find the other musketeers so that they can protect him and the queen. Since D'Artagnan is now poor and one of "the heroes of yesterday," teased by the young bloods of the day, he agrees. Although Aramis (Richard Chamberlain) and Athos (Oliver Reed) are delighted to see their friend, who still employs his old servant Planchet (Roy Kinnear). They do not wish to fight on the side of the cardinal. Athos criticizes D'Artagnan for being a mercenary. Only Porthos (Frank Finlay) chooses to join him, mainly because he needs the pay.

When Beaufort escapes, Porthos and D'Artagnan are detailed to recapture him. Their attempts are thwarted by Athos and Aramis, who are on the other side. Athos' adopted son Raoul (C. Thomas Howell) sees a headsman apparently assassinated by a young priest who turns out to be the beautiful Justine (Kim Cattrall) in disguise. She is the bastard daughter of Milady de Winter and Rochefort, who had been left in England as a baby by her mother; she is now a spy for Cromwell and determined to avenge her mother. Before being killed, the headsman had told her that the musketeers paid him for her mother's execution. Rochefort, in disgrace and terrified of the Bastille, begs Justine to take him to England with her. Her price: the identity of her mother's judges. She

is angry that he had not killed them himself, and he points to the wound where D'Artagnan had skewered him to a lectern and left him for dead. The musketeers are sent on a mission to London to save Queen Anne's brother King Charles I, but Justine and her father prevent the rescue and the king is executed. Returning to France, the musketeers discover that Cromwell had planned to blow them up in the middle of the English Channel and so they leave Justine and Rochefort on board as they escape.

Rochefort dies in the explosion but Justine escapes and, acting with the greedy scheming cardinal, using all her wiles on the self-important young king, she secretly takes him away to another castle where they can usurp his power and rule the country without the interference from French rebels who hold Paris in the grip of political unrest. The musketeers follow them and, employing the new hot air balloon technology, gain access to the castle. After much fighting with the cardinal's soldiers and Justine, who is an expert with the sword, they force the cardinal to sign a decree that grants concessions to the French rebels. He also signs decrees making Aramis a bishop, Porthos a baron with appropriate estates and wealth, Raoul a commissioned officer in the Guards and D'Artagnan an officer in any branch of the service he desires. Justine makes a spectacular escape. D'Artagnan starts to take leave of his friends to go and "fight in the wars" but they can't resist joining him and gallop off into the sunset. "One for all and all for one!"

Comment

Christopher Lee, who played Rochefort, commented in his autobiography, "*The Return* should never have been made. They attempted the impossible, trying to shoot a twelve-week picture in eight weeks. Much worse than the failure of the film, however, was the accidental death of Roy Kinnear, one of the most loved men in the business, who came off his horse on cobblestones taking a corner, as he rode with the musketeers over a bridge from Toledo castle. He had always been terrified of riding horses on the earlier films, and now he was fifteen years older and heavier" (Lee, 278). On the death of Kinnear, director Richard Lester's first instinct was to cancel the picture. A meeting of the stars and Mrs. Kinnear resulted in the conclusion that the project should go ahead as a tribute to the very talented and much loved actor; footage of Kinnear was interspersed with that of a double.

The two months' filming began on April 22, 1988. The budget was around $17 million, small for such a project. After two previews in the U.S., Universal Pictures sold the movie straight to cable television — not the best vote of confidence. There was a theatrical release in England but the critics felt much the same as the American previewers. Pauline McLeod in the *Daily Mirror*, July 7, 1989: "Our dear old musketeers — once dashing and dare-devil — are middle aged and graying"; *New Musical Express*, August 5, 1989: "Here is a film designed for Easter/Christmas snoozetime TV. There is very little genuine action, excitement or humor to disturb the slumbering viewer.... *Return* is merely a swaggering monotony. Personified, by and large, by old fool Oliver Reed who plays himself again as the 'drunk and disorderly' Athos. He dominates a desperate storyline"; *What's On in London*, August 2, 1989: "...Athos (Reed) is a rowdy drunk. Well, no great stretch there.... [T]he story is little more than an obvious excuse for the action and comedy scenes that make up the movie.... Another glaring fault is that the Musketeers are rarely all together yet this is when they are at their best. There are good moments, but sadly not enough"; *Variety*: "[It's] a stillborn event which looks as tired as its reassembled cast.."; *Screen International*: "Undoubtedly more fun to make than to watch.... [It has] the feel of a self-indulgent college reunion."

And Oliver Reed? "By now a life on the piss had taken its toll of his appearance; he was pot-bellied, gray-haired, lined and stooping like an old man; at times he looked like Father Christmas leaving an Alcoholics Anonymous meeting. It was a long way from the brooding sex symbol of the early '70s. His face was now 'a sad reflection of a dissolute life,' as one journalist put it, 'a Hogarthian example of debauchery's perils.' When in 1989 he played Athos once again[,] Reed looked positively prehistoric compared with his co-stars from the

original movie. But the hellraiser was still there" [Sellers, 247].

All the hard work of the cast and crew was to no avail; the clever inventions, the carefully crafted fight sequences, the gorgeous costumes and quirky historical touches fell by the wayside. Perhaps their hearts weren't really in it after Roy Kinnear's death.

Panama Sugar (1990)

(Aka *Panama Sugar and the Dog Thief*) Trinidad Film Production; Reteitalia; released by Delta to video in 1990 in the U.S.; no U.K. release

Crew— Director: Marcello Avallone; Writers: Marcello Avallone, Vincenzo Mannino, Roberto Parpaglione, Andrea Purgatori; Executive Producer: Enzio Palaggi; Associate Producer: Marisa Palaggi; Producer: Italo Zingarelli; Original Music: Gabriele Ducros; Film Editor: Adriano Tagliavia; Casting: Chiara Meloni; Art Director: Luciano Sagoni; Stunts: Massimiliano Urbaldi; Grip: Umberto Dessena; Stills Photographer: Franco Biciocchi.

Cast— Scott Plank (Panama), Oliver Reed (The General), Lucrezia Lante della Rovere (Liza), Vittorio Arnondola.

Synopsis

On a Caribbean paradise island, a group of young swingers dance away the day and drink away the night at their favorite bar. An American wheeler-dealer (Vittorio Arnondola) wants to buy the bar and transform the island into an international gambling den. He is backed in this venture by the island's strongman, the General (Oliver Reed). Panama (Scott Plank), the ultimate cool hero, sends packing various toughs when they try to intimidate the bar owner. He still finds time to romance Liza (Lucrezia Lante della Rovere), a beautiful visitor with a yacht. With the help of Pirate, a thieving dog, they convince the general that there is a treasure hidden on the island. The general, afraid of competition, sends the Americans on their way.

Comment

There's not much to say on this one. The authors were unable to obtain a video but the synopsis doesn't make the film seem promising. *Variety* (March 28, 1990) commented, "...Reed gets by with his usual Mussolini posturing, jutting jaw and bull neck, though he has a riveting intensity even in this caricatured role."

It's difficult to imagine that *Panama Sugar* was any better than the other nonsense that Reed was making at the time and it's unlikely that we'll ever find out.

Hired to Kill (1990)

Omega Entertainment; A Paramount video release in 1990; Technicolor; 100 minutes

Crew—Directors: Nico Mastorakis, Peter Rader; Writers: Fred C. Perry, Kirk Ellis, Nico Mastorakis; Executive Producer: Isabelle Mastroakis; Producer: Peter Rader; Associate Producer: Aladdin Pojhan; Original Music: Jerry Grant; Cinematography: Andreas Bellis; Production Design: Michael Stringer; Makeup Artist: Nina Kent; Sound Effects Editor; Steve Mann; Special Effects: Donn Markel; Stunt Coordinator: Mark Cuttin; Stunts: Clint Carpenter, Mark Cuttin, David Fisher, Gene Harrison, Michael Kane, Lee Lindquist, Phil O'Dell, Shawn O'Neil, Dan Rycerz, Alex Spinoulas, Marc Wolf; Aerial Camera Operator: Adam Dale; Aerial Coordinator & Helicopter Pilot: Marc Wolf; Key Grip: Mark Pickens; Runner: Andreas Garouniatis; Production Assistant: Tiffany L. Kurtz.

Cast— Brian Thompson (Frank Ryan), Oliver Reed (Michael Bartos), George Kennedy (Thomas), Jose Ferrer (Rallis), Michelle Moffett (Ana), Barbara Lee Alexander (Sheila), Jordana Capra (Joanna), Kendall Conrad (Daphne), Kim Lonsdale (Sivi), Jude Mussetter (Dahlia), Penelope Reed (Katrina), David Sawyer (Louis), Angela Gerekou (Tara), Fanny Xidis (Prison Guard), Alea Bair (Photo Model), Cynthia Lee (Arm Wrestler), Peter Rader (Busboy), John Holt (Young Guerrilla), Mark Pickens (Radio Operator), Mark Cuttin (Chopper Pilot).

Synopsis

Ex–government assassin Ryan (Brian Thompson) is called back to duty by Thomas (George Kennedy), who heads a secret organization that supersedes the CIA. The plan: The small European country of Cypra is ripe for revolution. If the rebels win, it will benefit the west. The elderly leader Rallis (Jose Ferrer) has been imprisoned by head of security Bartos (Oliver Reed); Thomas wants him freed. The cover: Ryan is to impersonate Cecil Thornton, a gay fashion designer, and enter Cypra with a team of "models"— Sheila (Barbara Lee Alexander), Joanne (Jordana Capra), Daphne (Kendall Conrad), Sivi (Kim Lonsdale), Dahlia (Penelope Reed), and Tara (Angela Gerekou). The women all possess deadly fighting skills (some have been in prison) and they have been trained by Ryan. They arrive in Cypra to introduce a new line of clothing and are wined and dined by Bartos who, seemingly, falls for their cover. Bartos wants Ryan to accept his mistress Ana (Michelle Moffett) as a model — but actually to plant false information. Ana is, in fact, a double agent and Ryan's contact. She tells him that Bartos is about to move Rallis to a more secure location. A further surprise: Daphne, under Thomas' orders, betrays her comrades and attempts to kill them when they storm the prison and release Rallis. Ryan has been ordered to kill Rallis if he seems unable to lead effectively — but Ryan can't go through with it, having learned of Thomas and Daphne's duplicity. After Bartos is placed in the rebels' hands, Ryan returns to America to deal with Thomas.

Comment

Hired to Kill sounds like it might be a film noir but is, in fact, a member of the *Dirty Dozen* family; in this case, though, it's *The Dirty Half Dozen*. Brian Thompson stars, quite capably, in "the former CIA agent who got sick of it all, reluctantly coming back to duty" role. And, instead of the twelve demented men assigned to him for the impossible mission, we get six psycho-degenerate women. Oddly enough, they're all beautiful, deadly and not against skimping on clothing. Filmed in Greece in 1990, *Hired to Kill* does not seem to have had an American or British theatrical release.

While hardly in the same league as *The Dirty Dozen*, *Hired to Kill* is the equal of most of the similar films that found theatrical bookings. It's professionally made with excellent photography, attractive locations, and convincing special effects and stuntwork. Thompson looks the part and plays it was well as anyone can play this kind of part. He's given decent support from his female counterparts who, unfortunately, are given little individuality and are tough to tell apart. Thompson is given more with which to work and gets across Ryan's world-weary cynicism. This is not *The Spy Who Came in from the Cold* but it raises *Hired to Kill* a few notches.

So does the supporting cast — at least on the video box. George Kennedy is effective in the "cynical CIA boss who isn't all he seems" role, but only has a few scenes. Jose Ferrer is on screen for about two minutes; it almost seems as though he was vacationing in Greece and had a day to kill and the producers signed him up.

Reed earned his second-billing. It's a legitimate role spread throughout the film. As Security Director Bartos, he looks menacing with long, slicked-back hair and a bushy moustache; he's easily at home in a helicopter holding a machine-gun or at a formal party holding a drink. As was so often true of Reed, his character projects the possibility of violence more than committing violence. He illustrates this perfectly: His only weapons are his voice, eyes and evil intentions, as in a very creepy scene where he confronts Ryan (who is posing as a gay fashion designer) and Ana (whose breasts he is fondling).

BARTOS: You fascinate me, Mr. Thornton.

RYAN: In what way, Mr. Bartos?

BARTOS: In the way you surround your whole life with beautiful women but you never avail yourself of their delights. Forgive my naïveté but I find this very strange.

RYAN: So did my parents.

BARTOS: And yet you say you find my Ana very beautiful.

RYAN: Forgive me, but my essential tastes lie in other areas, so to speak.

BARTOS: Oh, that's a pity, Mr. Thornton. Men are crude and violent and their love-making has force. Most of us lack a certain gentility in our lovemaking. We need women in our lives to give us balance.

As he's speaking, quietly, with his eyes never leaving Ryan, Bartos strips off the front of Ana's dress, fully exposing her breasts. After dismissing her, he walks over to Ryan and, incredibly, grabs his crotch and kisses him hard on the lips!

Hired to Kill has its share of violent scenes; there are plenty of well-staged fights and explosions. One of them seems to have gone wrong; the film is dedicated to helicopter pilot and stuntman Clint Carpenter.

Oddly for a film of this kind, both villains' fates are left to the viewers' imaginations. Bartos is last seen, from a helicopter, surrounded by rebels, and Thomas is last seen surrounded by Ryan and the remaining girls. One imagines both are in for a lot of trouble. *Hired to Kill* delivered what it promised and was one of the best movies Reed appeared in at this point of his career — which speaks as much for the stage of his career as it does for the film.

The Pit and the Pendulum (1991)

Full Moon Entertainment; Empire Pictures; released by Full Moon Entertainment in the U.S.; no U.K. release; 96 minutes

Crew— Director: Stuart Gordon; Producer: Albert Band; Executive Producer: Charles Band; Screenplay: Dennis Paoli; based on the short story by Edgar Allan Poe; Cinematographer: Adolfo Bartoll; Editor: Andy Horvitch; Sound: Giuseppe Mratori; Art Director: Giovanni Corridori; Special Effects Makeup: Greg Connom.

Cast— Lance Henriksen (Torquemada), Rona De Ricci (Maria), Jonathan Fuller (Antonio), Jeffrey Combs (Francisco), Tom Towles (Don Carlos), Stephen Lee (Gomez), Frances Bay (Esmeralda), Oliver Reed (Cardinal).

Synopsis

In medieval Spain, Torquemada (Lance Henriksen), author of the terrible Inquisition, mortifies his flesh on a daily basis while wreaking the vengeance of the church on hundreds of poor souls, most of whom do not deserve his dungeons or his tortures which are supposed to save "lost souls." Torquemada has no mercy — that part of Christian theology is entirely wasted on him; his surrounding groups bask in the fear and kudos that working for him brings. Public executions are the order of the day and overseen by Torquemada personally. And at one such execution his attention is drawn to Maria (Rona De Ricci), the saintly wife of the local baker. Maria does have pity for the condemned and when she tries to intervene in a nasty execution, Torquemada has her arrested — and plans to question her himself. He then becomes besotted with her. When she will not yield to his lust, he accuses her of bewitching him and has her locked up. Her husband gets into trouble trying to get her out of Torquemada's citadel and he is sentenced to death. Torquemada's servant and enforcer Gomez (Stephen Lee) believes his master is above earthly temptation; his faith is completely destroyed when he finds Torquemada trying to seduce Maria. However, Maria does have some kind of power, and discovers it when she is imprisoned with Esmeralda (Frances Bay), a practitioner of magic. Esmeralda teaches her to project her spirit to endure the torture.

To prevent Maria from revealing his fall from grace, Torquemada cuts out her tongue and traps her in a tomb. The cardinal, sent to conduct a review of Torquemada's inquisition, proves to be a drunkard and a devious politician. He intends to shut Torquemada down but finds himself, literally, on the sharp end of Torquemada's disapproval, and is killed. Using his new torture machine, the Pit and the Pendulum, Torquemada intends to execute the baker, but Gomez has other ideas, helps the baker escape and brings about Torquemada's demise on his own machine. Torquemada's clerk Francisco (Jeffrey Combs) frees the prisoners and helps reunite Maria and her loving husband.

Comment

This movie was filmed on location in Italy. This should be a horror story, but it is so absurd that Lance Henriksen, playing Torqumada, and Reed as the cardinal should have felt insulted by the offer of the parts. From Jeffrey Combs' anachronistic spectacles to the over-indulgent camera lingering on tortures and executions alike, it is a travesty.

Henriksen gives an intense performance, and if the film had been serious, it would have been magical. Reed took his cameo as the prince of the church who preferred the wine cellars to the torture chambers and made the viewer regard him with the same contempt as Torquemada. Who can take dialogue seriously when the cardinal is yelling at his host, "The good Lord wants us to love our neighbor — not roast him!" A mildly interesting 96 minutes, if you can take the gross background.

"For a pic dealing with premature burials, burnings at the stake, impalements, torture, and tongue slicing, *Pit* is remarkable unexciting. Except for Henriksen's intense performance and Reed's juicily hammy cameo, the performances are bland" (*Variety*, June 17, 1991); "*Re-Animator* director Gordon and co-scenarist Dennis Paoli have brushed the cobwebs off the familiar Edgar Allan Poe story, infusing all the gore and nudity missing from the very different Roger Corman movie. With its overheated acting and silly dialogue, this flick is closer in spirit to Mel Brooks and Monty Python" (*Video Review*, July 1991).

Prisoner of Honor (1991)

Dreyfuss/James Productions; Etude; Warner Bros. Productions; released in the U.S. by HBO; no U.K. release

Crew— Director: Ken Russell; Writer: Ron Hutchinson; Co-Producers: Michael Bendix, Colin Callender, Steven Nalevansky; Associate Producer: Christopher Chase; Producers: Richard Dreyfuss, Judith James; Line Producer: Ronaldo Vasconcellos; Original Music: Barry Kirsch; Cinematographer: Mike Southon; Film Editor: Mia Goldman; Co-editors: Margaret Goodspeed, Brian Tagg; Casting: Susie Bruffin; Production Design: Ian Whittaker; Art Director: Frank Walsh; Set Decoration: Jill Quertier; Costume Design: Michael Jeffery; Supervising Makeup Artist: Magdalene Gaffney; Makeup Artist: Ken Lintott; Supervising Hair Stylist: Stephen Rose; Hair Stylist: Tracy Smith; Production Manager: Peter Elford; Second Assistant Director: Callum McDougall; Third Assistant Director: Richard Whelan; Carpenters: Leon Apsey, Karl Apsey; Property Master: Barry Wilkinson; Dressing Properties: Joe Dipple, Peter Wallis, Reg Wheeler; Stagehand: Gary Evans; Construction Manager: Roy Evans; Assistant Art Director: Melanie Hall; Standby Props: Steve Wheeler, Gary Ixer; Property Storeman: Charles Ixer; Painter: Brendan Power; Foley Artist: Tim Chilton; ADR Mixer: David Gertz; Boom Operator: Mark Holding; Sound Editor: Richard S. Steele; Sound Recordist: Bruce White; Still Photographer: Sven Arnstein; Electricians: Ted Bird, Bob Brock, Jason Wall; Gaffer: Micky Brown; Playback Operator: Peter Eusebe; Clapper Loader: John Foster; Generator Operator: John Murphy; Focus Puller: Steve Parker; Best Boy: Richard Seal; Camera Grip: Malcolm Sheehan; Casting Assistant: Amanda Newland; Wardrobe Master: Anthony Black; Wardrobe Mistress: Louise Page; Wardrobe Assistant: John Scott; Music Editor: Stan Jones; Production Coordinator: Elaine Burt; Production Assistants: Jackson James, Simon Oxenham; Location Manager: Anne Glanfield; Choreographer: Anita Desmarais; Flying Effects: Nick Kirby; Script Supervisor: Sheila Wilson.

Cast—Richard Dreyfuss (Col. Picquart), Oliver Reed (Gen. De Boisdeffre), Peter Firth (Maj. Henry), Jeremy Kemp (Gen. De Pellieux), Brian Blessed (Gen. Gonse), Peter Vaughan (Gen. Mercier), Kenneth Colley (Capt. Dreyfus), Catherine Neilson (Eloise), Lindsay Anderson (War Minister), Christopher Ashley (Orator #1), Shauna Baird (Henry's Wife), David Bamford (Boy Prostitute), Duncan Bell (Army Doctor), John Bennett (Magistrate), John Cater (New War Minister), Simon Chamberland (Cabaret Piano Player), Imogen Claire (Cabaret Singer), Vernon Dobtcheff (Rennes Prosecutor), Paul Dufficey (Sketch Artist), Nick Edmett (Orator #2), Martin Friend (Emile Zola), Leslie Glazer (Boisdeffre's Artist), Michael Haughey (Esterhazy Inquiry Judge), Jonathan Howell (Billiard Player), Christopher Logue (Labori), Mac McDonald (Picquart's Lawyer), Michelle McKenna (La Belle France), Murray Melvin (Bertillon), Norman Mitchell (Court Usher), Nick Musker (Vampire Dreyfus), Anthony Newlands (Rennes Presiding Judge), Guy Nicholls (Degradation Sergeant), Carsten Norgaard (Col. Von Schwartzkoppen), Andrew Norman (Music Hall Picquart), Judith Paris (Madame Dreyfus), Andrew Powrie (Orator #3), Alex Richardson (Minister's Aide), Patrick Ryecart (Maj. Esterhazy), Sean Scanlan (Reporter), Stephen Simms (Eloise's Husband), Albert Welling (Capt. Cuignet), Leslie Bryant, Miranda Coe, Simon Shelton, Mack Walsh-Holme, Stephen Houghton (Male Prostitutes), Oliver Haden, William Haden, Felicity Hayes-McCoy, Paul Lowther, Peggy-Ann Jones (Audience Members).

Synopsis

In this tale of the Dreyfus Affair, the Jewish French army Captain Dreyfus (Kenneth Colley) was tried and convicted of espionage by a court-martial to cover up the shortcomings of another officer — the latter a Christian. Colonel Piquart (Richard Dreyfuss), a martial court's lawyer, is given the job of justifying the sentence, but instead uncovers the true culprit, a member of the general staff with "good" connections. The general staff, headed by General de Boisdeffre (Oliver Reed), close ranks against the upstart. Piquart's attempt to bring the true perpetrator to justice effectively ends his own military career. Writer Emile Zola (Martin Friend), who fought on Dreyfus' behalf, is convicted of libel.

Comment

This is a very entertaining and at times discomfiting retelling of one of France's unfinest hours. Ken Russell, for once, leaves his

tory to tell its own tale. The general staff quickly become aware that they have targeted the wrong man, but they are pressured by their superiors to pick on the Jew who has had too successful an army career for some of them. Only General De Boisdeffre (Oliver Reed) has a few moments of unease, but in the end, he follows the pack and withdraws his objections. Piquart (Richard Dreyfuss) is disgusted with them, but the honor of the corps and the dignity of France are more important to these old warhorses.

Russell, as usual, had a good eye for period; the locations are perfect, the costumes spot on. He invited Reed to join the mostly British cast of acting luminaries. "The two hadn't worked together for years and Russell saw in his old sparring partner that the spark he once loved had burned out. 'There was always an animal lurking under the surface and the animal had either been tamed or driven out of him. It wasn't the same Oliver. He was a different man.'" [Sellers, 258]: On the other hand, John Cater (appearing as the new war minister, whose job it was to try and right the injustice and set the army on an even keel again), told the authors, "I hadn't seen Oliver for a very long time. Of course, the years had mellowed him, but he was as charming and professional as ever. And obviously, very much in love with Josephine, his wife; he doted on her and I think she had made an enormous difference to his life. The old tiger was tamed — a contented old cat was in its place, enjoying the sun. He's greatly missed."

Severed Ties (1992)

Columbia Pictures Corporation; Fangoria Films; direct to video; 95 minutes; color

Crew— Director: Damen Santostefano; Screenplay: John Nystrom, Henry Dominic: Story: Damen Santostefano, David A. Casci; Producers: Rex Piano, Christopher Webster; Executive Producers: Norman Jacobs, Steven Jacobs; Music: Daniel Licht; Editor: Richard Roberts; Cinematographer: Geza Sincovics; Production Design: Don Day; Makeup–Special Effects: KND Effects Group; Casting: Kent Demarches.

Cast— Oliver Reed (Dr. Vaughn), Elke Sommer (Helene), Billy Morisette (Harrison), Garrett Morris (Stripe), Johnny Legend (Preach), Denise Wallace

(Eve), Roger Perkovich (Lawrence), Bekki Vain (Lila), Gerald Shidwell (Dr. Harrison), Julian Weaver (Policeman).

Synopsis

Brilliant — but insane — young scientist Harrison (Billy Morisette) is following the researches of his brilliant — but insane — father (Gerald Shidell) in the creation of a limb-regenerating gene plasma (and gene blender). His mother Helene (Elke Sommer) has not only killed her husband, she's taken up with the evil Dr. Vaughn (Oliver Reed), who's taken up with a neo–Nazi group, Nordkem. They plan to use Harrison's plasma to achieve world domination through organ regeneration. When Harrison quarrels with Dr. Vaughn over substandard lab equipment, Harrison's arm is accidentally severed by a sliding door. He injects himself with the plasma which contains genetic elements of a giant lizard and a serial killer. Harrison runs off and is taken in by Stripe (Garrett Morris), a derelict with one leg who lives with a colony of disabled malcontents. Harrison's arm has regenerated — as a snake with a hand for a head — with a life and a mind of its own. After the arm kills group leader Preach (Johnny Legend), Harrison decides to replicate the reproducing plasma to regenerate the degenerates. He sends Eve (Denise Wallace) and the arm to his old lab to steal the necessary equipment and restores Stripe's leg — with initially horrific results. Tipped by the police, Dr. Vaughn and Helene arrive at Harrison's new lab where she is disturbed to see her son with Eve due to her incestuous interest in the lad. She and Dr. Vaughn kidnap Eve — and steal the plasma — and return to the lab where they meet Nordkem agents Lawrence (Roger Perkovich) and Lila (Bekki Vain). Harrison and Stripe are in pursuit with an army of arms made from Preach's degenerate genes. Dr. Vaughn is killed when an arm impales his chest. Helene and Eve fall into the blender to be regenerated as a single being.

Comment

Fangoria is a "splatter film" magazine, perhaps the bible of the genre. It's totally insulting, tasteless, gross and highly entertaining, not unlike its first venture into film production. Both the magazine and its movie are guilty pleasures that one can really feel guilty about.

Severed Ties (aka *Army*— get it?) is actually very funny — intentionally so, we hope. Most of this is due to the expert performances of Reed and Elke Sommer who play it just straight enough (like Leslie Nielsen in the *Airplane!* movies) to be funny. The ludicrous, over-the-top special effects are just right too.

The two stars' scenes alternate between lust and disgust. Sommer was still incredibly attractive, Reed less so. Life had definitely begun to catch up with him; he looks tired and bloated. Only nine years and ten films remained for him, but the old pro was still in there trying.

> DR. VAUGHN: It's not as if Nordkem is some kind of Nazi concern!
>
> HELENE: Well, my dear, there was that Zylon gas contract.
>
> DR. VAUGHN (insulted): That was fifty years ago. Why can't people forgive and forget? Once we have regenerated the elderly, then we will have defeated death itself, haven't we?
>
> HELENE: You mean the slave-cloning facility?
>
> DR. VAUGHN (really insulted): Will you stop throwing that back in my face?

The two leads are well supported by Billy Morisette and Garrett Morris; all four understand that the movie is a sick, sick joke. It's really impossible to defend something like *Severed Ties* on any level; it's detrimental to both cinema and society in general. But it does have a crazy sort of charm ... and it is, believe it or not, fun. It was, not surprisingly, not reviewed by any major outlet and seems to have been released directly to video.

Severed Ties was probably the best movie ever filmed in Rhinelander, Wisconsin.

Russian Roulette — Moscow 95 (1995)

Belarusfilm; distributed by Central Cinema Company

Crew— Director: Menahem Golan; Writer: Andrew Sasmonof; Producer: Artur Brauner; Executive Producer: Wolf Brauner; Original Music:

Sergei Bubenko; Cinematographer: Yuri Marukhin; Costume Design: Ludmila Torshina; Second Assistant Director: Andrew Simonian; Sound: Sergei Bubenko; Foley Artist: Shamil Ismailov.

Cast— Oliver Reed, Barbara Carrera, Karen Moncrieff, Zachi Noy, James Pertwee, Frank Singer, Mariya Shukshina, Jan Michael Vincent.

Comment

The authors could find no copy of the film to view, no reviews, release dates or any information other than the above, which we offer to keep the filmography as complete as possible.

Superbrain (1995)

Central Cinema Company

Crew— Director: Menahem Golan; Producer: Artur Brauner; Production Manager: Timothy Tremper; Sound: Sergei Bubenko; Armorer: Alister Mazzotti

Cast— Oliver Reed, Torsten Lennie Munchow, Hanns Zischler

Comment

The authors were unable to find a copy of the film to view or any other data other than the above which we offer to keep the filmography as complete as possible.

Funny Bones (1995)

Hollywood Pictures; A Suntrust Films Production; released on March 24, 1995, in New York City and March 31, 1995, in the rest of the U.S.; released on September 29, 1995, in the U.K. by Buena Vista Pictures

Crew— Director: Peter Chesholm; Writers: Peter Chesholm, Peter Flannery; Producers; Peter Chesholm, Simon Fields; Co-producer: Laurie Borg; Executive Producer: Nicholas Frye; Associate Producers: Lester Berman, Peter McMillan; Original Music: John Altman; Cinematography: Eduardo Serra; Film Editor: Martin Walsh; Production Design: Caroline Hanania; Art Director: Andrew Munro; Set Decorator: Tracey Gallacher; Costume Design: Lindy Hemming; Chief Makeup Artist: Pay Hay; Makeup Artists: Barbara Jo Batterman, Yvonne Coppard, Helen Johnson; Chief Hair Stylist: Stephen Rose; Hair Stylists: Barbara Jo Batterman, Tracy Smith; First Assistant Directors: James LaRoca, Mike Zimbrich; Second Assistant Directors: Geoff Dibben, Toby Ford, Jeff Kay, Cliff Lanning, Andrew Wood, Greg Zekowski; Third Assistant Director:

Robert Grayson; Property Master: Gordon Fitzgerald; Construction Manager: Steve Ede; Dialogue Editor: Peter Elliott; Supervising Sound Editor: Glenn Freemantle; Special Effects Supervisor: Tom Harris; Wire Expert: Steve Crawley; Stunt Coordinator: Simon Crane; Crane Operator: Keith Manning; Camera Grip: Colin Manning; Casting: Mary Gail Artz, Barbara Cohen, Kate Dowd, Janey Fothergill, Maggie Lunn, Rena Lenhard; Assistant Costume Designer: Debbie Scott: Costume Supervisor: John Scott; Wardrobe Assistants: Nigel Egerton, Clare Spragge; Music Editor: Dina Eaton; Music Producer: Amanda Hughes; Choreographer: Christina Avery; Circus Consultant: David Barnes; Production Coordinator: Tania Windsor; Location Manager: Tony Clarkson; Script Supervisor: June McDonald.

Cast— Oliver Platt (Tommy Fawkes), Jerry Lewis (George Fawkes), Lee Evans (Jack Parker), Leslie Caron (Katie Parker), Richard Griffiths (Jim Minty), Sadie Corre (Poodle Woman), Oliver Reed (Dolly Hopkins), George Carl (Thomas Parker), Freddie Davies (Bruno Parker), Ian McNeice (Stanley Sharkey), Christopher Greet (Lawrence Berger), Peter Gunn (Nicky), Gavin Millar (Steve Campbell), William Hootkins (Al), Terence Rigby (Billy Mann), Ruta Lee (Laura Fawkes), Peter Pamela Rose (Jenny), Ticky Holgado (Battison), Olivier Py (Barre), Mouss (Poquelin), Peter McNamara (Canavan), Richard Platt (Bellows), Francois Domange (Pirard), Harold Nicholas (Himself), George Khan (Francesco), Ian Rowe (Ringmaster), Phil Atkinson, Nicholas Coppin (Policemen), Jona Jones (Security Guard), Tony Barton, Mike Newman (Comedians), Ruth Kettlewell (Camilla Powell), Peter Morgan (Gofor), Fred Evans (Mr. Pearce), George Raistrick (Club Owner), Mickey Baker (Mayor), Reg Griffiths, Duggie Chapman, Tony Peers, Andy Rashleigh (Reporters), Phil Kelly (Himself), Amir Fawzi (Little Tommy), Andy Thompson, Peter Brande, Frank Harvey, Anthony Irvine, Eileen Bell, Risty Goffe, Terri Carol, Fred Cox, Frank Cox, Shane Robinson, Benji Ming, Zipporah Simon, Maudie Blake, Andras Banlaki, Laci Endresz Jr., Brian Webb, Peter Martin, Chloe Treend, Andrea Bretherick, Lisa Henson, Rebecca Metcalfe, Camilla Simpson, Tina Yoxall (Entertainers).

Synopsis

In the Irish Sea, two boats converge, exchanging "magic" wax eggs containing an ancient powder that confers youth on its user. During an altercation, a French crook falls overboard, onto the propeller screw of the English boat, and dies. An English crook on the French boat has to jump for it and surfaces from the sea with one of the eggs and a floating foot.

Half brothers Tommy (Oliver Platt) and Jack (Lee Evans) are comedians, one American, the other English, and neither are aware of the other's existence. Tommy is the joke man; he employs writers and likes to analyze but he's lost because he lives in the shadow of his famous father, the legendary comedian George Fawkes (Jerry Lewis). Jack, George's illegitimate son, is the antithesis of Tommy; he is poor, without education, naturally funny but uncontrolled and dangerous to the point where he has been banned from working. He's almost literally barking mad and the only creature he feels comfortable with is his dog.

After a disastrous, heart-breaking opening night in Las Vegas, Tommy flees to the English seaside resort of Blackpool where he spent his early years. It is here that he sets out to "trade" in comedy material and to find out why he was taken away so suddenly when he was six years old. Tommy still believes that Blackpool is the mecca for comedians as it was in the 1950s; he remembers sunny days and funny people that his father worked with. He offers to pay whoever shows up with comedy material or an act. Since a sucker appears to be in town, all kinds of eccentrics crawl out of the woodwork, from a backwards talking man to the bastard son of Louis XIV. But Tommy's quest leads to Jack and the Parker Brothers, a troupe of comedians who were the funniest anyone ever saw. However they have not worked for fifteen years following Jack's killing someone in the circus ring while getting his biggest laugh.

Only when the Parkers audition for Tommy does he realize that this was the family he used to live with. Tommy discovers that Jack is his half brother and that George had an affair with Katie Parker (Leslie Caron) while she was married to one of the Parker Brothers. When she became pregnant, rather than face his responsibilities, George upped and left for the U.S., taking Tommy with him together with all the Parkers' comedy material which he claimed as his own, and leaving an illegitimate son behind. The Parker Brothers and Jack are revealed as the egg smugglers, selling the remaining five to gangster art collector Dolly Hopkins (Oliver Reed) who is not pleased that one egg is missing since the powder inside is supposed to give the user ten years of youth. When Tommy calls his father in Las Vegas, George decides to come clean and returns to Blackpool to attempt to make amends so that the Parkers can work again. Jack, however, is still banned from performing. As George puts it, a boxer kills a guy in the ring, he gets to fight again. With a comedian it might just be bad for business. But at the Parkers' big comeback show, they use the magic powder Jack has mixed in their stage makeup and get scarily youthful; Jack comes to the ring disguised as a drunk. He performs a death-defying and riotously funny act atop a 50-foot swaying pole. A policeman following Jack climbs the pole to bring him down. Jack strikes the policeman who seemingly begins to plunge to his death. At the last moment Jack reaches out to save him and the cop is revealed as Tommy, the new addition to the act.

Comment

It is hard to know what to make of this movie; its pedigree is phenomenal but it can't seem to decide if it's a thriller or a comedy or a hybrid of some kind.

British director Peter Chelsom says in the production notes, "*Funny Bones* is essentially a comedy but it is dark, wild, hard-edged, and my most personal film. The story is about a polarity, the two extremes present in all of us, as portrayed by the two half brothers. It's about the personal manager versus the wild beast."

Apparently the locals at a pub frequented by Reed complained that he drank the whole allocation of imported lager while working in Blackpool; recovered from a recent health scare, he was fit and raring to go again. Joanna Lumley was cut out of the film and most of Reed's part was removed during editing.

Sunday Telegraph Review, October 1, 1995: "Oliver Reed camps it up as a Mr. Big in mandarin's robes.... In the end *Funny Bones* is more of a *momento mori* than a laff-riot"; *Observer Review*, October 1, 1995: "There's too much plot in *Funny Bones* (including a redundant subplot involving Oliver Reed as a rich homosexual gangster in search of an Ancient Asian longevity powder) not all of it convincing or coherent." *Today*, September 29, 1995: "There's a sub-plot involving smuggled eggs [involving Reed], that presumably has been scissored within an inch of its life — which does little more than get in the way."

Chesholm in the production notes; "Oliver Reed has a tremendous presence and to cast him as this very precious, terribly neurotic character, was taking him into an area as an actor that he had never played before." So little remains that we cannot tell how successfully he fulfilled the brief. Enough for the producers to keep his name on the movie anyway.

The Bruce (1996)

Cromwell Productions Ltd.; released on DVD in Europe in 2004; no U.S. or U.K. release

Crew—Directors: Bob Carruthers, David McWhinnie; Original Music: Paul Farrer; Film Editing: Owen Parker; Art Director: Jeremy Freeston; Set Dresser: Charlie Rae; Camera: Paul Gavin; Stunt Performers: Ian Armstrong, Scott Cowan, Stuart Leggatt; Fight Arranger: Bill Little; Wardrobe: Neil Burn; Special Thanks: Tony Rotherham and the White Boar Fight Crew.

Cast—Brian Blessed (Edward I), Oliver Reed (Bishop Wisherton), Sandy Welch (Robert the Bruce), Hildegard Neil (Queen Eleanor), Richard Brimblecome (Edward II), Conor Chamberlain (Elizabeth Bruce), Steven Clark (English Soldier), Pavel Douglas (John "Red" Comyn), Ross Dunsmore (Nigel Bruce), Vincent Faber (Scottish Soldier), Heather Flannagan (Marjorie Bruce), John Hoye (Edward James), Michael Layton (Aubrey), Michael van Wijk (Henry De Bohun).

Synopsis

In the shadow of the pyramids, the Crusaders prepare to do battle against their foes. To give them courage, one of the Crusaders hurls a heart-shaped box at the opposing army.

The scene shifts to many years earlier. Edward I (Brian Blessed), king of England, is fighting the Scots for their country as he has done for many years. Scotland has two claimants for the throne: Robert the Bruce (Sandy Welch) and "Red" Comyn (Pavel Douglas), so-called because of his distinctive auburn hair. The two men agree to unite to fight Edward. During the battle, Comyn, who had secretly betrayed the Bruce by agreeing not to fight in exchange for being supported by Edward in the role of Scottish king, withdraws from the battle and leaves the Bruce in desperate straits. The Scottish army scatters to the winds and everyone believes that the Bruce has been killed.

The bishop (Oliver Reed) is heartbroken for he had supported the Bruce's claim to the Scots throne, short of joining the fighting. Comyn is to be Edward's puppet king (having told the Scots that the Bruce is dead) and it is imperative to make peace with Edward. The bishop withdraws from the council when he hears that Comyn is to be crowned within the week, declaring, "Treason! May the Lord have mercy on your soul!"

The Bruce is hiding in the Scottish Highlands to rest and search his soul for a way forward, realizing that Comyn has betrayed him. Aubry (Michael Layton) is told to organize the coronation but is so disturbed at the unrest of the Scots that he plans to have a spare crown made in case the real one should be spirited away. Comyn encounters the Bruce in the cathedral and a fight ensues; Comyn meets the fate of all traitors but the Bruce has committed sacrilege in killing him on sacred ground. The bishop is angry and sad but confirms that he cannot enter the armed struggle as his vow, made on a Crusade, was not to take up arms against Edward. He ought to excommunicate the Bruce for the sacrilege but decides not to; the Bruce vows to fight for the freedom of the Scots from the English, whatever the cost.

Edward, discovering that the Bruce is not dead after all, prepares to march into Scotland and put down the rebellion, despite being near to death. When he does die, his weak son is bullied by the proud Queen Eleanor (Hildegard Neil) and the English warlords to continue the fight. The Bruce and the bishop meet for a parlay; the bishop has dug out his Crusader clothes and is preparing to wear them in battle in support of his friend now that his vow is no longer binding. In the final great battle he acquits himself well in the thick of the fighting. This time the Scots do not scatter; the Bruce has won the day.

Many years later, the Bruce's heart, encased in a lead reliquary, leads the Scots Crusaders in the Holy Land.

Comment

According to producer Bob Carruthers in *The London Times* (February 18, 1995): "*Chasing the Deer* proved you can make a good film and have a lot of fun in the bargain. We hope *The*

Bruce will give ordinary people another chance to join in another great celluloid adventure. The role of the Bruce himself will make an unknown actor into a star. The producers have begun a countrywide search for the man who will be King. Somewhere out there [is] the Bruce."

The Bruce began filming in April 1995, with Sandy Welch in the lead. He didn't become a star but gives a star quality performance. The locations included Needpath Castle, Dunfermline Abbey, Blackness Castle, Houlgate Village and Doune Castle. A scene was even filmed in Egypt. The locations, sets, costumes and weaponry were the equal of any bigger budget film including *Braveheart*.

We first see Reed as the bishop as he addresses the Bruce (Welch), the would-be king of Scotland — if he isn't first assassinated by order of King Edward (Brian Blessed). Reed's Scots accent is perfect and but not surprisingly so; he was always good at accents. As he jokes with the crowd, the bishop reveals himself as a man of power and confidence, a man of his people, and a man totally committed to Scotland. He is also committed to the rebels, but only as far as the law will allow.

At the Bruce's coronation on Palm Sunday, the Bishop unites the country: "He's won the right through force of arms and the blessing of God. Let all good men see that Scotland has a king again." Reed adds a human touch to the proceedings, smiling and bouncing up and down with joy.

Brian Blessed is excellent throughout, especially so when he plays the "Oliver Reed role" after learning that the Bruce has been crowned.

The battle scenes are brilliantly staged because they don't seem staged at all. The soldiers were presented as what they were: men fighting, often clumsily, for their lives. The re-enactors have a pleasingly amateur look about them. There is no choreography or stylization; just the simple brutality of warfare. As the battle ends with the Scots' victory, the Bruce raises his sword and lowers the curtain on an excellent production.

The Bruce was given a world premiere at the Glasgow Odeon on March 1, 1996 (tickets at £50.00, black tie or full highland dress required). Proceeds were to aid the Wallace Clan Trust. *The Glasgow Herald* found the film "spectacular, convincing, and bloodthirsty." Reed was to play Sawney Beane, "infamous 16th century Scottish cannibal" in a film to be produced by the same team, but it was not to be.

Despite the quality of the film and his performance in it, *The Bruce* did nothing to advance Reed's career. He was off screen for two years until Michael Winner cast him in a small but effective role in *Parting Shots*. Reed made the bishop a totally believable character and gave the best performance of his career that few outside of Scotland ever managed to see.

The Incredible Adventures of Marco Polo (1998)

Avalanche Home Entertainment

Crew— Director: George Erschbamer; Writer: Peter Waelbeck (aka Harry Alan Towers); Producer: John Dunning; Original Music; Leon Aronson: Cinematography: Cliff Hokason; Film Editing: Jacques Jean; Casting: Susan Forrest, Andrea Kenyon, Art Director: Konstantin Zagorsky; Costume Design: Anya Kusnetsova; Hair Stylist–Makeup: Jules Korshoonoff; Supervising Sound Editor: Michael B. Bordeleau; Stunt Coordinator: Oleg Korytin.

Cast— Don Dimant (Marco Polo), Oliver Reed (Capt. Cornelius Donovan), Jack Palance (Beelzebub), John Hallam (Ali Ben Hassad), Cas Anvar (Youssef), Jeff Saumier (Nicolo), Garth Hunt (Grand Master), Gavin Abbott (Leader), Lara Bobroff (Princess Marita), Lyudmilla Brusentsova (Sylvia), Graham Stark (Old King), Viktor Polusmak (King's retainer), Julia Volchkova (Jasmine), Mikhail Shayevich (Rusticello).

Synopsis

A retelling of Marco Polo's voyage to the Far East in search of trade routes.

Comment

This was apparently released to Brazilian TV and went straight to video in the U.S. We were not able to find a copy to review, but that's probably a good thing. It was filmed on location in the Ukraine with loads of local talent. We hope that they appreciated working with Reed and that he enjoyed the experience.

Parting Shots (1999)

Michael Winner Films; Scimitar Films; released on May 14, 1999, in the U.K.; no U.S. release

Crew— Story-Producer-Director: Michael Winner; Writers: Michael Winner, Nick Mead; Assistant Producers: John Blezard, Timothy Pitt Miller; Associate Producer: Ron Purdie; Original Music: Les Reed; Cinematography: Ousama Rawi; Film Editor: Arnold Crust Jr. (aka Michael Winner); Supervising Editor: Chris Barnes; Casting: Noel Davis; Production Design: Crispian Sallis; Makeup Artist: Deborah Lindsell; Hair Stylist: Stevie Hall; First Assistant Director: Ron Purdie; Second Assistant Director: Antony Ford; Third Assistant Director: Toby Hefferman; Property Master: Brian Lofthouse; Props: Tim Prosser; Assistant Art Director: Tom Still; Production Buyer: Lucinda Sturgis; Graphic Designer: Carol Kupisz; Carpenter: Steve Challenor; Dressing Props: Dave Crawford; Stand-by Dressing Props: Andy Harris; Art Department Assistant: Joanna Foley; Sound Editor: Jim Roddam; Assistant Sound Editor: Peter Dansie; Boom Operator: Keith Batten; Dialogue Re-recordist: Venetia Crust; Sound Re-recording Mixers: Tim Cavagin, Dean Humphreys, Mark Lafbery; Assistant Camera: Mike Parker; Camera Grip: Peter Scorah; Still Photographers: Sophie Baker, Toby Corney, Tom Hilton; Electricians: Ray Bateman, Ken Lowe; Gaffer: John Haylen; Best Boy: Stuart King; Clapper Loader: Ulric Van den Bogaerde; Wardrobe Mistress: Emma Lock; Wardrobe Assistant: Maura McDermott; Wardrobe Supervisor: Sue Wain; Musician: Chris Rea; Music Arrangers: Les Reed, Max Middleton; Conductor: Barrie Guard; Production Accountants: Irena Butcher, David Maconochie; Script Supervisor: Hilary Fagg; Location Manager; Michael Harvey; Assistant Location Manager: Midge Ferguson; Production Coordinator: Christine Fenton; Production Assistants: Alan Grim-Wood, Toby MacDonald, Julia MacKenzie, Greg Turner; Office Assistant: Zoe Marie Vigus; Picture Vehicle Technician: Ian Clarke.

Cast— Chris Rea (Harry Sterndale), Felicity Kendall (Jill Saunders), Bob Hoskins (Gerd Layton), Ben Kingsley (Renzo Locatelli), Joanna Lumley (Freda), Oliver Reed (Jamie Campbell-Stewart), Diana Rigg (Lisa), John Cleese (Maurice Walpole), Gareth Hunt (Inspector Bass), Peter Davison (John), Patrick Ryecart (Cleverley), Edward Hardwicke (Dr. Joseph), Nicholas Gecks (D.C. Ray), Ruby Snape (Melissa), Nicola Bryant (Beverley), Brian Poyser (President Zlomov), Sheila Steafel (President's Wife), Trevor Baxter (Maitre D'), Timothy Carlton (Commissioner Grosvenor), Nicky Henson (Askew), Caroline Langrishe (Vanessa), Taryn Kay (Ruth Layton), Alison Reynolds (Zoe Layton), Michael Ayers (Young Harry), Crispian Belfage (Courier), Steven Bronowski (Officer), Steve Brownlie (Young Walpole), Nora Connolly (Mother of the Bride), Barney Craig (Policeman), Marc Crealmann (Guest), Roland Curram (Lord Selwyn), Daisy Donovan (Girl), Father Donovan (Vicar), Peter Gale (Ballistics Expert), Jack Galloway (TV Journalist), Mark Gillies (Policeman), Andrew Grainger (Best Man), David Griffith (Hotel Official), Mottel Hathaway (Bellboy), Alison Jack (TV Newscaster), Craig Jelley (Cleverley, aged 12), Tim Kelly, Jay Hammond (Boys), Jenny Logan (Lady Selwyn), David Marrick (Wine Waiter), Sarah Parish (Ad Agency Receptionist), Vanessa Perry (Bride), Sarah Reeves (Young Lisa), Christopher Routh (Young Policeman), Mildred Shay (Old Lady at Wedding), Anthony Smee (George), Donald Standen (Rick), Mark Stratford (Policeman), John Tordoff (Father of the Bride), Nathan Weaver (Harry, aged 12), William Wilde (Harry's Solicitor).

Synopsis

Harry Sterndale (Chris Rea), a failed photographer, is told that he has three months to live, as he apparently has an aggressive cancer. After mulling over his short future he decides that he will kill or destroy all the people who have ever crossed or hurt him. He assumes that he will be dead before any link can be made to him for the killings, so what the heck? To his surprise, he falls in love with Jill (Felicity Kendall). He hires an aging hitman, Jamie Campbell-Stewart (Oliver Reed), to kill him in the hopes of Jill profiting from his huge insurance policy. Harry wants to do the revenging himself, but the hitman is paid to kill him off when he's finished, so has to follow Harry like a bloodhound. But then the doctor recalls him to explain that there was a misdiagnosis — and the hitman is still there. After all, a contract's a contract.

Comment

Jamie Campbell-Stewart is of the old school, of military bearing and a bit the worse for wear. So was Oliver Reed at this point in his career. Only Michael Winner held him in any esteem and he threw his old friend the opportunity to work on his new project *Parting Shots*.

The film is a wonderful Winner concoction: great locations, lots of well-known faces popping up in cameo parts, and a rollicking good tale. But it was not well received by the critics; *Empire* magazine named it the 42nd worst film of all time. The authors particularly liked the scene where Harry and Jill are patronized by the customers and staff of an up-market restaurant when they are on a date; it brings Winner's recently axed TV cooking program deliciously to mind! The satire in the film is effective and on target even if in relatively bad taste.

"It takes great skill and judgment to gather together some of the best loved comedy actors in Britain and weave around them a movie as stunningly unfunny as this" (*Sun*, May 15, 1999); "It so closely resembles a home movie, casually improvised by ... Winner and his thesp friends for their private amusement, that I felt like an embarrassed intruder while viewing it" (*Observer Review*, May 16, 1999); "*Parting Shots* is a sad coda to a clearly ill Oliver Reed, who cameos as a hitman. Reed's work with Winner in the Sixties ... [and] Joseph Losey's *The Damned*, stand as a tribute to his feral screen charisma" (*Guardian*, May 14, 1999).

The whole thing is worth a viewing for the last glance of Jamie Campbell-Stewart before he walks away, exonerated and relieved of the contract, if not the fee. Reed, though in a tiny part, was in form and ready for more work. In fact, rumor had it that his daily appearance, sober and fully prepared for work, had not gone unnoticed in certain areas. He had proved himself fit, responsible and ready for a challenge — in fact, he was employable.

Orpheus and Eurydice (2000)

Pissanos International Film & TV Productions; Unizarre International Film & TV Productions; released by Pissanos International Film Distributors in Europe in 2000; no U.S. release

Crew— Director-Writer-Producer Paul Pissanos; Associate Producer: George Angelopoulos; Cinematographer: George Antonakis; Film Editor: Ilias Sgouropoulos; Casting: Tricia Evans, Lynn Merritt; Costume Design: Anna Ivanovna Kuznetsova; Production Manager: Elizabeth Pissano; Sound Mixer: Nikos Despotidis; Supervising Sound Editor: Mikhail Ivanovitch Reznitcenko; Special Effects: Costas Arpajanis, Rania Lada, Stelios Mamalis; Choreographer; Olympia Gelodari.

Cast—Andrew Bullock (Orpheus), Carolina Liriti (Eurydice), Oliver Reed (Narrator), David Bowles (Alcaeus), Ilia Nathanial (Musaeus), Francesca Agati (Aglaoniki), Christopher Radcliff (Hermes), Ted Merwood (Lycon), Joseph Gatt (Charon), Peter Theiss (Pluto), Chejon Fernandes (Aristaeus),

Olga Balaganova (Persephone), Anna Maria Economoy (Styx), Kyriakos Cosmides (Dionysus), Steve Chandras (Glaucus), Rika Dialina (Shepherdess), Angelika Vaena, Vassia Bizidi (Dancers).

Comment

The authors have no way of knowing how faithfully the filmmakers kept to the old tale because we could not find a copy to view. That Reed's narration was wonderful, we have no doubt, since that beautiful voice was masterly at conveying every nuance of the words in his script. We look forward to catching up with it one day.

Gladiator (2000)

DreamWorks SKG, Universal Pictures; Scott Free Productions; released by DreamWorks in the U.S. and U.K. in 2000

Crew— Director: Ridley Scott; Story: David Franzoni; Screenplay: David Franzoni, John Logan, William Nicholson; Producers: David Franzoni, Branko Lustig, Douglas Wick; Executive Producers: Laurie MacDonald, Walter F. Parkes, Ridley Scott; Associate Producer: Terry Needham; Original Music: Lisa Gerrard, Hans Zimmer; Cinematographer: John Mathieson; Film Editing: Pietro Scalia; Casting: Louis DiGiaimo; Production Design: Arthur Max; Set Decoration: Crispian Sallis; Costume Design: Janty Yates; Key Makeup Artist: Paul Engelen; Makeup Artists: Jo Allen, Melissa Lackersteen, Laura McIntosh, Trefor Proud; Key Hair Stylist: Graham Johnston; Hair Stylists: Anita Butler, Carmel Jackson, Alex King, Marese Langan, Emma Sheldrick; Sculptor: Rob Mayor; Unit Manager: Judi Bunn; Production Supervisors: Brian Cook, Zdravko Madzarevic, Ty Warren; Unit Production Manager: Branko Lustig; Post-Production Supervisor: Lisa Dennis Kennedy; First Assistant Director: Terry Needham; Second Assistant Director: Adam Somner; Second Unit Director: Alexander Witt; Drapery Master: Colin Fox; Drapesman: Stephen Ashby.

Cast— Russell Crowe (Maximus), Joaquin Phoenix (Commodus), Connie Nielsen (Lucilla), Oliver Reed (Proximo), Richard Harris (Emperor Marcus Aurelius), Derek Jacobi (Gracchus), Djimon Hounsou (Juba), David Scofield (Falco), John Shrapnel (Gaius), Tomas Arana (Quintus), Ralf Moeller (Hagen), Spencer Treat Clark (Lucius), David Hemmings (Cassius), Tommy Flanagan (Cicero), Sven-Ole Thorsen (Tiger), Omid Djalili (Slave Trader), Nicholas McGaughey (Praetorian Officer), Chris Kell (Scribe), Tony Curran, Mark Lewis (Assassins), John Quinn (Valerius), Alun Raglan (Praetorian Guard #1), David Bailie (Engineer), Chick

Allen (German Leader), Dave Nicholls (Giant Man), Al Hunter Ashton (Rome Trainer #1), Billy Dowd (Narrator), Ray Calleja (Lucius' Attendant), Giannina Facio (Maximus' Wife), Giorgio Cantarini (Maximus' Son), Alan Corduner, James Fiddy, Nic Main, Joao Costa Menezes, Neil Roche (Roman Soldiers), Ruth Frendo (Roman Girl), Antonio Meitin (Battlefield Medic), Norman Campbell Rees (Sedan Chair Carrier), Christian Simpson (Chief Catapult Operator).

Synopsis

In Germania in A.D. 180, Emperor Marcus Aurelius (Richard Harris) is engaged in a fierce battle against the barbarian tribes that would conquer Rome. His intensely loyal commander is General Maximus (Russell Crowe), a Spaniard. Maximus leads his troops to victory and is rewarded with the offer to lead the Empire after Marcus Aurelius' death. When the emperor's estranged — and diabolical — son Commodus (Joaquin Phoenix) discovers this, he murders his gravely ill father and orders Maximus to be killed.

Maximus escapes and returns to Spain where he finds his estate in ruins and his wife and son murdered. He is captured and sold into slavery to become a gladiator. In North Africa, along with Juba (Djimon Housou), he is bought by Proximo (Oliver Reed), a former champion and now a trainer of gladiators. Initially Maximus refuses to comply but he and Juba form a team and defeat all comers. Proximo is impressed with Maximus' prowess and realizes that the Spaniard could be his ticket back to Rome — and glory. The teacher wins over his pupil by telling Maximus that, if he is successful, he may one day stand before the emperor ... Commodus.

The new emperor is being pulled apart by his distrust of the Senate, his incestuous love of his sister Lucilla (Connie Nielson) and his own demons. Lucilla is terrified of her brother and his growing interest in — and influence over — her son Lucius (Spenser Treat Clark). Maximus enters Rome as a slave but soon becomes a sensation, idolized by the people, not least by Lucius. Commodus demands to meet the masked gladiator and is stunned to see his rival. Lucilla is equally dumbfounded; she and Maximus had been lovers. Commodus is torn between his hatred of Maximus and his desire to please his subjects who have elevated the gladiator to near godlike status. Senator Gracchus (Derek Jacobi) leads the opposition to Commodus and joins forces with Lucilla to free Maximus and reunite him with his still loyal troops. Commodus discovers the attempted coup and arrests Maximus after having Proximo murdered for giving his gladiator the opportunity to escape. Gracchus is also arrested and Lucilla is neutralized as Commodus takes Lucius hostage.

As a demonstration of his power, Commodus stages a fight to the death in the arena with Maximus — after first stabbing him while he's chained in a cell. Mortally wounded, Maximus kills Commodus, freeing Rome of his evil, and meets his murdered family in Paradise.

Comment

Gladiator, the Best Picture of 2000 — and one of the best of all time — began when producers Douglas Wick and Walter Parker came into director Sir Ridley Scott's office and deposited on his desk a copy of the painting "Police Veso (Thumbs Down)" which featured a gladiator in an arena. Scott said in the press release: "That image spoke to me of the Roman Empire in all its glory and wickedness. I knew right then and there I was hooked."

Parker had a screenplay by David Franzoni, John Longorn and William Nicholson on that very subject in his possession. Parker in the press release: "As the script came together, we realized the real challenge would be to find a filmmaker who could deal with the sheer physical size and spectacle of the movie with such mastery that the essential elements of character and story would not be overpowered by the setting. From the start, Ridley Scott was at the top of the list." Scott, again from the press release: "Entertainment has frequently been used as a tool of leaders as a means to distract an abused citizenry. The most tyrannical ruler must beguile his people even as he brutalizes them. Our story suggests that, should a hero rise out of the carnage of the arena, his popularity would give him tremendous power ... and were he to be a genuine champion of the people, he might threaten even the most absolute tyrant."

"Sword and sandal" movies have long been

a staple of the movie industry, but never, it seems, for long. They had last prospered in the 1950s on a "B" level, often starring Gordon Scott, Steve Reeves or Ed Fury. The genre got a huge upgrade in 1959 with Charlton Heston in *Ben-Hur,* then Kirk Douglas in *Spartacus* in 1960. The films continued on that high level with *Cleopatra* (1963) and *The Fall of the Roman Empire* (1964) but by the decade's end these epics had fallen into oblivion. Blockbusters of the 1970s tended to look forward, as with the *Star Wars* and *Star Trek* series. DreamWorks and Universal were gambling that the public was ready for a trip back in time, and gave that public one of the best films ever made.

Gladiator began production on February 1, 1999, in England at Shepperton Studios and Farnham, which stood in for Germania in the opening battle scene. Almost 30,000 arrows were fired during the fight. As luck would have it, the British Forestry Commission had designated the Bourne Woods, where many of the scenes' flaming arrows were fired, to be deforested. Scott was only too happy to comply.

The company moved next to Quarzato, Morocco, to film the marketplace where Maximus is sold, Proximo's gladiator school and the arena where Maximus and Juba practice their new trade. The next stop was Malta.

Reed had been on the set for a month and had, not surprisingly, become one of the best liked and most respected members of the cast. It was felt that he was delivering a powerhouse performance and that he had resumed his career. In the press release Reed said: "I'm responsible for finding out if Maximus can fight, taking him to Rome, and putting him into the big game. Proximo's a wonderful character — but then, if you're involved in something this big, you have to believe that your character can compete with everything else that's going on. An actor is only as good as the script he eventually gets. You can look at the old statues and paintings but the rest is in the script and the way the director uses his camera. Occasionally some filmmaker comes up with an idea that interests me and this was certainly one of those occasions."

But for all his bluster, Reed was, at this point of his fading career, unsure of what to do. He nearly did nothing. In addition to having

directed some of Reed's best films, Michael Winner proved to be an excellent judge of what was best for his old friend's career. Reed had kept that career more or less alive by alternating "guest appearances" in obscure films with larger roles in even worse ones. When he turned in an excellent performance in Winner's *Parting Shots,* the word went out that Reed still had it. According to Winner,

> It was that employment which alerted people in the industry to the fact that he was still around and that he was all right to work with because if Michael Winner would take him on, Oliver Reed was "safe." One day Oliver said to me, "Ridley Scott wants me to go read for him for a part in *Gladiator.* I can't audition, I'm a star." I said, "Oliver — read for Ridley Scott. You need a last act of your life. You need the money. You need the prestige" [Winner, 115].

Interviewee Reed said on the *Gladiator* DVD, "My agent phoned me up, as they do, and said that 'Ridley Scott would like to have you in a movie, and they're going to send you the script.' And so I opened the bag when it came through the door and the first thing that slipped out was 'The sending of this script does not constitute an offer.' So I thought, 'Fuck it.' And then my agent phoned up and said, 'He'd like you to read for it.' And I thought, 'I don't read for people. If he wants to see my work, he can see it ... talk to anyone.' And then I thought again — and I thought, 'Well, if he really does want me to read for it, perhaps I can get a free ticket to London — I can go see a show.' So I thought this is something that... "All right ... I never read ... but for Ridley, I'll do it.'"

In the end, Reed wisely read for and won the role that would provide him with the last act of his life. But not as Michael Winner envisioned.

On Sunday, May 2, 1999, Oliver Reed was kicking back, as was his custom, at The Pub in Valletta, Malta. With him was his wife Josephine, for whom he had just bought a gold bracelet for her 35th birthday. He was, as was also his custom, buying drinks for the house which on this day included the crew of HMS *Cumberland.* After several hours of drinking,

Reed went into cardiac arrest. Despite frantic attempts to revive him, both at The Pub and St. Luke's Hospital, he died.

Richard Harris said, "I got quite a shock when I heard it. It's a shame, because this movie could have revived his career" (Landau, 122). According to Russell Crowe, "Oliver went out the way he lived his life. I think it's one of the best performances ... so it can be a memorial to him" (122). Sir Ridley Scott said in *The London Times* (May 26, 1999): "Oliver Reed's death was a great loss to both me and the world of cinema." David Hemmings had a lovely remembrance of his old friend: "I had known Oliver for forty years, but hadn't seen him in a decade or so. When Oliver walked into the Phoenix Bar, ordering orange juice, he looked forever the gentleman he could some-times be. With gray, flowing hair, a silver beard, and a white linen jacket, he looked the quintessential expatriate, at home in Malta; swirling an arm at the assembled company, as if he were Her Majesty's representative, bestowing pleasure at the drop of his white fedora" (Hemmings, 400).

Reed's death was, less sentimentally, also a great loss to DreamWorks and Universal. He still had a key scene yet not filmed, giving the company two very unpleasant and expensive choices. One: scrap all of Reed's footage and hire another actor to reshoot the scenes. This would involve gigantic expenses; all the actors with whom Reed had appeared would have to be called back and sets would have to be rebuilt. Two: finish Reed's scene through computer generated imaging. This would also be expensive, time-consuming and difficult.

Fortunately for both the film and Reed's legacy, they went for choice number two.

"Reports of Oliver Reed's death may have been exaggerated," *The London Times* (May 26, 1999) somewhat disrespectfully announced. For many, the techno-wizardry that allowed Reed's performance to be completed also diminished the quality of that performance to that of a magic trick.

Steven Spielberg's DreamWorks technicians in Hollywood and Scott's at The Mill (Shepperton's special effects center) created a CGI Oliver Reed. Rob Delicate, head of production at The Mill, told *The London Times* (May 21, 1999): "We have the technology to replicate Reed. We can make a 3-D image by isolating his head from previous scenes and recomposing him in a different location. We can place an artist's mouth in Reed's head, but cutting together his own words from previous shots is hard. The whole process involves a lot of intense work, but fortu-

Oliver Reed as Proximo (one of his greatest performances) in *Gladiator* (Scott Free/Dreamworks/Universal, 2000).

nately Dreamworks have allocated a substantial special effects budget for the movie. He is quite a character within the film and although we could put a range of emotion on his face, it is not going to be the real Reed."

Scott said, "It was like a jigsaw puzzle. We reorganized three shots of his close-ups from three different scenes. I had his body double walk up to the camera stand, talk, and then I put Oliver's CGI head on the body" (Landau, 122). John Nelson, special effects supervisor, said, "When Oliver passed on, we were all pretty shaken. He had given such a great performance, but Ridley, Pietro (Scali-Ed) the producers and I knew we would have to use a few subtle [visual effects] to finish his part of the movie. Pietro selected footage of Oliver from existing shots and we put him into new backgrounds for the scenes we had left to do, in some cases changing the color of his costume. What we did was small compared to our other tasks on the film. What Oliver did was much greater. He gave an inspiring, moving performance. All we did was help him finish it" (Landau, 122).

Reed dominated each scene in which he appeared, which is incredible, as most of his screen time is shared with the equally dominating Russell Crowe, winner of the Best Actor Oscar. Reed's snub by the Academy — he wasn't even nominated — is hard to justify or to understand.

Josephine Reed wrote in *The Sunday Telegraph* (February 18, 2001): "Ollie was never part of the Hollywood scene. He was committed to the British Film Industry and made a conscious decision not to work in America. I think that may have gone against him."

Simon Reed wrote in *The Sunday Telegraph* (February 18, 2001): "The lack of an Oscar nomination is sad. It seemed a real possibility only a short while ago. The family had very high hopes. Ridley Scott took a big gamble when he offered him the role. I think Olly was determined to repay Ridley's faith and gave the best performance he possibly could." Michael Winner said, "It would be disgraceful if he had missed out on any honor because of his drinking. The awards are for acting, not sobriety. Oliver was a far better actor than people gave him credit for."

Looking back, one wonders why Oliver

Reed never received a single nomination. He was certainly up to that standard in *Women in Love* and *The Devils*....

Reed's big scene takes place in Proximo's school. He stands on a terrace looking at his small world when Maximus arrives. Reed is all blazing blue eyes and purring menace.

PROXIMO: You're good, Spaniard. But you're not that good. You could be magnificent.

MAXIMUS: I am required to kill. So I kill. That is enough.

PROXIMO: The young emperor has arranged a series of spectacles to commemorate his father, Marcus Aurelius.... So finally after five years of scratching a living in flea-infested villages, we're finally going back to the Colosseum ... fifty thousand Romans watching every movement of your sword — willing you to make that killer blow — the silence before you strike — and the noise afterwards.

MAXIMUS: You were a gladiator.

PROXIMO: Yes, I was.

MAXIMUS: You won your freedom.

PROXIMO: A long time ago, the emperor presented me with a wooden sword. He touched me on the shoulder and I was free.

MAXIMUS: You knew Marcus Aurelius?

PROXIMO: I did not say I knew him. I said he touched me on the shoulder once.

MAXIMUS: I too want to stand before the emperor as you did.

PROXIMO: Then listen to me. Learn from me. Win the crowd and you will win your freedom.

MAXIMUS: I will win the crowd. I will give them something they've never seen before.

Reed and Crowe gave the cinema audience something it sees only too rarely: two high-powered, deadly earnest actors at the top of their game. They could almost be talking about themselves — the world-weary old pro, looking for one more triumph, and the young upstart looking for his first.

Crowe had been on the brink of superstardom and *Gladiator* pushed him to the top. It was a wonderful performance, well deserving of the Oscar. Few actors have ever combined intense physicality with emotional sensitivity as convincingly. Supposedly Mel Gibson and Antonio Banderas were considered for the role. Crowe had gained fifty pounds for his role in *The Insider*— another terrific performance — and lost it for *Gladiator*, which was filmed a few months later, mostly by working on his Australian farm. Scott said, "He went from a paunchy, middle-aged scientist to a gladiator. Not bad. In other words, he's a real actor. Russell has an uncanny way of internalizing a role" (Landau, 122).

He certainly needed to be in top condition, fighting not only gladiators but also tigers (although he never got within fifteen feet of them — the illusion was carried out through CGI) and was almost pitted against a rhino. The crew created several ingenious shortcuts to help Crowe through the ordeal of his performance including making his armor of foam rubber. Twelve complete sets were created: breastplates, leg armor and helmets in various states of repair and disrepair. (In all, over 10,000 costumes were designed.) *The New Yorker* (May 8, 2000) described Crowe's Maximus as "stocky, sad and stubbled, with a low Neanderthal brow and quick eyes, educated in suspicion; though shorter than most of those around him, he has mastered the art of walking taller than any of them. Once or twice he tries a smile and it practically cracks the lens." Actually, Crowe had little to smile about when filming the arena scenes; the temperature often topped 100 degrees and he broke several bones in his foot and arm and tore both bicep tendons.

Also, his facial cuts after the opening battle scenes in Germania required no makeup; his horse bolted and ran him through some tree branches. It's fair to say that Crowe may have been more of a hero than the audience realized. That said, a hero is only as worthy as the villain he challenges, and Crowe was fortunate to be paired with Joaquin Phoenix's Commodus. Surely one of the most depraved characters ever seen on the screen, he murders his ailing father, lusts after his own sister, and stabs his helpless rival before dueling with him. It's difficult to sink much lower. Yet the genius of Phoenix's performance is that he — somehow — makes Commodus more pathetic than hateful. Almost. (Several of the *Gladiator* characters ac-

tually existed, including Commodus. He was the only Roman emperor to actually fight in the arena. But unlike the film's Commodus, he didn't actually die there; he was strangled in his dressing room by a gladiator named Narcissus.)

The entire cast is wonderful, a tribute to Scott and the acting talent assembled. Connie Nielsen is a standout as the beleaguered Lucilla; her revulsion at her brother's advances is chilling.

One of the biggest "stars" of the film was the stunning recreation of the Colosseum, courtesy of Dreamworks and The Mill. It took four months and three hundred technicians plus the magic of CGI to create the illusion with a great deal of ingenuity. In order to create realistic lighting effects, cinematographer John Mathieson had a velarion built — over 500 feet long and suspended on 14 steel towers to be raised or lowered to create the desired shadows. Inside the Colleseum were over 2000 extras mixed with over 30,000 CGId spectators. These are two small examples of the expertise required.

When *Gladiator* wrapped, DreamWorks offered to give the sets to the Maltese government to use as a theme park, but they were turned down and the sets were struck. *Gladiator* premiered in Los Angeles on May 1, 2000, and in the rest of the world between May 4 and June 1. Reviews for the film and its major contributors were, as one would expect, overwhelmingly positive.

"Mr. Reed seems to find it delicious that he is mentor to a character he might have played himself a long time ago in a galaxy far, far away. With a satisfied, sleazy purr and red still dancing in his eyes from the last party he attended, Mr. Reed still looks capable of malice" (*New York Times*, May 5, 2000); "This is truly a gladiator movie for our times. Our hero lives up to the film's title as coached by a sardonically benevolent Oliver Reed. The movie is dedicated to him, and a jolly monument it is too. Looking bronzed and fit, Ollie certainly doesn't look like a man who wasn't going to make the premiere. His performance is great, too" (*The Sunday Telegraph*, May 13, 2000); "Having cowered at his Bill Sikes in *Oliver!*, I thought Reed was a terrifying actor who never got his due; with his bullock's bulk and that soft, whispering sea roar of a voice, he could have trod the Burt Lancaster path. This last role is not quite meaty enough for a send-off, but I liked the sight of his blue eyes glazed with the tedium of daily massacre, opening a little wider as he first watches Maximus in the ring — gold dust glinting in the sand" (*The New Yorker*, May 8, 2000); "[I]t is Joaquin Phoenix's bravado turn as the saturnine weasel Commodus that delivers the biggest surprise in the cast. He gives the nine-year-olds in all of us someone who deserves our hissings" (*Newsday*, May 5, 2000); "It is one of the cinema's most ambitious and successful recreations of Imperial Rome" (*The Guardian* May 4, 2000).

A much more personal view came from Reed's widow Josephine, who found seeing her husband on screen traumatic. *The Sunday Telegraph* (May 14, 2000) reported, "It should have been a moment of pride and exhilaration, the triumphant return of her hell-raiser husband to cinema screen success. Instead, this week, in the seclusion of a private London cinema, Reed's widow could not bear to watch her husband's poignant final scene in his last film *Gladiator*. 'I just had to close my eyes in those moments. It was all too much for me. It seemed so strange to see Oliver up there on the screen even larger than in life.'"

Reed said in his final interview: "I wouldn't want to go anywhere without her. I can't stand being apart from her. She's a lovely woman and, do you know what? She's put up with me all these years. We like being with each other and she understands that, now and then, I like to have a drink or two."

Gladiator was the last word on Oliver Reed's career and his life. Perhaps the last word on the film should be, "This is why cinema was invented" (*The Sunday Telegraph*, May 13, 2000).

Note: a final credit reads "To our friend, Oliver Reed."

Afterword by Michael Winner, OBE

I miss Oliver terribly. I think of him many times. He was the most wonderful, kind, gentle (yes, I did say gentle) person. I'm glad that I helped his return to the big time even though it was sadly short-lived. He was doing *Parting Shots* for me and said, "Ridley Scott wants me to go and read for him. I don't read for parts, I'm a star." I said, "Oliver, you need a third act for your life. I told you to do TV with Ken Russell when you said to me in Austria I'd made you a movie star and you wouldn't do TV. Now I'm telling you to read for Ridley." Happily, he did.

Our last conversation was a few days before he died. I was sending the show business editor of *The Daily Mail*, a lady, to interview Oliver in Malta. I said, "Please, Oliver, don't throw her in the swimming pool!" He promised to behave. He was excited. He was going to play Uncle Silas on TV. "I've never done TV," he said. A couple of days later the phone rang. I was in the kitchen having a snack dinner. *The Daily Express* said, "Oliver Reed's dead." I literally cried out in sorrow. I couldn't believe it. I'd lost a friend of some forty years. We'd sat on film sets and gossiped in between takes day after day. In many countries. Now my friend was gone. I flew to Ireland for his funeral. I was the only person from show business who attended it. I didn't cry at my mother's funeral or my father's. Oliver's coffin sat in the church and I walked down the aisle and touched it. When I turned to go back to my seat, I was weeping.

The funeral cortege went through little Irish villages. The local people stood by the roadside and crossed themselves as it went by. It was very moving. We ended up in a field behind Oliver's favorite pub. Everyone was saying, "What a lovely place, those tall trees, the birds, the peace." Oliver's first wife, Kate, Irish and beautiful, was walking with me. "What a shithouse," she said, "the whole place is covered in cow dung. There's flies and midges, it's fucking awful." I imagined phoning Oliver the next day and talking about his funeral. I'd have told him what Kate said. I know he'd have answered very quietly, "She always had a great sense of humor."

I still talk to Oliver. He may be gone but he's not gone for me. Some newspapers wrote he'd had a wasted life. What rubbish! He was a great actor, he starred in many films, he loved life, had a drink or two (or fifty) now and then. He lived life to the fullest. I am honored and lucky to have been part of Oliver's life. He was as dear a friend as I ever had. He is not gone. He is not forgotten. He's with me every day. I still love him.

Michael Winner, OBE
London, April 17, 2008

Director Michael Winner gave Oliver Reed a starring role in The System *(1964) and would direct several of Reed's best performances including* The Jokers *(1966). Winner provided him with a late comeback role in* Parting Shots *(1999).*

Appendix:
Television Dramas

- 1959 *The Golden Spur*
- 1959 *The Invisible Man*—"The Mink Coat"
- 1959 *The Third Man*—"Toys of the Dead"
- 1962 *Play of the Week*—"The Second Chef"
- 1962 *Play of the Week*—"Murder in Shorthand"
- 1963 *The Saint*—"The King of the Beggars"
- 1964 *The Saint*—"Sophia"
- 1964 *The Third Man*—"A Question in Ice"
- 1965 *It's Dark Outside*—"The Prevalence of Liars"
- 1965 *R3*—*Good Clean Fun*
- 1966 *Court Martial*—"La Belle France"
- 1983 *Masquerade*—"Wolfen"
- 1985 *Black Arrow*
- 1985 *Christopher Columbus* miniseries
- 1987 *Dragonard*
- 1989 *The Lady and the Highwayman*
- 1989 *Master of Dragonard Hill*
- 1990 *Treasure Island*
- 1990 *A Ghost in Monte Carlo*
- 1993 *Return to Lonesome Dove* miniseries
- 1996 *Die Tunnelgangster von Berlin*
- 1998 *Jeremiah*

Bibliography

Baxter, John. *An Appalling Talent: Ken Russell.* London: Joseph, 1973.

Bilbow, Tony, Michael Aspel, and John Gau. *Lights, Camera, Action!: A Century of the Cinema.* Boston: Little, Brown, 1995.

Bryant, Christopher. *Glenda Jackson: The Biography.* New York: HarperCollins, 1999.

Caute, David. *Joseph Losey: A Revenge on Life.* London: Faber and Faber, 1996.

Ciment, Michael. *Conversations with Losey.* London: Methuen, 1985.

Court, Hazel. *Hazel Court, Horror Queen: An Autobiography.* Sheffield, England: Tomahawk Press, 2008.

Crawford, Michael. *Parcel Arrived Safely, Tied With String: My Autobiography.* London: Century, 1999.

Del Vecchio, Deborah, and Tom Johnson. *Peter Cushing: The Gentle Man of Horror and His 91 Films.* Jefferson, NC: McFarland, 1992.

Del Vecchio, Deborah, and Tom Johnson. *Hammer Films: An Exhaustive Filmography.* Jefferson, NC: McFarland, 1996.

de Rham, Edith. *Joseph Losey.* London: Andre Deutsch, 1991.

Goodwin, Cliff. *Evil Spirits: The Life of Oliver Reed.* London: Virgin, 2000.

Hemmings, David. *Blow-up and Other Exaggerations.* London: Robson Books, 2004.

Johnson, Tom, and Mark A. Miller. *The Christopher Lee Filmography: All Theatrical Releases, 1948–2003.* Jefferson, NC: McFarland, 2004.

Landau, Diana, ed. *Gladiator—The Making of the Ridley Scott Film.* New York: The New Market Press, 2000.

Lawrence, D. H. *Women in Love.* New York: Penguin, 1982.

Lee, Christopher. *Lord of Misrule: The Autobiography of Christopher Lee.* London: Orion, 2000.

Lentz, Robert J. *Lee Marvin: His Films and Career.* Jefferson, NC: McFarland, 2000.

Mathews, Tom D. *Censored.* London: Random House/Chatto & Windus, 1994.

Parkinson, Michael. *Parky: My Autobiography.* London: Hodder and Stoughton, 2008.

Reed, Oliver. *Reed All About Me.* London: Hodder and Staunton, 1979.

Rigby, Jonathan. *English Gothic: A Century of Horror Cinema.* London: Reynolds & Hearn, 2000.

Russell, Ken. *Altered States: The Biography of Ken Russell.* New York: Bantam, 1991.

Sellers, Robert. *Hellraisers: The Life and Inebriated Times of Richard Burton, Richard Harris, Peter O'Toole and Oliver Reed.* London: Preface, 2008.

Server, Lee. *Robert Mitchum: "Baby I Don't Care."* New York: St. Martin's Press, 2001.

Wapshott, Nicholas. *Carol Reed: A Biography.* New York: Knopf, 1994.

Winner, Michael. *Winner Takes All: A Life of Sorts.* London: Robson Books, 2004.

Publications

Fandom's Film Gallery.
Film Review.
Films and Filming.
The Horror Elite.
Kinematograph Weekly.
Little Shoppe of Horrors.
Monthly Film Bulletin.

Index

Entries in **_bold italics_** indicate films of Oliver Reed